GLOBAL PERSPECTIVES ON INTERCULTURAL COMMUNICATION

Edited by
Stephen M. Croucher

First published 2017
by Routledge
711 Third Avenue, New York, NY 10017

and by Routledge
2 Park Square, Milton Park, Abingdon, Oxon OX14 4RN

Routledge is an imprint of the Taylor & Francis Group, an informa business

© 2017 Taylor & Francis

The right of the Stephen M. Croucher to be identified as the author of the editorial material, and of the authors for their individual chapters, has been asserted in accordance with sections 77 and 78 of the Copyright, Designs and Patents Act 1988.

All rights reserved. No part of this book may be reprinted or reproduced or utilized in any form or by any electronic, mechanical, or other means, now known or hereafter invented, including photocopying and recording, or in any information storage or retrieval system, without permission in writing from the publishers.

Trademark notice: Product or corporate names may be trademarks or registered trademarks, and are used only for identification and explanation without intent to infringe.

Library of Congress Cataloging-in-Publication Data
Names: Croucher, Stephen Michael, 1978– author.
Title: Global perspectives on intercultural communication /
   Stephen M. Croucher.
Description: New York, NY : Routledge / Taylor & Francis Group, [2017]
Identifiers: LCCN 2016050424 | ISBN 9781138860773 (hardback) |
   ISBN 9781138860780 (pbk.)
Subjects: LCSH: Intercultural communication—Social aspect—
   Globalization. | Language and languages—Globalization. |
   Culture and globalization. | Sociolinguistics.
Classification: LCC P95.54 .C76 2017 | DDC 302.2—dc23
LC record available at https://lccn.loc.gov/2016050424

ISBN: 978-1-138-86077-3 (hbk)
ISBN: 978-1-138-86078-0 (pbk)
ISBN: 978-1-315-71628-2 (ebk)

Typeset in Classical Garamond
by Apex CoVantage, LLC

CONTENTS

List of figures viii
List of tables ix

PART 1
What is Intercultural Communication? 1

1 Why Intercultural Communication? 3
  STEPHEN M. CROUCHER, MASSEY UNIVERSITY, NEW ZEALAND

2 Intercultural Communication in South America 14
  JAVIER PROTZEL, UNIVERSIDADE DEL PACÍFICO, LIMA, PERU

3 Intercultural Communication: A European Perspective 21
  JOÃO CAETANO, UNIVERSIDADE ABERTA, PORTUGAL

4 Intercultural Communication in South Africa 25
  SABIHAH MOOLA AND BABALWA SIBANGO, THE UNIVERSITY OF SOUTH AFRICA, UNISA

5 Intercultural Communication: A West African Perspective 29
  ELVIS NGWAYUH, UNIVERSITY OF JYVÄSKYLÄ, FINLAND

6 Intercultural Communication: An Israeli Perspective 32
  YUVAL KARNIEL AND AMIT LAVIE DINUR, THE INTERDISCIPLINARY CENTER (IDC) HERZLIYA, ISRAEL

7 Intercultural Communication: An Iranian Perspective 37
  NOUROLLAH ZARRINABADI, UNIVERSITY OF ISFAHAN, IRAN

8 Intercultural Communication: A Chinese Perspective 40
  JIANG FEI, CHINESE ACADEMY OF SOCIAL SCIENCES, BEIJING, CHINA

9 Intercultural Communication: A Korean Perspective 47
  YOUNG-OK LEE, KYUNG HEE UNIVERSITY, SOUTH KOREA

10 Intercultural Communication: A Japanese Perspective 53
  JIRO TAKAI, NAGOYA UNIVERSITY, JAPAN

11　Intercultural Communication: An Australian Perspective　　58
TERRY FLEW, QUEENSLAND UNIVERSITY OF TECHNOLOGY,
BRISBANE, AUSTRALIA

12　Intercultural Communication: A Christian Perspective　　62
JANIE HARDEN FRITZ, DUQUESNE UNIVERSITY, PITTSBURGH, USA

13　Intercultural Communication: A Muslim Perspective　　66
HASSAN ABU BAKAR AND MUNIF ZARIRRUDDIN FIKRI NORDIN,
UNIVERSITI UTARA MALAYSIA, MALAYSIA

14　Intercultural Communication: A Buddhist Perspective　　71
TENZIN DORJEE, CALIFORNIA STATE UNIVERSITY, FULLERTON, USA

PART 2
Culture　　75

15　Culture and Values in Intercultural Communication　　77
STEPHEN M. CROUCHER, MASSEY UNIVERSITY, NEW ZEALAND

PART 3
Theoretical Domains　　95

16　Identity and Intercultural Communication　　97
STEPHEN M. CROUCHER, MASSEY UNIVERSITY, NEW ZEALAND

17　Language and Intercultural Communication　　129
TODD L. SANDEL, UNIVERSITY OF MACAU, CHINA

18　Intercultural Communication and Relationships　　155
CHIA-FANG (SANDY) HSU, UNIVERSITY OF WYOMING, USA

19　Culture and Conflict　　179
DALE HAMPLE AND MENGQI ZHAN, UNIVERSITY OF MARYLAND, USA

20　Intercultural Communication and Adaptation　　205
GINA BARKER, LIBERTY UNIVERSITY, USA

PART 4
Intercultural Contexts　　245

21　Intercultural Communication Competence　　247
CARMENCITA DEL VILLAR, UNIVERSITY OF THE PHILIPPINES,
DILIMAN, THE PHILIPPINES

22　Intercultural Communication and Organizations　　270
CHIN-CHUNG CHAO, UNIVERSITY OF NEBRASKA-OMAHA, USA
AND DEXIN TIAN, YANGZHOU UNIVERSITY, CHINA

23 Intercultural Communication and Health 315
DIYAKO RAHMANI AND CHENG ZENG, UNIVERSITY OF
JYVÄSKYLÄ, FINLAND

PART 5
Conclusion **353**

24 The Bases for Intercultural Communication in a Digital Era 355
SHIV GANESH, MINGSHENG LI, AND FRANCO VACCARINO,
MASSEY UNIVERSITY, NEW ZEALAND

Index 367

FIGURES

1.1	The Communication Process	6
8.1	World Culture under Four Perspectives	41
9.1	Cultural Index Values of South Korea and the United States	49
15.1	Three Layered Model of Culture	79
15.2	Ganesha	81
15.3	Traditionally dressed Laotian Hmong woman	84
15.4	Comicon Fans	86
16.1	A Traditional Finnish Sauna	101
16.2	French Protesters in the Wake of Terrorist Events	106
17.1	How to Say Thank You	129
17.2	Toasting as a Ritual Performance	133
17.3	Pronouns as Shifting Indexicals	138
17.4	Scoundrel: Mixed Codes on Social Media	142
20.1	Extended U-Curve Model of Intercultural Adjustment	210
20.2	Stress-Adaptation-Growth Dynamic	211
20.3	Relationships among Components of Acculturation	213
20.4	Integrative Theory of Intercultural Adaptation	214
20.5	Acculturation Strategies	216
20.6	Relative Acculturation Extended Model	219
20.7	Third-Culture Building	223
22.1	A Traditional Hierarchical Organization	279
22.2	A Team-Structured Organization	280
22.3	A Network-Structured Organization	280
22.4	A Matrix-Structured Organization	281
22.5	Downward, Upward, and Horizontal Communication	289

TABLES

15.1 Schwartz's Seven Cultural Value Types   89
22.1 Trends and Tensions in Organizational Change   275

PART 1
WHAT IS INTERCULTURAL COMMUNICATION?

The following 14 chapters each present different approaches to what is intercultural communication. Each chapter is written by a different author(s) from a different geographic, religious, theoretical, and/or methodological perspective. When asked to write these chapters, each of these authors approached this task differently. However, each was asked, and delivered on, one task, to discuss what is the intercultural from their point of view. I believed it was essential to offer different perspectives on what is "intercultural" and "intercultural communication," as opposed to the typical US, and Western, connotations provided in most intercultural communication textbooks. I hope you learn from and enjoy it.

In Chapter 1, "Why Intercultural Communication," I, Stephen Croucher, do a few things. First, I define a few key terms. I define these terms from predominantly a US-approach to intercultural communication, as this is the approach in which I was trained. I also introduce you to the other chapters in the book.

In Chapter 2, "Intercultural Communication in South America," Javier Protzel outlines how intercultural communication as a field of inquiry has developed in different South American nations. He also discusses the multicultural nature of the continent. In Chapter 3, "Intercultural Communication: A European Perspective," by João Caetano, you are introduced to the intricate links between interculturality and what it means to be a member of the European Union. Questions such as how integration, diversity, and wealth relate to intercultural communication are posed. In Chapter 4, "Intercultural Communication in South Africa," Sabihah Moola and Babalwa Sibango explore how intercultural communication can best be understood in its specific contexts. This chapter explores the unique historical background of South Africa and how intercultural communication relates to its history and present situation. In

Chapter 5, "Intercultural Communication: A West African Perspective," Elvis Ngwayuh offers an overview of the diversity of West Africa and how cultural differences shape this region. In Chapter 6, "Intercultural Communication: An Israeli Perspective," Yuval Karniel and Amit Lavie Dinur discuss the links between politics and culture in nation building. Their discussion combines historical and cultural elements to describe what is the intercultural from an Israeli perspective. In Chapter 7, "Intercultural Communication: An Iranian Perspective," Nourollah Zarrinabadi explores the development of the intercultural discipline and describes its place in Iranian culture. He also explains the aims of intercultural communication in Iranian culture. In Chapter 8, "Intercultural Communication: A Chinese Perspective," Jiang Fei sketches the landscape of intercultural communication research in China. He outlines various developments in China regarding intercultural communication research as a field of inquiry/scholarship. In Chapter 9, "Intercultural Communication: A Korean Perspective," Young-Ok Lee describes how in Korean society, the links between history, religion, and societal hierarchy are intrinsically linked to what makes the intercultural. In Chapter 10, "Intercultural Communication: A Japanese Perspective," Jiro Takai explores the history of intercultural communication as a discipline. In doing so he outlines how this discipline, and concept, have emerged, and still are emerging from other fields. In Chapter 11, "Intercultural Communication: An Australian Perspective," Terry Flew considers how history, geography, demography, social policy, and political economy all shape a distinctively Australian perspective on intercultural communication. In Chapter 12, "Intercultural Communication: A Christian Perspective," Janie Harden Fritz describes how intercultural communication has been part of the Judeo-Christian tradition since its beginnings and has always been an integral part of the Christian doctrine. In Chapter 13, "Intercultural Communication" A Muslim Perspective," Hassan Abu Bakar and Munif Zarirruddin Fikri Nordin explain how a basic tenet for Muslims is to communicate. Thus, the significance of intercultural communication as essential to Islam is outlined in this chapter. In Chapter 14, "Intercultural Communication: A Buddhist Perspective," Tenzin Dorjee describes how intercultural communication includes interdependent origination, nonviolence, and mindfulness, among other things.

1 WHY INTERCULTURAL COMMUNICATION?

Stephen M. Croucher, Massey University, New Zealand

Chapter Outline

- Book Outline
- The Complex Nature of Communication
  - Communication Defined
  - Models of Communication
- The Need for Intercultural Communication
  - Review of Intercultural Communication Definitions
- The Needs for and Benefits of Intercultural Communication

Book Outline

While working on this book the European Union has grappled with an unprecedented influx of migration. More than one million migrants in 2015 escaped ISIS and/or the war in Syria and conflicts in Africa, and entered the EU (Migrant crisis: Migration to Europe explained in graphics, 2016). Upon entering the EU, many migrants have experienced vast cultural differences, physical challenges, legal challenges, economic challenges and opportunities, etc. Communication has been integral to the entire management and interpretation of the migrant crisis. Many of the migrants who have entered the EU speak different languages than those in their new host nation(s), have different cultural/social practices, and the press coverage of the crisis has varied significantly from nation to nation in the EU. As a consequence, it has been common to see clashes between migrants and host nations (Greece, Germany, Finland, France, etc.), migrant violence toward the host nation (Germany), and the introduction/proposal of various anti-immigration and migrant resettlement/deportation proposals throughout the EU (e.g., Sweden, France, and the United Kingdom) (Fiaola, 2015; Migrant Crisis: Finland's case against immigration, 2015; Wintour, 2015). Ultimately, the migrant crisis in the EU has renewed the call for heightened cultural awareness, communicative competence, and intercultural communication.

In this chapter we will examine intercultural communication from my point of view. I stress that it is from my point of view because, as you will find throughout this textbook, multiple points of view on what *is* intercultural communication are presented. This is done to show you, the reader, the depth and breadth of the field. To facilitate this examination we will first explore communication itself. In this first section we will define communication and describe the different models of communication. In the second section of the chapter we will delve into why we need intercultural communication, and what it is. In the following chapters in this textbook you will be introduced to various definitions and approaches to intercultural communication. All of these chapters and approaches will further address the why and what of "intercultural communication."

The Complex Nature of Communication

Communication Defined

In one form or another communication has been around for thousands of years; but what is it? Well, there is not one singular definition of communication. Littlejohn (1999) asserted, "communication is difficult to define. The word is abstract and, like most terms, possesses numerous meanings" (p. 6). To better understand the variety of approaches to defining communication, take a look at the following list of five classic definitions of communication:

1. "All of the procedures by which one mind can affect another." (Weaver, 1949, p. 95)
2. A verbal interchange of thoughts or ideas. (Hoben, 1954)
3. A process through which we try to understand individuals and have them understand us. The process is dynamic and continually changing in response to the situation. (Andersen, 1959)
4. The transmission of ideas, information, emotions, skills, etc. through symbols, words, pictures, etc. (Berelson & Steiner, 1964)
5. The central interest of communication is to transmit a message to a receiver with conscious intent to affect the receiver's behavior(s). (Miller, 1966)

Each of these definitions provides different, and some overlapping perspectives on what is communication. While some of the definitions are narrower in scope than others, for example Hoben's (1954) only considers verbal exchanges, others consider all aspects of human behavior that influence another person (Weaver, 1949). Most modern-day communication researchers tend to follow a combination of the definitions provided by Andersen (1959) and Berelson and Steiner (1964). In this case, **communication** is a dynamic process through which we share meaning with others through various message channels (Croucher & Cronn-Mills, 2015).

There are three key elements of communication that should be reviewed before we can progress any further, each of which are common to most definitions of communication. First, communication involves the sharing of symbols via signs. A **sign** is an object (e.g., letter, word, phrase, action, event, etc.) that represents something else. To understand how signs work we need to define two terms: **signifier** and **signified**, using the example "computer." The signifier is the word "computer." The signified is the physical object that is the "computer," all of the electronic and metal parts that make up the "computer." The relationship between the signified and the signifier is the sign. In most cases this relationship is easily understood and does not need explanation; we have mental concepts/ideas of what these signs represent, what Ogden and Richards (1927) called **referents**. For example, when you see a "computer" you may think of a device to log onto the Internet, do homework, connect to social media, etc., while others may see it as work; it all depends on our experiences with the sign.

Second, most researchers view communication as a process. Communication is ongoing and ever-changing. Consider the following example. An employee asks his/her employer for a raise. This request is not a one-time communication event. In fact, when the employer considers the request, the employer thinks about many things the employee has done since working at the company. Our past deeds influence the final decision as to whether or not we get a raise, as well as the financial situation of the company. Are we a good employee? Does the boss like us or not? How well do we communicate that we are an effective employee? There are countless questions that go into this decision. Our past interactions with the boss will have a huge impact on the final decision. Ultimately, how we communicate is greatly influenced by our past and present situations/interactions when we realize that communication is a process.

Third, communication is often regarded as transactional, or a back and forth between a sender and receiver. Essentially, feedback is critical to communication. Yet, a transactional approach to communication takes more into consideration than just feedback. Burgoon and Ruffner (1978, p. 9) noted that the participants in communication have a great impact on one another:

> People are simultaneously acting as source and receiver in many communication situations. A person is giving feedback, talking, responding, acting, and reacting continually through a communication event. Each person is constantly participating in the communication activity. All of these things can alter the other elements in the process and create a completely different communication event. This is what we mean by transaction.

Models of Communication

To better understand the transactional approach to communication let's look back at the employer/employee interaction over a raise. When thinking about this interaction look to Figure 1.2 below as a model of communication. Each of the individuals is a sender of messages, while at the same time being a receiver of messages. Both communicators are **encoding** (processing messages to send out), and **decoding** (processing messages received). In this particular case their communication channel is verbal and non-verbal communication (voice, talking, eye contact, and gestures). However, they could also have this interaction over another communication channel, such as Facebook, or via texting for example. No matter what communication channel they use, the other person receives their messages and gives them feedback, more than likely through the same communication channel. However, as we all know from communicating with people, we often misinterpret communication messages, we can decode messages incorrectly. This can be attributed to many things, one being noise. **Noise** is any physiological, physical, psychological, and/or semantic factor that interferes with our understanding of a communication message. Physiological noise includes hunger, fatigue, headache, depression, medications, and other issues that affect how we feel. Physical noise includes things that physically disrupt the communication, like loud sounds and bright lights. Psychological noise is the issues within us that limit our abilities to decode properly, such as prejudice, being defensive, being bored, being in love, etc. Semantic noise is when words cannot be understood. This transactional approach to communication considers the complexities of communication. All of us have had a hard time getting our message across at one time or another; look to the model in Figure 1.2, considering how communication is symbolic and a process, and hopefully you will have an improved understanding of communication.

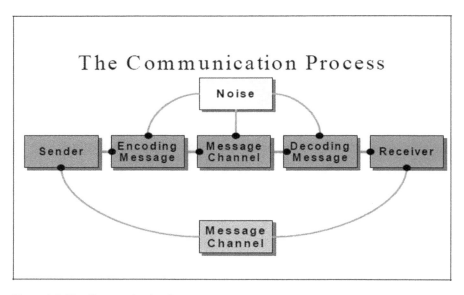

Figure 1.1 The Communication Process

The Need for Intercultural Communication

With a basic understanding of the communication process, we can now turn to one kind of communication, intercultural communication. In the rest of this book you will be introduced to numerous approaches and definitions of intercultural communication. Each of these reveals the depth and breadth of the field of intercultural communication. Moreover, each of these researchers demonstrates the economic, political, and cultural/societal needs for and benefits of intercultural communication.

Review of Intercultural Communication Definitions

Intercultural communication is communication (verbal and/or non-verbal) between individuals from different cultures. Essential to intercultural communication are two concepts: communication and culture (Martin & Nakayama, 2014). Historically, with the research of scholars like Edward T. Hall (1959, 1966), this meant individuals from different nations. However, as the field has developed, the concept of "different cultures" has also expanded (Gudykunst, 2004; Neuliep, 2015). In Part 1 of this textbook you are introduced to a variety of approaches to intercultural communication. Each of these approaches details how "intercultural communication" is broadly studied and defined in a different region, and/or from a different philosophical point of view. Collectively, these chapters emphasize the significance of communication and culture in "intercultural communication," and the broad nature of the field of inquiry. The next part focuses on the notion of culture; however, the authors in the first part when discussing "intercultural communication" highlight the following cultural notions, which have driven the study of the "intercultural": religion, ethnicity, politics, gender, history, race, subgroups, geography, nationality, socioeconomic status, customs, habits, and community all being cultural elements that shape how we as societies define and study the intercultural. Moreover, it is important to note that from all of the perspectives, various forms of media, from interpersonal to group interactions, and storytelling, to name but a few, are all viewed as key ways in which communication takes place on an intercultural level.

It should also be noted that you may encounter in your studies three closely related sub-fields of intercultural communication: cross-cultural, interethnic, and international communication, all of which are closely related fields of intercultural communication. **Cross-cultural communication** is comparing communication across cultures (Gudykunst, 2004). In this kind of study a researcher would compare how the same kind of communication issues occur in different cultures. For example, Oetzel and Ting-Toomey (2003) found approaches to conflict differed between China, Germany, Japan, and the United States. **Interethnic communication** is communication between individuals from different ethnic groups. For example, Hecht, Ribeau, and Alberts (1989) explored how African-Americans perceive communication with Whites. **International**

communication is the study of media's use to facilitate communication across international borders. Historically, it focused on communication between nation-states. However, it increasingly focuses on other types of communication: political, economic, corporate, social, etc. Boyd-Barrett (2000) for example explored the extent to which national and local news agencies influence processes of globalization and localization.

The Needs for and Benefits of Intercultural Communication

Economically, the ability to communicate effectively in the global marketplace/workplace is an increasingly essential competency. With increased migration workforces are becoming more and more diverse in many nations. Issues of multiculturalism, diversity, etc., are of greater importance to companies hoping to achieve profits and growth. The ability of individuals to effectively communicate with individuals from different cultural groups is shown to lead to more effective workplace teams, and in turn lead to more corporate profits (Matveev & Milter, 2004). Furthermore, research increasingly shows that in the United States for example, migration raises the standard of living and wages, and boosts the US economy (Matthews, 2013). Another way to look at the influence of intercultural communication on the US (as one national example) is to consider its top 10 trading partners in 2015 (in terms of imports and exports, in order, China, Canada, Mexico, Japan, Germany, South Korea, the United Kingdom, France, Taiwan, and India) (U.S. Census, 2015). Together these 10 nations represent vastly different cultural groups, different linguistic groups, different ways of doing business, and are from different geographic regions. As foreign trade increases globally, effective intercultural communication will be essential to helping corporations, nations, and individuals realize their full economic potential.

Politically, the need for intercultural communication is immense. Almost every nation in the world today is grappling with **multiculturalism**, or the political, social/cultural acceptance, promotion, or rejection of multiple cultural groups residing in the same society. In essence, it is how much a society tolerates or promotes diversity and the co-existence of different groups within that society. The member states in the European Union are in the midst of a multiculturalism crisis, as individuals, political parties, and governments ask what to do with all of the new migrants. Should the states open their borders to the migrants or close their borders? Once the migrants arrive what kinds of considerations, if any, should be given to them in terms of language training, integration services, etc. (Fiaola, 2015; Wintour, 2015)? These same questions have been asked for more than a century in the U.S. regarding immigrants: German, Irish, Italian, Asian, Mexican, etc., all have faced similar questions. In response to such questions, issues of migration and movement of people have become highly politicized. Political parties often use the fear of multiculturalism to their advantage, painting immigrants and minorities as threats to society: immigrants/minorities will take away your jobs, make society unsafe, hurt the economy, and/or change *our* culture or way of life. Such plays on the dominant culture's fears of the "other" have helped many far-right nationalist parties in Europe achieve political gains and influence since 2010 with many parties now controlling more than 20% of their national parliaments: Jobbik in Hungary 20.2%, New Flemish Alliance in Belgium 20.3%, Freedom Party of Austria 20.5%, Danish People's Party in Denmark 21.1%, Swiss People's Party in Switzerland 26.6%, Law and Justice in Poland 37.6%, and Internal Macedonian Revolutionary Organization–Democratic Party for Macedonian National Unity (VMRO-DPMNE) 43% (Nordsieck, 2014; Swiss election sees nationalist party lose share of votes, 2011). The belief that national identity and culture are under threat has led to many of these parties gaining strength. In fact, in Finland, where the Finns Party (formerly known as the True Finns) has 17.6% of the Parliament in 2015, one of its members of Parliament went to Facebook in 2015 to post his thoughts (and those of many of his supporters) about multiculturalism (Finnish MP calls for fight against "nightmare of multiculturalism", no comment from party leadership, 2015):

> I'm dreaming of a strong, brave nation that will defeat this nightmare called multiculturalism. This ugly bubble that our enemies live in, will soon enough burst into a million little pieces. Our lives are entwined in a very harsh times. These are the days that will forever leave a mark on our nations [sic] future. I have strong belief in my fellow fighters. We will fight until the end of our homeland and one true Finnish nation. The victory will be ours.

The Finnish government denounced the remarks, with the Prime Minister Juha Sipilä, a member of the Centre Party, publicly denouncing the comments as not representing the government or the multicultural nation he wants to build as Prime Minister. These political issues demonstrate the political need for intercultural communication. As migration continues, and in many places grows, we continually face the challenging political questions of migration. Through effective intercultural communication we can be better equipped to understand diversity and respond to our more multicultural and ever-changing world.

There are also cultural/societal reasons why we need and will benefit from having better intercultural communication. Societies are rife with stereotypes, ethnocentrism, and unnecessary/harmful conflict. Intercultural communication is needed to help address these problems. A **stereotype** is how members of one group expect members of another group to behave/act (Stephan & Stephan, 1993). Stereotypes, particularly negative ones, inhibit communication and promote fear between groups (Verkuyten, 1997). For example, since 9/11 many media outlets and pundits have painted Muslims as violent, and linked the entire religion and culture to terrorism (Jaakkola 2009), an extremely negative stereotype indeed. Negative stereotypes do not encourage healthy communication between groups, as this form of communication promotes misunderstandings between individuals from different cultural groups. The more we can try to break free from stereotypes and try to understand the individual for who they really are, the more likely we can have a more honest and fruitful conversation.

Similarly, **ethnocentrism**, or the feelings of superiority and preferences for one's own cultural group (Adorno, et al., 1950; Neuliep, et al., 2001) hinders effective communication. Ethnocentrism creates boundaries among social groups. Thus, intergroup relations can be limited as people do not see others as worthy of their time or energy. Moreover, ethnocentrism leads to **prejudice**, or predetermined opinions we have about individual or groups before we know the facts. This prejudice often leads to conflict between individuals and groups, because unfortunately we do not understand, and/or do not want to understand one another.

Conflict, or the "expressed struggle between at least two interdependent parties who perceive incompatible goals, scarce resources, and interference from the other party in achieving their goals," is inevitable (Hocker & Wilmot, 1991, p. 12). While interpersonal conflicts, such as between friends or romantic partners have their own unique elements to them, once an intercultural element is added, the conflict has a whole new dimension to it. Nussbaum (2007) for example explored religious differences in India and found that the conglomeration of different traditions, customs, and religions created both a land of vast opportunities and intense conflicts. In the case of India, and many other nations, one way in which cultural issues are approached for many is through religious lines, through what Akbar (2003) and Mukherji (2007) called the "politics of communalism"; essentially, conflicts are often interpreted through religious lines. What this shows is that it is essential to have effective intercultural communication.

Looking forward in this textbook, you will see in the following chapters how intercultural communication is defined, broadly speaking, in various geographic areas, and among different religious groups. Each of these chapters in Part 1, "What is Intercultural Communication," presents a snapshot, and is not meant to be the conclusive point of view from a particular perspective. However, these authors are presenting alternative points of view on what is the intercultural, often ignored in intercultural communication textbooks and journal articles.

Part 2, "Culture," includes one chapter on culture and values, and their place in intercultural communication. You will be introduced to many different approaches and perspectives on what is culture, and what are values throughout the textbook. However, this chapter provides standard definitions and theoretical approaches to help guide you through Parts 3–5.

Part 3, "Theoretical Domains," includes five chapters that delve into five different theoretical and conceptual areas of intercultural communication. Chapter 16, "Identity and Intercultural Communication," describes key theories on identity and how they relate to intercultural communication. Chapter 17, "Language and Intercultural Communication," focuses on the links between language and intercultural communication. Chapter 18, "Intercultural Communication and Relationships," focuses on the intricate links between culture, communication, and relationships. Chapter 19, "Culture and Conflict," discusses the interplay between culture and conflict. Chapter 20, "Intercultural Adaptation" describes adaptation processes and how they relate to intercultural communication.

Part 4, "Intercultural Contexts" includes three chapters that place intercultural communication in different communicative contexts. Chapter 21, "Intercultural Communication Competence," explores how intercultural communication links to communicative competence. Chapter 22, "Intercultural Communication and Organizations," discusses the growing links between organizations and interculturality. Chapter 23, "Intercultural Communication and Health," looks into how our health and health care is intrinsically linked to intercultural communication.

Part 5, "Conclusion" closes the textbook with Chapter 24, "The Bases for Intercultural Communication in a Digital Era," in which future directions of research and implications for the field are discussed.

Key Terms

Communication
Decoding
Intercultural communication
Multiculturalism
Sign
Stereotype

Conflict
Encoding
Interethnic communication
Prejudice
Signified

Cross-cultural communication
Ethnocentrism
International communication
Referents
Signifier

Activities

1. Google the term "intercultural communication." Choose 10 of the definitions you find. How are these definitions similar and how are they different?
2. Break up into groups of 3–5 of your peers. Watch the following short video: http://uk.businessinsider.com/big-misconceptions-about-islam-religion-politics-muslim-2016–1?r=US&IR=T

    What are some stereotypes the video is attempting to disprove? Does it do a good job or not? Do you believe the stereotypes the video is trying to disprove? Do some research on these stereotypes and discuss your results with your group.

References

Adorno, T. W., Frenkel-Brunswik, K., Levinson, D., & Sanford, R. N. (1950). *The authoritarian personality*. New York, NY: Harper & Brothers.

Akbar, M. J. (2003). *India: The siege within: Challenges to a nation's unity*. New Delhi, India: Roli Books.

Andersen, M. P. (1959). What is communication? *Journal of Communication*, 9, 5.

Berelson, B., & Steiner, G. A. (1964). *Human behavior*. New York, NY: Harcourt, Brace & Company.

Boyd-Barrett, O. (2000). National and international news agencies: Issues of crisis and realignment. *International Communication Gazette*, 62, 5–18.

Burgoon, M., & Ruffner, M. (1978). *Human communication*. New York, NY: Holt, Rinehart, & Winston.

Croucher, S. M., & Cronn-Mills, D. (2015). *Understanding communication research methods: A theoretical and practical approach*. New York, NY: Routledge.

Fiaola, A. (16 August, 2015). Germany unnerved by scores of xenophobic attacks against refugees. *The Washington Post Online*. Retrieved from: https://www.washingtonpost.com/world/europe/germany-unnerved-by-scores-of-xenophobic-attacks-against-refugees/2015/08/16/eada9284-3fb1-11e5-b2c4-af4c6183b8b4_story.html

Finnish MP calls for fight against "nightmare of multiculturalism", no comment from party leadership. (26 July, 2015). *YLE Online*. Retrieved from: http://yle.fi/uutiset/finnish_mp_calls_for_fight_against_nightmare_of_multiculturalism_no_comment_from_party_leadership/8182155

Gudykunst, W. B. (2004). *Bridging differences: Effective intergroup communication* (4th ed.). Thousand Oaks, CA: Sage.

Hall, E. T. (1959). *The silent language*. Garden City, NY: Doubleday.

Hall, E. T. (1966). *The hidden dimension*. Garden City, NY: Doubleday.

Hecht, M. L., Ribeau, S., & Alberts, J. K. (1989). An Afro-American perspective on interethnic communication. *Communication Monographs*, 56, 385–410.

Hoben, J. B. (1954). English communication at Colgate reexamined. *Journal of Communication*, 4, 76–86.

Hocker, J., & Wilmot, W. (1991). *Interpersonal conflict* (3rd ed). Dubuque, IA: Wm. C. Brown.

Jaakkola, M. (2009). *Maahanmuuttajat suomalaisten näkökulmasta. Asennemuutokset 1987–2007. (Immigrants Finnish point of view. Changes in attitude 1987–2007.)* Helsinki: City of Helsinki Urban Facts Research Series.

Littlejohn, S. (1999). *Theories of human communication*. Boston, MA: Wadsworth Publishers.

Martin, J., & Nakayama, T. (2014). *Experiencing intercultural communication: An introduction* (5th ed.). Columbus, OH: McGraw Hill.

Matthews, C. (30 January, 2013). The economics of immigration: Who wins, who loses and why. *Time online*. Retrieved from: http://business.time.com/2013/01/30/the-economics-of-immigration-who-wins-who-loses-and-why/

Matveev, A. V., & Milter, R. G. (2004). The value of intercultural competence for performance of multicultural teams. *Team Performance Management: An International Journal*, 10 (5/6), 104–111.

Migrant crisis: Finland's case against immigration. (9 September, 2015). *BBC News Online*. Retrieved from: http://www.bbc.com/news/world-europe-34185297

Migrant crisis: Migration to Europe explained in graphics. (28 January, 2016). *BBC News Online*. Retrieved from: http://www.bbc.com/news/world-europe-34131911

Miller, G. R. (1966). On defining communication: Another stab. *Journal of Communication*, 16, 88–98.

Mukherji, N. (2007). Contemporary communalism: Textuality and mass culture. In I. Habib (ed.), *Religion in Indian history* (pp. 263–283). New Delhi, India: Tulika Books.

Neuliep, J. W. (2015). *Intercultural communication: A contextual approach* (6th ed.). Thousand Oaks, CA: Sage.

Neuliep, J. W., Chaudoir, M., & McCroskey, J. C. (2001). A cross-cultural comparison of ethnocentrism among Japanese and United States college students. *Communication Research Reports*, *18*, 137–146.

Nordsieck, W. (2014). *Parties and elections in Europe.* Retrieved from: http://www.parties-and-elections.eu/macedonia.html

Nussbaum, M. C. (2007). *The clash within: Democracy, religious violence, and India's future.* Cambridge, MA: Harvard University Press.

Oetzel, J. G., & Ting-Toomey, S. (2003). Face concerns in interpersonal conflict: A cross-cultural empirical test of the face negotiation theory. *Communication Research*, *30*, 599–624.

Ogden, C. K., & Richards, I. A. (1927). *The Meaning of Meaning.* New York, NY: Harcourt, Brace, & Company.

Stephan, W. G., & Stephan, C. W. (1993). Cognition and affect in stereotyping: Parallel interactive networks. In D. M. Mackie & D. L. Hamilton (eds.), *Affect, cognition, and stereotyping: Interactive processes in group perception* (pp. 111–136). Orlando, FL: Academic Press.

Swiss election sees nationalist party lose share of votes. (23 October, 2011). *The Guardian Online.* Retrieved from: http://www.theguardian.com/world/2011/oct/23/swiss-election-nationalist-party-result

U.S. Census Bureau. (2015). *Foreign Trade.* Retrieved from: https://www.census.gov/foreign-trade/statistics/highlights/top/top1512yr.html#total

Verkuyten, M. (1997). The structure of ethnic attitudes: The effect of target group, region, gender, and national identity. *Genetic, Social, and General Psychology Monographs*, *123*, 261–284.

Weaver, W. (1949). Recent contributions to the mathematical theory of communication. In C. Shannon & W. Weaver, *The mathematical theory of communication.* Urbana, IL: University of Illinois Press.

Wintour, P. (3 September, 2015). Britain should not take more Middle East refugees, says David Cameron. *The Guardian Online.* Retrieved from: http://www.theguardian.com/world/2015/sep/02/david-cameron-migration-crisis-will-not-be-solved-by-uk-taking-in-more-refugees

2 INTERCULTURAL COMMUNICATION IN SOUTH AMERICA

Javier Protzel, Universidade del Pacífico, Lima, Peru

> **Chapter Outline**
> - Studies and Institutions
> - Hybridation and Interculturality
> - Bilingual Intercultural Education
> - Environment Issues, Intercultural Unrest and Politics
> - Conclusion

Studies and Institutions

Intercultural communication (ICC) is usually understood in South America either as an anthropologist's task, a foreigner's (and maybe national) experience of local exoticism, or as the living result of biological miscegenation, i.e., the blend of different biological phenotypes (races) through human reproduction, but mostly not as concrete and distinct interactions of Self with an Other, defined by linguistic and behavioral differences, as it would happen in a modern multiculturalist setting or in an international business meeting. The underlying concepts of culture seem to differ from each other insomuch as the positions occupied by the actors vary. In a United States discourse about ICC the Self is clearly situated 'outside' Otherness, while in Brazil, Mexico, Bolivia, Peru or Colombia it might well be deeply 'inside': the result, for a considerable part of the southern subcontinent's population of a four-century long process of miscegenation among Iberic, African, and Amerindian peoples. Thus, the concept of 'a' culture gets blurred. Moreover, the theoretical equivalence of nation to culture taken for granted in some areas of the world (US, Korea, Japan, Germany, for instance) becomes a critical issue. There is a conceptual cost when trying to fit cultural heterogeneity into a unitary nation-state; the heuristic value of almost any ICC research with pretensions of achieving nation-wide conclusions would decrease (Levine, Park, & Kim, 2007).

ICC studies about cultural affinities/differences between interacting individuals/groups of diverse nations do exist in South America, but on a reduced scale (corporate communication, marketing research and international business private education), and academically oriented both to undergraduate and graduate students. It is useful for the training of managers who travel abroad or receive visitors. Rather than being focused on communication within the vast sub-continental cultural and linguistic diversity, it is more congruent with the US conception of ICC set by Hall (1989).

South American mainstream studies and research, on the contrary, concern mostly three kinds of institutions: governments, universities, and NGOs, focused on domestic realities. When ICC was already distinct from anthropology north of the continent, on the south only anthropology was undergoing intensive growth as a science. Its focus on intercultural issues would be based on a secularized version, free of domination purposes, of the centuries-long Iberic tradition of study and communication with native populations aiming at massive conversions to Christianity (Marzal, 1998). Likewise, from the mid-1970s on, departments and schools of communications flourished in South America including in most of them intercultural matters among their subjects, under different names. By 2015, some 400 South American schools of communication may be counted, as well as specific institutions directed to indigenous peoples for the study and practice of ICC.

Hybridation and Interculturality

By 2011, approximately 45% of the Latin American population was either *mestizo* (mixed phenotype of European and Amerindian) or Amerindian, and 16% of African descent according to self-qualification (Latinobarómetro, 2011). The Amerindian and *mestizo* may account for up to 79% in the Andean countries,[1] making ethnic and race variables dramatically overlap social classes. Except for the Southern Cone (Argentina, Chile and Uruguay), social classes are racially stratified: upper and upper-middle classes mostly white, while the rest occupy a wide range going from mainly *mestizo* or *mulatto* (mixed phenotype of African and European) lower-middle- and up-going urban lower classes to marginal Amerindian communities. Thus, the criteria to define Self and Other may vary according to context.

There are three distinguishable population sectors relevant for ICC. The first of these sectors comprises lower- to lower-middle class urban dwellers of a *mestizo*, yet modern culture, also named 'hybrid'. To a lesser or greater extent indigenous, they arrived from the savannahs, highlands, grasslands or jungles mostly from the mid-20th century on. They are the majority. Distinct from the first sector are the minorities, scattered across several regions, namely Andes, Amazon, Chaco, Continental Caribbean, Orinoco, and Patagonia. Andean Amerindian peasants (75% of South America's aboriginal population) are mostly grouped in rural communities of Bolivia, Ecuador, Peru, plus Chilean, Colombian, and Argentine minorities. This second sector is connected to the former; it conserves the native languages (Quechua, Aymara, and Guaraní with the most speakers), religious syncretism, rituals and other symbolic features. Many tend to migrate and yield to the impact of modern markets. Third, there are the native ethnic communities ('*pueblos*') less integrated into modern society, inhabitants of the rainforests of Brazil, Bolivia, Ecuador, Peru, Colombia, Paraguay, and Venezuela, some of which remain voluntarily isolated, as in southern Argentina and Chile. They speak 347 languages, including the three mentioned above. They also keep their clothing, hairstyle, body expression, and build. For the whole of South America these indigenous peoples add up to 355 languages (Sichra, 2009), of which around 70% live in the Amazon. Chosen or not, symbolic markers have become ethnic and social classifiers in this clearly high-context sub-continent. Despite urban modernization and formal democratic equality, centuries-old Iberic hierarchies survive, downgrading black, *mestizo* and Amerindian populations. Such post-colonial behavior reinforces a contemporary dilemma among the aboriginal peoples of Brazil, Bolivia, Ecuador, Peru, and Colombia. It is either to choose between the avoidance of traditional ethnical markers for a transit towards assimilation, whereby they may integrate the new *mestizo* urban middle-class, which is the majority's option, or rather to assume fully the challenge of keeping their Amerindian ethnicity, requiring recognition of cultural rights and undertaking an intercultural dialog with the state, without having to renounce the essentials of their identity.

Beyond scientific research on the field of communications at universities, ICC's South American equivalent is in the fieldwork of anthropologists and/or the interaction with the last sector mentioned above, the Amazon/Chaco/Orinoco/Patagonia indigenous peoples, and to a minor degree, the highland peasant communities, more integrated into their respective national societies. From the 1950s through the 1990s studies about indigenous peoples underwent a gradual shift. Studying the Other-inside-the-country had previously been a political commitment of South American élite social scientists (a task shared with U.S. and European researchers). The idea of an 'internal colonialism' (*colonialismo interno*) gave a Marxist bias to the interpretation of intercultural relations during the 1960s and 1970s. This was comparatively progress with respect to *indigenismo*, the Mexican-born pro-Amerindian esthetical and political movement, guided by middle-class intellectuals. *Indigenismo* was originated around 1915, spread southward until the 1950s, and influenced a first generation of anthropologists (Favre, 1998). However, those efforts were surpassed from the 1980s onward by an activation and organization of diverse Amerindian groups from almost all of the sub-continent who demanded dialog and respect. This overflow pushed national states, modern civil societies, and researchers to intercommunicate with them and promote indigenous citizenship on behalf of an ideal 'diverse Us' (*nosotros diverso*) (Degregori, 2000).

Henceforth the term 'interculturality' started to be used in a series of interdisciplinary practices, especially by anthropologists and communicators, focused on promoting indigenous identities. The enhancement of dialogue and mutual understanding through bilingual intercultural education was accompanied by health assistance and by recognition of their human and territorial rights.

Bilingual Intercultural Education

Bilingual intercultural education[2] (BIE) is for sure a major issue of intellectual debate in those countries with sizable indigenous and comparatively isolated populations. The close correlation between Amerindian identities and illiteracy and extreme poverty was overlooked for more than a century. As the Amazon territories of Bolivia, Brazil, Ecuador, Colombia, and Peru were considered 'empty' during the mid-19th century, the nation-states promoted the arrival of European settlers to whom land would be freely awarded. Mapuches, the southernmost ethnic group of the Americas resisted the colonization of their territory by the Argentine and Chilean State until until the 'conquest' by these respective armies. As the end of the past century approached, most experts agreed upon the qualities of bilingual intercultural education, which was implemented in all countries having indigenous populations, each under its singular features. Situations vary considerably from one country to another. The immense linguistic variety and dispersion contrasts with the national rates of indigenous population. Taking the whole of South America and the Caribbean, there are only five Amerindian languages spoken by more than one million people, and 706 by 1,000 persons or less. Ecuador, Bolivia, and Peru have 26% of their populations speaking one of the (only) four predominant native languages, while less than 1% of Brazilians are Amerindians, but they are linguistically very diverse with 186 languages.

Access to literacy through the mother tongue (previous to Spanish/Portuguese) helps indigenous adults and children read and write by using their own mental tools, which is better for a clearer native outlook into reality, and likewise for the general self-esteem of the ethnic groups concerned. For some nation-states such as Peru and Ecuador this meant a national integration no longer based on 'civilizing' native communities through 'Spanization' ('*castellanización*'), thus an historical re-interpretation of national identity, whereby linguistic and cultural plurality become a necessary component to define it (Zúñiga & Gálvez, 2002).

However, different proficiency levels bring uneven country results. Contents may vary critically, from simple translations of western-based contents to locally-based knowledge. In some cases, colleges located in Amazon areas will invite aboriginal leaders to campus to get them trained as teachers, or rather go to their settlements, as in Brazil. However, the results of intercultural education must not be considered as the generation of a cultural blend. More realistically it may lead to a bi-cultural pattern.

Environment Issues, Intercultural Unrest and Politics

Most generally intercultural contacts do not occur in South America in harmonious or peaceful contexts. BIE did not appear spontaneously; it was mostly subsequent to pressures upon national governments and activism by black and native movements during the 1980s and 1990s (Albó, 2009). They formed unions and national confederations in Ecuador, Brazil, Bolivia, Argentina, Chile, and Colombia, proclaiming they were not 'peasants' but 'ethnic nations'. This is surprising in a country such as Argentina whose self-perception had always been of a white, European country with very few Amerindians and no blacks (Briones et al., 2007). The political background of this issue is the increasing interest of the global economic powers in extractive activities (i.e. oil, mining, gas, wood). Most of those resources are in the Andean mountains and under the Amazon soil, particularly inside ancestral Amerindian territories. According to ILO's (International Labor Organization) Convention 169 on Indigenous and Tribal Peoples in Independent Countries (1989), native inhabitants should be previously consulted about investments on their territories. This frequently does not happen; subsequently some environments get damaged (oil leaks, tailing basins) by the extractive ventures by transnational corporations, which foster frequent conflicts. Amerindian communities may even have clashes with their national states by reason of their autonomous internal rules, mythical beliefs, and adscription to territory which reach stages of physical confrontation when rivers and prairies get polluted, cattle, fish and birds die, and sizable portions of the rainforest are destroyed (Tovar, 2007).

Intercultural communication becomes increasingly politicized. Its specific concerns get connected with environmental issues and violence. The intercultural level might relate more to communication between taut negotiating contenders than to peaceful encounters trying to know each other better. It is usual for ethnic communities to ask consultants from NGOs, mainly anthropologists, about relations with the government or with foreign investors, who count on the assessment of hired anthropologists. Cultural identities might not have a lineal descent from the past, or their real origins may have faded from the collective memory, so traditions and the consciousness of belonging may have been reinvented. For instance, the black communities (*comunidades negras*) from the Colombian Pacific coast, mostly descendants from slaves who paid for freedom or simply fled, took refuge since the 19th century in this jungle, building entirely Afrocolombian settlements where they reinvented their African traditions with a mythical conception of ownership of the rainforest and of mutual protection with nature. The national government bestowed on them a status such as the one aboriginal peoples from other regions of Colombia received: a double condition of ethnic communities and of protectors of the environment (Rivas, 2004).

A somewhat opposite situation is still ongoing in Bolivia, the country with the highest proportion of indigenous peoples in the Americas (nearly 70%). After being elected president in 2006, Evo Morales, the Aymara leader of the native coca farmers' unions, enacted a new Bolivian constitution. This republic was renamed 'pluri-national', committed to defend the Aymara and Quechua, and their ethnic ties with Andean soil, itself the mythic goddess *pachamama* (*Madre Tierra*, or Motherland). But this radical anti-western *indigenista* governance neglected other smaller and marginal Amerindian groups. The Moxeño, Yuracaré and Tsimanes, all three from inside the national park of Isiboro-Sécure on the eastern Bolivian jungle are opposed to the construction of a new road, a future short-cut from Bolivia to Brazil, but an ecological and cultural threat, which nevertheless favors migrant Aymara coca producers, who outnumber the original people from Isiboro-Sécure. This entailed inter-ethnic struggles wherein the Aymara majorities, together with Brazilian corporate interests, have confronted those minorities (Muñoz, 2013).

These scenarios are more intense in Peru due to the high volume of Quechua people from the cold highlands who since the mid-1950s left their mountains and came down to the tropical rainforest. More integrated into national society than the Amazon groups, many of these 'colonizers' (*colonos*) migrated eastbound seeking to work on market-oriented products (tea, coffee) but later moved to plant, sell and/or process coca to be illegally exported as cocaine. They fit into a *mestizo* Spanish-speaking pattern, linked to or controlled by powerful mafias which exploit the neighboring Amazon communities and occupy their territories. Likewise, the illegal timber industry is driving 'colonizers' directly to share responsibilities for deforestation and ethnocide. The cultural existence of the Ashaninka, Mashco-Piro, Yanesha, Matsiguenga and other peoples is menaced, particularly to the southeast, where an illegal gold rush overruns the state, destroys sustainable territories and transforms the jungle into an intercultural inferno.

Conclusion

South American ICC studies differ in two aspects from how they are portrayed in English-speaking industrialized societies. First, its academic practice mainly aims at the mutual understanding between modern society and comparatively isolated and/or socially downgraded ethnic groups within the same country. It is either a matter of anthropological university study and research, or of promotional projects by NGOs and governments. Although schools of communication have ICC as a subject, they are mostly not addressed as issues of cultural and linguistic assimilation of foreign visitors or migrants. An explanation would be the coexistence of a modern Self with radical Otherness inside the same territory. Latin America as a whole is the most unequal region of the world. Even if its modern middle-classes have dramatically increased after the turn of the century, traditional non-western cultures keep a significant role in public life. Second, conflicts arisen from racial and linguistic segregation, on the one hand, and clashes due to territorial, corruption and environmental concerns, on the other, are considerably more typical of intercultural relations than encounters looking forward to mutual understanding.

Notes

1 Broadly defined, a South American *mestizo* may not be only someone of a mixed biological phenotype (i.e., European and Aymara Amerindian in Bolivia). Frequently he/she may also be of a full Amerindian phenotype that abandons his native traditions and crosses an ethnic border while adopting Spanish or Portuguese (both South American *lingua francas*) as a Westernized cultural *habitus*.
2 This term (*educación intercultural bilingüe*) was created at an international meeting of indigenous peoples held at Pátzcuaro, Mexico in 1980 (Zúñiga & Gálvez, 2002).

References

Albó, X. (2009), Etnicidad y política en Bolivia, Perú y Ecuador. In Sandoval, P. (Ed.) In *Repensando la subalternidad* (pp. 497–560). Lima, Peru: SEPHIS/IEP.

Briones, C., Cañuqueo, L., Kropff, L., & Leuman, M. (2007). Escenas del multiculturalismo neoliberal. Una proyección desde el Sur. In Grimson, A. (Ed.). *Cultura y Neoliberalismo* (pp. 265–299). Buenos Aires, Argentina: CLACSO.

Degregori, C. I. (2000). *No hay país más diverso. Compendio de antropología peruana*. Lima, Peru: IEP/PUCP/UP.

Favre, H. (1998), *El indigenismo*. Mexico City, Mexico: Fondo de Cultura Económica.

Hall, E. T. (1989), *Beyond culture*. New York: Anchor Books.

Latinobarómetro (2011). *Informe 2011*. Santiago: Chile: Corporación Latinobarómetro.

Levine, T. R., Park, H. S., & Kim, R. K. (2007). Some conceptual and theoretical challenges for cross-cultural communication research in the 21st century. *Journal of Intercultural Communication Research*, 36, 205–221.

Marzal, M. (1998). *Historia de la antropología. Vol. I Antropología Indigenista*. Quito, Ecuador: Ediciones Abya-Yala.

Muñoz, M. J. (2013), El conflicto en torno al territorio indígena Parque Natural Isiboro Sécure: Un conflicto multidimensional. *Cultura y representaciones sociales*, 7 (14). Retrieved from: http://www.scielo.org.mx/scielo.php?pid=S2007-81102013000100004&script=sci_arttext

Rivas, N (2004). Ambientalismo y surgimiento de nuevos actores étnicos en el Pacífico Sur. In Barbary, O. & Urrea, F. (eds.), *Gente negra en Colombia. Dinámicas sociopolíticas en Cali y el Pacífico*. Medellín, Columbia: Cidse/Ird/Colciencias.

Sichra, I. (2009). Introducción. In *Atlas sociolingüístico de pueblos indígenas en América Latina*. FUNPROEIB Andes-UNICEF (pp. 3–16).

Tovar, M. (2007). *Régimen socio-político de los pueblos indígenas*. In Brunelle, D. (ed.) *Gobernabilidad y democracia en las Américas* (pp. 119–137). Loja, Ecuador: Universidad Técnica Particular de Loja.

Zúñiga, M. & Gálvez, M. (2002). Repensando la educación bilingüe intercultural en el Perú: bases para una propuesta de política. In Fuller, N. *Interculturalidad y política. Desafíos y posibilidades* (pp. 309–329). Lima, Peru: Red para el desarrollo de las Ciencias Sociales en el Perú.

3 INTERCULTURAL COMMUNICATION
A EUROPEAN PERSPECTIVE
João Caetano, Universidade Aberta, Portugal

Chapter Outline
- Multiculturalism and Diversity
- Place of Intercultural Communication in Europe
- Conclusion

Multiculturality and diversity are typical European features. Not only is Europe a multicultural continent but also the European countries are multicultural, either because they host many nations and languages, or because they received along their history successive waves of immigration and other strong cultural influences. Given the free movement of persons within the European Union, it is much easier today to promote contact between Europeans. Also, Europe continues to attract, as in the past, people from all over the world, because of its high levels of development and overall well-being (economic, political, social, etc.). Many of these people move to Europe fleeing poverty and also because of political or religious persecution in their countries of origin. There are also people who move to Europe for work, educational or cultural reasons.

Multiculturalism and Diversity

Europe is as rich and diverse culturally, which raises communication difficulties. Jean Monnet, one of the founders, after World War II, of the present European Union, wrote in his *Mémoires* (1976) a self-critique, where he takes his share of responsibility for the choice of the European integration model being based on the economy, while also defending that the European project should have started on cultural terms and not on economic terms because culture establishes the communication basis between people and the rulers of countries.

The current difficulties of the European integration process, increased by the international financial crisis of 2008 and the refugee crisis of 2013–2016, are mainly problems of intercultural communication caused by economic reasons. Many Europeans in northern Europe, including the governments of those countries, do not understand the behaviors of the people of southern Europe. The EU is aware of this fact, which is the reason why it financially supports scientific projects able to promote the understanding of cultural differences between Europeans and making a positive use of them, which is a major challenge.

Not only do Europeans behave differently, but they perceive reality differently. Knowledge in social sciences differs among societies and cultural contexts, which raises an important political and social question: is it possible, or not, to have intercultural understanding? A question to which different people have different answers.

The questions of understanding, acceptance, and political management of cultural differences put in contrast Western reason and other universals of discourse, but it is also at the very heart of Western reason born in Europe. Indeed, communication difficulties of a European or American with a Chinese are not necessarily bigger than the communication difficulties of a German with a Greek, as is apparent in contemporary European politics. Some authors and the media (de Quetteville, 2015; Greene, 2000, 2015) point out that Greece is closer to Russia or even to its traditional enemy Turkey, all marked by the common Byzantine culture, than to Europe and the EU.

Place of Intercultural Communication in Europe

Intercultural communication theories arise out of the concern about the lack of effective cultural communication skills among people who do not share the same life experiences, values or language (that's to say, a lack of public trust between cultures). The EU, as a political community, needs to create and strengthen political and cultural conditions for communication between people who live together but think and behave differently –consider, e.g, the different way northern European states and southern European states react to austerity or how the Europeans react to the phenomenon of refugees.

The knowledge of reality depends on reality. On the basis of the explanatory discourses of societies, there are contextual differences immediately expressed in the construction of language as a communication tool and the existence of different behaviors and social practices. The plasticity of English stems from the fact that it incorporates many elements of Latin and Anglo-Saxon cultures and languages, which is reflected in the practices of its speakers. But all languages and cultural practices have their own contributions to better understanding humanity as a whole.

On the basis of intercultural communication theories there is a need to understand cultural differences in order to explain and assess individual routes and community, which makes them important political and social instruments for peace and development. There is in intercultural communication theories a relativism that justifies the existence of different human behaviors according to cultural differences to which individuals are subject. It is by understanding more deeply the characteristics of difference and unity that it is possible to improve and better establish rules for communication between individuals.

The possibility of intercultural understanding is based on scientific research that shows there is something like a rational community, which could be shared by all people (Winch, 1990). On this basis, it is understood that humanity has created a pluralistic world culture (Winch, 1990), learning from experience and especially from the mistakes of the past.

Authors such as Wittgenstein (1953), Winch (1990), Pitkin (1973), and Habermas (1984, 1987) laid the foundations for a critical epistemology that underlies the possibility of an intercultural knowledge based on arguments that claim at the same time the differences and the confluences of cultures, which enable democratic dialogue. All of these authors were born in Europe and the majority of them emigrated, mainly due to political persecution. They also contributed to the discussion of the concept of democracy as the reality of the multiple and diverse.

The complexity of contemporary societies is reflected in the structure and viability of communicative processes. Traditionally, communication was done directly between people. Currently, communication can be made between people with the mediation of machines, without the need for physical mobility, which raises new problems of communication and changes the assumptions of the communication process.

A few years ago the Brazilian newspaper *Estado de S. Paulo* classified Europe as the World Museum because it has created both the major Western political institutions and its great cultural wealth. However, Europe not only lost the capacity to decisively influence world politics, but it is also facing very serious internal problems arising from cultural differences within it. Thus, Europe is today an excellent test-bed for the possibility of effective intercultural communication. Can Europe solve its own problems due to the difference of behaviors between people? Can Europe open up to the world in respect to its differences?

Conclusion

In terms of intercultural communication, a question emerges now in the European context, with repercussions beyond Europe. There are cultural characteristics of certain European peoples that generate greater wealth. Will thus the maintaining of that cultural diversity require further efforts to ensure that this diversity, especially in terms of wealth creation capacity, is not too strong so as to difficult the possibility of people living together. According to the economist Eric Beinhocker (2006), wealth is useful information. Will European states be able to work together in a spirit of openness and solidarity or, even harder, will they be able to compete towards self-improvement in a non-violent productive way?

Despite being a globally rich continent, there are strong economic disparities across Europe, and also a serious threat to EU peace because of cultural incompatibilities. If the combination of economic and cultural difficulties causes the collapse of the EU, this would be the failure of the most advanced European peace initiative in the last hundred years.

References

Beinhocker, E. D. (2006). *The origin of wealth: Evolution, complexity, and the radical remaking of economics*. Boston, MA: Harvard Business School Press.

de Quetteville, H. (16 June, 2015). We can't afford to lose Greece to Russia, *The Telegraph Online*. Retrieved from: http://www.telegraph.co.uk/news/worldnews/europe/greece/11679455/We-cant-afford-to-lose-Greece-to-Russia.html

Greene, M. (2000). *A shared world: Christians and Muslims in the early modern Mediterranean*. Princeton, NJ: Princeton University Press.

Greene, M. (2015). *The Edinburgh history of the Greeks, 1453 to 1768: The Ottoman Empire*. Oxford, UK: Oxford University Press.

Habermas, J. (1984). *The theory of communicative action: Reason and the rationalization of society* (Vol. 1). Boston, MA: Beacon Press.

Habermas, J. (1987). *The theory of communicative action: Live world and system: A critique of functionalist reason* (Vol. 2). Boston, MA: Beacon Press.

Monnet, J. (1976). *Mémoires*. Paris, France: Fayard.

Pitkin, H. (1973). *Wittgenstein and justice: On the significance of Ludwig Wittgenstein for social and political thought*. Berkeley, CA: California University Press.

Winch, P. (1990). *The idea of a social science and its relation to philosophy* (2nd ed.). London, UK: Routledge.

Wittgenstein, L. (1953). *Philosophical investigations*. London, UK: Basil Blackwell.

4 INTERCULTURAL COMMUNICATION IN SOUTH AFRICA

*Sabihah Moola and Babalwa Sibango,
The University of South Africa, UNISA*

Chapter Outline
- The South African Context
- Intercultural Communication
- Approaches to Intercultural Communication
- Conclusion

Intercultural communication can be best understood in its specific contexts. Various countries may experience intercultural communication differently due to a number of factors such as history, inequalities, and/or politics. South Africa as a country has a unique historical background which has impacted on intercultural relations in this country.

The South African Context

South Africa has its historical roots embedded in both colonialism and apartheid. The colonial eras saw individuals being grouped into four distinct 'races', namely, – White, Indian, Coloured, and Black. These groups occupied unequal positions, both on an economic and a social level. Whites were the superior race, Indians and Coloureds occupied the intermediary position and Blacks were the most inferior amongst all the races. Each race group was further divided into ethnic groups. Among whites, there are two main ethnic groups, namely – English and Afrikaans-speaking whites. Among Indians, the dominant ethnic groups are Tamils, Hindus and Muslims. Coloureds also differ based on origins. Some for example descended from Black and White origins, East-Indians and white, or the Khoi-san and White. Among Blacks there are nine ethnic groups – Zulu, Sotho, Xhosa, Ndebele, Shangaan, Tswana, Venda,

Swati, and Pedi. It should also be noted that relations among these ethnic groups were also marked by tensions, such as the Anglo-Boer War (1899–1902), which took place amongst Whites and the Difaqane (the crushing) wars (1818–1835), which occurred amongst Black ethnic groups.

The Group Areas Act (which was repealed in 1991) ensured all races lived separately – schools, residential areas and certain cities were designated for specific race groups. However, there were also individuals who defied apartheid laws and lived amongst other race groups although they faced harsh punishments from the government. Some apartheid heroes even sacrificed their lives in the struggle for freedom.

Apartheid officially ended in 1994, and individuals from different groups were now free to live together as a 'Rainbow Nation'. The concept of the Rainbow Nation in South Africa symbolises 'unity in diversity', a peaceful existence of diverse cultures in one nation (Habib, 1997). New laws were drafted; and the new Bill of Rights ensured all citizens were to be treated as equals. The Truth and Reconciliation Committee (TRC) was developed to allow people to speak up against the crimes committed and aimed to 'heal' the new South Africa (Moller, et al., 1999).

The notion of the racial hierarchy was demolished and policies such as Affirmative Action (AA) were created to support previously disadvantaged racial groups by creating job opportunities. Affirmative action however has become a sensitive issue amongst the remaining races (Indians, coloureds and whites) who feel disadvantaged by such policies and refer to these policies as being apartheid in reverse. Each race group is marked by inequalities, even today after South Africa's 20 years of democracy, the country still has a long road ahead before the inequalities and injustices of the past can be removed. It should be noted that Whites in general hold economic dominance, followed by Indians, Coloureds, and lastly Blacks – these are inequalities inherited from apartheid and will take many years to disperse.

Intercultural Communication

After apartheid was dismantled in 1994, the concept of the Rainbow Nation emerged under the leadership of President Nelson R. Mandela (the apartheid activist and hero of the country). Tensions emerged after South Africa became the 'new' South Africa; intercultural politics occurred amongst the different races. More than 20 years after democracy individuals are only now becoming accustomed to living with other groups. For some, however, this is not the case – there are a number of interracial incidents in post-apartheid South Africa, such as interracial fights, arguments and even racism.

Intercultural communication is communication between individuals from different cultures. Intercultural communication is thus built on two main concepts – culture and communication (Martin, et al., 2013).

Culture in South Africa encompasses race, ethnicity, religion, gender, class, sexuality, physical (dis)ability, and a wide-range of (sub) groups. Culture distinguishes one group from another – for example ethnic groups differ in terms of language or 'looks'. Culture has been defined by various authors as a set of beliefs, values or norms shared by a group of people. This definition implies each culture has its set of beliefs or values that are not shared by other cultures. Culture is also understood as dynamic, flexible or changeable, that is, culture changes with changing times or contexts. Cultures also differ in terms of social and/or economic power – that is, some cultural groups have more power than others. Cultures are also conceived as a creation of the powerful elite – who categorise individuals based on skin colour or beliefs.

Communication on the other hand is any attempt to create a shared meaning between individuals. That is, individuals have to communicate in a language they both understand. Approaches to intercultural communication in South Africa are based on the definitions of culture as discussed above. These approaches to intercultural communication are discussed below.

Approaches to Intercultural Communication

Intercultural communication is communication that occurs between different cultural groups with varying communication styles, values, norms or beliefs between dominant and non-dominant groups (Collier, 2007). Intercultural communication is considered to be: communication which occurs between individuals from various ethnic groups (example, Zulu and Tswana among Blacks) and/or different religions, classes or even within the same race groups. Although intercultural communication can be considered both tension-filled as well as harmonious in different contexts, intercultural communication aims to build the country and educate the masses on how we all can live in unity through diversity.

Some individuals, such as politicians and researchers, suggest that denouncing culture or race contributes to national identity. That is, individuals should label themselves as 'South African' instead of using their racial or ethnic labels, to reduce segregation. This view was dominant during the Mandela term as President. Some, however, suggest individuals should embrace their cultural identities but must still show respect towards other cultures by embracing them too. The term 'Rainbow Nation' for instance was coined to show individuals can be 'united in their diversity'.

Another dominant view is that different racial groups should adopt critical diversity (Steyn, 2010). That is, individuals should acknowledge inequalities among and within racial groups and bridge them. Indeed, some political figures and scholars believe there can be no social cohesion without social equality.

Another view is that South Africa should be Africanised and de-westernised. This means the country should adopt African culture as the country's culture, for example, by using African languages in schools. This was the key theme during President Thabo Mbeki's (1998–2008) term as demonstrated in his 'I am an African' speech.

Conclusion

Intercultural communication in South Africa is a complex scenario. While some progress has been made in de-segregating the once divided cultures this country still has a long way to go. Apartheid-inherited inequalities have yet to be bridged, current policies have made some progress in this regard but the inequalities still remain and intra-racial inequalities are on the rise.

References

Collier, M.J. (2007). Context, privilege, and contingent cultural identifications in South African group interview discourses. *Western Journal of Communication, 69*, 295–318.

Habib, A. (1997). South Africa: The rainbow Nation and prospects for consolidating democracy. *African Journal of Political Science, 2*(2), 15–37.

Martin, J.N., Nakayama, T.K., Schutte, P., & Van Rheede Van Oudtshoorn, G.P. (2013). *Experiencing intercultural communication – South African edition*. London, UK: McGraw Hill.

Moller, V., Dickow, H., & Harris, M. (1999). South Africa's "Rainbow people", national pride and happiness. *Social Indicators Research, 47*, 245–280.

Steyn, M. (ed). (2010). *Being different together*. Cape Town, South Africa: INCUDISA.

5 INTERCULTURAL COMMUNICATION
A WEST AFRICAN PERSPECTIVE

Elvis Ngwayuh, University of Jyväskylä, Finland

Chapter Outline

- West Africa and Intercultural Communication
- Conclusion

Over the past two decades, migration to Western countries has skyrocketed (Meuleman, et al., 2009). The current refugee crisis (2013–2016) for example has led to the migration of more than one million asylum seekers into the European Union from countries such as Syria, Afghanistan, Eritrea, Somalia, Iraq, and countries experiencing conflict, widespread violence, and insecurity (BBC, 2015; UNICEF, 2015). Moreover, every year, there are numerous international students and professionals from different countries who relocate to Western countries in pursuit of better educational and professional opportunities. Because of this, the demographic composition of most Western countries has changed considerably within the last few decades. Western societies have become culturally diverse. By culturally diverse, I mean the coexistence of multiple national cultures (nationalities) or identities. Within this context of cross-national migration, intercultural communication is most often understood as communication processes between people from different national cultures. This is also evident in the literature and studies in the field of intercultural communication. It is also true that from the inception of the field of intercultural communication (ICC), it has emphasized contact between "national" cultures. I consider this to be off course and limited in its scope. Even though I know the term "intercultural" is a very complex one, I would like to use this opportunity to introduce, emphasize, or highlight a West African context.

West Africa and Intercultural Communication

First, I would like to state here that Africa is not a country. Africa is a continent with 54 different countries. You might be surprised to know how many people think Africa is a country and that the language spoken there is Afrikaans. West African countries include countries such as Cameroon, Central African Republic, Burundi, Congo, Chad, Rwanda, Equatorial Guinea, Gabon, Angola, South Sudan, and Sao Tome and Principe. Since most of these countries have experienced very little cross-national migration of the culturally dissimilar compared with most Western countries, people tend to ignore or lose sight of how intercultural most of these countries are within themselves. Sometimes it seems to me that if we were to eliminate the idea of cross-national migration, most European countries would no longer entertain the idea of "intercultural." Unlike most Western countries, within most countries in West Africa, there exist several distinct cultural and ethnic tribes, groups, or identities with a wide variety of unique cultural practices, traditions, rituals, symbols, art, music, dance, and language (verbal and nonverbal communication), to name just a few. The ethnic diversity within these countries and the distinctiveness of their respective cultural identities and practices, and the intercultural experiences among them, warrant more attention and research in the field of intercultural communication. These different ethnic groups coexist together in a shared context and possess a common national identity but yet very distinct and strong ethnic or tribal identities and cultures. Intercultural communication within this geographical and sociological context should not only be limited to the processes of interaction between people from different countries (national cultures) as it is often understood, especially in most Western countries. But it should also encompass the intercultural experiences of people from different ethnic, tribal, or cultural groups within an ethnically and culturally diverse country.

In Nigeria for instance, the most populated country in Africa, there are over 250 ethnic groups with the most populous and politically influential being Hausa and Fulani 29%, Yoruba 21%, Igbo 18%, Ijaw 10%, Kanuri 4%, Ibibio 3.5%, and Tiv 2.5% in descending order. Even though English is the main official language, there are up to 500 additional local or indigenous languages spoken within the country. Some of the most popular ones are: Hausa, Yoruba, Igbo (Ibo), and Fulani. Moreover, in addition to English as the main official language in Ghana, there are close to 100 linguistic groups corresponding to over 100 ethnic groups within the country. Senegal is also a West African country that is ethnically diverse. There are about 36 different ethnic groups and languages within the country. French is considered the most spoken language while Wolof is the main official language of the country (Info.publicintelligence.net). When it comes to the Ivory Coast, there are over 60 ethnic groups speaking close to 80 different indigenous languages (Landinfo, 2006). In Burkina Faso, there are over 60 ethnic groups speaking a variety of languages (Ourafrica.org). Similarly in Cameroon, my home country, French and English are the main official languages but there are over 250 different languages spoken within the country corresponding to over 250 ethnic groups. I remember so clearly several times I encountered misunderstandings in the process of communication with Cameroonians from another ethnic group. For example, I come from an ethnic group called Oku and I have had the opportunity to live with a friend from another tribe called Bayangi. We sometimes experience some form of conflict because of our different ways of interpreting non-verbal communication symbols.

Conclusion

This ethnic, linguistic, and religious diversity in West Africa represents interesting intercultural communication experiences, but yet unexplored. Intercultural communication should be studied at the "interethnic" level as well. The point here is intercultural communication should not be seen solely in the limited light of communication between people from different (national cultures). It should encompass the intercultural experiences in a culturally and ethnically diverse nation like most in West Africa. Little research in the field of intercultural communication has focused on this West African context or perspective. But it is my desire that researchers in the field will pay more attention to this.

References

BBC (2015). *Migrant crisis: One million enter Europe in 2015*. Accessed 28/02/2016. http://www.bbc.com/news/world-europe-35158769

Info.publicintelligence.net. *Senegal culture field guide*. Accessed 28/02/2016. https://info.publicintelligence.net/MCIA-SenegalCultureGuide.pdf

Landinfo, 2006. Report: Cote d´Ivoire: Ethnicity, Ivoirité and conflict. Accessed 28/02/2016. http://www.landinfo.no/asset/514/1/514_1.pdf

Meuleman, B., Davidov, E. & Billiet, J. (2009). Changing attitudes toward immigration in Europe, 2002–2007: A dynamic group conflict theory approach. *Social Science Research*, 38, 352–355.

Ourafrica.org. *Our Africa, people and culture*. Accessed 28–02–2016. http://www.our-africa.org/burkina-faso/people-culture.

UNICEF (2015). *Refugee migrants in Europe; Consolidated emergency report 2015*. Accessed 28/02/2016. https://www.unicef.org/ceecis/160322_RO_CEE-CIS_-_Refugee_and_Migrant_Crisis_in_Europe_-_Regional_Cons....pdf

6 INTERCULTURAL COMMUNICATION
AN ISRAELI PERSPECTIVE

Yuval Karniel and Amit Lavie Dinur,
The Interdisciplinary Center (IDC) Herzliya, Israel

Chapter Outline

- Multiculturalism and Media in Israel
- Seven Prominent Rifts in Israel
- Conclusion

Israel is an intriguing and unique case of a Jewish nation state that faces complex challenges emerging from the encounters and communications involving the cultures it contains. The State of Israel was founded as a Jewish state in 1948, after the Jewish Holocaust in Europe, and according to its Basic Laws, Israel is defined as a Jewish, democratic state that is committed to equality and civil rights (Karniel, 2006).

Multiculturalism and Media in Israel

Multiculturalism is a prominent trend in contemporary western society and culture, and is also evident in full force in Israel. As a result of changes in the composition of the population and in the media, as well as political, economic, and technological developments, Israel contains religious, ethnic, national, and gender groups whose cultures transcend the geographic borders of the Israeli nation state.

Since Israel's foundation, diversity and multiple rifts have characterized Israeli society, with its ethnic, religious, and national groups embroiled in a moral, ideological battle over the identity of the state and the allocation of its resources. Over time, the attitude of Israeli society to the cultural differences that it contains has changed (Avraham, 2003). In the first years after statehood, Zionist ideology was a salient feature of Israeli society. Israeli culture was a melting pot that aimed to shape a uniform collective Israeli identity that blurred the cultural uniqueness of Israel's ethnic groups (Yuchtman-Yaar, 2005). This cultural trend was further engrained in society due to state broadcasting systems, as well as privately owned and party-affiliated newspapers promoting the government's melting-pot policy.

The media colluded in the efforts to disregard the various tribes of Israeli society, especially the Palestinians, the state's Arab citizens, and Haredi Jews, the state's ultra-orthodox Jewish citizens. Israel focused on absorbing Jewish immigration from all over the world and its population grew from 600,000 in 1948 to 8 million today.

Following the political reversal of 1977, at which time the political right wing won the elections for the first time, Israeli media increasingly featured new voices that demanded political and media representation, status, rights, and resources for various ethnic, religious, national, and gender groups in Israeli society. Over the past two decades the Israeli media has become increasingly privatized, which led to greater variety and decentralization of media channels. This interactive revolution, together with globalization being on the rise, plays a key role in the process by which groups are consolidating distinct collective identities. This has led to those groups mobilizing the support of their members, thus successfully obtaining satisfaction of their demands from the government.

Based on these trends, Israel now has separate media in Arabic for its Palestinian citizens, in Russian for new immigrants from the former Soviet Union, religious media, and media for every significant political stream. In addition, there is evidence of increased representation and participation of the various cultures in Israel's hegemonic mainstream media led by the popular television channel, Channel 2 (Karniel & Lavie-Dinur, 2011).

These changes are immediately linked to two wars, the Six Day War of 1967 and the October War of 1973, which had a significant impact on Israeli society and on the depiction of the government in the Israeli media. Prior to the Six Day War, the national mood in Israel was apprehensive and filled with despair. The military victory opened Israel up to myriad influences: Israel was engulfed by a flood of young men and women, Jews and non-Jews, who came to volunteer on the country's kibbutzim or spend a year in the country. These young people brought their customs, faiths, and habits of dress to Israel, which was relatively isolated until then. Israel's first television broadcasts were launched immediately after the war and exposed society to new influences. The sixties were a decade of liberated attire, psychedelic music, and drug use all over the world. After the development of oral contraception and before the AIDS era, this period was characterized by commitment-free sexual relations. Young Israelis were exposed to—and adopted many of—the beliefs, attitudes, and customs of the volunteers who came to Israel in this period from all over the world. Israel had opened up to the world.

The October War of 1973 triggered growing criticism of the government and a significant change in the media's treatment of government messages. Previously, Israeli media conducted itself as "mobilized media" that was responsive to government requests for censorship, especially on security-related matters. As a result, in order to prevent public panic, the media failed to inform the Israeli public of the military preparations of Egyptian and Syrian armies for war in violation of the cease-fire agreements. Then-Prime Minister (PM) Golda Meir similarly refused to approve wide-scale mobilization of reservists for fear of arousing a public response. Instead of informing the public of these developments and preparing them for the anticipated war, the media, through what was known at the time as the high-profile Editors' Committee, acceded to government requests to conceal the information. The October War of 1973 caught the Israeli public and the army unprepared. The enormous shock that reverberated through Israeli society also affected the media. From that point onward, the Israeli media became more critical and suspicious of the government.

Cultural diversity and fragmentation may lead to multicultural pluralism that embraces diversity as an integral part of Israeli society, yet conserves Israel's definition as a Jewish and democratic state and a joint—but not homogeneous—framework. However, these developments may also exacerbate polarization, mutual negation, alienation, hatred, divisions, and discord among the different sections of Israeli society, to the point where they undermine Israel's potential to exist as a Jewish, democratic state. Both these trends are observable in Israel concurrently.

Presently, it is clear that the melting pot policy—the desire of Israel's founder and first PM David Ben Gurion to view all Israelis as a single, homogeneous group—was never achieved. Today, more than ever, Israel has made room for diversity (Khazzoom, 2003).

Seven Prominent Rifts in Israel

The seven prominent rifts in Israeli society today are based on nationality (Jews–Arabs), religion (observant and secular Jews), ethnicity (Ashkenazi and Sephardi Jews), status (poor and rich), tenure in Israel (long-standing citizens and new immigrants), politics (right and left), and gender (men, women, and the LGBT community). In Israel, several tribes exist alongside each other, in separate political frameworks, and typically maintain distinct media: Palestinian Arab citizens of Israel, who largely identify with the Palestinian nation that is outside Israel's borders and is involved in occasional aggression against Israel; orthodox Jews; national-religious Jews, some of whom are settlers in the Occupied Territories; new immigrants from the former Soviet Union countries who still speak Russian; dark-skinned Sephardi Jews from North Africa and other Arab countries; light-skinned Ashkenazi Jews from Europe and the Americas; and the LGBT community that has significant presence in the media (Avraham, 2003; Bar-Yosef, 1980; Caspi, et al., 2002; Lavie-Dinur & Karniel, 2013; Loshitzky, 2001; Shohat, 2010).

The aforementioned groups however are not homogenous units either, even though over time some dilution between them has occurred. Some examples of this include Arab Israelis speaking Hebrew, immigrants from the former Soviet Union listening to Israeli music, and secular Ashkenazi Jews fasting and going to temple on Yom Kippur, the holiest day of the Jewish calendar. This dilution in part also shapes the political landscape of Israel. Parliament in Israel is made up of a vertigo-inducing number of parties that range from the far left on the political spectrum to the far right, with the Haredi party Shas (religious conservatism) splitting recently due to an ideological rift, the Arab Israelis having several parties as well as secular Israelis being divided into many groups based on their opinions on the peace process, and moreover whether they have socialist or capitalist ideals when concerned with economics. So while dilution of the cultural identities leads to the Israeli sub-cultures constantly evolving and changing, due to immigration and new trends, Israeli culture overall does not become more uniform, but rather more diverse. While Israel is far from embracing diversity and tolerance of others, Israeli society has made much progress, and today tolerance of minority groups is much greater than ever before.

For example, until the 1990s, the few occasions on which homosexual males appeared on television were in stereotyped contexts. Even in foreign comedy series aired on Israeli television, such as *Are You Being Served*, Mr. Humphreys was a caricature of an effeminate male and the object of ridicule. In the second half of the 1990s, queer characters underwent normalization. In Israel, the change was marked by the popular dramatic television series *Florentine*, with lovers Iggy and Tomer, and continued with the successful film *Yossi & Jagger*, which contained not only insinuations but an actual male couple—two officers planted firmly in the heart of the Israeli consensus—the military (Yosef, 2005). The media played a role in establishing a positive attitude toward homosexuals as a group in Israeli society. Today the gay community is a prominent and an influential group located at the heart of the Israeli media consensus, and its members frequently appear on popular prime time commercial television shows.

Conclusion

Other minority groups such as Haredi Jews, new immigrants from Russia, and even Palestinian Arab citizens, feature in Israeli media today more than ever. These representations, although limited and occasionally stereotyped, create hope that Israel is moving toward a more multicultural society, at least with respect to its Jewish citizens.

References

Avraham, E. (2003). *Behind media marginality: Coverage of social groups and places in the Israeli press.* Baltimore, MD: Lexington Books.

Bar-Yosef, R. W. (1980). Desocialization and resocialization: The adjustment process of immigrants. In E. Krausz (ed.), *Studies of Israeli society,* 1: *Immigration, ethnicity and community* (pp. 19–27). Piscataway, NJ: Transaction Books.

Caspi, D., Adoni, H., Cohen, A. A., & Elias, N. (2002). The Red, the White and the Blue: The Russian media in Israel. *International Communication Gazette, 64,* 537–556.

Karniel, Y. (2006). Balancing the protection of civil liberties during wartime: How the Israeli Supreme Court shaped Palestinian freedom of expression during the Second Intifada. *Government Information Quarterly, 22,* 626–643.

Karniel, Y., & Lavie-Dinur, A. (2011). Entertainment and stereotypes: The representation of Palestinian Arab citizens in reality shows on Israeli television. *Journal of Intercultural Communication Research, 41,* 65–87.

Khazzoom, A. (2003). The great chain of Orientalism: Jewish identity, stigma management, and ethnic exclusion in Israel. *American Sociological Review, 68,* 481–510.

Lavie-Dinur, A., & Karniel, Y. (2013). 'Esti Ha'mechoeret': Ugly Esti. In: J. McCabe & K. Akass (eds.), *TV's Betty goes global: From telenovela to international brand* (pp. 167–174). London, UK: IB Tauris.

Loshitzky, Y. (2001). *Identity politics on the Israeli screen.* Austin, TX: University of Texas Press.

Shohat, E. (2010). *Israeli cinema: East/West and the politics of representation.* London & New York, NY: IB Tauris.

Yosef, R. (2005). The national closet: Gay Israel in Yossi and Jagger. *GLQ: A Journal of Lesbian and Gay Studies, 11,* 283–300.

Yuchtman-Yaar, E. (2005). Continuity and change in Israeli society: The test of the melting pot. *Israel Studies, 10*(2), 91–128.

7 INTERCULTURAL COMMUNICATION
AN IRANIAN PERSPECTIVE

*Nourollah Zarrinabadi,
University of Isfahan, Iran*

Chapter Outline

- Purpose of Intercultural Communication Research in Iran
- Popular Intercultural Topics in Iran
- Conclusion

The study of intercultural communication may be one of the most important topics in the social sciences/humanities. Communication among members of various cultures has always been important and is more and more needed. Intercultural communication was formerly needed for purposes such as trade but it is a matter of survival for human beings today (Kim, 2010).

Communication with people of other cultures in Iran has been investigated under different terms such as "interactional," "intercultural," and "cross-cultural" communication. Although considered necessary by researchers, authorities, and decision-makers, intercultural communication as an academic field has not gained much importance to be taught as a university major. It is still considered as an area of research within other related fields such as communication, linguistics, and media and journalism.

Purpose of Intercultural Communication Research in Iran

The official language of Iran is Persian, and Islam is the official religion. Iranian society is recognized as highly diverse due to the existence of various linguistically, ethnically, and culturally diverse groups such as Kurds, Turks, Baluchis, Lurs, and Arabs. Iranian cultures are different from non-Iranian cultures, specifically the Western ones, due to various differences: language, literature, religion, value systems, ethnicity, lifestyle, rituals, and attitudes and beliefs. This diversity in cultural systems makes it difficult to draw any conclusions about the status of intercultural communication research in the country. It is, however, possible to claim that the study and practice of intercultural communication in Iran has had two main purposes. First, the research and practice of intercultural communication has been encouraged by policy-makers as a way to increase national cohesion and integrity. Consequently, intercultural communication for an Iranian mainly refers to communicating with a compatriot from a different ethnic, religious, or linguistic background. Iranians believe the outcome of such interactions should enhance national cohesion and friendship among different ethnicities, religious groups, and cultural systems. This perception is, of course, influenced by Islamic virtues, which state that all human beings are equal and Muslims and non-Muslims should live together peacefully and enjoy social justice and equity. More than 10 principles in the constitution state that people are free to have their own language, religion, and rituals and require the media and educational system to foster national integration by making members of society familiar with other cultural groups. The educational system pays special attention to different cultures in the country and tries to encourage friendly relations with others. Moreover, the media, particularly national TV, attempt to cover the language, norms, and rituals of all groups. Therefore, research on intercultural communication has mainly focused on investigating intercultural sensitivities, intercultural perceptions, and methods for intercultural education to develop intercultural competence and provide practical implications to facilitate intercultural interactions.

Second, intercultural communication is also perceived as understanding the process of delivering and receiving message while communicating with people or groups of people from cultures of foreign countries. Intercultural communication research in this sense mainly compares and contrasts communication processes in Iran with those of other nations. The following can be expressed as the aims of this view of intercultural communication in Iran (Ameli & Mohammadkhani, 2009):

1. To broaden the knowledge of history, culture, institutions, and lifestyle of foreign countries
2. To develop critical awareness of the norms, values, and beliefs of own and other cultures
3. To provide the conventions which govern the communicative behaviour of foreigners in specific environments
4. To understand the relationship between context, culture, and the language
5. To become aware of sensitivities and other variables that hinder successful intercultural communication.

Popular Intercultural Topics in Iran

In recent years, there has been an increasing amount of literature on diverse aspects of intercultural communication in Iran. Iranian intercultural researchers took the mainstream theoretical frameworks in intercultural communication as their guiding compass and tried to test them in the Iranian multicultural and multilingual context. The majority of these studies have been of a theory-testing nature or follow-up studies, which tried to investigate the status of the phenomena in Iran. Researchers have tried to compare and contrast their findings with those of the Western contexts to see the extent to which their findings are similar to or different from the Western data. The following are some of the most popular topics in intercultural communication research for Iranian scholars:

1. *The role of culture in intercultural communication research*: The ways in which different aspects of Iranian culture may influence intercultural communication with people of other nations.
2. *The role of language in intercultural communication*: cross-cultural metaphor awareness or realization of different speech acts (e.g., apologizing, requesting, and inviting) in Persian and their seminaries and differences with other languages.
3. *Adaptation and acculturation studies*: studies related to psychological and socio-cultural adaptation of Iranian international students in English-speaking countries such as Australia, Canada, and the US.
4. *Intercultural communication competence*: Assessing different models of intercultural communication competence among Iranian English language learners, or investigating the relationship between intercultural communication and other individual variables such as anxiety and motivation.
5. *Communication traits*: Investigating communication traits such as willingness to communicate, self-perceived communication competence, and communication apprehension in the Iranian context and comparing the findings with those of other nations.

Conclusion

In summary, intercultural communication arguably seems to be one of the most serious issues confronting Iranian people due to the government's ideological orientations and the recent changes in Iranian foreign policy to expand international relations with other nations including Western ones. This seems to increase the interest in intercultural communication research in the country and open up numerous research trends and avenues in which intercultural communication can be investigated to assist the development of relationships with other cultures on the one hand and contribute to the global understanding of intercultural communication on the other hand.

References

Ameli, S. R. & Mohammadkhani, N. (2009). Intercultural communication and Iranian legal, educational, and media discourse. *Iranian Journal of Cultural Research*, 4, 41–78.
Kim, M. (2010). Intercultural communication in Asia: current state and future prospects. *Asian Journal of Communication*, 20, 166–180.

8 INTERCULTURAL COMMUNICATION
A CHINESE PERSPECTIVE
Jiang Fei, Chinese Academy of Social Sciences, Beijing, China

Chapter Outline

- The First Gate of the Labyrinth
- The Romance of the Three Kingdoms
- Mainstreams in Communication Research in China
- Academic Resources

As Samovar and Porter (1972) said, one must be both ambitious and arbitrary to include an article in or exclude it from an Intercultural Communication Reader. Now I am facing almost the same challenge; although I have sketched out the intercultural communication research landscape in more or less 40,000 Chinese words (Jiang, 2012), to give you the whole picture of Chinese intercultural communication within very limited words is an all-or-nothing game. Here I try to shoulder the burden and sort out an Ariadne's Thread to help you go through the labyrinth.

The First Gate of the Labyrinth

The very first gate of the labyrinth is to locate Chinese intercultural communication studies in world history and cultural studies, and understand the post-colonial context for intercultural communication scholars in China (Jiang, 2005). Since the middle of the 20th century after World War II, world culture has largely been preoccupied with the problematic of colonial times. If you go back to the history of how different cultures interact, we can see four stages (Figure 8.1).

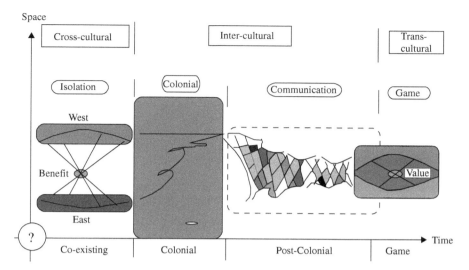

Figure 8.1 World Culture under Four Perspectives

1. Cultural co-existence, where East and West had low levels of cultural self-consciousness. Different cultural subjects interacted through trade and individual visits.
2. Colonial times. The general process of human cultural evolution was taken over by cultural supremacy because of colonialism. A culture that has been taken over is hard to rest in peace: it rests in pieces. As Fanon wrote, the colonial era changed the whole cultural situation, 'The Black man wants to be white. The white man slaves to reach a human level', and even worse, 'the white man is sealed in his whiteness, the black man in his blackness'(Fanon, 1968, p. 9).
3. Post-colonial time. Critical theory, starting with *Orientalism* (Said, 1979), evokes world wide cultural consciousness. In addition to the great works from mass media, the field of communication-between-cultures turns out to be a shadow less lamp, highlighting the direction of disenchantment with a deep-lying unbalanced cultural situation on the one hand, and on the other hand, like a shuttle flies back and forth on the loom, other than providing messages and entertainments, the mass media plays a role of weaving a new cultural 'tapestry' (Leeds-Hurwitz, 2002, p. 70) through neo-knowledge production (Jiang, 2012).

We believe problems cannot be tackled solely on one's own. The fourth stage in terms of trans-cultural communication philosophy, targeted on unresolved supremacy along with new but unresolved problems such as cultural hegemony, is coming. When you look at China, it's crucial to realize the post-colonial context is an unlatched door. The ebb and flow of research on communication between cultures and other related practices in China go on as usual, but if you ignore the door, you may become lost in the overcomplicated categories of China's cultural jungle: different emotions and policies mingled with de-westernization, localization, De-Chinese, Re-Chinese, cultural inferiority, consciousness, ambition, and so on. I believe you will have to retreat and knock on the door again.

The Romance of the Three Kingdoms

Communication-between-Cultures is a trans-disciplinary field in China in which at least three main disciplines are deeply involved: Linguistics, International relations, and Communication research. They share the same categories of research perspective: Communication-between-Cultures, whether cross-cultural, intercultural, or trans-cultural, is translated as a single Chinese concept: "kua wen hua" (in Chinese, "跨文化"). When linguistics researchers translate "Communication," they prefer to use "jiao ji" (in Chinese, "交际") to put their research focus on interactions when individuals meet from different cultures. The mainstream team of researchers comes from multi-language teachers in departments of languages in universities. International relations researchers, for their part, prefer to use "jiao liu" (in Chinese, "交流") to highlight their emphasis on cultural communication on the national/state level (Guan, 1996).

For scholars in the field of media and communication studies, "chuan bo" (in Chinese, "传播") defines their research subject as information flow. The focus of their energy is on media and medium studies, and they embrace more perspectives from other disciplines, for example, anthropology, comparative literature studies, and even comparative cultural studies.

Mainstreams in Communication Research in China

The mainstream of China communication-between-cultures research is in the field of media and communication studies. We can trace one of the basic trends in communication studies. In general terms, its focus moved from result oriented to cultural context oriented. After Hall put "intercultural" and "communication" together in the 1950s (Hall, 1959), intercultural communication was a normal course being taught in university classes in the 1960s, and booming in the 1970s in the United States, and it was introduced into the mainland of China and Taiwan in the 1980s (Duan, 1988; Hu, 1988; Wang, 1982). From this point, we can conclude that intercultural communication research was transplanted effectively in at least three disciplines in the culturally shifting context, being embedded in media and communication theory, following the research paradigm from the US. In fact, the process of introducing communication-as-a-field into China itself is a process of intercultural communication and a research subject for intercultural communication studies.

From the year 2000 onwards, China's intercultural communication studies show the following characteristics:

1. The number of papers on intercultural communication study history rose steadily (Guan, 2006; Luo & Si, 2004).
2. Systematic approaches to the middle-level intercultural communication research emerged, for example, concerns about the construction mechanism of intercultural communication in terms of globalization and glocalization (Chen, 2001); scholars investigated how to find the basic starting point and standpoint for Chinese intercultural communication practices based on understanding of western philosophy (Ja, 2007; Jiang, 2004; Lee, 2004).
3. Efforts were redoubled to construct a fundamental research framework for intercultural communication studies (Liu & Yu, 2000; Wu, 2000).
4. More intercultural communication readers appeared (Emmerson, 2007; Yu, 2006).
5. Intercultural communication through new media attracted more and more consideration (Dan & Shi, 2008; Hu, 2005; Peng, 2005).
6. Some well-known key intercultural communication concepts were interpreted and deeply studied, for example, high/low context (Liu & Cheng, 2007), culture shock (Hu & Wen, 2006), cultural community (Jiang & Huang, 2013, 2014) etc.
7. Some new concepts and research paradigms, which are well rooted in Chinese culture, appeared when dealing with Chinese local intercultural communication practices and theory. For example, "antibody," a specialized word from preventive medicine, was borrowed and redefined as "cultural antibody" to describe the situation of China's construction of counter-power against Western modernity and cultural invasion in general (Li, 2008). "Neo-knowledge production theory" for Chinese intercultural communication practices and studies is easier to understand from this point (Jiang, 2010); Guanxi, which was regarded as the "lifeblood of Chinese business communities" (Ramasamy, Goh, & Yeung, 2006) was applied in demonstrating a model of international relationships with Chinese characteristics; "Cultural Other" (capitalizing the word "other") was academically defined as a research subject of intercultural communication as distinct from "Cultural other" (Jiang, 2007).

Academic Resources

The first and only national intercultural communication association, the Chinese Intercultural Communication Association, was founded in 1995 within the field of linguistics. Together with the regular association committee conference, they initiated a biannual international I-C conference, which has so far convened ten times. In the field of media and communication studies, the first national congress was organized by the Institute of Journalism and Communication at the Chinese Academy of Social Sciences in 1982. They discussed intercultural communication in some sections in the early 1990s. Starting from 2004, the Institute of Journalism & Communication from Wuhan University collaborated with Bordeaux III University from France, and initiated another biannual international intercultural communication conference with participants mostly from media and communication studies. It has been held seven times so far. The fourth important IC conference platform is under the aegis of the China Information Office of the State Council and is organized by the Center of International Communication under the CIPG, China International Press Group. It was entitled the "Intercultural Forum" in 2006, but changed into the "National and International Communication Congress" in 2009. Its topic shifted from "How to Build a Modern Communication System in China" (2009), to "New World Landscape and International Communication: Chinese Approaches" (2011), and from "Global Communication: New Trends, New Media, New Action" (2013) to "China International Discourse System Construction" (2015). Other academic sources on Chinese intercultural communication are rather limited. The only monthly published journal called *International Communications*[1] is sponsored by the Center for International Communication under the CIPG. It is actually a summary-and-report-oriented magazine targeted at Chinese officials in the field of international propaganda rather than intercultural communication academic research. The intercultural communication research situation took a favorable turn in 2013, when Professor Hu Zhengrong from the Communication University of China established the first Blue Book to record Chinese International Communication practices annually. I established a program entitled the China Intercultural Communication Research & Training Program in July 2013, and put out a new annual book recording Chinese Intercultural Communication academic research. It is modeled on the *International/Intercultural Communication Annual*, which was established by the Speech Communication Association of the US in 1974. The first issue (*China Intercultural Communication Annual, CIC Annual*) came out in June 2015; it was published by the China Social Sciences Press both in English and Chinese, and also starting from 2015 the Institute of Journalism and Communication under the Chinese Academy of Social Sciences will accredit an Intercultural Communication Ph.D. It is a tangible signal that Chinese intercultural communication is to some extent reaching new heights.

As intercultural communication scholar Ting-Toomey from the US described in the preface of her book, we are all cultural animals like fish swimming in an aquarium oblivious to the importance of water and the tank. But once we are challenged by another whose cultural background is totally different from ours, we will feel anxious and finally realize the importance of preparing intercultural knowledge and skills (Ting-Toomey, 1999). The awkward facts for Chinese intercultural communication scholars, which are hard to gloss over, are the intercultural communication knowledge and skill gap between research and practice: the government of China has gone too far in promoting international communication through state projects such as building new centers for CCTV in Kenya and the Confucius Institutes, while simultaneously neglecting the lessons that the USA experienced in the 1950s. These have been recorded in many intercultural communication books including Hall's *The Silent Language*, which was translated into Chinese in 1991. There is no new thing under the sun, but despite this, China is becoming one of the best research targets in the study of intercultural communication.

Note

1 Introduction for the magazine from the website in Chinese: http://baike.baidu.com/link?url=4Zoiv9V3hxCvCE2HkVxyUt4XnXIEkz4UooU-9e9AyBnjTKI4LX_xclfk6NAbupys73sDjHBEAf-UT-I4foMJa_. Access date: February 2, 2015.

References

Chen, W. X. (2001). Globalization context for intercultural communication [跨文化传播的全球化背景]. *Journal of International Journalism [国际新闻界]*, 2.

Dan, H. J., & Shi, Y. B. (2008). Intercultural communication study from Internet Social Theory Perspective [网络社会理论视角下的跨文化传播思考]. *Journal: Theory Studying and Exploration [学习与探索]*, 4.

Duan, L. C. (ed.). (1988). *Introduction of international/intercultural communication.* Beijing, China: China Building Industry Press

Emmerson, J. Z. (Ed.). (2007). *International intercultural communication research reader [国际跨文化传播精华文选]*. Hangzhou, China: Zhejiang University Press.

Fanon, F. (1968). *Black skin, white masks* (C. L. Markmann, Trans.). New York, NY: Grove Press, Inc.

Guan, S. J. (1996). *Intercultural communication: A field help to promote international communication skills [跨文化交流学：提高涉外交流能力的学问]*. Beijing, China: Peking University Press.

Guan, S. J. (2006). Ten-year review and prospect for China intercultural communication research [中国跨文化传播研究十年回顾与反思]. *Journal for International Communication [对外大传播]*, 12.

Hall, E. T. (1959). *The silent language.* New York, NY: Doubleday and Company.

Hu, C. (2005). *Intercultural communication: Paradigm and competence construction in E-time [跨文化交际：E时代的范式与能力构建]*. Beijing, China: China Social Sciences Press.

Hu, L. X., & Wen, Z. Y. (2006). Cultural shock study in intercultural communication [论跨文化传播中的'文化休克'现象]. *Southeast Communication [东南传播]*, 3.

Hu, W. Z. (Ed.). (1988). *Intercultural communication and English study*. Shanghai, China: Shanghai Translation Publishing House.

Ja, L. (2007). Immanuel Wallerstein World System Theory's intercultural communication and its revelations [资本全球化视域中的文化同一性探究——沃勒斯坦"世界体系"理论的跨文化传播及其启示]. *Social Science Abroad [国外社会科学]*, 5.

Jiang, F. (2004). Post-colonial context for intercultural communication [跨文化传播的后殖民语境]. *Journal for Journalism and Communication [新闻与传播研究]*, 1.

Jiang, F. (2005). *Post-colonial context for intercultural communication*. Beijing, China: Renmin University Press.

Jiang, F. (2007). Move from academic frontier to theoretical axis: Exploration of the object for intercultural communication research [从学术前沿回到学理基础——跨文化传播研究对象初探]. *Journal for Journalism and Communication [新闻与传播研究]*, 3, 31–37.

Jiang, F. (2010, February, 2). Neo-knowledge production from a Chinese perspective (in Chinese). *Chinese Social Sciences Today*.

Jiang, F. (2012). An intercultural communication study from China's perspective [跨文化传播研究的中国视角]. In A. Fung (Ed.), *The imagination of Chinese communication [华人传播想像]* (pp. 137–194). Hong Kong: The Chinese University of Hong Kong Press.

Jiang, F., & Huang, K. (2013). Community media in China: Communication, digitalization, and relocation (in English). *Journal of International Communication*, 19(1).

Jiang, F., & Huang, K. (2014). Communication grey zones and the humanistic approach in communication studies. ["'传播灰色地带'与传播研究人文思考路径的探寻"]. *Nanjing Journal of Social Sciences [南京社会科学]*, 4, 122–130.

Lee, C. C. (2004). *Beyond West supremacy: Media and China cultural modernity [超越西方霸权——传媒与文化中国的现代性]*. London, UK: Oxford University Press.

Leeds-Hurwitz, W. (2002). *Wedding as text: Communicating cultural identities through ritual*. Mahwah, NJ: Lawrence Erlbaum Associates Inc.

Li, S. W. (2008). Cultural anti-body in intercultural communication: Starbucks event in China Forbidden City as a case [跨文化传播中的文化抗体研究——以故宫星巴克咖啡传媒事件为个案]. *Journal for Journalism and Communication [新闻与传播研究]*, 5.

Liu, J., & Cheng, L. (2007). Context Control Theory's intercultural communication [语境控制理论的跨文化传播意]. *Journal of Northeast Normal University (Social Science) [东北师大学报(哲学社会科学版)]*, 4.

Liu, S., & Yu, W. X. (2000). *Intercultural communication: Dismantling the cultural wall [跨文化传播：拆解文化的围墙]*. Haerbin, China: Heilongjiang Renmin Press.

Luo, Y. C., & Si, J. X. (2004). *Review and prospect of intercultural communication research in Mainland of China [中国大陆跨文化传播研究的回顾与展望]*. Paper presented at the Asian Media Forum [年亚洲传媒论坛], Beijing.

Peng, L. (2005). A primary study on intercultural communication through Internet [网络与跨文化传播问题初探]. Retrieved February 20, 2008, from 紫金网 http://www.zijin.net/blog/user1/118/archives/2005/266.shtml.

Ramasamy, B., Goh, K. W., & Yeung, M. C. H. (2006). Is Guanxi (relationship) a bridge to knowledge transfer? *Journal of Business Research*, 59(1), 130–139.

Said, E. W. (1979). *Orientalism*. New York, NY: Random House.

Samovar, L., A., & Porter, R., E. (eds.). (1972). *Intercultural communication: A reader*. Belmont, CA: Wadsworth Publishing Company, Inc.

Ting-Toomey, S. (1999). *Communicating across cultures*. New York, NY: The Guilford Press.

Wang, G. (1982). *Culture and communication*. Taiwan: SanMinShuJu.

Wu, Y. M. (2000). Research boundary and practical concern for intercultural communication research [跨文化传播的研究领域与现实关切]. *Journal of Shenzhen University (Humanities & Social Sciences) [深圳大学学报：人文社科版]*, 1.

Yu, W. H. (Ed.). (2006). *Intercultural research reader [跨文化研究读本]*. Wuhan, China: Wuhan University Press.

9 INTERCULTURAL COMMUNICATION
A KOREAN PERSPECTIVE

Young-Ok Lee, Kyung Hee University, South Korea

Chapter Outline:
- The Korean Context
- Cultural Aspects of Korean Society
- Conclusion

According to the *New Millennium Dictionary of Korean Language and Culture*, Korea is an old nation with a long history of more than 4000 years (Suh, 2003). As in the case of any country with a long history, Korean history is not a peaceful one—it has been marked by a succession of struggles by outsiders to gain control of the Peninsula and Koreans kept fighting to recover their sovereignty. After the Korean War (1950–1953) and the nationwide movement for democracy, it finally established a bona fide democratic regime and the economy has developed at speeds no other country has outstripped. As was testified by Huntington (2000), just within the period of 40 years or so after the war, South Korea has become an industrial giant with the 14th largest economy in the world, multinational corporations, major exports of automobiles, electronic equipment, and other sophisticated manufactures. It is a wonder—and some would even describe it as a miracle—to achieve such an economic feat for a country with its small land divided into South and North Korea, and only limited natural resources. The answer to such an extraordinary development may be found in their unique culture, as was suggested by Huntington.

The Korean Context

Thus, while Koreans have a deep respect for their long history, their value system represented in their communication patterns and other behaviors for important matters underwent a big change in the huge upheavals of the sociopolitical order and economic situation. In this 21st century of knowledge and the information era, the importance of the English language as the lingua franca has further increased and it is felt by a country like South Korea whose economy greatly depends on exports and trades. According to a recent report by Yunhap, the South Korean economy has the highest trade dependence rate among the Group of 20 (G-20) leading countries. It reported that exports accounted for 43.4 percent of South Korea's gross domestic product (GDP) in 2009 (*Yunhap News*, September 13, 2010).

With increasing contact with other cultures, especially English-speaking Western cultures, Korean cultures are rapidly changing in every aspect of their lifestyle and belief systems, and the Christian and modern democratic and rational Western ideology emphasizing individualism and rationalism (Wierzbicka, 2006) is in stark contrast to the traditional Korean value system. However widespread and strong Western influence may be, the deep-seated cultural characteristics are not so easily erased or changed because the basic elements crucial to the culture are fused into their thought and language patterns. For example, Korean sentence structures and diverse constructions incorporate the relative social status of the interactants and referents, and there are typical vocabulary items reflecting cultural specifics. Proverbs and idioms are some instances of fixed expressions that reflect the common shared memories of the past which are very important in establishing identity and culture.

Christianity has spread widely in Korean society, and about 14.3 million Koreans are of various Christian denominations (*Economist*, August 12, 2014). It is a remarkable phenomenon, considering traditional Korean society was characterized by its collectivistic Confucian culture, which is keen to keep social harmony with every member following ethical codes of conduct strictly ordained by rule-like social norms. As was asserted by Samovar et al. (2013) and Morrison and Conaway (2007), Confucianism in Asian cultures maintains that the ultimate ideal is one of harmony in relationships and the stability of society is based on unequal relationships between people. Do (2006) asserted that the basic guidelines for human relationships in various situations, namely, the Three Bonds and Five Relationships (三綱五倫) worked as a justification for ruling class people's oppression of the lower classes. The Three Bonds and Five Relationships are supposed to be three fundamental principles and five moral disciplines required to be observed in the following five relationships: master–follower, father–son, elder brother–younger brother, husband–wife, and senior friend–junior friend. As Hofstede explained (2001), these relationships contain mutual and complementary obligations and these ideas are still used as guidelines for people to follow in dealing with other people. Under this prevailing Confucian ideology, traditionally Koreans, accustomed to the long-lasting monarchy and governed under the system of strict social hierarchy, put great value in preserving the family line along the male offspring of the same family name. This strong concept of male supremacy and the patriarchal system encompassing every corner of people's lives has played a very significant role in forming the value system and related rituals and social institutions in Korea.

Cultural Aspects of Korean Society

The most significantly powerful and prevailing core values representing the two cultures may be collectivism for Korean culture and individualism for US culture, respectively. According to Hofstede's (2001) comparative study of cultural features representing different countries over the world in terms of four major dimensions, Korea is designated relatively high in Power Distance (60) and Uncertainty Avoidance (85), but low in Individualism (18) and Masculinity (39). These index values show interesting contrast with those of the United States, which is relatively low in Power Distance (40) and Uncertainty Avoidance (46), but high in Individualism (91) and Masculinity (62). Long-Term Orientation also represents the two cultures as opposed to each other: relatively high for South Korea (75) but fairly low for the US (29). The differences in the two countries' relative cultural index values may be clearly revealed in Figure 9.1.

Israeli psychologist Shalom Schwartz, before his extensive survey of schoolteachers and students in 44 countries finished in 1994, suggested ten categories of value clusters: power, achievement, hedonism, stimulation, self-direction, universalism, benevolence, tradition, conformity, and security. If we apply Schwartz's (1992) value clusters to the present Korean society with a mixture

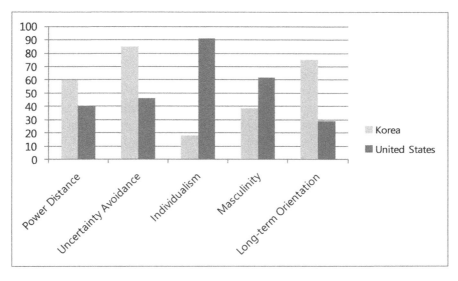

Figure 9.1 Cultural Index Values of South Korea and the United States

of the traditional values and the newly introduced American values, we may characterize it as strong in power, achievement, hedonism, universalism, tradition, conformity, and security while still weak in such categories as stimulation, self-direction, and benevolence.

According to Hulbert (1969/1906), the first American scholar who recorded the behavioral patterns of Koreans from the perspectives of Westerners, the most remarkable and unique characteristics of the Koreans was to take trouble to keep or save their face. He wrote that he was very surprised to see Koreans donate a large sum of money for the purpose of justice or to treat guests with the generous hospitality rarely found in other people.

While specific cultural features of a country may undergo changes along with various outward factors, deep-seated ethos or characteristics are hard to change. Most of all, the language and the way of thought reflected in linguistic expressions are interrelated to each other, reinforcing their influence on the basic culture. Thus, as was elaborated by Lee (2010, 2013a, 2013b), the Korean language has developed some unique sets of lexical items for distinguishing social status or intimacy between the interactants along with systems of morphological devices for derivation. In other words, the Korean language structure reflects its collectivistic culture, which regards oneself as inescapably connected with the life of other people, especially one's family and close relatives. So they keep observing the people around them ready to modify their behavior according to their senior's taste or decision.

Diverse expressions used to designate Koreans' characteristics like the following may all be subsumed under the keyword of connection with other people, the core value of collectivism: face, harmony with others, respect for the elderly, understanding of others' wishes without verbal expressions—the main characteristic of high-context culture. These basic values are realized in various behavioral patterns, of which the most remarkable one is discriminating against women, such as discriminating treatment against daughters—(because the male family line is the important mechanism to be connected with other family members under male supremacy or patriarchy), sharing liquor with close male colleagues or friends (it may be an important ritual for male company workers to relieve the stressful tension they have gathered every day in their strictly hierarchical organizations), filial piety (along with ancestral worship, this is a very important virtue or duty imposed on the son and the daughter-in-law, another important example of male-chauvinistic discrimination against women), or their propensity to accomplish things in a hurry (it is important to serve their senior's wishes immediately without making them wait).[1]

Now with a woman elected president in 2013, Korean society is rapidly changing and the past heritage of male-chauvinistic attitudes discriminating against women is also undergoing a great and inevitable change, even though the gender gap is still very low (111st out of 136 countries in 2013).[2] Other important Korean traits like enjoying music, dance, and art with lots of famous and outstanding young artists both in pop arts[3] and classical arts are also to be listed as important elements and traditional values that Koreans cherish.

The noble ideas of generosity towards others, compassion, purity, preserving nature, and sharing with others are among the positive features frequently mentioned as unique to Koreans.[4]

We may point out many cases exemplifying a high degree of uncertainty avoidance for Koreans. The most revealing example of uncertainty avoidance may be found in the recent history of the Chosun Dynasty when Regent Heungseon Daewongun (1820–1898) adopted a closed-door policy, which was to guard the country against foreign influence to reduce unpredictability and ambiguity. The fact that traditionally various religious practices are performed may also be counted as an example of the Koreans' propensity for uncertainty avoidance. Korean people rarely make decisions on important matters alone. Young people tend to ask their parents' opinion about specific details regarding their marriage, even the selection of their spouse. Although these days it has changed greatly with Western influence, in the past free dating between young men and women was not allowed as in present Korean society; matchmakers used to play an important role for parents to choose their daughters- or sons-in-law.

Another important characteristic of the Korean people, the unique concept of "Jeong (情)" should not be neglected. This may be translated into the English word "empathy" but a more humanistic and widely shared ethos of Korean people. One example of this "Jeong" may be illustrated by the anecdote of a family told by one witness of the Catholic persecution in the 1800s.[5] When a constable arrived at the house of the so-called "criminal Catholic" for arrest, the mother treated the constable with a warm meal to show human sympathy or "Jeong." It is well known that Korean villagers used to treat strange travelers to free meals; they would invite them to share their meals when they spotted travelers pass by their homes. That may be a clear example of the Koreans' empathic attitude toward other fellow humans once they are within the same community.

Conclusion

In conclusion, in contrast to American or other Western cultures characterized as individualistic, rational, rule-oriented with low-context style of communication preferring clear and explicit verbal expressions, Koreans may be characterized as collectivistic, hierarchical, compassionate, hedonistic, and creative with positive and negative features for each of them with high-context style of communication in which lots of important messages are not verbally expressed but assumed to be understood by the group members.

Notes

1 See Lee (2008), where the concepts of time in different cultures are discussed to show how they are realized in various aspects of verbal and nonverbal communication.
2 World Economic Forum, *The Global Gender Gap Report 2013*.
3 Psy's *Gangnam Style*, which achieved world-record views on Youtube, K-Pop group singers, and Korean dramas very popular around the world are some examples.

4 See Baek, et al. (2010).
5 This anecdote was told by Kim Joon-Cheol, a priest of Donamdong Catholic Church at the morning mass of October 26, 2014.

References

Baek, S-.K., Kim, E., Lee, H.-S. (2010). *Real Korea in the world*. Seoul, South Korea: Idam Books.

Do, H.-C. (2006). Seonglihak-yeu Suyong-kwa Chosun-yeu Jibae Inyeom (The Acceptance of Seonglihak and the ruling ideology of the Chosun Dynasty). In *Hanguk Sasangsa Ipmun (The introduction to the history of Korean thoughts)* (pp. 187–210). Ed. by The Association of the History of Korean Thoughts. Seoul, South Korea: Seomun Munhwasa.

Economist (August 12, 2014). Why South Korea is so distinctively Christian. Retrieved from http://www.economist.com/blogs/economist-explains/2014/08/economist-explains-6.

Hofstede, G. (2001). *Culture's consequences: Comparing values, behaviors, institutions and organizations across nations*. Thousand Oaks, CA: Sage Publications.

Huntington, S. P. (2000). Cultures count. In L. E. Harrison & S. P. Huntington (eds.), *Culture matters* (pp. xiii–xiv). New York, NY: Basic Books.

Hulbert, H. (1969/1906). *The passing of Korea*. Seoul, South Korea: Yonsei University Press.

Lee, Y.-O. (2008). Chronemics. In M.-S. Park & D. W. Klopf (eds.), *Communicating nonverbally: An introduction to nonverbal communication* (pp. 55–80). Seoul, South Korea: Thaehaksa.

Lee, Y.-O. (2010). Cultural differences reflected in personification in Korean and English: Focusing on speech act expressions. *Research on Communication Studies*, *18*,(4), 5–30.

Lee, Y.-O. (2013a). Numericals and classifiers in Korean and English. *The Journal of Translation Studies*, *14*(3), 111–135.

Lee, Y.-O. (2013b). Korean and English cultural differences reflected in figurative expressions: Focusing on "Maeum" and "Mind". *Research on Translation and Interpretation*, *17*(2), 169–193.

Morrison, T. & Conaway, W. A. (2007). *Kiss, bow, or shake hands: Asia*. Avon, MA: Adams Media an F+W Publications Company.

Samovar, L., Porter, R., McDaniel, E., & Roy, C. (2013). *Communication between cultures*. International Edition: Wadsworth.

Schwartz, S. H. (1992). Universals in the content and Structure of Values: Theoretical advances and empirical tests in 20 countries. *Advances in Experimental Social Psychology*, *25*, 1–65.

Suh, C. S. (Ed.) (2003). *New millennium dictionary of Korean language and culture*. Seoul, South Korea: Hansebon.

Wierzbicka, A. (2006). *English: Meaning and culture*. Oxford, UK: Oxford University Press.

World Economic Forum. (2013). *The Global Gender Gap Report 2013*. Retrieved from http://www3.weforum.org/docs/WEF_GenderGap_Report_2013.

Yunhap News. (September 13, 2010). S. Korea's trade dependence highest among G-20 nations. Retrieved from http://english.yonhapnews.co.kr/business/2010/09/13.

10 INTERCULTURAL COMMUNICATION
A JAPANESE PERSPECTIVE
Jiro Takai, Nagoya University, Japan

Chapter Outline

- Higher Education Deregulation and the Rise of Schools of Communication
- Academic Societies Pertaining to Intercultural Communication
- Research in Intercultural Communication
- Conclusion

Intercultural communication in Japan has a very interesting history, since communication has never been recognized as a full-fledged academic discipline, such as psychology and sociology. While there are plenty of faculty who possess a PhD in communication, they are not concentrated in one department, and while many universities offer genuine courses in communication, there are no departments that offer a coherent curriculum in the communication discipline as it is known worldwide. Nonetheless, there are a variety of academic societies and associations that take on the name "communication," and while most of them are actually based on the communication discipline, these associations have not been fully successful in convincing the domestic universities about the *real* concept of Communication, and the need for a comprehensive, and independent major.

Despite this cultural background, intercultural communication has always had a special emphasis in this country, as the majority of PhD holders in communication did their dissertations in either rhetoric or intercultural communication. New doctorates would return home to Japan, but they would soon realize their university would view them as English language teachers, not research specialists in their academic discipline. Intercultural communication, hence, is thought to be language proficiency, especially in the lingua franca,

English. The following describes the historical, cultural, and societal factors that have led to this dismal state of the art of the discipline, with special focus on the intercultural field.

Higher Education Deregulation and the Rise of Schools of Communication

The Japanese Ministry of Education had traditionally not allowed universities to name their Schools using foreign language terms ("communication" included), specifically, labels that utilize *katakana*, the writing form reserved for foreign words. In 1991, however, it amended the Standards for Establishment of Universities, which allowed universities greater liberty to design original curricula, and therefore, to name their Schools in accordance with these new curricula (Japanese Ministry of Education, Culture, Sports, Science and Technology, 2015). At the same time, the amendment recommended the integration of general education into the four year undergraduate program, rather than requiring students to spend their first two years taking solely general education courses.

Many universities had a separate College of General Education, with a full set of faculty in Languages, Arts, Humanities, and Sciences, and with the amendment, these Colleges were to be dissolved, or restructured into new Schools. This resulted in a mixed cast of professors with nowhere to go, and with the new freedom in designing Schools, many universities formed Schools utilizing the keyword "communication," including intercultural communication. In essence, these Schools of Communication consisted of faculty who had taught foreign languages, specializing in foreign philosophy, history, and literature. Universities would rationalize their choice of "Intercultural Communication" by claiming culture was communicated through the teachings of these faculties. Communication, then, became a convenient label for Schools established based on integrating a disparate aggregate of existing faculty, rather than hiring a coherent new set of faculty based on the concept of communication as a discipline.

Academic Societies Pertaining to Intercultural Communication

With this societal misconception of the academic discipline of Communication, the role of academic associations dealing in communication is undoubtedly important. The single comprehensive communication society has been the Communication Association of Japan (CAJ), which was established in 1971 as the Communication Association of the Pacific (Miyahara, 2011). The membership of this association consists mainly of rhetoric and intercultural specialists, but at times, the majority of the membership is composed of English language teachers. In recent years, CAJ has concerted its efforts into catering to scholars of communication proper, but still, the bias toward the aforementioned two areas remains. CAJ's constituents have typically received their graduate education in the United States, hence their interests toward cultural issues. The CAJ journal is the *Japanese Journal of Communication Studies*, which publishes twice a year. Membership numbers around 500.

The second largest intercultural communication related association is SIETAR (Society for Intercultural Education, Training, and Research) Japan, established in 1985. The Japanese name of this society is 異文化コミュニケーション学会, which translates to Intercultural Communication Association. This association specializes in intercultural communication matters, in particular, intercultural education and training. It is interesting that the majority of those committed to SIETAR Japan do not participate actively in CAJ, indicating their identity is not with the communication discipline as a whole, but toward the field of intercultural communication only. It publishes the *Journal of Intercultural Communication* once annually. Membership numbers about 400.

One other society dedicated to intercultural communication is Japan Society for Multicultural Relations (JSMR). Established in 2002, this society is relatively young, but boasts 350 members, and publishes the journal *Multicultural Relations* once a year. This society is more interdisciplinary in nature than the other two, catering to sociologists, political scientists, and anthropologists, aside from communication scholars, whose main interests are in intergroup relations, not communication per se.

Perhaps the most crucial shortcoming of these associations in failing to realize communication's recognition as a bona fide academic discipline is that their interests are not in the whole discipline itself, but in narrow fields within the discipline. Interpersonal and small group communication research has by and large been conducted by social psychologists, while sociologists have done much of the work in mass communication, and business administration experts have studied organizational communication. The Japanese population of communication scholars has been fractionalized by particular interests, and little attempt has been made to integrate these interests into one single, comprehensive community of communication specialists.

Research in Intercultural Communication

Japanese articles dealing with intercultural communication can not only be found in the journals published by the above mentioned associations, but in social psychology (*Japanese Journal of Experimental Social Psychology*, *Japanese Journal of Social Psychology*), and in education (*Intercultural Education*) journals, amongst others. Clear trends in Japanese intercultural communication research are evident. Perhaps the peak efforts were made in the 1980s, when there was a scholarly boom on indigenous communication styles driven by *Japanology*, which celebrated the rise of Japan as an economic power threatening American dominance. *Japanology* became the dynamo for generating articles and books on Japanese communication theories and concepts, such as Doi's (1982) *amae*, Ishii's (1984) *sasshi* and *enryo*, and Okabe's (1983) *awase*, which were introduced during this time. According to Kawakami (2009), intercultural communication established itself as a research field in Japan by the 1990s.

The 1980s heyday of intercultural communication has also seen a barrage of *cross*-cultural communication studies, mainly by Gudykunst and his associates (see for reference Gudykunst & Nishida, 1994), who based their studies on cross-cultural theories, such as individualism–collectivism, comparing the Japanese against the Americans. In the new century, however, the trend has turned from empirical approaches toward post-modern and post-post-modern, such as cultural studies, and critical theories, as is the case in intercultural communication in the United States. Also, pressures toward globalization have warranted research in "global competence" of the Japanese, and schools and universities have launched education programs geared toward self-assertion and argumentation (see Sonoda, 2014, for example).

Conclusion

While societal factors have impeded the recognition of communication as an academic discipline in Japan, the field of intercultural communication has enjoyed much attention, in the form of university student majors, and in academic societies dedicated to its advancement. While progress has been made to separate intercultural communication from language education, modern globalization has brought back the perception that intercultural communication is indeed competence in communicating in the English language. It remains to be seen if the cells of communication scholars can unite into a single community to give the discipline its rightful citizenship within Japan's academic disciplinary ranks.

References

Doi, T. (1982). The Japanese patterns of communication and the concept of Amae. In L. A. Samovar & R. E. Porter (Eds.), *Intercultural communication: A reader 3rd Edition* (pp. 218–223). Belmont, CA: Wadsworth.

Gudykunst, W. B., & Nishida, T. (1994). *Bridging Japanese/North American differences*. Thousand Oaks, CA: Sage.

Ishii, S. (1984). Enryo-sasshi communication: A key to understanding Japanese interpersonal relations. *Cross Currents*, *11*, 49–58.

Japanese Ministry of Education, Culture, Sports, Science and Technology (2015). 大学設置基準の一部を改正する省令の施行等について (*Application of the ministerial ordinance regarding revision of the Establishment Standards of Universities*). http://www.mext.go.jp/b_menu/hakusho/nc/t19910624001/t19910624001.html. Retrieved May 10, 2015.

Kawakami, H. S. (2009). A history and development of the intercultural communication field in Japan (1950–present). Retrieved from ProQuest Dissertations and Theses. (Accession Order No. 3390819.)

Miyahara, A. (2011). Prologue. In Communication Association of Japan (ed.), *Communication studies in Japan: The state of the art* (pp. 3–10). Tokyo: Sanshusha.

Okabe, R. (1983). Cultural assumptions of East and West: Japan and the United States. In W.B. Gudykunst (ed.), *Intercultural communication theory: Current perspectives* (pp. 21–44). Beverly Hills, CA: Sage.

Sonoda, T. (2014). An investigation of assertiveness in university students: Comparison of students of the United States, China, Thailand, and Japan. *Intercultural Education*, *40*, 128–137.

11 INTERCULTURAL COMMUNICATION
AN AUSTRALIAN PERSPECTIVE

Terry Flew, Queensland University of Technology, Brisbane, Australia

Chapter Outline

- Australian Colonisation and Intercultural Communication
- Australian Multiculturalism and Political Economy
- Conclusion

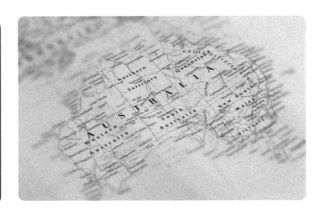

A distinctively Australian perspective on intercultural communication arises from consideration of the nation's history, geography, demography, social policy, and political economy. In broad terms, one can distinguish three main phases of intercultural communication in Australia:

- the colonial and early nation period (1788–1945), where there was the active construction of a European monoculture, often by exclusion or force;
- the post-World War I period (1945–1975), where the nation became increasingly diverse culturally, but where there continued to be resistance to transforming official cultures to better reflect such changes;
- contemporary multicultural Australia (1975–present) where active recognition of cultural diversity is seen as enhancing the nation both socially and economically. The latter period also sees the opening up of the Australian economy to greater trade with Asia, and increasing connection to China as a leading global economic power.

Australian Colonisation and Intercultural Communication

Australia was founded as a *settler colonial* society (Veracini, 2010), with European settlement on indigenous lands taking place from the first arrival of British convicts in Sydney Cove in 1789, under Governor Arthur Philip. The historian Marilyn Lake observed that a common feature of countries as otherwise diverse as Australia, New Zealand, the United States, Canada, South Africa, Kenya, and Rhodesia (Zimbabwe) has been their 'imaginative coherence' as a 'white man's country', where 'a spatial politics of segregation and exclusion was common to them all, and the "white man" ruled over the "natives"' (Lake, 2003, p. 352).

Australian colonisation of indigenous lands and dispossession of indigenous people was frequently brutal and was widely resisted throughout the frontier (Reynolds, 1996). The highly dispersed nature of Aboriginal tribal groupings and very different conditions across Australia meant that there was never any single treaty signed between settlers and the indigenous population, as with the Treaty of Waitangi in New Zealand. One of the big issues in intercultural communication in Australia is the recognition of prior Aboriginal ownership of land and the ongoing role played by Aboriginal people in Australian society and culture. While some advances have been made, such as Prime Minister Kevin Rudd's Apology to the 'Stolen Generations' (those children taken from their Aboriginal parents and placed under state-administered welfare) in 2008, the need for some form of treaty or other Constitutionally relevant statement that addresses issues of indigenous sovereignty continues to be an obstacle to reconciliation between indigenous and non-indigenous Australians.

Australian Multiculturalism and Political Economy

Australia in the 19th and early 20th century was racially exclusionary in other ways, most notably through the 'White Australia' policy, which particularly restricted Asian migration to Australia, and was not finally repealed until 1963. Australia had been established as a colony of the British Empire, becoming an independent nation in 1901, but its demographic composition changed considerably in the aftermath of World War II, as it took in substantial numbers of migrants and refugees from Europe, particularly from southern European nations such as Italy, Greece and what was Yugoslavia. Australia's history and its political institutions reflected a British heritage to which new migrants were expected to assimilate, but it was becoming increasingly apparent from the 1970s that wider cultural changes were required to respond to a more ethnically and culturally diverse population.

Multiculturalism was first proposed as government policy in the 1970s, and was consolidated in the 1980s and early 1990s. Australian multiculturalism has, as Pakulski (2014) has argued, been relatively pragmatic in its nature, promoting social integration and national cohesion rather than celebrating cultural diversity as an end in itself. The National Agenda for a Multicultural Australia, published in 1989, emphasised multicultural citizenship, which 'impose[d] obligations as well as conferring rights: the right to express one's own culture and beliefs involves a reciprocal responsibility to accept the right of others to express their views and values' (Department of the Prime Minister and Cabinet, 1989, p. 9). Australian multiculturalism has been criticised for being more concerned with facilitating ethnic community leaders' engagement rather than promoting social justice and addressing race-based inequalities, and for being insufficiently concerned with diversifying 'core' cultural and political institutions (Castles et al., 1988; Hage, 1998). These policies have survived major challenges, most notably the rejection of the whole concept by the nationalist One Nation Party, headed by Pauline Hanson.

One enduring feature of Australian multiculturalism has been the Special Broadcasting Service (SBS). SBS Radio commenced in 1978, and SBS Television in 1980, as a government-funded multicultural broadcaster with a Charter remit to 'provide multilingual and multicultural radio and television services that inform, educate, and entertain all Australians, and, in doing so, reflect Australia's multicultural society' (quoted in Ang et al., 2008, p. xiii). In their history of the SBS, Ang et al. identify its distinctive understanding of intercultural communication within a media organisation, as 'it *begins* from the idea of difference and diversity as normal . . . it assumes that what Australians have in common *is* diversity and that the role of public media is to create spaces where the connections and differences between particular groups and perspectives can be understood and negotiated' (Ang et al., 2008, p. 3). One important way in which SBS has 'mainstreamed multiculturalism' is by ensuring that all non-English language programming is subtitled in English, meaning that the programs in question do not cater to any single cultural or linguistic community, but are potentially available to all Australians. SBS has also been particularly important in providing forums in which Australian multiculturalism and diversity can be discussed and debated: this has been a feature not only in news, current affairs and documentaries, but in its drama, comedy and light entertainment programs.

Conclusion

Australia has always been geographically located within the Asia-Pacific, but its history and culture has been linked to Europe, and its major political and economic ties have been to the United Kingdom and the United States. In the 21st century, Australia's political economy is now largely tied to Asia, and various policy documents have sought to address this, such as the 2012 *Australia in the Asian Century* White Paper (Department of Prime Minister and Cabinet, 2012). To take one example, 20–25% of students enrolled in Australian universities are from other countries: of these, by far the largest number is from China, followed by India, South Korea, Vietnam, Indonesia, and Thailand. China also became Australia's largest trading partner in 2013, with Japan and South Korea being among the top four trading nations, along with the United States. This economic shift towards Asia creates an imperative that all Australians become more 'Asia-literate', which requires a better understanding of Asian culture and customs as well as language.

References

Ang, I., Hawkins, G. & Dabboussy, L. (2008). *The SBS story*. Sydney, Australia: UNSW Press.

Castles, S., Kalantzis, M., Cope, B. & Morrissey, M. (1988). *Mistaken identity: Multiculturalism and the demise of nationalism in Australia*. Sydney, Australia: Pluto Press.

Department of the Prime Minister and Cabinet (1989). *National Agenda for a Multicultural Australia: Sharing our future* (Canberra: Australian Government Printing Service).

Department of the Prime Minister and Cabinet (2012). *Australia in the Asian century*. Canberra, Australia: AGPS.

Hage, G. (1998). *White nation: Fantasies of White supremacy in a multicultural society*. Sydney, Australia: Pluto Press.

Lake, M. (2003). White man's country: The transnational history of a national project. *Australian Historical Studies*, 122, 346–63.

Pakulski, J. (2014). Confusions about multiculturalism. *Journal of Sociology* 50, 23–36.

Reynolds, H. (1996). *Frontier: Aborigines, settlers, and race*. Sydney, Australia: Allen & Unwin.

Veracini, L. (2010). *Settler colonialism: A theoretical overview*. Basingstoke, Australia: Palgrave Macmillan.

12 INTERCULTURAL COMMUNICATION
A CHRISTIAN PERSPECTIVE

Janie Harden Fritz, Duquesne University, Pittsburgh, USA

Chapter Outline

- Early Intercultural Communication and Christianity
- Intercultural Communication and Christianity Today
- Conclusion

Paul in Athens (Acts 17) by Raphael

Christianity is one of the world's major religions, with adherents in every continent (Pew Forum, 2011). Christianity's core teaching is that Jesus Christ came into the world to restore humanity's broken relationship with God (e.g., Donovan, 1978; Moreau, et al., 2014). The death and resurrection of Jesus, which happened over 2,000 years ago and is recorded in the New Testament of the Christian Bible, is the good news—the gospel—that members of the Christian church, whether Catholic, Orthodox, or Protestant, live out in their daily lives and have a responsibility to share with the rest of the world. Christians believe all cultures simultaneously reflect God's goodness and contain elements that fail to reflect it, that all human beings—and all cultures—need to be restored to a right relationship with God, and that God longs to restore that relationship.

Early Intercultural Communication and Christianity

Intercultural communication has been part of Christian tradition from its beginnings in Jerusalem. Examples from the early church include the recognition that the gospel message was for both Jewish and non-Jewish persons and the church's need to address diversity among its members. Jesus's charge to the disciples to take the gospel to all nations, known as the Great Commission (Matthew 28: 16–20), the account in the book of Acts describing how persons of many cultures heard the gospel in their own languages on what is celebrated in the Christian church as the feast (or holy day) of Pentecost (Acts 2: 1–13), and Peter's visit to Cornelius, a non-Jew (Acts 10), an event that highlighted God's welcome to all people, represent early foundations for Christian approaches to intercultural communication with audiences external to the church. The aim of intercultural communication in these contexts was to communicate the message of God's forgiveness to people from all over the world who have not yet heard it, inviting belief in the Christian message and establishment of a Christian community and subsequent participation in the life of the church. In another instance from the early church, also recorded in the book of Acts (6:1), Greek-speaking believers brought complaints against Hebrew-speaking believers because of perceived inequality in the distribution of daily food allotments to Greek-speaking widows. This incident illustrated the church's need for internal intercultural communication—in this case, to resolve conflict and restore peace, modeling the love and unity that the church was designed to show to the world as a sign of the validity of the Christian message.

Intercultural Communication and Christianity Today

Today, Christian theologians and missiologists—people who study missionary work—have developed models to explain the interrelationship of communication, culture, and faith. Some models address ways to communicate the Christian faith to persons in cultural contexts with no framework of meaning for Christian concepts such as individual-level sin. Other models address issues relevant to intercultural communication within the church itself, such as embracing cultural differences among members and fighting racism and other injustices stemming from historic power imbalances (e.g., Perkins, 1976).

Moreau et al. (2014), working from an evangelical Protestant position, integrated intercultural communication and theology/missiology by tracing the history of Christian approaches to the contemporary field of intercultural communication back to the 1950s and identified issues facing Christian intercultural communication today. From their perspective, the mandate for intercultural communication stems from our nature as communicating creatures, God's communication to human beings, and the command from Jesus to share the good news of the gospel with others (Moreau et al., 2014, p. 1). The second Vatican Council, which took place in the 1960s under the leadership of Pope Paul VI, included explicit teachings for the Catholic Church recognizing the value of cultural differences, termed an inculturation perspective. Pope Benedict XVI, in a document called *Verbum Domini* ("the Word of the Lord"), reiterated the importance of culture: "The word of God, like the Christian faith itself, has a profoundly *intercultural* character; it is capable of encountering different cultures and in turn enabling them to encounter one another" (Benedict XVI, 2010, italics in the original). Culture is part of human existence and God's creation. God always communicates in a concrete cultural situation, but the word of God is passed on in different cultures; therefore, specific responses to the gospel message will show variety and difference, although always in a way consistent with the foundational message of the gospel (see also Donovan, 1978).

Moreau et al. (2014) defined communication as dynamic, irreversible, proactive, interactive, and contextual, shaped by cultural, social, and personal factors; culture is understood as dynamic, interconnected, learned, transmitted, symbolic, shared, and necessary for interpretation of others' behavior. Intercultural communication addresses meaning systems, which are made up of a common human core, or cultural universals, that every human being shares generally, such as language, authority structures, and institutions; cultural specifics, or particular ways of seeing the world and specific instances of cultural universals developed by a given culture; personal specifics, and encounter specifics, all of which are involved in the coding, interpretive, and response system happening between two persons (Moreau et al., 2014). This model of intercultural communication is consistent with secular, or nonreligious, approaches. However, Christian and secular approaches also tend to diverge significantly. Secular approaches typically take a noninterference approach, considering any attempt to influence another culture's religious beliefs to be unethical. However, Christian scholars note that intercultural encounters have historically involved exchanges of ideas, technology, and practices; there is no intercultural contact that does not, by definition, involve some form of influence. The key issue is approaching others with openness to learning from difference and a desire to work alongside others while sharing the message of the gospel (Moreau et al., 2014).

Conclusion

An example of working alongside and learning from others from almost a millennium ago is Ramon Llull, a thirteenth-century rhetorician and missionary who spent years learning Arabic and reading works of Islamic and Jewish scholars, seeking common ground with other cultures in order to find points of connection with the gospel (Boone, 1995). Contemporary examples emerge from the context of short-term missions in the context of global Christianity, in which groups from countries representing the "old center" of Christianity, such as the United States, visit Christian communities in countries in the rapidly-emerging new centers of Christianity (Offut, 2011), such as Japan (e.g., Barber, 2015). Hosts from the countries to which mission teams travel hope to work alongside guests, who often come with their own expectations about what is to take place during the trip and the nature of the tasks to be done in the host location. Guests must listen carefully so as to avoid imposing their own agendas on hosts and develop intercultural sensitivity to avoid offending their hosts and creating negative impressions of Christianity among non-Christians in the host country. Differences in communication patterns across cultural and religious traditions, such as expectations for the amount and nature of self-disclosure (Croucher, et al., 2012) and appropriate communicative behavior in public contexts (Barber, 2015) require openness to learning, a key ethical requirement in this historical moment (Arnett, et al., 2009).

References

Arnett, R. C., Fritz, J. M. H., & Bell, L. M. (2009). *Communication ethics literacy: Dialogue and difference.* Thousand Oaks, CA: Sage.

Barber, R., Jr. (2015). Host-directed short-term missions: Interviews with Japanese liaisons. *Missiology: An International Review, 43,* 309–323. DOI:10.1177/0091829615581930

Benedict XVI. (2010, September 30). Post-synodal apostolic exhortation *Verbum Domini.* Retrieved from http://w2.vatican.va/content/benedict-xvi/en/apost_exhortations/documents/hf_ben-xvi_exh_20100930_verbum-domini.html

Boone, G. M. (1995). Mystical Unity and hierarchical difference: Ramon Llull's rhetoric of conversion. *Journal of Communication & Religion, 18*(1), 49–59.

Croucher, S. M., Faulkner, S. L., Spencer, A. T., & Long, B. (2012). A comparative analysis of the relationship between religion and self-disclosure in the U.S. and India. In S. M. Croucher & T. M. Harris (eds.), *Religion and communication: An anthology of extensions in theory, research, and method.* New York: Peter Lang.

Donovan, V. (1978). *Christianity rediscovered.* Maryknoll, NY: Orbis.

Moreau, A. S., Campbell, E. H., & Greener, S. (2014). *Effective intercultural communication: A Christian perspective.* Grand Rapids, MI: Baker Academic.

Offut, S. (2011). The role of short-term mission teams in the new centers of global Christianity. *Journal for the Scientific Study of Religion, 50,* 796–811. DOI: 10.1111/j.1468-5906.2011.01600.x

Perkins, J. M. (1976). *Let justice roll down.* Ventura, CA: Regal Books.

Pew Forum. (2011). Global Christianity – A report on the size and distribution of the world's Christian population. Retrieved from: http://www.pewforum.org/2011/12/19/global-christianity-exec/

13 INTERCULTURAL COMMUNICATION
A MUSLIM PERSPECTIVE

Hassan Abu Bakar and Munif Zarirruddin Fikri Nordin, Universiti Utara Malaysia, Malaysia

Chapter Outline

- Islam and Relationships
- Relationships and Communications with Human Beings
  - Communication between Muslims
  - Communication with Non-Muslims
- Intercultural Communication in Majority Muslim Countries

The meaning of Islam comes from the Arabic word, which means to submit, accept or surrender to only one God; that is Allah, and in addition Islam also means peace (Ramadan, 2012). A Muslim refers to a person who engages in the act of submission, acceptance or surrender, or promotes peace. Therefore, a Muslim is a person who submits to the will of Allah (God) or can also be referred to as a follower of Islam. There are two key elements of Islam that act as a guide for a Muslim. The first element is the supporting and inter-locking of behavior and practices of submission towards only one God, firmly and unequivocally located in one book that is, the holy Quran. The second element is the life of the Prophet Muhammad Peace Be Upon Him (PBUH), which constitutes the *sunnah*. The *sunnah* consists of the Prophet Muhammad's (PBUH) behaviors, words, and values. The combination of these two elements forms the path for a Muslim to Islam that is, total submission, acceptance, or surrender to Allah (God) and also promotes peace among human beings (Ahmed, 2002). The holy Quran and the *sunnah* set a basic rule for a Muslim to form and communicate with other Muslims and non-Muslims, which will be the main focus of this chapter.

Islam and Relationships

The defining role of relationships between Muslims and Allah (God), between a Muslim and another Muslim and Muslims and non-Muslims in Islam is based on the notion of establishing peace and bringing about happiness for all human beings in both this world and the eternal world. The relationship between a Muslim and Allah (God) is based on the principle of *iman*. The word *iman* is derived from an Arabic word; *a-m-n*, meaning to be at peace, to believe and have faith in God. The holy Quran sets six principles of *iman* or beliefs for a Muslim, which are the Oneness of Allah (God), His Angels, His Prophets, His revealed books (Torah, Zabur, Bible and Quran), the concept of the Hereafter, and belief in destiny. This belief is translated into five pillars of Islam, which is a combination of an act and communication of a Muslim to Allah, which means to worship no other God except Allah and to declare that Muhammad (PBUH) is His messenger, to perform prayers five times a day, to fast in the month of Ramadhan, to give *zakat* (alms) and to perform Haj. In addition, a Muslim also communicates with Allah through *zikir* (chanting the names of Allah or His attributes) and *du'a* (supplication, for example, to seek forgiveness from Allah) (Hamdan, 2007). The relationships of a Muslim to another Muslim go beyond ethnicity, race, culture or nation. All Muslims are united into one *ummah*. In the concept of *ummah*, each Muslim has responsibility towards each other. A Muslim is a brother or a sister to another Muslim. In the relationships with non-Muslims, the teaching of Islam emphasizes that a Muslim respects the right of non-Muslims, based on the said non-Muslim's religious obligations or cultural values. In fact, the holy Quran and the Prophet Muhammad (PBUH) emphasize that Muslims should respect the rights of "the people of the book" (the Jew and Christian) to perform their religious responsibilities and rituals. The relationships and interactions with non-Muslims are also a potential act of worship if it is done with "pure" intention and within the limits prescribed by Allah in the holy Quran and the Prophet Muhammad (PBUH) in the *sunnah* (Beekun & Badawi, 2005).

Relationships and Communications with Human Beings

This section will summarize the communicative actions and behaviors of a Muslim based on the holy Quran and the Prophet Muhammad's (PBUH) *sunnah*. These communications and behaviors are known as *akhlaq* or *adab*.

Communication between Muslims

The communication acts or behaviors for a Muslim to another Muslim are as follows:

- To give *salam* (greeting) to another Muslim, or to join or to leave a group of Muslims with "*As-salaamu alaikum!*" (I wish you peace and tranquility in this life)

- To accept an invitation (to any ceremonial event) from another Muslim
- To give advice to another Muslim if he/she seeks advice
- To make *du'a* (supplication) to Allah (God) for the whole Muslim *ummah*. The *du'a* is mainly a request for a better life for Muslims in this world and the eternal world
- To visit another Muslim if he or she is sick
- To bury and perform prayer for another Muslim who dies
- To avoid unkind remarks to another Muslim; this type of communication is considered sinful in Islam.

Communication with Non-Muslims

The communication acts or behaviors for a Muslim to non-Muslims are based on wisdoms that promote the best manners of a Muslim (al-Qardawi, 2004; Ramadan, 2004). These communication activities are as follows:

- To assure that Muslims should not force others to accept Islam
- To assure peace and harmonious relationships and coexistence with non-Muslims in society
- To respect non-Muslims' rights
- To assure freedoms to perform non-Muslim rites and rituals
- To assure that there is no enmity or hatred to non-Muslims regardless of their social status or ethnicity
- To promote brotherhood in relationship with non-Muslims
- To respect the differences between Muslims and non-Muslims.

Intercultural Communication in Majority Muslim Countries

The teaching of Islam supports the fact of cultural diversity and differences in human being, for example in *Al-Qur'an*, Surah Al Hud, reveals: "If thy Lord had so willed, He could have made mankind one nation: but they will not cease to differ" (Hud, 11: 118, Quran.com). Thus, the Qur'an as the vision of God clearly recognizes diversity, which in turn presumes cultural differences. Because *Al-Qur'an* and As Sunnah exist in a context (Arabic culture), the Islamic values and interpretation are also influenced in part by the national culture. Thus, national culture makes interpretation of Islam differ from one culture to another. For example, the practice of Islam in countries like Malaysia, Indonesia and Brunei differs significantly from countries of South Asia (Pakistan and Bangladesh) and West Asia (Arab countries).

Malaysia, for example, is a plural society based on uneven ethnic distributions mainly of Bumiputra (the Malay), the Chinese and the Indians (Abdul Rashid & Ho, 2003). In Malaysia, ethnic divisions are coterminous with linguistic, cultural, religious and economic differences. While there is very little cultural homogeneity between the three ethnicities in Malaysia, their value differences converge under the nation of Malaysia (Selvarajah & Meyer, 2006;

2008). Religion is closely tied to ethnicity in Malaysia. For example, the majority of Malays are Muslims, most Indians follow Hinduism, and the majority of Chinese practice a combination of Taoism and Buddhism, mixed with values associated with Confucianism. There are also small minorities of Chinese and Indians who follow Christianity and Islam, respectively (Abdullah, 2001).

The Muslim Malay majority not only shapes the cultural norms of society but also shapes inter-ethnic communication behavior in Malaysia (Bakar, et al., 2014). Generally, the ideas of intercultural communication in Malaysia as noted by Kennedy (2002) are based on harmonious relationships between ethnic groups, respect for other religions, and belief in face-saving. These communication characteristics in Malaysia are in line with the main principles of Islam. In fact Muslim Malays when communicating with others (other Malays, Chinese, or Indian) emphasize modesty and face-saving as emphasized in Islamic principles. Specifically, the Muslim Malay will not highlight either their successes or failures, when communicating with others; failures would not be mentioned in an attempt to save face, particularly for those who are responsible for the failed effort.

To sum up, communication from the Muslim perspective is based on the notion of establishing peace, tolerance, and respect (al-Qardawi, 2004; Ramadan, 2012) and bringing about happiness for all human beings. The communication with Allah (God) is based on the principle of *iman* through the act of the five pillars of Islam, *zikir* and *du'a*. The communication between a Muslim and another Muslim is to ensure all Muslims are united into one "*ummah*." Communication between Muslims and non-Muslims emphasizes the rights and the coexistence of non-Muslims in society and the maintenance of harmonious relationships. In addition, the teachings of Islam encourage pluralism and recognize diversity; in fact any communication and relationship efforts are encouraged as long they are not against the basic principles of Islam.

References

Abdul Rashid, M.Z., & Ho, J.A. (2003). Perceptions of business ethics in a multicultural community: The case of Malaysia. *Journal of Business Ethics, 43,* 75–87.

Abdullah, A. (2001). Influence of ethnic values at the Malaysian workplace. In A. Abdullah & A. Low (eds.), *Understanding the Malaysian workforce: Guidelines for managers* (revised edition ed., pp. 1–25). Kuala Lumpur, Malaysia: Malaysian Institute of Management.

Ahmed, A.S. (2002). *Discovering Islam: Making sense of Muslim history and society.* New York, NY: Routledge.

Al-Qardawi, Y. (2004). *Khitabuna al-Islami fi 'asr al-'awlamah.* Cairo: Dar al-Syuruq.

Bakar, H.A., Walters, T., & Halim, H. (2014). Measuring communication style in the Malaysian workplace: Instrument development and validation. *Journal of Intercultural Communication Research, 43,* 87–112.

Beekun, R.I., & Badawi, J.A. (2005). Balancing ethical responsibility among multiple organizational stakeholders: The Islamic perspective. *Journal of Business Ethics, 60,* 131–145.

Hamdan, A. (2007). A case study of a Muslim client: Incorporating religious beliefs and practices. *Journal of Multicultural Counseling and Development, 35*, 92–100.

Kennedy, J. C. (2002). Leadership in Malaysia: Traditional values, international outlook. *Academy of Management Executive, 16*, 15–26.

Ramadan, T. (2004). *Western Muslims and the future of Islam*. Oxford, UK: Oxford University Press.

Ramadan, T. (2012). *The quest for meaning: Developing a philosophy of pluralism*. London, UK: Penguin Books.

Selvarajah, C., & Meyer, D. (2006). Archetypes of the Malaysian manager: Exploring ethnicity dimensions that relate to leadership. *Journal of Management & Organization, 12*, 251–269.

Selvarajah, C., & Meyer, D. (2008). One nation, three cultures: Exploring dimensions that relate to leadership in Malaysia. *Leadership & Organization Development Journal, 29*, 693–712.

14 INTERCULTURAL COMMUNICATION
A BUDDHIST PERSPECTIVE

Tenzin Dorjee, California State University, Fullerton, USA

Chapter Outline

- Interdependent Origination and Intercultural Communication
- Nonviolence and Intercultural Communication
- Mindfulness and Intercultural Communication

Mt. Kailash, "Gang Rinpoche" (Precious Mt.)

Intercultural communication (ICC) is contextual in that communicators are expected to appropriately adapt their verbal and nonverbal communication symbols according to different cultural values and norms for shared understanding and to fulfill their needs (e.g., relational and instrumental goals). Intercultural communication scholars have theorized and investigated it largely from a Eurocentric perspective. There is minimal research on intercultural communication from a Buddhist perspective. Arguably, a Buddhist perspective on ICC includes understanding interdependent origination, nonviolence, and mindfulness, among other things.

Buddhism originated in India over 2500 years ago. According to His Holiness the Fourteenth Dalai Lama of Tibet, Buddhism can be classified into three domains: Philosophy, Science of Mind, and Religious Practice. The first two domains are universal and cross-cultural domains because interested people can study and follow them regardless of their religious or secular background. The last domain is the business of Buddhist devotees and practitioners. From a Buddhist perspective, ICC can be defined as a process of encoding and decoding messages in an intercultural context characterized by understanding interdependent origination, nonviolence, and mindfulness among other things.

Interdependent Origination and Intercultural Communication

Interdependent origination (*Pratitsamudpad*) is a central philosophy in Buddhism and it describes the ontological status of reality or phenomena. There is no intrinsic reality or truth. Nothing exists in and of itself because everything exists dependently. Interdependent origination can be explained in three different ways: causality, relativity, and arbitrariness. Many things we experience in life are created by their causes and conditions such as pain and pleasure, and failure and success. But many things simply exist in relation to each other such as good and bad, and short and tall. Finally, everything exists arbitrarily. There is no intrinsic relationship between phenomena and their names or labels. This reality of arbitrariness is called emptiness (*Shunyata*) in Buddhism. For example, "Football" means soccer in most countries around the world, but it means American football in the United States. Heart Sutra states, "Form is empty. Emptiness is form . . ." This non-duality embodies the subtlest meaning of interdependent origination.

Everything is nominally and interdependently existent. ICC is no exception. All the things including identity, relationship, values, norms, and conflicts that we study in intercultural communication are conceptually established phenomena or arbitrary realities. Things may seem to exist objectively in us or out there, but in reality they exist nominally. In the Western system of education Cartesian dualism is taken for granted and promoted. In contrast, Buddhism contends that subject and object are interdependently related. Relating this to ICC, a message is socially constructed and its meaning/s need to be decoded in a given context based upon things that influence communication processes at and across different levels (i.e., macro, exo, meso, and micro). This holistic perspective allows for different meaning interpretations in ICC.

Nonviolence and Intercultural Communication

Science of Mind in Buddhism provides extensive knowledge of the mind, its types, functions, and subject–object relationships (Rinpoche, 1981). The mind is a formless, clear, and cognitive phenomenon. It consists of six primary types of consciousness, and many mental attitudes. The mind can be positive (love and compassion), negative (anger and hostility) or neutral (equanimity and sleep). Nonviolence (*Ahimsa*) is a positive mental attitude and it is central to Buddhism. It essentially means not to harm others and it is rooted in compassion (*Karuna*). According to Buddhism, ICC has to be ethical or nonviolent communication. Intercultural communicators should verbally and nonverbally communicate to each other nonviolently. Nonviolent communication involves concern for others such as respect and acceptance. Inspired by the Dalai Lama, many scientists are today engaged in dialogues with contemplative scholars and experiments on the effects of compassion and mindfulness on our psychosomatic well-being (Mind and Life Org.).

Nonviolence is directly related to peace, **harmony**, dialogue, intergroup and intercultural conflict resolution. Violence breeds violence. In interpersonal and intercultural interactions people who are compassionate or inclined to nonviolence are likely to solve problems and conflicts through dialogue. Nonviolent communication is antithetical to the dark side of communication such as hurtful and deceptive communication. Dorjee (2013) discussed nonviolence and dialogue to resolve even intractable conflict such as the Sino-Tibetan conflict. The world is more interconnected and interdependent and this is the new reality. Global peace, harmony, prosperity, and survival are inextricably bound with resolving issues through nonviolence and dialogue.

Mindfulness and Intercultural Communication

In Buddhism mindfulness (*Smriti*) is explained among the Eightfold Paths and the Sutra of Mindfulness discusses four types of mindfulness relating to body, feelings, mind, and reality (*Dharma*). Mindfulness can mean "awareness," "recollection," and "retention." Mindfulness is central to meditational practices for mental stability and sharp cognition. In ICC, mindfulness can be recognized as focused meta-cognition, meta-communication, and meta-sensation attunement work needed for effective communication (Ting-Toomey & Dorjee, 2014).

In today's world people need to develop effective ICC skills to relate to each other interpersonally and interculturally. Effective ICC involves communicating appropriately, competently, and adaptively according to different cultural values, norms, and situational contexts. Mindfulness is important to successfully connecting ICC theoretical knowledge and skills with practice. Gudykunst (2005) theorized that effective ICC is possible if intercultural communicators mindfully manage their anxiety and uncertainty in interactions. Mindfulness enables intercultural interactants to be ethnorelative and situationally adapt to the pragmatic needs while respecting each other's communication styles. Mindfulness leads to shared intercultural understanding.

In short, a Buddhist perspective on ICC embodies understanding interdependent origination, nonviolence, and mindfulness. Holistic, nonviolent and mindful ICC can contribute to global peace, stability, harmony, and intercultural understanding.

References

Dorjee, T. (2013). Intercultural and intergroup conflict resolution: Nonviolence and middle way approaches. In J. G. Oetzel & S. Ting-Toomey (eds.), *The Sage handbook of conflict resolution: Integrating theory, research, and practice* (2nd ed., pp. 687–712). Thousand Oaks, CA: Sage.

Gudykunst, W. (2005). *Theorizing about intercultural communication*. Thousand Oaks, CA: Sage.

Mind and Life Org. Retrieved from: www.mindandlife.org.

Rinpoche, L. (1981). *Mind in Tibetan Buddhism* (trans. & ed. E.S. Napper), Ithaca, NY: Snow Lion.

Ting-Toomey, S., & Dorjee, T. (2014). Language, identity, and culture: Multiple identity-based perspective. In T. Holtgraves (ed.), *Oxford handbook of language and social psychology* (pp. 27–45). New York, NY: Oxford University Press.

PART 2
CULTURE

Part 2 is a short part, I know. However, it includes a critical chapter for this book. Chapter 15, "Culture and Values in Intercultural Communication" introduces you to key definitions, concepts, and theories related to culture and values. As you have already found in Chapters 1–14, the role of culture is integral to our understanding of intercultural communication. We all view culture differently. Moreover, we all have different value systems that have a profound impact on our cultural systems. Together, our culture, cultural understanding(s), and values all relate to how we approach and understand intercultural communication.

15 CULTURE AND VALUES IN INTERCULTURAL COMMUNICATION

Stephen M. Croucher, Massey University, New Zealand

Chapter Outline

- Culture
  - Culture Defined
  - Components of Culture
  - Subcultures
- Cultures and Values
  - Hofstede's Cultural Dimensions
  - Hall's Context, Time, and Space Dimensions
  - Schwartz's Value Theory
- Chapter Summary

Our eyes are windows into our souls. This is a popular phrase that captures a feeling many of us have when we look at another person; we often feel as though we can tell a lot about a person by simply looking into his/her eyes. The Christian *Bible* refers to the significance of the eyes as way to judge a person's soul. Matthew 6:22 states, "The eye is the lamp of the body; so then if your eye is clear, your whole body will be full of light. But if your eye is bad, your whole body will be full of darkness." Cicero also stated, "The face is a picture of the mind as the eyes are its interpreter." Researchers have historically looked for links between our eyes (color, shape, etc.), health, and personality. Some research has even attributed pain threshold, risk of diabetes, intelligence, and coordination to eye color (Naish, 2014).

The eyes might be doorways or windows into interpreting or understanding human behavior but for some, our culture(s) is a critical feature of our human nature. Hall (1966, p. x) stated culture is "those deep, common unstated experiences which members of a given culture share, communicate without knowing, and which form the backdrop against which all other events are judged." While we all come from different cultures we all view the world through cultural lenses; we see the world from our own points of view. In this chapter we will thus first define culture and its various components. Second, we will look to the relationship between cultures and values, paying close attention to the works of Hofstede, Hall, Schwartz, and Kluckhohn and Strodtbeck.

Culture

Culture Defined

The word "culture" originates from the Latin "cultura," which comes from the verb "colere," or "to till," as in till the soil or land. The word shares its etymology (history or origins) with other words you may be familiar with, such as agriculture and cultivate. Over time the word "culture" began to include aspects of the human condition (mind and being), and developed into the term we associate it with today. In trying to define culture, there are hundreds of definitions. Each of these definitions shares many components, and differs in some ways too. Linton (1945) defined culture as "a configuration of learned behaviors and results of behavior whose component elements are shared and transmitted by the members of a particular society" (p. 32). Moving more toward a biological point of view, Parsons (1949) defined culture as consisting of "those patterns relative to behavior and the products of human action which may be inherited, that is, passed on from generation to generation independently of the biological genes" (p. 8). Hall (1959) stated "culture is communication and communication is culture" (p. 159). This definition clearly shows the inseparable link between culture and communication. Hall (1976) later defined culture as "a series of situational models for behavior and thought" (p. 13). Geertz (1973) later defined culture as a web people spin. He stated:

> Culture is the fabric of meaning in terms of which human beings interpret their experience and guide action; social structure is the form that action takes, the actually existing network of social relations. Culture and social structure are then but different abstractions from the same phenomena.
> (p. 145)

Hofstede (1984) defined culture as the "collective programming of the mind which distinguishes the members of one category of people from another" (p. 51). Lederach (1995) described culture as the "shared knowledge and schemes created by a set of people for perceiving, interpreting, expressing, and responding to the social realities around them" (p. 9). Gudykunst and Kim (2003) borrowed Keesing's (1974) definition when conceptualizing culture:

> Culture, conceived as a system of competence shared in its broad design and deeper principles, and varying between individuals in its specificities, is then not all of what an individual knows and thinks and feels about his [or her] theory of what his [or her] fellows know, believe and mean, his [or her] theory of the code being followed, the game being played, in the

society into which he [or she] was born ... Culture in this view is not ordered simply as a collection of symbols fitted together by the analyst but as a system of knowledge, shaped and constrained by the way the human brain acquires, organizes, and processes information and creates "internal models of reality."

(p. 89)

Considering all of these definitions (and many not mentioned in this chapter), the similarities and differences, this chapter defines **culture** as the learned way of life of a group of people which consists of the shared experiences, behaviors, thoughts, traditions, values, beliefs, rituals, worldviews, and modes of communication of that group. This definition stresses the following aspects of culture: it is learned, shared, and consists of various components.

Components of Culture

Cultures consist of various components/elements. Dodd (1998) explained how a culture can be divided into three layers: the inner core of a culture, which consists of the group's beliefs, history, identity, values, and worldviews; the intermediate layer, which consists of the activities of the group that make up the culture, such as art, communication(s), customs, stories, and rituals; and the outer layer, which are the larger cultural systems representing the culture, such as economic, educational, family, health, political, religious, and other systems unique to a cultural group. See Figure 15.2 for a model of these three layers, adapted from Dodd (1998).

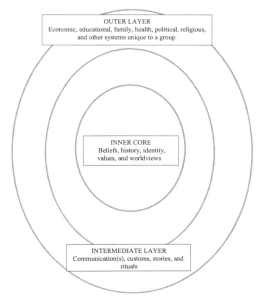

Figure 15.1 Three Layered Model of Culture

The inner core consists of a culture's beliefs and values, history, identity/identities, and worldviews. These elements of culture are the most difficult to change, as they are the most central to individuals. Beliefs and values are critical to a culture. Beliefs are mental representations of an attitude viewed through a cultural lens, which are felt to be true. Sigel (1985) for example stressed how beliefs are mental constructions that are "integrated into schemata or concepts that are held to be true and that guide behavior" (p. 313). In this sense, our **beliefs** are representations or constructions of reality (which we believe to be true) that are shaped by our cultural groups, which in turn guide our behaviors. For example, traditional Finnish culture is closely linked to nature. Many older (and younger Finns as well) believe that the best way to cure a cold, flu, or other ailment is to spend time in nature, the woods in particular. This belief in the power of nature comes from Finland's strong and historical links to nature.

Closely linked to beliefs are values. **Values** are personally and socially shared ideas of what is acceptable and good behavior or ideas, which determine how a person should or should not behave or act in a group (culture) (Graber & Osborne Kilpatrick, 2008; Rokeach, 1973). Values differ in different cultural groups. For example, in Finnish culture, college tuition for all Finnish citizens is free. The idea is that education is a right for all Finns. This is not the case in the US, where college tuition costs continue to be a political and social issue of debate. Ultimately, for Finnish society it is not appropriate to charge for what they consider a right, while in the US college education is not a right for all; thus, it is valued less.

A culture has a shared history. This history is the heritage, the development, and the origin of the culture. This history is passed on through various means, such as customs, stories, literature, rituals, heroes, and other forms of communication, which will be discussed in the intermediate layer of culture. Our history makes us who we are. Think about the United States. While writing this chapter the Republicans and Democratic candidates are embroiled in tough primary election battles. Many of the candidates have told stories about the Founding Fathers. The term "Founding Fathers" evokes images of key figures (all male) forming the US while fighting against the tyrannical British crown. Even my description here is based on my own narrative and historical understanding, and jesting. Granted, many of the stories the current candidates have told, and quotations, have been incorrect. However, this is irrelevant. When telling a historical narrative the facts are not always 100% essential; the imagery and emotions bind group members together around a common understanding. These shared stories and interpretations told over generations build a cultural narrative, a culture, and a shared identity.

Our identities are multifaceted. There is a more in-depth discussion of identities in Chapter 18 by Sandy Hsu. However, for now, researchers (e.g., Gudykunst, 2004; Gudykunst & Kim, 2003; Turner, 1987) have delineated identities into various types: human, personal, and cultural/social. Each of these identities influences how we perceive our culture and our place in a given culture (Turner, 1987). Our **human identity** is how we view ourselves in relation to other humans, as we are all part of this planet Earth (Turner, 1987). Our **personal identity** includes those aspects of ourselves that make us different from the other people in our ingroup, or group of people with a shared identity or interest. For example, compared to others in my group I see myself as smart, good-looking, affectionate, adventurous, etc. The study of our cultural/social identities has received a great deal of attention. A **cultural/social identity** is a perception of ourselves that we believe we share with other members of an ingroup. Gudykunst and Kim (2003) explained how cultural/social identities may:

> be based on the roles we play, such as student, professor, or parent; the demographic categories in which we are categorized, such as nationality, ethnicity, gender, or age; and our membership in formal/informal organizations, such as a political party, organization, or social club.
>
> (pp. 27–28)

A more in-depth discussion of the significance of identities is provided in Chapter 18.

Dodd (1998) also discussed how a culture's **worldview**, or beliefs about how the world and universe work, is essential to understanding the behaviors, attitudes, beliefs, values, thoughts, and actions of a culture. Let's take Hinduism as an example. Hinduism is a pantheistic religion; it equates God with the universe. At the same time Hinduism is polytheistic; there are many gods and goddesses who personify aspects of God, which allows Hindus many ways to worship. Since Hinduism is pantheistic individuals can worship in many ways based on their family traditions, regional practices, etc. Each of these variations in Hinduism influences a Hindu's worldview, which is one reason why Hinduism is such a diverse religion/culture.

The intermediate layer of culture consists of the group activities that make up the culture, such as art, literature, communication(s), rules, customs,

Figure 15.2 Ganesha

stories, rituals, and other forms of expression (holidays, music, technology, etc.). Take art for example. Japanese art has historically focused less on the physical form of humans and more on nature and natural settings. While European artists (from the ancient Greeks and Romans to the Renaissance) were focusing on the human form, many Japanese artists were focusing on animals, gardens, and other natural scenes. This natural scenery reflects the importance of nature and natural beauty in Japanese culture.

Rituals are another key activity that differentiates cultures from one another. In Japan, unlike in the United States, it is common for individuals to practice *Ocha*, or a tea ceremony. A tea ceremony is a ritualized preparing and serving of Japanese green tea called Matcha along with Japanese sweets. Preparing tea and sweets in this fashion has its own philosophy, which is hard to understand for those not from Japanese culture. The tea ceremony philosophy includes: *wa*, *kei*, *sei*, and *jaku*. *Wa* means harmony, *kei* means respect, *sei* is purity, and *jaku* is tranquility. All of these elements are striven for in the *Ocha*, a unique cultural experience.

How we communicate is also a key element of what defines us as a culture. As stated earlier in this chapter, "culture is communication and communication is culture" (Hall, 1959, p. 159). Take the verbal language that you speak. In Chapter 17, Todd L. Sandel discusses the links between culture and language. However, for now, consider the following. The language we are brought up in influences how we see the world. I was brought up primarily speaking English in the US. In the US it is fairly common for intimate couples (and even friends and parents and children) to express the phrase "I love you" to one another on a regular basis. It is also common for people to express their "love" of other objects, such as food, animals, things, objects, places, etc. However, after moving to Finland I learned that "*rakastaa*" the Finnish version of "to love" is used *very* sparingly. In fact a few Finnish friends of mine laughed when another friend of mine commented on how she loved a certain food and an airport. Their response was how can you love a food or place? For many Finns, "love" is a very intimate statement that really is reserved for very intimate others, and is rarely stated; as the person who deserves to hear it should know you "love" them, which explains why many intimate couples rarely say it . . . it is almost sacred. So now, whenever I go to the US and hear people say "I love you" I feel as if they are throwing the phrase out like "I like you." I have culturally changed in how I use and understand language.

The outer layer of culture consists of the macro-cultural systems representing the culture, such as the economic, educational, family, health, political, religious, and other systems unique to a cultural group. One significant cultural system that binds together members of a culture, provides its members with an identity, beliefs, values, a worldview, customs, rituals, etc. is religion (Dodd, 1998). A **religion** is "a unified system of beliefs and practices relative to sacred things, that is to say things which are set apart and forbidden – beliefs and practices which unite into one single moral community called a Church, all those who adhere to them" (Durkheim, 1976, p. 47).

Religions, and particularly the teaching and texts of a religion guide individuals and societies in how they see and judge the world. For example, how individuals manage/negotiate conflict is influenced by religious texts and teachings. The *Qur'an*, the holy book of Islam:

> urges believers to have patience (sabr) (e.g., 2: 153; 16: 127). It is through patience, particularly in tough times (such as conflicts), that one should trust in Allah's plans (3:200; 40: 77). Instead of rushing to judgment during a conflict, sabr implies that one should contemplate the situation; pray for God's help to deal with it; seek guidance from others, such as a neutral third party; and/or allow the situation/conflict to settle down before engaging in it.
>
> (Croucher, 2013b, pp. 567–570)

Our beliefs about health and health practices are also culturally based. Many societies rely on more modern, Western ideas regarding health care. The belief that medical practitioners, who have a medical degree and rely on Western medicine (prescriptions, surgeries and other procedures, etc.), is vastly different than those cultures that rely more on traditional medicine. In traditional Hmong culture, shamans, or healers/medicine men are often used to diagnose and treat those Hmong who are ill. Shamans will conduct a more holistic assessment of an individual's emotional, physical, mental, and religious state before considering a diagnosis and whether treatment is needed. If treatment is needed, shamans will treat their patients with a variety of methods: prayers, rituals, plants and herbs, and other more natural and spiritual approaches. In a traditional Western approach to medicine medical practitioners are more likely to assess only a patient's physical state and then treat with prescriptions or other medically/scientifically proven methods. Such differences in approaches have caused conflicts when Hmong encounter Western medicine. Fadiman (1997) in her book, *The spirit catches you and you fall down*, retold the story of Lia Lee (a young child diagnosed with epilepsy), her Hmong refugee family, and the tragic clashes they experienced when they encountered Western medicine in a California hospital.

There are many other systems that represent a culture, such as its political system. It is more common to hear criticisms of socialism in the US, where capitalism and a free-market society has been the tradition since the Founding Fathers, while in the Nordic countries socialism is a much more common and acceptable form of government and economics. The family system is also culturally bound. As a case in point, historically in China it was common for families to care for the elderly members of their families. The extended family was regarded as extremely important. However, with increased urbanization, rising living costs, and a falling birth rate as a consequence of the one-child policy, fewer families are caring for their elderly family members (Yoon, 2013). Collectively, as described by Dodd (1998), culture establishes and reveals itself on three levels: inner core, intermediate, and outer layers. Exploring each of

Figure 15.3 Traditionally dressed Laotian Hmong woman

these components/levels of a culture helps us understand how cultures function, and how they differ from one another.

Subcultures

Within every culture there are smaller, microcultures, or subcultures. **Subcultures** are membership groups within a larger group that hold different values and/or norms, or behave differently than the larger (typically defined as dominant) group. Schaefer (2012) identified five characteristics of a subculture. First, members possess some cultural or physical characteristics that distinguish them from the dominant culture. In the case of the Sami people in the Nordic nations, they are ethnically and linguistically different than the dominant Finnish, Swedish, and Norwegian populations. African-Americans are a minority in the US, and Whites are considered to be the group with the most economic and political power. Second, membership is often not voluntary, but is some cases it can be. In India individuals are born into a particular caste (social hierarchy), and it is extremely difficult to change your caste. You are born White, Asian, etc., which can have political, social, and economic implications. However, in some cases, which you will see below, some people choose membership in a subculture. Third, many members of subcultures practice endogamy, or marrying within the ingroup. In many cultural groups arranged marriages are still practiced, and it is not common to marry outside of the ingroup. Moreover, many people are simply more comfortable marrying within their own group. Fourth, members of the subculture are aware of their membership in the group. When an individual is born into a subculture, which inherently has less political and economic power than the dominant culture, they are aware of their status. Minority status in fact often brings members of subcultures together as a community. Finally, subcultures often unfortunately experience discrimination. There are countless examples of minorities throughout history being persecuted due to their minority status. Subcultures also give members identity distinct from the dominant culture through various means: language, dress, rituals, art, history, shared activities, media, and many other means.

Before discussing one particular subculture (which many of you have heard about or seen), there are two different types of membership groups that we should briefly define: ethnic and social groups. An **ethnic group** is a group with distinctive cultural, linguistic, religious, or national characteristics, which is socially constructed by its members (the ingroup) and the outgroup (those who do not share the group's characteristics) (Gudykunst & Kim, 2003). For example, Muslims are a growing religious group in the United States, which is historically a Christian majority nation. In Finland in 2015, in the wake of the 2015 refugee crisis in the European Union, Somalis are a growing immigrant group, which is a vastly different group when compared to the traditional Protestant, Caucasian Finn. A **social group** is a group that shares similar social (organizational, political, economic, etc.) interests or characteristics. For example, individuals in the US who identify as Republican or Democratic are identifying with a social group, a political party (a subculture). Those who identify with these political parties understand (probably) the platform/beliefs of these political parties and how the two parties differ. Being a Mets or a Yankees fan—you really can't be both. If you do not know what I am talking about that is because you are either not a fan of American baseball or you have never heard of these two professional baseball teams. In the world of sports people often identify with one team over others, Barca/Real Madrid in European football, Montreal/Toronto in the NHL, or Auburn/Alabama in college football.

An example of a subculture based on shared social interests is the Trekkie subculture. Trekkies are an example of one of many fan-based subcultures. Here is a short list of some others: Beatlemaniacs (Beatles fans), Furries (fans of the furry genre), Bondians (fans of James Bond), K-pop fans, Manga fans, Parrotheads (Jimmy Buffet fans), Potterheads (Harry Potter fans), Star Wars fans, and Whovians (Doctor Who fans), just to name a few. **Fandom** refers to a group of people (fans) who have a shared sense of camaraderie with one another over a common interest, and these people spend a significant amount of their time (and often resources) on this interest as part of a social group. Trekkies, or fans of the Star Trek franchise, are a classic example of fandom. Since the late 1960s thousands of Trekkies have attended film openings, gathered at science fiction conventions, attended book signings, and other activities. Trekkies have their own unique history, anthropology, heroes, stories, rituals, costumes, and language, just to name a few elements of a culture. In fact, Jindra (1994) compared Trekkie fandom to a religious culture. He stated that the fandom of Trekkies resembles a religious-type movement, as it has an origin myth and a set of

Figure 15.4 Comicon Fans

beliefs, to name just two aspects of its structure. Die-hard Trekkies have also been noted to know everything about the franchise, from the obvious to the obscure (Hale, 1975; Jenkins, 1992). The Trekkie subculture has also faced discrimination and stereotypes, with many of its members being called obsessive, scary, nerds, and maladjusted (Jenkins, 1992; Kozinets, 2001). However, this subculture continues to provide many of its members with positive role models and a sense of community (Kozinets, 2001).

Cultures and Values

As indicated earlier, a culture is the learned way of life of a group of people that consists of the shared experiences, behaviors, thoughts, traditions, values, beliefs, rituals, worldviews, and modes of communication of that group. That particular group will be similar and different in some ways from another group; cultures differ. To clarify the differences and similarities between cultures it is essential to have a way to talk about these issues. It makes no sense to say, "Jussi is quieter because he is Finnish" or "Stephen talks a lot because he is American." These statements do not tell us why each person is the way they are, or why we perceive them to be the way they are. There are dimensions of culture that might be similar or different in Finland and the US that could explain the differences in communication styles. These dimensions are cultural variability. Two researchers in particular have shaped our understanding of cultural variability, Hofstede and Hall.

Hofstede's Cultural Dimensions

In a monumental 1980 study, Hofstede analyzed the occupational attitudes/ feelings of more than 160,000 IBM employees in more than 50 different nations. In this first study he defined four cultural dimensions that influenced behaviors: individualism–collectivism, masculinity–femininity, **power distance**, and uncertainty avoidance. In a follow-up study a fifth dimension, long–short-term orientation was added (Hofstede & Bond, 1988), and then in 2010 a sixth dimension was added, indulgence-restraint (Hofstede, Hofstede, & Minkov, 2010).

The individualism–collectivism continuum is probably the most researched dimension of cultural variability. **Individualism** is a preference for loose social networks, and an individual preference for taking care of themselves and their immediate families. For individualists there is a clear preference for individual goals over group goals and the promotion of self-realization. **Collectivism** is a preference for more tightly knit social networks, and an individual preference for individuals to care for members of their ingroup in exchange for what Hofstede and Bond (1988) call "exchange for loyalty" (p. 419). For collectivistic individuals there is a preference for group goals over individual goals and the promotion of belonging to the group. Hofstede's research, and subsequent research by others has often found East Asian nations (Japan, China, and Korea for example) tend to score higher on collectivism, while Western European nations (Germany, the United Kingdom, and the US for example) tend to score higher on individualism (see the Hofstede Center for a sample of national scores: http://geert-hofstede.com/countries.html).

Masculinity–femininity is the second dimension of cultural variability offered by Hofstede (1980, 2001). Cultures higher in **masculinity** tend to be more assertive, competitive, strive more for achievement and heroism, and more highly value success. Cultures higher in **femininity** tend to be more cooperative, modest, care more for the weak, and strive for higher quality of life for all. It is more common in highly feminine cultures to see initiatives such as maternity and paternity leave having more support, as such initiatives are seen as caring for all. East Asian nations have been found to typically score as more masculine, while Nordic nations (Norway, Sweden, Denmark, and Finland) have tended to score higher on femininity.

Power distance is the third dimension of cultural variability provided by Hofstede. **Power distance** is the extent to which less powerful members of a society accept and expect power to be distributed equally/unequally. Cultures high in power distance easily accept **hierarchy**, where people have their place in society. It is common in high power distance cultures for the gap between those who have power and those who do not to be large, and this gap is often accepted and not challenged, as challenging is often seen as futile. Low power distance cultures have hierarchy; however, structures within the culture strive to balance the distribution of power within society. It is common in low power distance cultures for the gap between those who have power and those who do not to be small, as power inequalities should be justified. Research has consistently shown that East Asian and African nations tend to be high power distance, which Western European and Nordic nations tend to be lower power distance.

The fourth original cultural dimension is uncertainty avoidance. **Uncertainty avoidance** is the degree to which people feel uncomfortable with ambiguity and uncertainty. How a culture and its members deal with the unknown future is significant. Cultures high in uncertainty avoidance have strict codes and/or rules for behavior that must be followed, and these cultures can be intolerant when these codes and/or rules are broken. Cultures low in uncertainty avoidance tend to have fewer codes or rules for behavior. Many Mediterranean and South American nations score high on uncertainty avoidance. The Nordic nations, and some Asian nations (e.g. Singapore) tend to score low on uncertainty avoidance.

The fifth cultural dimension is long–short-term orientation. Cultures with a **short-term orientation** consider the past or the present as more important than the future. Such cultures value tradition, current hierarchies, and prefer immediate gratification. Cultures with a **long-term orientation** focus more on the future. Such cultures are willing to go without short-term gratifications, are thriftier, and more willing to save for the future. The US and other Western European nations tend to score high on short-term orientation, while East Asian nations score higher on long-term orientation.

The final, and newest, cultural dimension is indulgence versus restraint. **Indulgence** means the culture allows free gratification of natural and basic human drives related to having fun. In essence, the culture encourages its members to seek out their needs and desires. **Restraint** means the culture suppresses the gratification of needs and desires, and regulates members through social norms. Western European nations tend to score higher on indulgence, while East Asian and African nations tend to score more on the side of restraint.

While Hofstede's dimensions of cultural variability have had a profound impact on communication and social scientific research, researchers have criticized these dimensions for various reasons: for being hegemonic, too culturally generic, for not applying to culture at all, for being inconsistent, and for lacking empirical support and transparency (Baskerville, 2003; Croucher, 2013a; Fougère & Moulettes, 2007; McSweeney, 2002: Signorini, et al., 2009). All in all, these dimensions are starting points for cultural comparison.

Hall's Context, Time, and Space Dimensions

Edward T. Hall (1976) described three distinct cultural factors: context, time, and space. Hall discussed how cultures fall on a continuum between high and low context. In **high context** cultures, there are many contextual aspects/elements that help people understand the norms and/or rules in society. Thus, communication is often taken for granted and implied. Asian nations, Brazil, and France tend to be higher context. In **low context** cultures, very little is taken for granted, as communication is more explicit, and little is left for misinterpretation. This type of communication is more common in most European nations and the US.

Hall (1976) also discussed how cultures differ in their use of time. He described two types of time use: monochronic and polychronic. In a

monochronic time culture people are more likely to do one thing at a time, and planning is essential. This type of time management is more common in low context cultures. In a **polychronic** time culture people are more likely to multi-task more, value human interaction more than time, and have less concern for getting things done than on how they get them done. This time management is more common high context cultures.

Hall (1966) also described people's relationship within their space. He defined this area of research as **proxemics** or the study of the use of space. Hall explained how each of us needs a different amount of personal space to be comfortable. When others violate our personal space, our bubble or territory, we see this violation as a threat because it violates our **territoriality**, or concern for space, which is culturally specific. Hall (1966) divided cultures into high and low territoriality. Cultures with high territoriality have high concern for ownership, mark their territory, and use words like "mine." This concern for space is most common in low context cultures. Cultures with low territoriality have less concern for ownership, boundaries are less important for them, and they typically share ownership of things. This concern for space is most common in high context cultures.

Schwartz's Value Theory

The final approach to understanding how cultures differ is from a values approach. Schwartz (1994, 1999) argued that understanding an individual's value priorities could explain their behaviors. Schwartz (1999) identified seven types of values on which to compare cultures: **conservatism**, **egalitarian commitment**, harmony, hierarchy, **mastery**, **affective autonomy**, and **intellectual autonomy**. Table 15.1 below defines each type of value.

Table 15.1 Schwartz's Seven Cultural Value Types

Type	Definition
Conservatism	A society that strives to maintain the status quo and tradition and that emphasizes harmonious relations
Egalitarian commitment	A society emphasizing the wholeness of selfless interests
Harmony	A society that focuses on harmony with nature
Hierarchy	A society that stresses hierarchy, roles, and resource allocation
Mastery	A society that stresses active control of the social environment and a person's right to get ahead of other people
Affective autonomy	A society that acknowledges people as autonomous people who are free to pursue their own pleasure-seeking, interests and desires
Intellectual autonomy	A society that acknowledges people as autonomous people who are free to pursue their own intellectual *dreams and desires*

Schwartz (1999) summarized these seven values into three macro categories, or continua. Cultures that place higher on one side of the continuum have more of a preference for that value, and perceive the other value as less important: (1) mastery versus harmony, (2) hierarchy versus egalitarianism, and (3) autonomy versus embeddedness. The relationship humankind has with nature is the essence of mastery versus harmony. Cultures that value mastery strive to control and change the world. Such cultures typically exploit the Earth to "advance" their interests. Values such as ambition, competition, and success are highly valued in these cultures. India and China are ranked very high on mastery. Cultures that value harmony strive to live harmoniously with nature. In these cultures it is essential to be stewards of the environment, and to do as little harm as possible to the Earth. Values such as preservation and caring are more common. The Nordic nations tend to score high on harmony.

Preserving the social needs and order of a society is the second issue Schwartz (1999) addressed with hierarchy versus egalitarianism. This dimension is very similar to Hofstede's power distance dimension. Cultures that value hierarchy see the distribution of hierarchy and power in economic, political and social structures as justified and necessary to maintain social order. Such structures are necessary for rules to exist. Southeast Asian and many African nations tend to be more hierarchical. On the other hand, egalitarian cultures see the distribution of hierarchy and power in structures as unjust. People in these cultures are encouraged and taught to move beyond hierarchies and work for one another. The Nordic nations and many Western European nations tend to be more egalitarian.

The relationship between the individual and the group is the third issue all people face. Autonomy versus embeddedness is similar to Hofstede's individualism/collectivism continuum. In more autonomous cultures people are more independent (intellectually and emotionally) and are encouraged to express their independence. Typically Western European nations and the US encourage autonomy the most. In more embedded cultures people are more dependent on one another and identify more with the larger group. People are more likely to identify with a shared way of life or community. Conservatism is much higher in an embedded culture, as it protects the group mentality. Many East Asian cultures and African cultures tend to be more embedded.

Chapter Summary

Culture is a complex concept. This chapter defined culture as the learned way of life of a group of people, which consists of the shared experiences, behaviors, thoughts, traditions, values, beliefs, rituals, worldviews, and modes of communication of that group. Breaking down this definition you can see there are many elements to explore. We are all part of various cultures at the same time. These numerous cultures we are a part of impact our identities, worldviews, and behaviors. While we are also part of many cultural groups (our ingroups), there are many cultural groups we are not part of (outgroups). We differentiate ourselves, in these instances we learn at a very early age to recognize those we perceive as like us and those who are not part of our culture(s). In the next chapter we will look in more depth into how and why we identify ourselves in certain ways.

Key Terms

Affective autonomy	Beliefs	Collectivism
Conservatism	Cultural/Social identity	Culture
Egalitarian commitment	Ethnic group	Fandom
Femininity	Harmony	Hierarchy
High context	Human identity	Individualism
Indulgence	Intellectual autonomy	Long-term orientation
Low context	Masculinity	Mastery
Monochronic	Personal identity	Polychronic
Power distance	Proxemics	Religion
Restraint	Short-term orientation	Social group
Subcultures	Territoriality	Uncertainty avoidance
Values	Worldview	

Activities

1. In a group of 3–5 people, go online and find 10 definitions of culture. What are the commonalities and differences you find in the definitions? Compare these definitions to the definitions in the chapter. What is your definition of culture? Justify your definition.
2. Identify a subculture, any subculture. What makes it a subculture? What are the characteristics that make it distinct from the dominant culture?
3. Looking at your cultural group, where do you place your group on Hofstede's dimensions? Compare your thoughts about your group or another group using Hofstede's Country Comparison Tool: http://geert-hofstede.com/countries.html

References

Baskerville, R. F. (2003). Hofstede never studied culture. *Accounting, Organizations and Society, 28*, 1–14.

Croucher, S. M. (2013a). Communication apprehension, self-perceived communication competence, and willingness to communicate: A French analysis. *Journal of International and Intercultural Communication, 6*, 298–316.

Croucher, S. M. (2013b). Religion and conflict: An emerging field of inquiry. In J. G. Oetzel, & S. Ting-Toomey (eds.), *The SAGE handbook of conflict communication: Integrating theory, research, and practice* (pp. 563–584). Thousand Oaks, CA: Sage.

Dodd, C. H. (1998). *Dynamics of intercultural communication* (5th ed.). Boston, MA: McGraw-Hill.

Durkheim, E. (1976). *The elementary forms of religious life*. London, UK: Harper Collins. First published in French 1912.

Fadiman, A. (1997). *The spirit catches you and you fall down: A Hmong child, her American doctors, and the collision of two cultures*. New York, NY: Farrar, Straus and Giroux.

Fougère, M. & Moulettes, A. (2007). The construction of the modern west and the backward rest: Studying the discourse of Hofstede's *Culture's consequences*. *Journal of Multicultural Discourses*, 2, 1–19.

Geertz, C. (1973). *The interpretation of cultures*. New York, NY: Basic Books.

Graber, D. R., & Osborne Kilpatrick, A. (2008). Establishing values-based leadership and value systems in healthcare organizations. *Journal of Health & Human Services Administration*, 31, 179–197.

Gudykunst, W. B. (2004). *Bridging differences: Effective intergroup communication* (4th ed.). Thousand Oaks, CA: Sage.

Gudykunst, W. B., & Kim, Y. Y. (2003). *Communicating with strangers: An approach to intercultural communication* (4th ed.). Boston, MA: McGraw Hill.

Hale, B. (April 26, 1975). Believing in Captain Kirk. *Calgary Herald*. Retrieved from: https://news.google.com/newspapers?id=LnBkAAAAIBAJ&sjid=nX0NAAAAIBAJ&pg=2771,3366878&hl=fi

Hall, E. T. (1959). *The silent language*. New York, NY: Doubleday.

Hall, E. T. (1966). *The hidden dimension*. Garden City, NY: Doubleday.

Hall, E. T. (1976). *Beyond culture*. New York, NY: Anchor Books.

Hofstede, G. (1980). *Culture's consequences: International differences in work-related values*. Beverly Hills, CA: Sage.

Hofstede, G. (1984). National cultures and corporate cultures. In L. A. Samovar & R. E. Porter (eds.), *Communication between cultures* (pp. 51–63). Belmont, CA: Wadsworth.

Hofstede, G. (2001). *Culture's consequences: Comparing values, behaviors, institutions and organizations across nations* (2nd ed.). Thousand Oaks, CA: Sage.

Hofstede, G., & Bond, M. H. (1988). The Confucius connection: From cultural roots to economic growth. *Organizational Dynamics*, 16, 5–21.

Hofstede, G., Hofstede, G. J., & Minkov, M. (2010). *Culture's consequences: Comparing values, behaviors, institutions, and organizations across nations* (3rd ed.). Thousand Oaks, CA: Sage.

Jenkins, H. (1992). *Textual poachers: Television fans and participatory culture*. New York, NY: Taylor & Francis.

Jindra, M. (1994). Star Trek fandom as a religious phenomenon. *Sociology of Religion*, 55, 27–51.

Keesing, R. (1974). Theories of culture. *Annual Review of Anthropology*, 3, 73–97.

Kozinets, R. V. (2001). Utopian enterprise: Articulating the meanings of Star Trek's culture of consumption. *The Journal of Consumer Research*, 28, 67–88.

Lederach, J. P. (1995). *Preparing for peace: Conflict transformation across cultures*. Syracuse, NY: Syracuse University Press.

Linton, R. (1945). *The cultural background of personality*. New York, NY: Appleton Century.

McSweeney, B. (2002). Hofstede's model of national cultural differences and their consequences: A triumph of faith – a failure of analysis. *Human Relations*, 55, 89–118.

Naish, J. (June 9, 2014). Can't hold a drink or cope with pain? Blame the colour of your eyes. *The Daily Mail Online.* Retrieved from: http://www.dailymail.co.uk/health/article-2653300/Cant-hold-drink-cope-pain-Blame-colour-eyes.html

Parsons, T. (1949). *Essays in sociological theory.* Glencoe, IL: The Free Press.

Rokeach, M. (1973). *The nature of human values.* New York, NY: Free Press.

Schaefer, R. T. (2012). *Racial and ethnic groups* (13th ed.). Upper Saddle River, NJ: Prentice Hall.

Schwartz, S. (1994). Beyond individualism/collectivism: New cultural dimensions of values. In U. Kim, H. C. Triandis, C. Kagitcibasi, S. C. Choi, & G. Yoon (Eds.), *Individualism and collectivism: Theory and method, and applications* (pp. 85–119). Thousand Oaks, CA: Sage.

Schwartz, S. (1999). A theory of cultural values and some implications for work. *Applied Psychology: An International Review, 48,* 23–47.

Sigel, I. E. (1985). Parental concepts of development. In I. E. Sigel (ed.), *Parental belief systems: The psychological consequences for children* (pp. 83–105). Hillsdale, NJ: Erlbaum.

Signorini, P., Wiesemes, R., & Murphy, R. (2009). Developing alternative frameworks for exploring intercultural learning: A critique of Hofstede's cultural difference model. *Teaching in Higher Education, 14,* 253–274.

Turner, J. H. (1987). *A theory of social interaction.* Stanford, CA: Stanford University Press.

Yoon, E. (October 22, 2013). How China's one-child policy hurts the elderly. *CNBC Online.* Retrieved from: http://www.cnbc.com/2013/10/22/

PART 3
THEORETICAL DOMAINS

Part 3 focuses on Theoretical and Conceptual Domains in Intercultural Communication. The following five chapters discuss key theoretical and conceptual areas of intercultural communication. You will find one interesting element at the end of each of these chapters, a sample student paper. This student paper is a real student paper that has been included to provide an example of what can be done in an intercultural communication when asked to write a review of literature or argument paper related to theory. These are real students, who come from different levels of experience in communication. The students come from different majors, and some of the students are native and some non-native English speakers. Each of the authors has also commented on the student papers so you can see ways in which the student papers are strong, and ways in which the papers could be improved. We all would like to thank the students for allowing us to include their papers in this textbook.

In Chapter 16, "Identity and Intercultural Communication," I describe key theories on identity and how they relate to intercultural communication. In Chapter 17, "Language and Intercultural Communication," Todd L. Sandel focuses on the links between language and intercultural communication. In Chapter 18, "Intercultural Communication and Relationships," Sandy Hsu focuses on the intricate links between culture, communication, and relationships. In Chapter 19, "Culture and Conflict," Dale Hample and Mengqi Zhan discuss the interplay between culture and conflict. In Chapter 20, "Intercultural Adaptation," Gina Barker describes adaptation processes and how they relate to intercultural communication.

16 IDENTITY AND INTERCULTURAL COMMUNICATION

Stephen M. Croucher, Massey University, New Zealand

Chapter Outline

- Identity
  - Identity Defined
  - Formation of Identities
  - Kinds of Identities
- Identity Theories
  - Social Identity Theory
  - Ethnolinguistic Identity Theory
  - Face Negotiation Theory
- Chapter Summary
- Student Paper

ADVICE FROM A CATERPILLAR

In Lewis Carroll's 1865 classic *Alice's Adventures in Wonderland* we are introduced to a myriad of characters as Alice falls through a rabbit hole and then encounters numerous strange (to put it nicely) anthropomorphic creatures. In my favorite chapter of the book, Chapter V, "Advice from a Caterpillar," a miniaturized Alice encounters a caterpillar smoking a hookah sitting on a mushroom. The caterpillar questions Alice about her identity and the identity crisis she has been going through while in Wonderland. The following is a short excerpt from their conversation:

> The Caterpillar and Alice looked at each other for some time in silence: at last the Caterpillar took the hookah out of its mouth, and addressed her in a languid, sleepy voice.
> "Who are you?" said the Caterpillar.
> This was not an encouraging opening for a conversation. Alice replied, rather shyly, "I—I hardly know, sir, just at present—at least I know who I was when I got up this morning, but I think I must have been changed several times since then."

"What do you mean by that?" said the Caterpillar sternly. "Explain yourself!"

"I can't explain myself, I'm afraid, sir" said Alice, "because I'm not myself, you see."

"I don't see," said the Caterpillar.

"I'm afraid I can't put it more clearly," Alice replied very politely, "for I can't understand it myself to begin with; and being so many different sizes in a day is very confusing."

"It isn't," said the Caterpillar.

"Well, perhaps you haven't found it so yet," said Alice; "but when you have to turn into a chrysalis—you will someday, you know—and then after that into a butterfly, I should think you'll feel it a little queer, won't you?"

"Not a bit," said the Caterpillar.

"Well, perhaps your feelings may be different," said Alice; "all I know is, it would feel very queer to me."

"You!" said the Caterpillar contemptuously. "Who are you?"

This over 150-year-old literary dialogue illustrates the dynamic nature of identities. The question of "Who am I?" has been asked for thousands of years. The different ways in which we see/perceive ourselves are our identities. Castells (1997) said that while we have multiple identities, these identities give us a sense of place and being. Moreover, Giles and Hewstone (1982) explained that we are continually negotiating and reconstructing our identities, emphasizing the integral nature of communication to identity. Thus, in this chapter we will explore the multifaceted nature of identity. In the first section we will define identity and discuss different kinds/types of identities. In the second section we will review key identity management, negotiation, and other identity theories. The third section of the chapter includes a student paper on identity. This paper is included to demonstrate to you one way you could write a short paper on identity for an intercultural communication class.

Identity

Identity Defined

Identity is a person's self-concept in relation to the world around himself/herself. You might consider your identity to be how you view yourself, and how you think, and want others to view you. It is essential to understand, and we will keep coming back to this point, that the self does not create identities alone. Identities are co-created through our communication with others (Martin & Nakayama, 1997), which demonstrates the integral nature of communication to identity. Our identities emerge when we interact with others through communication. Collier (1997) explained that our identities are enacted in interpersonal communication/contexts through two processes: avowal and ascription. Avowal is the self that we portray: "I am Stephen. This is who I am. I am X." Ascription is the process through which others attribute an identity to us, for example through stereotyping. We avow our identities, and are ascribed identities in many ways, through symbols, norms, labels, etc. For example, what cultural symbols come to mind when you think about the United States? You might think about the American flag, baseball, and a multitude of other stereotypical "American" symbols. Such symbols and norms avow and ascribe "Americanness."

Research has overall shown that we tend to have three general types of identities: human, personal, and social (Turner, et al., 1987). **Human identities** include those elements, views, or commonalities of ourselves that we think we share with all other humans. As people we do not survive alone, we socialize with other humans. As Fuentes (1992, back cover) said, we are "born or reborn in contact with other men and women, with men and women of another culture, another creed, another race. If we do not recognize our humanity in others, we shall not recognize it in ourselves."

Personal identities are those perceptions or views of ourselves that separate/differentiate us from others in our ingroup. An **ingroup** is a group of people "about whose welfare [we are] concerned, with whom [we are] willing to cooperate without demanding equitable returns, and separation from whom leads to discomfort or even pain" (Triandis, 1988, p. 75). Essentially, this is a group to which we feel cohesion, have shared experiences, a future, and trust. An **outgroup** on the other hand is a group to which we feel less cohesion, have fewer shared experiences, do not have a shared future, and have less trust in such groups. Our personal identity differentiates us in some way from the ingroup, like our personality characteristics: being smart, tall, having glasses, having brown hair, etc.

Social identities are those perceptions or views of ourselves that we share with other members of our ingroups. For example, social identities can be based on our demographic characteristics (sex, age, race/ethnicity, nationality), membership in organizations (religious affiliation, social clubs, sports team), roles we have (parent, spouse, friend), professions (professor, lawyer, doctor, waiter), or membership in a stigmatized group (homeless, having HIV/AIDS).

Formation of Identities

We develop, maintain, and refine our identities through various stages and processes throughout our lives. Theorists have proposed various models to describe how we develop our identities. Most researchers agree that a critical time for identity development is adolescence. Tanti, et al. (2011) described how during adolescence (particularly in Western cultures) we are in an optimal time and place for self-categorization and comparison of ourselves to others. It is during this time that we undergo a great deal of identity development, facilitated by family, social groups, media, and other surrounding cultural elements. As our social world changes around us, we are also during adolescence affected by two other major transitions in life, that have major effects on our identities: a shift from primary to secondary school, and a shift from secondary school to university or work. It is through these shifts and through the changing social world during adolescence that much of our "adult" identity is shaped. Think back to your adolescence, it might not have been that long ago for some of you. What events or groups affected how you think about who you are, your identity?

Hardiman (2001) proposed four stages to social identity development (particularly in Western cultures again), this model further illustrates the complexities of how our identities develop and change over time. In the first stage we have an unexamined identity. This identity is shaped by the norms of the dominant culture, as the dominant culture shapes our identity and makes us who we are. In the second stage we accept the identity the dominant culture shapes for us. In the third stage we begin to question the dominant cultural paradigms. With this questioning we also begin to question and redefine our identity because we have a reinterpretation of the dominant culture. The fourth and final stage, particularly for Western cultures, is integration. This is where white individuals in particular, as described by Hardiman, become aware of their special privilege in society and integrate an awareness of minority cultures into their social identity. This final stage is often not reached in identity development, as it is a heightened form of identity development. Hardiman pointed out that this process is not linear, and there is no set time period for an individual to be in any stage.

There are two ways to approach identity in intercultural communication: the traditional and the modern (Banks & Banks, 1995). The traditional paradigm asserts that communication is an internal source of conflict and identity stress during which time we try to reduce fear and anxiety (Hall, 1992). Identity is a multidimensional concept consisting of psychological and social factors (Merino & Tileagă 2011), and negotiated until we reach mutual understanding and agreement on our identity (Ting-Toomey, 1993). However, the modern paradigm argues that identity is an animated and dynamic notion, whose form is dependent on social context and time (Hoffman, 1989). Considering these two approaches to identity, scholars have proposed different types of identity, such as national (Hofstede, 1980), cultural, ethnic (Khakimova, et al., 2012; Ting-Toomey, et al., 2000), religious (Koschmann, 2013), sexual (Koller, 2012; Motschenbacher, 2013), and gender (Back, 2014; Hall & LaFrance, 2012), to mention a few. The following section of this chapter describes some of these numerous identities we might have.

Kinds of Identities

In Hofstede's (1980) landmark study he explored cultural variability among IBM employees around the world. In his final analysis he divided the employees based on their nation. These studies, and many subsequent studies, have equated culture with an individual's national identity. **National identity** is an individual's perception of himself/herself as a member of a nation. When

Figure 16.1 A Traditional Finnish Sauna

considering national identity we should recognize that identifying with a nation has two elements. First, members share common characteristics: common history, language(s), culture, and common systems (economic, legal, and political for example). For example, most Finns speak either Finnish, Swedish, or Sami, know something about Finnish history, understand more about Finnish culture than non-Finns, understand the economic, social, legal, and political systems in Finland more than non-Finns do (outgroup members), and definitely know something about Finnish sauna.

Second, a critical element of national identity is that when we identify as part of a nation we inherently differentiate ourselves from those who are not one of us: ingroup/outgroup differentiation. While I am writing this book (in 2016) the United States is in the midst of an election for the next president. The rhetoric of many of the candidates for the Republican nominee for President, particularly Donald Trump, is differentiating between those who are "real" Americans, and those who are not. In many of Trump's speeches he has described how immigrants to the US, even if they are citizens, are not "real" Americans, as being able to identify as "American" for Trump is essentially reserved for those Caucasian-Christians born in the US. This rhetoric illustrates how the dominant culture often has the power to determine who is and is not in the ingroup.

Cultural identity includes our social identities based on cultural group memberships. While we are part of many groups (national, religious, ethnic, sexual, etc.), we attach different levels of emotional significance to these groups. My spouse and I were both born in the United States. We moved to Finland in 2012 and have since met many foreigners living in Finland. All of these individuals have different perceptions of what it means to be "American" and perceive Finland differently. For example, many of the immigrants we have met who identify more with their nation and culture of origin tend to more strongly maintain their original cultural beliefs, values, norms, etc., and are less likely to adopt Finnish culture. On the other hand, I have met some Americans who weakly identify with American culture, and thus they tend to pick up or accept Finnish culture rather quickly.

Our sense of belonging or identification with an ethnic group is our **ethnic identity**. While we often used terms like race and ethnicity interchangeable, they are in fact different. Race is based on an individual's biological characteristics. Ethnicity on the other hand is based on the cultural characteristics (nation of origin, language, culture, religion, etc.) that a group of people share. In the United States it is common to hear people identify themselves as African American. This identification represents a multifaceted identity. First of all, the person is identifying as an "American" (national identity). Second, the person is also identifying themselves as having African ethnicity. In this case, the person is also identifying with "African" culture. When I have done research in France among North African Muslim immigrants I have found that ethnicity is not the same concept as it is in the US. It is not common for individuals to identify as "African-French," as there is a long history of cultural and migration policies that have led people to not associate such concepts together. Instead, it is more common for minorities to declare that they are "Algerian-French" or "Muslim-French" (Croucher, 2008; Croucher & Cronn-Mills, 2011). In the French case, as with most other non-US nations, it is more common for ethnic identity to be associated with religious or origin nation, as opposed to cultural background, as with the US.

Geertz (1973) stated religion is an integral part of the human experience. Durkheim (1976) defined a **religion** as a "unified system of beliefs and practices relative to sacred things, that is to say, things which are set apart and forbidden—beliefs and practices which unite into one single moral community called a Church, all those who adhere to them" (p. 47).

Religion binds people together and is an expression of our social experiences. Our **religious identity** is the extent to which we identify with a religious group. So, we can say that I am "X" religion, and this is asserting an identity with this religion. If a person for example says they are a Muslim then this identity means they accept the overall beliefs, values, practices, norms, rules, etc. of Islam. Moreover, a self-proclaimed Muslim is most likely going to practice Islamic rituals (prayer, fasting during Ramadan, and will attempt to make a pilgrimage to Mecca once in their lifetime) and uphold Islamic traditions. Religious identities can carry immense emotional strength/salience, as a religious identity is often very significant for people with religious faith. In fact, an individual's religious identity and background are critical parts of his/her socialization. Research demonstrates religious groups, as cultures, perceive the world differently, which has profound effects on our identity development and worldview (Casmir, 1997; May & Sharratt, 1994).

An identity that is part social and part personal is our gender identity. **Gender identity** is the extent to which a person identifies with their gender. Gender and sex are different. **Gender** involves the social roles and norms that society has set forth for the sexes. For example, historically many cultures have deemed it more appropriate for boys to play with trucks and girls to play with dolls (we typically play with gender-specific toys by age 5–6), and men to be doctors and women to be nurses. Essentially, gender asks basic questions such as, what does it mean to be a real man or woman in a society, and what is masculine or feminine. More recently many people have tried to de-gender us from such norms, starting with children. It is more common today for parents, particularly in Western nations like the US and Western Europe, to allow their children to play with whatever toys they want in an attempt to not force gender roles on their young children. **Sex** on the other hand is a biological category that is determined at birth, such as chromosomes, hormones, and internal and external organs.

Ultimately, we have multiple identities. Our identities are multifaceted and constantly evolving. These identities are evolving and changing in response to various internal and external factors. As Hall (1959, 1977) explained, our identities are internally and externally crafted by ourselves and by others through the process of communication. The following section details a few of the many theories of identity, which help to describe how our identities are shaped and reshaped.

Identity Theories

Social Identity Theory

Social identity theory (SIT), originally proposed by Tajfel and Turner (1979, 1986) proposes that an individual's identity is made up of both personal and social identities. Personal identities are those perceptions or views of ourselves that separate/differentiate us from others in our ingroup, while social identities are those perceptions or views of ourselves that we share with other members of our ingroups. The primary tenet of SIT is that individuals keep and accentuate the identity that links them to desired groups. Such identities strengthen our positive self-image (Tajfel & Turner, 1979). In the event that we feel as though our identity is unsatisfying to us, we often seek out a new group identity. Social identities such as gender/sex, profession, nationality, ethnicity, religion, political affiliation, and so on all have unique shared cultural aspects (values, norms, etc.). Identifying with one or more of these groups creates a sense of belonging to that group, and not to the other group(s). When we feel like we belong to one group, and not to another, we begin to categorize those people not in our group. In relation to SIT, Roozen and Shulman (2014) argued that "ingroup/outgroup designations affect self-esteem, intergroup relationships, and under certain conditions intergroup conflict" (p. 166).

Research on SIT has collectively found that our social identities have a significant impact on our group biases. It is commonly accepted that group members tend to think that their ingroup is superior to other groups (Mullen, et al., 1992; Sumner, 1906). Research has demonstrated that many people seem to feel better about their own social identities after differentiating themselves, and their group, from others (discriminating in some cases) (Rubin & Hewstone, 1998). For example, describing your group as better than another group differentiates you from them and strengthens your social identity. Research has also shown that the more salient a social identity is the more likely a person is to view other members of their ingroup as interchangeable with one another. In essence, the ingroup takes on a collective nature, particularly when compared to the outgroup, which further illustrates ingroup/outgroup biases (Hogg & Abrams, 1988; Turner et al., 1987; Yuki, 2003). Research on SIT has been explored and applied (and overwhelmingly supported) in many contexts, such as social media, organizations, interpersonal communication, leadership, and group relations (Bergami & Bagozzi, 2000; Bryan Fuller, et al., 2003; Cheung, et al., 2011; Hogg, 2001; Terry, et al., 1999; Van Knippenberg, 2000).

Ethnolinguistic Identity Theory

Another theory of identity that considers how we categorize ourselves and our ingroup in comparison to others is ethnolinguistic identity theory (ELIT) (Giles & Johnson, 1981, 1987). ELIT focuses on minority ethnic groups and their language use in social contexts, particularly when they interact with members of the dominant culture. The original form of the theory concerned explaining the interethnic setting in which a specific group of individuals chooses a specific language strategy and at the same time it tried to study the reason a group of people choose a different strategy than the other group, i.e. they diverge to the outgroup language instead of accentuating their own language. This theory predicts "if an individual perceives high ingroup identification, cognitive alternatives to ingroup status, strong group vitality, and hard, close boundaries, intergroup differentiation will occur" (Abrams, et al., 2002, p. 230). ELIT is guided by four propositions, which emphasize the significance of ingroup identification being subjective, the dialectical nature of language, the importance of context, and human nature.

In research I conducted with Cronn-Mills (Croucher & Cronn-Mills, 2011) we found that both Christians and Muslims in France and the United Kingdom tended to feel as if their identities were threatened by one another. The Christians in France and the UK expressed how their way of life and sense of "Christianness" was under attack by the presence of Muslims, while Muslims stated they were being forced to abandon their Muslim identity to assimilate into the British and French cultures. The differences between Muslims and Christians in France and the UK help to illustrate the following propositions from ELIT.

Initially, research has shown an open social identity is one where we are more attracted to outgroups, open to intergroup communication, and tend to be less prejudiced. When our social identity is threatened we are more attracted to our ingroup, more dependent on the ingroup, less open to intergroup communication, and we tend to be more prejudiced against outgroup members (Jackson, 1999; Jackson & Smith, 1999). Thus, the first proposition of ELIT is that (Abrams et al., 2002, p. 215):

> 1a: Individuals who are highly dependent on their group, consider it central to their being, feel high solidarity for it, and possess a threatened social identity are likely to perceive intergroup encounters in intergroup terms.
> 1b: Individuals who are not dependent on their group, do not consider it central to their being, feel little solidarity for it, and possess an open social identity are not likely to perceive intergroup encounters in intergroup terms.

ELIT's second proposition focuses on the significance of language in maintaining a distinct social identity. Language can create power. Tong, et al. (1999) explained how when Hong Kong speakers converged to the official language of the Chinese mainland those speakers were regarded less favorably by self-identified "Hong Kongers." Self-identified "Chinese" on the other hand regarded the speaker more favorably for converging to Chinese. In this case switching language led to a new group identification; the minority group member abandoned their minority group language for that of the larger group, which had a significant effect on intergroup relations. The same language dynamics were observed in France among North African Muslim immigrants. Immigrants who described themselves as "very Algerian," or proud of their Algerian or North African heritage were more likely not to use Parisian colloquialisms or phrases more common in Paris to fit in with the dominant group (Croucher & Cronn-Mills, 2011). The second proposition of ELIT is that (Abrams et al., 2002, p. 216):

> 2a: Groups high in vitality will be more likely to express ingroup attraction and negative intergroup perceptions, and they will be more likely to use language strategically to achieve or maintain a positive and distinct social identity.
> 2b: Groups low in vitality will be less likely to express ingroup attraction and negative intergroup perceptions, and they will be less likely to use language strategically to achieve or maintain a positive and distinct social identity.

When studying ELIT it is important also to study the social and political histories between the dominant and minority groups. Not only is historical fact important in intergroup relations, but also perceptions of fact (Abrams et al., 2002). In the case of Muslims and Christians in France, the Algerian Civil War has left lingering distrust, prejudice, and hate between Muslims and Christians in France. During interviews with Christians in France many of them discussed how they are unable to trust a group of people (Algerians) who come from a nation that betrayed France. On the other hand, many Algerians discussed how they believe they must stick together, maintain their identity, and stand up to the aggressors who colonized their homeland. Moreover, the sociopolitical climate at the time (2009–2010) was ripe with anti-North African rhetoric, primarily from far right political parties, like the National Front (Croucher & Cronn-Mills, 2011). The climate has become even more complicated since the January 2015 Charlie Hebdo shootings and the November 2015 attacks in Paris.

The third proposition of ELIT is that (Abrams et al., 2002, p. 217):

3: Group-based efforts at vitality and positive distinctiveness will prompt interpretations of history and shifts in identity consistent with the sociohistorical and sociopolitical context.

Finally, ELIT focuses on the perception of closed, hard group boundaries. The primary issues here are the extents to which individuals can move between one group and another, or are identifiable as a member of one group or another. Many members of the dominant culture in France, self-identified Catholics, asserted they could spot Muslims in France by just looking at them because Muslims are not white. When pressed on this issue, as many Muslims in France are White, and many Catholics are non-white, the typical response in English was "I'm right most of the time." In response to such sentiments, often portrayed in French media, many Muslims in France have asked why even try to culturally adapt? In this case, physical appearance, whether right or wrong, was used as a way to separate members of the dominant from the minority culture. Thus, the boundaries established by the dominant culture are rather

Figure 16.2 French Protesters in the Wake of Terrorist Events

hard and closed in this particular case. The fourth proposition of ELIT is that (Abrams et al., 2002, p. 217):

> 4a: The perception of hard, closed boundaries contributes to trait-based intergroup distinctions consistent with cultural values and optimally suited for positive distinctiveness.
>
> 4b: The perception of permeable boundaries is not associated with trait based intergroup distinctions that conflict with an implicit theory of human nature as malleable and thus are not optimally suited for positive distinctiveness.

Studies into ELIT have linked this theory to various genres of communication studies, such as media studies (Vincze & Freynet, 2014; Vincze & Holley, 2013), nation-building and minority integration (Bekus, 2014; Olsen & Olsen, 2010), multilingualism and language policies (Brownie, 2012), and education (Taylor-Leech & Liddicoat, 2014), to mention a few. Collectively, such ELIT studies have shown how our identities are influenced by intergroup behavior and particularly how minority and dominant group identities influence one another.

Face Negotiation Theory

Face is "a claimed sense of favorable social self-worth that a person wants others to have of her or him" (Ting-Toomey & Kurogi, 1998, p. 187). Cultural norms, rules, and values impact on how we manage face and conflict situations. Social interactions embed conflict situations when we need to save lost face because of things such as attacking or teasing. Ting-Toomey (1985, 1988) asserted conflict is a face-negotiating process whereby we have our identities or "faces" threatened. Ting-Toomey's (1985) Face Negotiation Theory (FNT) explains how various factors contribute to manage these conflicts (Kirschbaum, 2012). According to Ting-Toomey and Kurogi (1998), face and facework (the communicative behavior individuals do to save their face) are universal, yet vary in different cultures. The updated version of FNT (Ting-Toomey, 2005) includes seven assumptions and 24 propositions. For example, FNT stresses the importance of culture in its seven basic assumptions (Ting-Toomey, 2005):

1. Communication in all cultures is based on maintaining and negotiating face.
2. Face is problematic when identities are questioned.
3. Differences in individualistic vs. collectivistic and small vs. large power distance cultures profoundly shape face management.
4. Individualistic cultures prefer self-oriented facework, and collectivistic cultures prefer other-oriented facework.
5. Small power distance cultures prefer an "individuals are equal" framework, whereas large power distance cultures prefer a hierarchical framework.

6. Behavior is also influenced by cultural variances, individual, relational, and situational factors.
7. Competence in intercultural communication is a culmination of knowledge and mindfulness.

Taken together it is clear that FNT considers face and facework to be universal phenomena. However, how face and facework are handled does differ culturally. This is where the theoretical propositions of FNT come in to explain the inner workings of the theory. Ting-Toomey's (2005) revision of FNT described how face and facework, particularly in regards to conflict, differed culturally and individually. Culturally, 12 propositions were proposed:

1. Individualistic cultures express more self-face maintenance interests than collectivistic culture members do.
2. Collectivistic cultures are more concerned with other-face maintenance than members of individualistic cultures.
3. Members of collectivistic cultures are more concerned with mutual-face maintenance than individualistic cultures.
4. Members of individualistic cultures use more direct and dominating facework strategies in conflict.
5. Collectivistic cultures use avoidance strategies more than individualistic cultures do.
6. Members of collectivistic cultures use integrative facework strategies more than individualistic culture members do.
7. Individualistic cultures prefer dominating conflict styles more than collectivistic cultures do.
8. Individualistic cultures use emotionally expressive conflict styles more than collectivistic cultures do.
9. Individualistic cultures use aggressive conflict styles more than members of collectivistic cultures.
10. Collectivistic cultures use avoidance techniques more than members of individualistic cultures.
11. Collectivistic cultures use obliging conflict styles more than members of individualistic cultures.
12. Collectivistic cultures utilize compromising styles of conflict more than members of individualistic cultures.

On an individual level, ten propositions were proposed to explain how facework and face is handled:

1. An independent self is positively associated with self-face concern.
2. An interdependent self is positively associated with mutual-face concern.
3. Self-face maintenance is associated with the dominating conflict style.

4. Other-face maintenance is associated with the avoiding and obliging conflict styles.
5. Other-face maintenance is associated with the compromising and integrating conflict styles.
6. An independent self-construal is associated with the dominating conflict style.
7. An interdependent self-construal is associated with the avoiding and obliging conflict styles.
8. An interdependent self-construal is associated with the compromising and integrating conflict styles.
9. A bi-construal is associated with the compromising and integrating conflict styles.
10. Ambivalence is associated with neglect/third-party.

Research has supported differences between cultures high in collectivism and those high in individualism on how face is negotiated, in that the former use other-oriented face-saving and other-face approval-enhancement strategies as their conflict management style while individualist cultures tend to use more self-oriented face-saving and self-face approval-seeking (Oetzel & Ting-Toomey, 2003; Zhang, et al., 2014). Studies of face negotiation theory have covered varied communication fields such as health communication (Heisler & Butler Ellis, 2008; Kirschbaum, 2012), interpersonal and intercultural conflict (Oetzel, 2003; Oetzel, et al., 2001), online media studies (Lim, et al., 2012), and organizational conflict management (Oetzel, et al., 2003).

Chapter Summary

Identity is a multifaceted and constantly changing and evolving part of our lives. This chapter defined identity as a person's self-concept in relation to the world around himself/herself. There are many kinds of identities, ranging from human, personal, social, to national, ethnic, and gender. While we develop our identities in our adolescence, these self-concepts are continually being managed. Different theories have been proposed to explain how we develop and manage our identities through communication. Social identity theory introduces us to the notion that we seek out social identities that satisfy us and give us a positive image, and based on this image we categorize ourselves and others into groups. The ethnolinguistic identity theory focuses on minority ethnic groups and their language use in social contexts, particularly when they interact with members of the dominant culture. Finally, the face negotiation theory describes how we manage our identities in the face of identity challenges/conflicts. Ultimately, as each of these theories, and this chapter shows, our identities and communication are intrinsically linked; they reinforce one another, no matter what culture we are in. In the next chapter, we will look at the relationships between culture and language.

Key Terms

Cultural identity	Cultural identity theory	Ethnic identity
Ethnolinguistic identity theory	Face	Face negotiation theory
Gender	Gender identity	Human identities
Identity	Ingroup	National identity
Outgroup	Personal identities	Religion
Religious identity	Sex	Sexual identity
Social identities	Social identity theory	

Activities

1. Write down as many identities you have. Next to each identity write a brief description of why you identify with this self-concept. Where does this identification come from? Why do you identify with this group?
2. Think about your national identity. Write down the elements (norms, values, etc.) that make your group what it is and others not part of this group. Then get together with a group of 5–7 other people and discuss your results about what it means to be X. For people from the same nation, ask yourselves whether you have the same descriptions. If so, why? If not, why not? For those from other nations what were your thoughts about what it meant to be from their nation?
3. On a daily basis what steps do you take to negotiate your identity? Look to the Face Negotiation Theory and in a group of 3–5 people discuss how you each negotiate face on a daily basis.

References

Abrams, J., O'Connor, J., & Giles, H. (2002). Identity and intergroup communication. In W. B. Gudykunst & B. Mody (eds.), *Handbook on international and intercultural communication* (pp. 225–240). Thousand Oaks, CA: Sage.

Back, M. (2014). "They say I'm like that but they don't know me": Transcultural discourses of masculinity. *Journal of Multicultural Discourses, 9,* 104–118.

Banks, A., & Banks, S. P. (1995). Cultural identity, resistance, and "good theory": Implications for intercultural communication theory from Gypsy culture. *Howard Journal of Communications, 6,* 146–163.

Bekus, N. (2014). Ethnic identity in post-Soviet Belarus: Ethnolinguistic survival as an argument in the political struggle. *Journal of Multilingual & Multicultural Development, 35,* 43–58.

Bergami, M., & Bagozzi, R. P. (2000). Self-categorization, affective commitment and group self-esteem as distinct aspects of social identity in the organization. *British Journal of Social Psychology, 39,* 555–577.

Brownie, J. (2012). Multilingualism and identity on Mussau. *International Journal of the Sociology of Language, 214,* 67–84.

Bryan Fuller, J., Barnett, T., Hester, K., & Relyea, C. (2003). A social identity perspective on the relationship between perceived organizational support and organizational commitment. *Journal of Social Psychology, 143*, 789–791.

Casmir, F.L. (1997). Some introductory thoughts. In F.L. Casmir (ed.), *Ethics in intercultural and international communication* (pp. 1–5). Mahwah, NJ: Lawrence Erlbaum. Castells, M. (1997). *The power of identity.* Oxford, UK: Blackwell.

Cheung, C.M.K., Chiu, P.-Y., & Lee, M.K.O. (2011). Online social networks: Why do students use Facebook. *Computers in Human Behavior, 27*, 1337–1343.

Collier, M.J. (1997). Cultural identity and intercultural communication. In L.A. Samovar & R.E. Porter (eds.), *Intercultural communication: A reader* (pp. 36–44). San Francisco, CA: Wadsworth.

Croucher, S.M. (2008). *Looking beyond the hijab.* Cresskill, NJ: Hampton Press.

Croucher, S.M. & Cronn-Mills, D. (2011). *Religious misperceptions: The case of Muslims and Christians in France and Britain.* New York, NY: Hampton Press.

Durkheim, E. (1976). *The elementary forms of religious life.* London, UK: Harper Collins (first published in French 1912).

Fuentes, C. (1992). *The buried mirror.* Boston, MA: Houghton Mifflin.

Geertz, C. (1973). *The interpretation of cultures.* New York, NY: Basic Books.

Giles, H., & Hewstone, M. (1982). Cognitive structure, speech, and social situations. *Language Sciences, 4*, 187–219.

Giles, H., & Johnson, P. (1981). The role of language in ethnic group relations. In J. Turner & H. Giles (eds.), *Intergroup behavior* (pp. 199–243). Oxford, UK: Basil Blackwell.

Giles, H., & Johnson, P. (1987). Ethnolinguistic identity theory: A social psychological approach to language maintenance. *International Journal of the Sociology of Language, 68*, 69–99.

Hall, B.J. (1992). Theories of culture and communication. *Communication Theory, 2*, 50–70.

Hall, E.T. (1959). *The silent language.* Garden City, NY: Doubleday.

Hall, E.T. (1977). *Beyond culture.* Garden City, NY: Doubleday.

Hall, J., & LaFrance, B. (2012). "That's gay": Sexual prejudice, gender identity, norms, and homophobic communication. *Communication Quarterly, 60*, 35–58.

Hardiman, R. (2001). Reflections on white identity development theory. In C.L. Wijeyesinghe & J.B. Bailey (eds.), *New perspectives on racial identity development: A theoretical and practical anthology* (pp. 12–34). New York, NY: New York University Press.

Heisler, J.M., & Butler, Ellis, J. (2008). Motherhood and the construction of "mommy identity": Messages about motherhood and face negotiation. *Communication Quarterly, 56*, 445–467.

Hoffman, D.M. (1989). Self and culture revisited: Culture acquisition among Iranians in the United States. *Ethos, 17*, 32–49.

Hofstede, G. (1980). *Culture's consequences: International differences in work-related values.* Beverly Hills, CA: Sage.

Hogg, M.A. (2001). A social identity theory of leadership. *Personality and Social Psychology Review, 5*, 184–200.

Hogg, M.A., & Abrams, D. (1988). *Social identifications: A social psychology of intergroup relations and group processes.* London, UK: Routledge.

Jackson, J. W. (1999). How variations in social structure affect different types of intergroup bias and different dimensions of social identity in a multi-intergroup setting. *Group Processes & Intergroup Relations, 2*, 145–173.

Jackson, J. W., & Smith, E. R. (1999). Conceptualizing social identity: A new framework and evidence for the impact of different dimensions. *Personality and Social Psychology Bulletin, 25*, 120–135.

Khakimova, L., Zhang, Y., & Hall, J. A. (2012). Conflict management styles: The role of ethnic identity and self-construal among young male Arabs and Americans. *Journal of Intercultural Communication Research, 41*, 37–57.

Kirschbaum, K. (2012). Physician communication in the operating room: expanding application of face-negotiation theory to the health communication context. *Health Communication, 27*, 292–301.

Koller, V. (2012). How to analyse collective identity in discourse-textual and contextual parameters. *Critical Approaches to Discourse Analysis across Disciplines, 5*, 19–38.

Koschmann, M. A. (2013). Human rights collaboration and the communicative practice of religious identity. *Journal of Communication & Religion, 36*, 107–133.

Lim, S. S., Vadrevu, S., Chan, Y. H., & Basnyat, I. (2012). Facework on Facebook: The online publicness of juvenile delinquents and youths-at-risk. *Journal of Broadcasting & Electronic Media, 56*, 346–361.

Martin, J. N., & Nakayama, T. K. (1997). *Intercultural communication in contexts*. Mountain View, CA: Mayfield.

May, L., & Sharratt, S. C. (1994). *Applied ethics: A multicultural approach*. Englewood Cliffs, NJ: Prentice Hall.

Merino, M., & Tileagă, C. (2011). The construction of ethnic minority identity: A discursive psychological approach to ethnic self-definition in action. *Discourse & Society, 22*, 86–101.

Motschenbacher, H. (2013). "Now everybody can wear a skirt": Linguistic constructions of non-heteronormativity at Eurovision Song Contest press conferences. *Discourse & Society, 24*, 590–614.

Mullen, B., Brown, R., & Smith, C. (1992). Ingroup bias as a function of salience, relevance, and status: An integration. *European Journal of Social Psychology, 22*, 103–122.

Oetzel, J. G. (2003). Face concerns in interpersonal conflict: A cross-cultural empirical test of the Face Negotiation Theory. *Communication Research, 30*, 599–624.

Oetzel, J., Meares, M., Myers, K. K., & Lara, E. (2003). Interpersonal conflict in organization: Explaining conflict styles via face-negotiation theory. *Communication Research Reports, 20*, 106–115.

Oetzel, J. G., & Ting-Toomey, S. (2003). Face concerns in interpersonal conflict: A gross-cultural empirical test of the face negotiation theory. *Communication Research, 30*, 599–624.

Oetzel, J. G., Ting-Toomey, S., Masumoto, T., Yokochi, Y., Pan, X., Takai, J., & Wilcox, R. (2001). Face and facework in conflict: A cross-cultural comparison of China, Germany, Japan, and the United States. *Communication Monographs, 68*, 235–258.

Olsen, K., & Olsen, H. (2010). Language use, attitude, and linguistic identity among Palestinian students in East Jerusalem. *International Multilingual Research Journal, 4*, 31–54.

Roozen, B., & Shulman, H. C. (2014). Tuning in to the RTLM: Tracking the evolution of language alongside the Rwandan genocide using social identity theory. *Journal of Language & Social Psychology, 33*, 165–182.

Rubin, M., & Hewstone, M. (1998). Social Identity Theory's self-esteem hypothesis: A review and some suggestions for clarification. *Review of Personality and Social Psychology, 2,* 40–62.

Sumner, W. G. (1906). *Folkways.* New York, NY: Ginn.

Tajfel, H., & Turner, J. C. (1979). An integrative theory of intergroup conflict. In W. G. Austin & S. Worchel (eds.), *The social psychology of intergroup relations* (pp. 33–47). Monterey, CA: Brooks-Cole.

Tajfel, H., & Turner, J. C. (1986). The social identity theory of intergroup behavior. In S. Worchel & W. Austin (eds.), *Psychology of intergroup relations.* Chicago: Nelson Hall.

Tanti, C., Stukas, A. A., Halloran, M. J., & Foddy, M. (2011). Social identity change: Shifts in social identity during adolescence. *Journal of Adolescence, 34,* 555–567.

Taylor-Leech, K., & Liddicoat, A. J. (2014). Macro-language planning for multilingual education: Focus on programmes and provision. *Current Issues in Language Planning, 15,* 353–360.

Terry, D. J., Hogg, M. A., & White, K. M. (1999). The theory of planned behavior: Self-identity, social identity and group norms. *British Journal of Social Psychology, 38,* 225–244.

Ting-Toomey, S. (1985). Toward a theory of conflict and culture. In W. B. Gudykunst, L. Stewart, & S. Ting-Toomey (eds.), *Communication, culture, and organizational processes* (pp. 71–86). Beverly Hills, CA: Sage.

Ting-Toomey, S. (1988). Intercultural conflicts: A face-negotiation theory. In Y. Y. Kim & W. B. Gudykunst (eds.), *Theories in intercultural communication* (pp. 213–238). Newbury Park, CA: Sage.

Ting-Toomey, S. (1993). Communicative resourcefulness: An identity negotiation perspective. In R. L. Wiseman & J. Koester (eds.), *Intercultural communication competence* (pp. 72–111). Newbury Park, CA: Sage.

Ting-Toomey, S. (2005). The matrix of face: An updated Face-negotiation theory. In W. B. Gudykunst (ed.), *Theorizing about intercultural communication* (pp. 71–92). Thousand Oaks, CA: Sage.

Ting-Toomey, S., & Kurogi, A. (1998). Facework competence in intercultural conflict: An updated face-negotiation theory. *Journal of Intercultural Relations, 22,* 187–225.

Ting-Toomey, S., Yee-Jung, K. K., Shapiro, R. B., Garcia, W., Wright, T. J., & Oetzel, J. (2000). Ethnic/cultural identity salience and conflict styles in four US ethnic groups. *International Journal of Intercultural Relations, 24,* 47–81.

Tong, Y.-Y., Hong, Y.-Y., Lee, S.-L., & Chiu, C.-Y. (1999). Language use as a carrier of social identity. *International Journal of Intercultural Relations, 23,* 281–296.

Triandis, H. C. (1988). Collectivism vs. individualism. In G. Verma & C. Bagley (eds.), *Cross-cultural studies of personality, attitudes, and cognition.* London, UK: Macmillan.

Turner, J. C., Hogg, M., Oakes, P., Reicher, S., & Wetherall, M. (1987). *Rediscovering the social group.* Oxford, UK: Blackwell.

Van Knippenberg, D. (2000). Work motivation and performance: A social identity perspective. *Applied Psychology, 49,* 357–371.

Vincze, L., & Freynet, N. (2014). Objective vitality as moderator of ethnolinguistic identity gratifications. *Communication Research Reports, 31,* 117–123.

Vincze, L., & Holley, P. (2013). Making news between cultures: Ethnolinguistic identity and journalism in four minority language daily newspapers. *Communication Reports, 26,* 61–72.

Yuki, M. (2003). Intergroup comparison versus intragroup relationships: A cross-cultural examination of Social Identity Theory in North American and East Asian cultural contexts. *Social Psychology Quarterly*, 66, 166–183.

Zhang, Q., Ting-Toomey, S., & Oetzel, J. G. (2014). Linking emotion to the conflict face- negotiation theory: A U.S.-China investigation of the mediating effects of anger, compassion, and guilt in interpersonal conflict. *Human Communication Research*, 40, 373–395.

Student Paper

The Becoming and Changing of Cultural Identity Theory

Ann C. Beiroth
University of Jyväskylä

"Who am I?", "What makes me 'me'?" "How would I define myself in relation to others?" These questions are probably as old as humanity itself, and almost everybody has wondered about them at some point in their lives. They all relate to identity. Academically, scholars have studied this concept under many different angles.

Personally, I have lived for a year each in three countries other than my home country now, and each has affected me to some degree. Especially my first year, in the US, affected me deeply and still affects me to this day. I feel like I have integrated into my personality aspects from all three countries that I lived in. This, however, covers only the aspect of national culture. Cultural identity covers so much more: ethnicity, gender, my relationship to the people involved in a specific situation, and many other factors.

> It is nice how Ann provides a personal link to why she is interested in writing this paper

In this literature review, I follow Collier and Thomas's (1988) definition of culture, which is a "historically transmitted system of symbols, meanings, and norms" (Collier, 1989, 295). It is thus not limited to national cultures, but does not specifically exclude these either. Cultural identities, then, are defined as "identifications with, and perceived acceptance into a group which has a shared system of symbols and meanings, as well as norms/rules for conduct" (Collier, 1989, p. 296).

(Continued)

Jameson (2004) distinguishes cultural identity from social identity by saying that the latter concerned only the present, while the former also considered what an individual had learnt in the past and how he or she wanted to act in the future.

In this literature review, I will explore the Cultural Identity Theory, originally introduced and then altered by Collier. I will review first premises of identity that preceded this theory or that were influenced by it, including Ting-Toomey's Identity Negotiation Theory and Hecht's Communication Theory of Identity, respectively. Then I will explain the original concept and follow its development over time to the Cultural Identity Negotiation Theory. My approach will be mostly chronological, at least as far as this is possible, since some theories were developing around the same time. All the while, I will include scientific articles in intercultural communication that have used this theory, or something very close but not specifically named, explain how the theory ties in with the study, and discover recurrent themes in identity-related literature.

Preceding and Related Identity Theories

The following identity theories have influenced Cultural Identity Theory, as Collier adopted some elements. Hecht's theory then evolved from Cultural Identity Theory, adopting some of its aspects. Also coming from the interpretive spectrum, they share some similarities and are thus important to look at when studying the becoming of Cultural Identity Theory.

Chronologically, the first theory to come out was Identity Negotiation Theory in the 1980s, later reviewed in 2005. Identity, for Ting-Toomey, is flexible self-images that are constructed by individuals according to the culture and situation (Ting-Toomey, 2005). People have multiple images of themselves, which are constantly affected by different kinds of identity (personal, social, and

---

This is a very clear introduction to the paper. In this introduction she defines the key concepts she will cover in the paper and also provides the reader with a concise preview of the paper.

This is one of the many ways you can approach a review of literature—chronologically.

(Continued)

cultural) (Toomey et al., 2013) and can change or be challenged during an interaction (Ting-Toomey, 2005). To Ting-Toomey, identity is so important because by understanding it better, we can understand much better who others are and thus communicate better (Ting-Toomey, 2009). According to her, only after that will intercultural communication be successful.

Cultural identity theory has then itself been a source for other theories. One example for this is Hecht's Communication Theory of Identity developed in the 1980s and 1990s. It takes into account both the individual and society, as well as performance and relationship (Hecht et al., 2005). Hecht proposes 10 basic assumptions about identities' properties (Hecht et al., 2005). Most of them also appear in Collier's framework, for instance the assumptions identities are both stable and flexible, that they are affective, cognitive, behavioral, and spiritual, that they involve both subjective and ascribed meaning, and that they are important to define membership to real or imagined communities (Collier & Thomas, 1988; Hecht et al., 2005).

The new element of this theory is that identities, constructed in communication with others, are seen to have four frames: personal (i.e., how a person sees themselves), enactment (identities are acted out in communication), relational (people change their behavior according to who they are communicating with, and are influenced by the other person), and communal (groups that also have identities with particular characteristics) (Hecht, 1993; 2009; Hecht et al., 2005). The frames of identity are not separate, but they are interwoven and can all be important in a given context.

Because of some criticism concerning interpenetration of identities, Jung and Hecht (2004) added the concept of identity gaps to the theory. They defined identity gaps as "discrepancies between or among the four frames of identity" (p. 268) that are omnipresent in communication. An identity gap could for example occur if others see you in a

(Continued)

different light than you see yourself (Jung & Hecht, 2004). These gaps influence the outcome of interactions, such as communication satisfaction, or the feeling of being understood (Jung & Hecht, 2004). Hecht's theory borrows from Collier's in that their identities are multiple and dynamic, that communication is important for the concept, the existence of ascription, and that identities have a relational aspect. Communication Theory of Identity concentrates more on identity as a whole, moving away from the purely cultural perspective.

A few examples of studies focusing on different identity approaches will follow. These authors do not focus on Collier's approach, but also make identity issues their theme in their research. Hence, they are interesting to look at.

Most focus on the cultural identity of minority groups. Razak (1995) was interested in the preservation and active protection of the native Arubian cultural identity. Through interviews, the author found some central cultural symbols this group definitely wanted to preserve, e.g. language, religion, the arts, and social rituals. Viewing their mixed cultural heritage and outside influences, their cultural identity is always under construction (Razak, 1995). Nevertheless, the Arubians recognize what they have acquired from others and construct their identity as opposed to the Other (Razak, 1995). In 2005, Maeda followed suit and looked at the construction of Asian American identity. He stated that long repression and the following fight against oppression constituted an important part in forming a distinct cultural identity (Maeda, 2005). More specifically, he argued that "black performance" (he named different groups as examples, like Frank Chin and the Red Guard Party) helped Asians as well, because it was for all non-whites (Maeda, 2005). However, he also found that their fight against oppression and assimilation was based on too much of an emphasis of masculinity, which led to the marginalization of women and homosexuals (Maeda, 2005). Craft Al-Hazza

> This is a nice transition from one main point to the next. It is good to sign post for the reader. What follows is a review of a few studies that look at cultural identities in various settings/contexts.

(Continued)

and Bucher (2008) also looked at cultural identity building of a minority in the US, but at that of Arab Americans, by analyzing children's literature in an elementary school classroom. They found there was but little literature used on Arabs in school readings, which they denounced because, as explained by the models for cultural identity that they relied on (Ting-Toomey, 2005), it is important for children to develop a sense of belonging to their larger cultural group and to learn about this group's behavior. They called for more Arab or Arab American literature in the classroom to help these children build their cultural identity (Craft Al-Hazza & Bucher, 2008).

Shannon took a slightly different approach. She analyzed (2009) African American cultural identity by looking at plays written by African American playwright August Wilson. She found an emphasis on being African as a positive trait in the plays and the emergence of positive "African" personality traits (loyalty, honor, and reverence of ancestors, just to name a few) (Shannon, 2009). She also discovered other symbolic elements of African American culture, such as special belief systems that accept the unlikely (Shannon, 2009). She claimed that the plays in general contributed toward affirming African American cultural identity during the Civil Rights Movement of the 1960s in the US (Shannon, 2009).

Finally, Slay and Smith chose to focus on professional identity construction (2011). They were also interested in how cultural stigma affects this. Professional identity building in this study is not defined too differently from identity building in general (a self-concept made up of values, beliefs, etc.), so this article is deemed appropriate. The authors analyzed 20 reports written by African American reporters talking about their experiences. Stigmatized minority groups have a lower starting point in identity, so to speak, because they are at a disadvantage outside of the work context (Slay & Smith, 2011). They found

(Continued)

redefinition (of self, of the profession and of the stigma) is found to be more helpful than adaptation (Slay & Smith, 2011).

Cultural Identity Theory

Along with Thomas, Collier proposed her Cultural Identity Theory in the late 1980s (1988). This theoretical framework can be located in the interpretive spectrum. It is out to explain the communicative processes in the individual to construct and negotiate their cultural group identity, as well as their identity in relationship with others (Collier, 2009b). Since its first introduction, it has undergone significant changes and been used in numerous case studies. Usually researchers use it along with qualitative research methods such as interviews or focus groups (Collier, 2009b).

The original version of this theory focuses on common contextual symbols as signs for culture (Collier & Thomas, 1988). Hence, culture is emergent in communication, when the symbols are being used (Collier & Thomas, 1988). Culture itself is defined as "a historically transmitted system of symbols, meanings, and norms" (Collier, 1989, p. 295). These symbols are subject to change during the course of an interaction (Collier & Thomas, 1988). The authors saw them as relatively stable over time, but flexible at the same time during an interaction. Hence, this model does not view culture as a static element, like many older researchers do, and it does not limit culture to nationalities. Culture can mean background, heritage, and emergent behavior in a specific situation, using a specific thematic identity (Collier 1989). Cultural identities are "identifications with and perceived acceptance into a group which has shared systems of symbols and meanings as well as norms/rules for conduct" (Collier 1989, p. 296). Identity can thus refer to nationality, but also to gender, relationship, or professional position. This again goes to show that identity,

---

> While Ann does a really nice job of reviewing these studies, she could have done a little bit more at the start of this section to explain why these particular studies were chosen for inclusion in the paper. Why discuss these studies and not others?

(Continued)

once adopted, can be managed and negotiated during an interaction. Collier and Thomas assumed that people have multiple types of cultural identities, like national, ethnic, or class identities. It would be too easy, they continued, to assume people judge each other based solely on nationality. It may be more important that the participants of an interaction are all women, or that they have a working relationship. Collier and Thomas found these different identities to be positioned in three dimensions, scope (how many people may share that identity), salience (how important the identity is, relatively speaking to other identities), and intensity (which is the strength of communication of an identity). These are positioned according to situational context, time, and relationship (Collier & Thomas, 1988). Considering that one individual always has several identities (e.g. gender, ethnicity, cultural), Collier (1989) found it interesting to study which identity takes precedence over the other, when, and why. She also found the combination of identities and resulting codes of behavior resulted in a positive overall identity, if the outcome of the interaction is positive (Collier, 1989).

Another very important aspect of this theory is the concepts of avowal and ascription of particular cultural identities. Avowal describes how people portray themselves, whereas ascription refers to the identities and characteristics attributed to a person by others (Collier, 2009b). According to her, these identities and characteristics are involved in the process of identity formation. Identity and characteristics depend on the situation, context, and relationship between the interacting parties, or the topic, they may vary in intensity (Collier, 2009b).

The ultimate goal of this approach is to understand "why particular conduct is viewed as appropriate and effective and what can be learned to help individuals improve the quality of their own experience" (Collier, 1989, p. 295). Communication,

> This paragraph was a really nice description of Collier and Thomas' theory.

according to Collier, is intercultural, if the participating parties view themselves as culturally different (Collier, 1989). She thus defined cultural competence as the behavior that is appropriate and effective for both partners when interacting with the identities employed at one given moment, and it is implicitly assumed that people will know how to behave (Collier, 1989). She said intercultural competence is higher, if there is more cultural difference between participants, and if the match between avowal and ascription is higher (Collier, 1989). The participants of an interaction can also negotiate competence, together, if the researcher asks them to tell which behavior would be appropriate for the chosen cultural identities (Collier 1989).

Collier herself did a number of studies using her cultural identity theory. I would like to give several examples of her research and of that of others to illustrate the interesting research results they have been able to procure using this theory.

The first example is Collier's article on ethnic friendships (2003). It is a study on the relationship between friendship values and ethnic background done on Asian, African, Latino, and Anglo Americans, both in and between these groups. Her theory came into play in that the participants of friendly interaction co-construct identity together. She was interested in how friendly behavior varied in across social groups and how identity came into play. She used the cultural identity theory to explain the different background identities (ethnic and others) the participants had. She used the method of questionnaires with open-ended questions leading to extensive answers about their friendships and appropriate behavior. After doing a content analysis with help from other researchers, she found several similarities, but also differences. Asian Americans placed value on the exchange of ideas and mutual support, Latinos put more emphasis on relational support, African Americans valued respect and

> You may notice throughout the paper that Ann is writing in the first person. This is something that really depends on the author. Some writers use first person, while others do not. I recommend that you speak with your instructor and ask if it is ok for you to write in the first person. In this particular case, Ann was told that it was acceptable to write in the first person. ☺

(Continued)

consideration, and Anglo-Americans mentioned most often disclosure and advice as valued aspects in their friendships (Collier, 2003).

Moss (2010) did a case study using mostly the traditional cultural identity framework as her guidance as well. She examined the effect of mural arts representations of African Americans on cultural identifications in intercultural communities in Philadelphia. She found the murals served mostly as inspiration for the future, or as rejections of depictions in mainstream media (Moss, 2010). Therefore, they have mostly positive effects on cultural identity of African Americans, helping them to renegotiate who they want to be.

Other researchers have concentrated more on education. Lu (2001), for instance, relied on Collier and Thomas's (1988) model of cultural identity in his study about how communication practices in Chinese schools around Chicago can play a role in the development of a bicultural identity of Chinese immigrants. He linked this theory to acculturation theories to examine immigrants' positions. Participation, observation, and interviews yielded the desire for a bicultural identity in these people, but they rejected association with Chinatown. The author concluded that biculturalism was preferable to Americanization (Lu, 2001). Schall (2010), in the face of growing diversity in the US, called for a better and more in-depth training for children, ensuring they understand cultural identity and culture in general, and do not focus on superficial elements such as clothing or holidays. According to her, mapping engagements will help children understand the realities better and include traditions, values, and belief systems, by making them think about priorities to put on their maps.

All this research is now considered the "early version" of Cultural Identity Theory (Collier, 2009b, p. 260). Due to critiques that mention the dangerous influence of ascription, this theory morphed into the Cultural Identity Negotiation

> As before, this is a solid review of a few studies using this theory. However, Ann could do a bit more to frame her argument. Why include these studies and not others? Much of a review of literature is about justification. Justify the inclusion of these pieces a bit more.

(Continued)

Theory (CINT) that still has interpretive elements, but combines them with critical perspectives, thus focusing more on hierarchical and power issues (Collier, 2009b). Contextual identity negotiation became more important, and a bigger focus was put on finding out and warning against injustice (Collier, 2009b).

Scholars have done CINT research, for example, on overt and subjacent racism discourse by personnel in US courtrooms (Myers & Collier, 2005). In general, research using CINT analyzes opinions of marginalized minority groups. In 2009, Collier used this new framework in a study analyzing interview discourse from female participants in a US peace-building program in the Middle East. Group membership, explicit or implicit, was important in this study, and avowal and ascription occur both all the time when these groups come together (Collier, 2009a). The method was qualitative once more by analyzing semi-structured interviews. The results showed participants managed multiple identifications and the context of the peace-building program at the same time enabled and counteracted their intergroup relationships (Collier, 2009a). This more critical approach also called future research to take into account context and history, and generally called for change of the present tense situation (Collier, 2009a). Critical and interpretive, Collier called for researchers to "uncover their own systems of oppression" (Collier, 2009b, p. 263) and to make changes accordingly, in all areas of life, also in the private life. Together with Thompson, Collier looked at intersecting identities in interracial couples in the US (2006). They found couples' identities changed over time, but the couples always did their utmost to protect their relationship and their partner from discrimination. Through qualitative interviews, they collected a variety of important themes, such as dissociation from the race-theme in relationships, race in the workplace, and race in personal relationships (Thompson & Collier, 2006).

(Continued)

Another research focus is group identity. Collier (2009c) used her altered framework on a study on group identity of two Northern Ireland intercommunity groups. She found out how these identities are negotiated simultaneously as different kinds of privileged positions, how participants placed themselves in their discourse in relation to different leaders and the importance of tensions and contradictions resulting from being a member of two community groups at once. It is obvious her present approach is more critical than before, simply by her focus and by her positioning herself as the researcher in the paper. Another example of the new framework in action is the study done by Chen and Collier (2012) on people involved in some way with two identity-based nonprofit organizations. Through interviews, the researchers found that the most frequently avowed and ascribed characteristic was Asianness, and how relationships and hierarchies are negotiated.

In addition, another study was by Simmons and Chen in 2014. Guided by Cultural Identity Theory, they proposed six-word memoirs (6WM) for students in order to be more aware of and to reposition their cultural identities. This pedagogical way of storytelling will, according to the authors, help students think about their avowals and ascriptions, and make them reflect on how their identities influence the way they think about the world. The authors found their own students were divided in two groups: members of the majority tended to select more individual characteristics and identities for their 6WM, while minority group students tended to pay more attention to their minority status (Simmons & Chen, 2014).

Of course, not all is rosy in the world of Cultural Identity Theory. There has been some criticism. One example is Jameson's article to reconceptualize cultural identity in the business world (2007). In it, she acknowledged the importance of understanding oneself, but criticized, among other models, Collier's Cultural Identity

---

In discussing a critique of Cultural Identity Theory, Ann is showing the reader that she not only understands the main arguments of the theory, but also understands what others think about the theory. This is a crucial part of many reviews, the critique part.

(Continued)

Theory. According to her, Collier's approach is too layered and fragmented, one "part" of identity taking over in any given situation, whereas individuals tend to see themselves as whole units. For Jameson, Collier's theory is mainly convenient for researchers because it allows focusing on one specific sub-identity, at the expense of others. Jameson proposed a different model focusing more on the individual perspective, likened to a pie chart where the different components may vary in importance, but always add up to 100%. She concentrated on a business context and included six parts: vocation, class, geography, philosophy, language, and biology. The identity then needs to be more than just a sum of the parts. However, Jameson valued some aspects of Collier's theory, such as avowal and ascription, and the fluid negotiation of identity. However, as far as I know, Collier never stated her different subparts of identity are clearly separated. On the contrary, she depicted them as dynamic and flexible, and was aware "persons do not categorize one another on the basis of national affiliation" (Collier, 1989, p. 298).

> It is good to see that Ann is acknowledging that she is not 100% familiar with the theory. She is saying as far as she knows.

Conclusion

This review showed what Cultural Identity Theory by Collier is and how it developed. It becomes evident that saying "cultural identity" does not always mean authors refer to Collier, as there are many other concepts out there that have not been explored here for reasons of brevity. However, even if they do not directly reference to it, they follow a concept that seems similar to Collier's in many ways and many factors coincide with Collier's theory. Their approach is, most often, to study cultural minority groups. Those that do refer directly to the old version of Cultural Identity Theory, including Collier herself, seem to focus on the study of cultural identity of ethnic minorities in the US. They do this in multiple contexts, such as friendship or education. Studies on the

(Continued)

newer and more critical version of the theory focus on racism, group identity in communities and organizations, or on education. Critique emerges against the fragmented nature of identity in this theory that may endanger real-life applicability, as people can be more entities than layers of identities.

In conclusion, one sees that this theory of cultural identity has undergone several changes over the years, both in definition and in literature. Emerging from other identity theories, it later morphed into a more critical theory, although it can still be interpretive. This review presented the forming and changing of cultural identity theory, and looked at several research studies that rely on this theory as their theoretical framework. It is obvious the method used in studies with this theory is most often qualitative, usually interviews. I found very few articles that even remotely resembled quantitative work, and those were usually not directly mentioning Collier's theory. Even though the topics were diverse, researchers put a strong focus on the cultural identity of ethnic minority groups. Usually, these studies are either descriptive or critical. Overall, it might be necessary to broaden the scope of research a little bit to include other aspects of identity as well mentioned in the original theory, such as nation, gender, and profession.

> This is a really sound review/conclusion of the review. What Ann has done is summarized her main points and offered a further analysis of CIT before she ends the paper.

References

Chen, Y.-W. & Collier, M. J. (2012). Intercultural identity positioning: Interview discourses from two identity-based nonprofit organizations. *Journal of International and Intercultural Communication*, 5, 43–63. DOI:10.1080/17513057.2011.631215

Collier, M. J. & Thomas, M. (1988). Cultural Identity: An interpretive perspective. In Y. Y. Kim & W. B. Gudykunst (Eds.), *Theories in Intercultural Communication* (pp. 99–120). Newbury Park, CA: Sage Publications.

Collier, M. J. (1989). Cultural and intercultural communication competence: Current approaches and directions for future research. *International Journal of Intercultural Relations*, 13, 287–302.

Collier, M. J. (1996). Communication competence problems in ethnic friendships. *Communication Monographs*, 63, 314–336.

(Continued)

Collier, M. J. (2009a). Contextual negotiation of cultural identification and relationships: Interview discourse with Palestinian, Israeli, and Palestinian/Israeli young women in a US peace-building program. *Journal of International and Intercultural Communication, 2,* 344–368.

Collier, M. J. (2009b). Cultural Identity Theory. In S. W. Littlejohn & K. A. Foss (Eds.), *Encyclopedia of Communication Theory* (pp. 260–262). Thousand Oaks, CA: Sage Publications.

Collier, M. J. (2009c). Negotiating intercommunity and community group identity positions: Summary discourses from two Northern Ireland intercommunity groups. *Negotiation and Conflict Management Research, 2,* 285–306.

Craft Al-Hazza, T. & Bucher, K. T. (2008). Building Arab Americans' Cultural Identity and acceptance with children's literature. *The Reading Teacher, 62,* 210–219. DOI:10.1598/RT.62.3.3 I

Hecht, M. L. (1993). 2002 – a research odyssey: Toward the development of a communication theory of identity. *Communication Monographs, 60,* 76–82.

Hecht, M. L., Warren, J. R., Jung, E. & Krieger, J. L. (2005). The Communication Theory of Identity: Development, theoretical perspective, and future directions. In W. B. Gudykunst (Ed.), *Theorizing About Intercultural Communication* (pp. 257–278). Thousand Oaks, CA: Sage Publications.

Hecht, M. L. (2009). Communication Theory of Identity. In S. W. Littlejohn & K. A. Foss (Eds.). *Encyclopedia of Communication Theory*. Thousand Oaks, CA: Sage Publications.

Jameson, D. A. (2007). Reconceptualizing cultural identity and its role in intercultural business communication. *Journal of Business Communication, 44,* 199–235.

Jung, E. & Hecht, M. L. (2004). Elaborating the communication theory of identity: Identity gaps and communication outcomes. *Communication Quarterly, 52,* 265–283, DOI:10.1080/01463370409370197

Lu, X. (2001). Bicultural identity development and Chinese community formation: An ethnographic study of Chinese schools in Chicago. *Howard Journal of Communications, 12,* 203–220. DOI:10.1080/106461701753287723

Maeda, D. J. (2005). Black Panthers, Red Guards, and Chinamen: Constructing Asian American identity through performing blackness, 1969–1972. *American Quarterly, 57,* 1079–1103.

Moss, K. L. (2010): Cultural representation in Philadelphia murals: Images of resistance and sites of identity negotiation. *Western Journal of Communication, 74,* 372–395. DOI:10.1080/10570314.2010.492819

Myers, M. A., & Collier, M. J. (2005). Cultural ascriptions displayed by restraining order court representatives: Implicating patriarchy and cultural dominance. *Women's Studies in Communication, 28,* 258–289.

Razak, V. (1995). Culture under construction. The future of native Arubian identity. *Futures, 27,* 447–459.

Schall, J. M. (2010). Cultural exploration through mapping. *The Social Studies, 101,* 166–173.

(Continued)

Shannon, S. G. (2009). Framing African American cultural identity: The bookends plays in August Wilson's 10-play cycle. *College Literature*, *36*, 26–39.

Simmons, N. & Chen, Y.-W. (2014). Using six-word memoirs to increase cultural identity awareness. *Communication Teacher*, *28*, 20–25. DOI:10.1080/17404622.2013.839050

Slay, H. S. & Smith, D. A. (2011). Professional identity construction: Using narrative to understand the negotiation of professionals and stigmatized cultural identities. *Human Relations*, *64*, 85–107.

Thompson, J. & Collier, M. J. (2006). Toward contingent understandings of intersecting identifications among selected U.S. interracial couples: Integrating interpretive and critical views. *Communication Quarterly*, *54*, 487–506.

Ting-Toomey, S. (2005). Identity Negotiation Theory: Crossing Cultural Boundaries. In W. B. Gudykunst (Ed.), *Theorizing About Intercultural Communication* (pp. 211–233). Thousand Oaks, CA: Sage Publications.

Ting-Toomey, S. (2009). Identity Theories. In S. W. Littlejohn & K. A. Foss (Eds.), *Encyclopedia of Communication Theory* (pp. 492–496). Thousand Oaks, CA: Sage Publications.

Toomey, A., Tenzin, D. & Ting-Toomey, S. (2013). Bicultural identity negotiation, conflicts, and intergroup communication strategies. *Journal of Intercultural Communication Research*, *42*, 112–134.

17 LANGUAGE AND INTERCULTURAL COMMUNICATION

Todd L. Sandel, University of Macau, China

Chapter Outline

- Language
  - Language Defined
  - Language in Time and Space
- Language and Culture
  - Cultural Discourse Analysis
  - Language Socialization
  - Language and Categorical Perception
  - Language Ideologies
  - Language and Identity
- New and Mixed Languages
  - Online Language
- Chapter Summary
- Student Paper

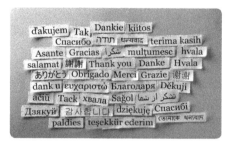

Figure 17.1 How to Say Thank You

A friend from Taiwan, who learned to speak English fluently before moving to the United States, was puzzled the first time an American said to her, "You bet!" Was this really a request to make a bet? Once I pulled up my car at a filling station in Taiwan and said to the attendant, in Chinese: "High gasoline 500"—a short-hand and common way to request: "I would like you to add 500 NT dollars [about 20 USD] of high grade gasoline." The attendant looked at me confused and did not respond. I repeated my request, and the attendant continued to look at me, speechless. I then said, "I'm speaking to you in Chinese. I want you to add 500 NT of high grade gasoline." Only then did the attendant respond and add fuel to the tank.

These two examples illustrate some of the challenges that arise in moments of intercultural communication. In the first, the literal, or **denotative** meaning of the words, "You bet" obscured the implied, or **connotative** meaning,

"I agree" or "You're right." This was meant to be conveyed through the use of **contextualization cues**, "the surface features of message forms" that are used to signal and interpret an activity, and how it relates to talk that precedes and follows (Gumperz, 1982, p. 131). Meanings can be conveyed by both nonverbal (e.g., a smile) and verbal cues (e.g., prosody, or a marked use of intonation, stress, and pitch) to convey that "You bet!" is meant to express agreement. Yet these cues were not understood. In the second case, when speaking with the filling station attendant, the listener was also using a contextualization cue—the nonverbal, physical appearance of the speaker (white, non-Chinese male)—to interpret the meaning of the message; but in this case the cue led to an initial moment of confusion.

In this chapter we examine the role of language in intercultural communication. Much has been written on this topic, and there are many theories that could be explored. Yet to make this chapter more manageable, I have selected a few theories and related key terms to help us better understand the role of language in intercultural communication.

Language

Language Defined

What is language? One scholar whose work has greatly influenced how we understand and study language is the Swiss scholar, Ferdinand de Saussure (1857–1913). He understood language to be the ordered arrangement of **signs** (De Saussure & Baskin, 1959). A sign is comprised of two parts: (1) the **signifier**, the outward symbol, or sound that is produced when a person speaks, and (2) the **signified**, the inward mental image that is produced in a person's mind when hearing a sound. For example, if an English language speaker hears the sound for "tree," this then maps onto an idea, or image of something that in that person's mind may look like [picture of a tree]. The combination of the signifier, or sound for "tree," and the signified, or mental image that the sound produces, produces the "sign" for tree. Yet Saussure also pointed out that if we compare signs across languages we see that most are **arbitrary**. For instance, the French speaker would look at [picture of a tree] and call it "*arbre*"; the Mandarin Chinese speaker would call it "*shu*" (with a sharply falling tone). The sign for the same object, when compared across languages, may vary greatly.

Another feature of signs is that they are organized and arranged according to collectively understood patterns, or rules of **grammar** and **syntax**. For instance, English sentences are structured according to the pattern: Subject + Verb + Object. We see this in the simple sentence: "I see a tree." "I" is the subject, "see" is the verb, and "a tree" the object. If these three signs were arranged differently and followed the pattern of Subject + Object + Verb, they would produce the sentence: "I a tree see." This would seem odd. However, the Japanese speaker would not perceive it that way, as a rule of Japanese syntax, the object, "a tree" comes before the verb, "see." Therefore, just as individual signs are arbitrary, when we look across a range of languages, we also see that the rules for how to arrange signs can also be arbitrary. While this is not problematic when people of the same language communicate, we can now see how speakers may misunderstand each other. How can shared meaning be achieved?

Language in Time and Space

The work of Mikhail Bakhtin (1895–1975) helps us answer this question. Bakhtin was a scholar whose primary interest was in analyzing works of literature, such as the novel. Influenced by Einstein's work in relativity, Bakhtin thought of a novel as an **utterance**, or communicative expression unique because it was situated in a particular space and time (Bakhtin, 1981). Yet this uniqueness did not mean that shared understanding was impossible. Two features of utterances help.

One is the stability of forms within utterances, or what Bakhtin called **speech genres** (Holquist, 1990). Consider, for example, J. K. Rowling's Harry Potter novels. While the events and characters of each novel are unique, we can identify passages that observe recognizable forms. For instance, in the first novel Harry's life changed when he received an "acceptance letter" to begin his studies at Hogwarts School of Magic. While the message itself was unique, the form was "stable" as it was like many other "acceptance letters" that are written in the non-magical world. In another novel the journalist, Rita Skeeter, interviewed Harry for an article in the newspaper, *The Daily Prophet*. The content of each of her columns was unique. Yet the interview as a journalistic practice, and the written columns published in the newspaper observed the forms and structures of other interviews and articles of non-magical-world newspapers. Meaning is achievable because the reader can see links between the unique texts of these novels, and the stable forms of other writings.

The second feature is the concepts of **addressivity** and **dialogue**. Addressivity is based upon the premise that a person is not simply a passive receptacle, but an "event" who is "addressed," and who responds to and shapes utterances. **Dialogue** is the understanding that we see the world comparatively and in conversation with others. Drawing upon Einstein's famous "train and platform" illustration of relativity, Bakhtin developed a similar analogy to illustrate dialogue. Imagine there are two people watching a train. The first is watching the train, and the second is observing the first person watching the train. Each person's point of view and field of vision is unique. Yet if the second person engaged in dialogue with the first, and shared this other perspective, new insights and understandings could be created, and yield what Bakhtin described as a **"surplus of vision"** (Morson & Emerson, 1990, p. 241). When two people are engaged in dialogue they can "see" more of the train than one watching it alone. If we extend Bakhtin's ideas to intercultural communication, we can then see a benefit of this form of communication: when people of different cultures and languages are engaged in dialogue, they may gain a surplus of vision that lets them see and know more about the world.

Language and Culture

In the 1970s the McDonald's corporation opened its first franchise restaurants in Hong Kong (Watson, 2006). A recognizable key to McDonald's success was its **Fordist methods** of food production, meaning that the same menu of items was produced in a standardized way, and offered across all restaurants. Yet McDonald's standardization was more than just how food is produced, it also involved how the food was served, and the style of interaction between customers and employees. Therefore, when entering the Hong Kong market, McDonald's introduced both its style of food production and customer service.

The local, cultural practice of customers at food stalls in Hong Kong—a type of restaurant similar to a McDonald's service counter—was *not* to stand in an ordered line; instead customers tended to "scrum" when waiting to place an order. Thus, when people in Hong Kong first began to visit McDonald's restaurants they would scrum at the service counter. This problem was solved with "queue monitors" who taught customers to line up properly; in time this practice was adopted and became accepted at McDonald's and other similar service counters at establishments across Hong Kong. When McDonald's, however, tried to introduce another practice—the behavior of food service personnel—it failed. McDonald's taught their employees to offer what is known as "friendly service": greet customers with a "smile" and "vary . . . 'Thank you' phrases so that customers receive what appear to be personalized messages" (Watson, 2006, p. 31). This did not catch on. To Hong Kong people a service person's smile, or politely uttered "Thank you" is not seen as "friendly." Instead, customers think this meant such a person was "playing around" or "laughing" at their expense.

The experience of McDonald's in Hong Kong illustrates that **cultural practices** and their associated meanings are not universal, and may appear—as we see in Saussure's analysis of the sign—to be quite arbitrary. This has implications for intercultural communication.

Cultural Discourse Analysis

The communication scholar, Donal Carbaugh, developed **cultural discourse analysis** as a tool to help us understand how culture shapes communication, and how it may impact **interaction** (Carbaugh, 2007). This theory is built upon the premise—similar to Bakhtin's concept of speech genres—that within each culture there are ritualized, **social interactions** that follow and display repeated, sequential forms. Such examples include greetings, joking sessions, or "good-byes" (p. 170). For example, Nuciforo (2013) studied a distinctly Russian **ritual performance** that may serve as a greeting and/or good-bye: toasting and drinking. At some time during a gathering, a person will initiate the sequence by announcing "well, come on, let's get to it!" (p. 165). The initiator then makes sure everyone has something to drink, and pours alcohol into everyone's glasses. The toast is uttered, and then everyone drinks. Nuciforo explained that while there can be great variation in the wording of a toast, each touches on "symbolic anchors," such as (1) pointing to the shared occasion that brought everyone together (e.g., birthday, national holiday), (2) addressing another person as "you" who is thanked or praised during a round of reciprocal toasts, (3) using the word "us" to index a shared bond as friends or relations, and/or (4) wishing a positive quality such as good health or joy to all. This ritual communication was perceived by Russians to be an important cultural performance, and may strengthen the interpersonal bonds of those who participate.

In moments of intercultural communication, when people of different cultures interact according to ritualized, sequential acts, miscommunication may occur. For instance, when Americans and Finns interact, Americans may seem superficial and Finns silent (Carbaugh, 2005). This is because Americans like to smile and engage in "small talk" with strangers or acquaintances as a way to "break the ice" and potentially lead to a deeper relationship. They prefer to talk about such "neutral" topics as the weather or sports teams, or express a personal opinion about a place or other persons—without having a strong commitment to that opinion—as a way to "explore" the issue. Finns, on the other hand, would rather remain silent than talk with friends or strangers about such "obvious" topics as the weather or sports; if they do talk, the topic should be something worthy of everyone's attention, and anything that is expressed should reflect a personal commitment to what is

Figure 17.2 Toasting as a Ritual Performance

said. Thus, Finns and Americans interacting may perceive each other as difficult to understand, or even impolite.

Language Socialization

The above examples demonstrate that the forms of everyday practices may differ across cultures. But this begs the question: How and why might such differences occur? An area of research that has investigated this question is **language socialization**. Two early scholars in this field, Elinor Ochs and Bambi Schieffelin (1995), from their respective fieldwork in Western Samoa and Papua New Guinea, observed that both the social situation involving child-caregiver interaction, and the language learning process, differed from accounts of child language acquisition studied in European American contexts. In the US the child was often exposed to language in a child-centered manner: "mothers hold their infants in such a way that they are face-to-face and gaze at them. [They] address . . . infants, vocalize to them, ask questions, and greet them" (p. 479). But in other contexts, such as Papua New Guinea, children were bystanders to adult conversation, and not expected to engage in talk: "Kaluli mothers [believe] that infants 'have no understanding' and never treat their infants as partners . . . [A] mother and infant do not gaze into each other's eyes" (p. 483). Such children were engaged in what is called "**situation-centered** learning environments" (Sperry, Sperry, & Miller, 2015).

To illustrate, consider the case of Western Samoa: society was highly stratified, and individuals were ranked on the basis of having a title or not (Ochs & Schieffelin, 1995). Children, who do not have titles, when they made a request of someone who has a title, were ignored. Instead, they first made a request of a lower-ranked person, such as a young adult; this person then passed on the request to the chief; the chief then replied to the young adult, who then replied to the young child. Likewise, high ranked persons were not expected to "find out" news and information by themselves; rather, they received reports from lower ranked people. As children got older, they were taught to be "messengers" to convey reports to adults. To deliver a report meant that not only must they learn the language—vocabulary, grammar, and syntax—of the report, they must also learn the social strata of society, and how to behave and properly address higher and lower ranked individuals. Based upon this work, Ochs and Schieffelin defined **language socialization** as the study of how novices (e.g., children) are socialized *through language* to communicate politely and appropriately, and socialized how to *use language* across a range of social situations.

While it was not the focus of her study, we could apply a language socialization paradigm to Nuciforo's (2013) study of Russian toasting and drinking. Consider that children and novices (e.g., an American who goes out with Russian friends), in order to perform a toast well, must learn not only the language of the toast, but also the acts and sequence of a toast. This can be learned by passively watching and observing how others do it, or having a competent toaster teach what words to say, and how to do a toast. Language would serve as the key tool to teach cultural routines and participant roles.

Language and Categorical Perception

Until this point we have looked at theories and practices that work mainly at the descriptive level, showing that when we look across a range of languages, we find sequences and acts arranged in patterned ways, and these differ. Now we turn our attention to examine how language works at the level of perception, and what impact this may have on intercultural communication.

In Taiwanese (also called Hokkien, Southern Min, Tai-gi), a southern Chinese language (also called a dialect of Chinese, see Sandel, 2015), the words for male and female differ in interesting ways. If we write these words phonetically, using common English language spelling, the word for male would look like "*za-bo*," and the word for female also "*za-bo*." Yet to Taiwanese speakers these words, and the sounds used to produce them, are markedly different. The "bo" in male is pronounced as a middle tone, and the "b" sound is a *non-vocalized* bilabial plosive. The "bo" in female is a high-falling tone, and the "b" sound is a *vocalized* bilabial plosive. To make a vocalized plosive means you must utter the sound while "voicing" it. A close approximation is that it sounds something like "mb." Yet, if we compare these words with sounds and words of English, we notice that marking words by tone, and distinguishing between vocalized and non-vocalized consonants, are not meaningful in English. When I (as a native English speaker) began learning Taiwanese I found it more challenging to learn than Mandarin, because it has more tones (seven in Taiwanese versus four in Mandarin), and a number of consonant sounds that do not occur in English, as explained in this short video: https://www.youtube.com/watch?v=B92YEXe68vQ. Yet many of my Taiwanese friends told me that Taiwanese was easier to learn than Mandarin. Why would they say this?

The answer lies in something observed by the scholar Edward Sapir (1884–1939). When studying a range of languages, he observed that even fluent speakers may be unaware of some sound differences, but highly attuned to others. For instance, English speakers rarely noticed the varieties of sound represented by the letter *l* (e.g., du*ll* sounds darker and c*l*ear sounds lighter), yet they did notice differences between *l* and *r* sounds (e.g., fa*ll* and fa*r*), that speakers of some other languages, such as Japanese, did not. These units of sound are known as **phonemes**; and the ways speakers differentiate them is based upon "**categorical perception**": objectively distinct sounds are put into similar categories for social purposes (O'Neill, 2015). These linguistic examples illustrate a psychology of language, that language is a system for filtering objectively different sounds into subjectively constructed categories of meaning. This explains why a Taiwanese friend, who learned the language at home as a child, and then later learned Mandarin in school (Sandel, 2003), would subjectively believe Taiwanese to be simpler than Mandarin, despite the objective evidence that Taiwanese is linguistically more complex than Mandarin. Thus, language plays a powerful role in shaping our mental perceptions and understandings of the objective world, a claim made by both Sapir and his best known student, Benjamin Whorf (1897–1941).

When performing his non-academic job as a fire prevention engineer for the Hartford Fire Insurance Company, Whorf saw that the language of the workplace was a contributing factor in fires. In one incident a fire broke out when "empty gasoline drums" were ignited by carelessly tossed cigarette stubs, because workers were not aware that "empty" drums contained invisible and highly explosive vapors. Likewise, an insulating material made from "spun limestone," when exposed to acid fumes and heat, was converted to an inflammable substance. Workers were surprised when this "stone" caught on fire (Whorf, 1956). Likewise, and in more recent times, people in the US concerned with traffic safety wanted to change the language used to describe traffic "accidents." They claimed that the word "accident" may "trivialize" the event and underplay the fact that most are caused by human error; thus, they wanted everyone to use the word "crash" instead of accident, and believed this would lead to fewer crashes (Richtel, 2016).

The power of language to shape human behavior—also called the **Sapir–Whorf hypothesis** (O'Neill, 2015)—involves more than the use of individual words. The structure of a language can also impact subjective perception. When contrasting English and other European languages with Hopi—a Native American language—Whorf found that Hopi did not mark time linearly, or use discrete units such as "hours" and "days": instead, Hopi marked time as a cyclical process. Thus, Hopi would not say, "I will meet you in three days," whereby each "day" was counted as a singular event; instead they would say, "I will meet you on the third day." When spoken this way a day was perceived to be a recurrent event that was counted sequentially.

The anthropologist Edward T. Hall, who as a young man worked in the US Southwest with Hopi and Navajo tribes, illustrated this Native American concept of time well. He wrote a story of how one Navajo man came to be called "Little Sunday." Hall began by explaining that Navajo had "difficulty getting used to the fact that we [sic] Europeans divided time into strange and unnatural periods instead of having a 'natural' succession of days which began with the new moon and ended with the old" (Hall, 1959, p. 12). Thus, some Navajo, who traveled long distances on horseback to reach a store operated by "white traders," arrived on a day when it was closed, Sunday. The Navajo did not use the "white" way to mark days, and to them "Sunday" did not have the same perceived meaning. Thus, finding the store closed, a Navajo would bang on the door until the trader opened it. One Navajo man, who was the most frequent Sunday visitor, was called "Big Sunday." "Little Sunday" was the name given to the second most frequent Sunday visitor.

Language Ideologies

In seventeenth century England, a religiously motivated group of people known as the Quakers decided that they would change the second person pronouns used to address people. The linguistic practice of the day was that the pronouns "ye" or "you" were used to address social superiors (e.g., a farmer to a lord), or persons of equally high rank (e.g., government ministers). The pronouns "thou" and "thee" were used to address social inferiors, or as a way to show solidarity or friendship with someone (Silverstein, 1995a). The Quakers, based upon a belief that all people are equal, consciously used thou and thee as pronouns to address all persons on all occasions. They believed this not only matched how they perceived the social world, but also had the power to change society and make it become more egalitarian. In response non-Quakers stopped using the pronouns thou and thee, as these were associated with Quakers. Over time the English language changed and the pronouns thou and thee dropped out of the language.

Silverstein (1995a) claimed this was an example of a change in language based upon a **language ideology**, or strongly held belief about the link between language and behavior. The Quakers believed that by changing language practices, they could change society. For similar reasons, Silverstein explained that in the late twentieth century we again saw a language ideology influencing a shift in pronoun use. Many feminists, believing like the Quakers that a change in language could change society, objected to the use of the masculine pronoun to refer to both women and men as found in such expressions as: "Everyone has a right to his opinion." Thus, he/she constructions were introduced ("Everyone has a right to his or her opinion") or the feminine pronoun she/her used instead of he/his ("Everyone has a right to her opinion"). Over time he/she phrases (sounding cumbersome) came to be replaced with a simpler solution, namely the third person pronoun, they/their/them, as a way to refer to both women and men. Thus, "Everyone has a right to his opinion" became: "Everyone has a right to their opinion."

These examples demonstrate that language is comprised of signs that are both **referential**, and refer to or name things (i.e., language maps onto an objective world of things), and **indexical**, that point to some state of affairs, and are assigned meanings based upon the context and subjective interpretation of reality (Silverstein, 1995b). Pronouns are a case of indexical words that can be assigned meaning only in context. Consider the sentence: "I am talking to you." *I* points to the speaker, and *you* to the listener, but the identities of I and you shift, depending on the identities of speaker and listener (Figure 17.3).

Similarly, features of a language, such as the way a word is accented, can be subjectively interpreted as indexing or pointing to a category of persons, and identifying a person as friend or foe. This we see recorded several thousand

Figure 17.3 Pronouns as Shifting Indexicals

years ago in the book of Judges, when people who pronounced the word "shibboleth" as "sibboleth," were believed to belong to an enemy tribe, and were singled out and killed. More recently, in 2016 a male airline passenger in the US, who was overheard speaking Arabic on the phone, was taken off his flight because another passenger, who thought that when he said *"inshallah"*—a common expression meaning "if god [Allah] wills"—meant that he was planning an act of terror (Stack, 2016).

Language and Identity

Because language is a powerful tool for constructing social reality, in moments of intercultural communication people can make false assumptions not only about what individual words mean, but also what are the identities and allegiances of people who speak different languages. Prior to the World Wars of the twentieth century, in many cities and states across the US the German language was widely spoken. German language newspapers were common, and bilingual education in German and English was found across many cities and states, with Ohio a leader "because of a law that permitted a German language program wherever a sufficient number of parents asked for one" (Alba & Nee, 2003, p. 145). Yet after the United States went to war with Germany, this practice ended quickly. People who spoke German were suspected of being disloyal to the US (Gavrilos, 2010). Speaking English was perceived to index an "American" identity, and by the end of World War I, "26 states had passed laws against the use of German" (p. 96). In the following decades German and immigrant groups "assimilated," and the pattern was established in the US that by the third generation, most children of immigrants could no longer speak their heritage language (Fishman, 1991).

A perceived link between language and identity, however, is not limited to the US. In many countries across the world there are **language policies** that promote a single "national language" (some nations, such as Canada, have two or more official languages). This is based upon the belief, or ideology, that a unified, and standardized language, creates the nation (Kroskrity, 2000). Thus, bi- or multilingual, non-standardized forms of language may be suppressed, such as was the experience of government-led efforts targeted against Native American tribes and Australian aborigines (Diamond, 1992). Or the "failure" of a "nation" to develop may be attributed to the lack of a unified and standard language, as was commonly perceived to be the cause of political unrest in the Balkan region of Europe and parts of Africa (Irvine & Gal, 2000.

New and Mixed Languages

Yet, despite the efforts of governments and educational institutions to standardize languages and/or reduce or eliminate **linguistic diversity**, new language forms arise. This happens for three reasons: one is that a language is not the property of the individual mind, but of the social group (Labov, 2012); the second is that language can be a resource for building and constructing alliances and identities; the third is that people—led by youth—desire to create new and novel forms of expression. We discuss each of these in turn.

Labov explained the importance of the **social group** in the following way:

> We are programmed to learn to speak in ways that fit the general pattern of our community. What I, as a language learner, want to learn is not "my English" or even "your English" but the English language in general. In this sense, the language learning faculty is outward bound, searching for a community consensus rather than an individual model.
> (Labov, 2012, p. 6)

Evidence to support this can be seen in the **dialect** (or accent) learned by children who grew up in the homes of first generation US immigrants: they did not learn to speak the version of English that they were exposed to at home—a "foreign" accented English—but learned the accent of their peers; they were perceived by others to have "no accent" when speaking English—because they learned the accent of their social group.

In mixed situations, where people speak more than one language, they may strategically use that language (or code) to create affiliation. This was something the scholar John Gumperz observed. Once, after a teaching a graduate seminar, an African American student approached the professor in the presence of both black and white students, and said: "Could I talk to you for a minute? I'm gonna apply for a fellowship and I was wondering if I could get a recommendation?" This was spoken in "standard" American English dialect. The professor replied and told the student to come to his office and "tell me what you want to do." After the professor left the group of students, the African American student "turning his head ever so slightly to the other students [said] . . . 'Ahma git me a gig! (Rough gloss: 'I'm going to get myself some support'.)" (Gumperz, 1982, p. 30). This last phrase was uttered in African American Vernacular English (AAVE), directed not to the professor, but to fellow students. Thus, AAVE was used as an **interactional resource** for speaking to peers and marking in-group solidarity.

Not all members of the same language community, however, may share a sense of affiliation, or shared identity. For instance, from a study of bilingual speakers in central Java, Indonesia, Wolff (1997) found distinctions between the ways *Peranakan* (ethnic Chinese) and *Pribumi* ("native" Indonesians) would **code-switch** (speak two or more languages). While both frequently mixed both Javanese and Melayu (Bahasa Indonesian), *Peranakan* spoke Melayu as a way to mark social status and difference, and Javanese for closeness; *Pribumi* did the opposite: they spoke Javanese to mark difference and Melayu for closeness. These diverse ways of using language indexed and created difference between these two co-present communities.

In Papua New Guinea, the anthropologist Don Kulick (1992) studied a very small tribe of 100 people, the Gapun, who in addition to a range of other languages, spoke their own language, called Tai-ap. Kulick came to understand that ideologies, or beliefs about languages, impacted their communication, especially across generations when parents decided which language to speak and/or teach their young children. One part of this ideology was that words and speech had magical, symbolic power; it was believed that if a language was understood by others, it may lose its power. Thus, in interactions with people who were perceived to be enemies, it was an advantage to conceal words and meanings, and people may consciously change their language so as to not be understood. Kulick reported that in 1978 the linguist K. McElhanon witnessed such an event. During a meeting of "Selepet speakers" who lived in the village of Indu, they made a conscious decision to be different and "would immediately stop using their usual word for 'no,' *bia*, which was shared by all their fellow speakers of Selepet. Instead they would begin by saying *buŋɛ*, which they did and have continued doing since this time" (pp. 2–3).

This last point demonstrates a point made above, namely that for many people there is a desire to develop or change language. It may be done, as in the case of both the Gapun and the Peranakan-Pribumi of Indonesia, in order to demonstrate and/or create differences across ethnic groups. Or, as happens more often, language change is motivated by the desire to speak in new ways, much in the way that rap artists do in their lyrics (Pennycook, 2007). And young people are most often at the vanguard of language change.

In a study of students at "Belten High School" in a Detroit suburb of the US, Eckert (1989) observed what she and Labov (2012) called the "Northern Cities Shift," or a change in the pronunciation of certain vowel sounds. From a year of ethnographic study she found differences that were associated with gender and class: linguistic shift was greater among girls than boys; it was also greater for "burnouts" (rebellious youth) than "jocks" (popular youth). Those most extreme in their burnout behavior, "the Burned out Burnouts" (p. 4) were the most extreme in their vowel shift. Eckert explained that jocks were more likely to conform to adult norms of speech, while "burnouts" were against them. Thus, burnouts, and more importantly girl burnouts, led the vowel shift as they spoke in ways that differed most from adults and conforming peers. The implication, as Labov (2012) explained, is that the speaking behavior of the non-conforming members of a social group, or in this case the shift in vowels, is an important symbolic marker of identity that carries social meaning.

Online Language

In this last section we turn our attention to look at a context where language is changing most rapidly: the language of the Internet and social media, also called **computer mediated communication** (CMC). The recent and rapid development of technologies that allow users to connect and communicate (e.g., computers, tablets, smart phones), has led to a range of new communicative **affordances**—an interaction between the objective qualities of a technology and subjective perceptions of its use—that may alter communicative practices and/or habits (Schrock, 2015, p. 1232). Consider, for instance, a typical scene at a cafeteria or eatery on a university campus. Four classmates are seated at a table, not looking at each other, but at their mobile phones. They alternately talk to each other and send messages via their phones to others not physically present. Ten years ago such a scene would be rare and 20 years ago unimaginable.

In the 1990s, when communication scholars began to look at CMC, they wanted to know, if—as most believed—CMC was inferior to face-to-face communication. In a series of studies, Walther (1992; 2012) demonstrated that CMC was not inferior, if measured by the ability to communicate affect or like for another person. According to the theory he developed, **Social Information Processing Theory**, CMC was not inferior given the following conditions: (1) participants were given more time to communicate, (2) users expressed like or dislike through the words in their communication, and (3) users took advantage of resources at hand, such as emoticons (:-) that could be entered on the keyboard (Walther, 1992).

With the development of new technologies CMC users now have far more resources than the initial generation of users (e.g., audio, video). CMC serves to lessen the perceptual boundaries of time and space across national, cultural, and linguistic boundaries (Sandel, 2014). Furthermore, **social media** platforms, such as WeChat (popular in China), afford both one-to-one (chat) and one-to-many communication (sharing pictures and text via "Moments") that expand perceptual boundaries, and may flatten social distance in relationships (Sandel & Ju, 2015). These technologies may also impact language, by affording the creation of novel expressions, the greater use of vernacular language, and **mixed codes**.

One such example of mixed language comes from messages collected in China's Pearl River Delta Region that includes Hong Kong, Macau, and Guangdong Province. The most widely spoken language is Cantonese. Mandarin Chinese is also used widely, as well as English and a range of other non-Chinese languages. In Figure 17.4 we present one screenshot of a mixed-code conversation.

Figure 17.4 is a screenshot of a WeChat user-defined group of five members. Turn 1, written in simplified Chinese, began with the question: "How did it appear in this group?" This was followed by a computer generated message

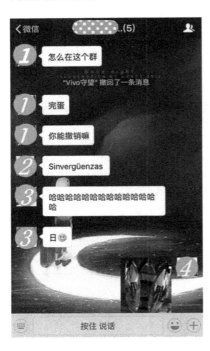

1. How did it appear in this group?

2. Text generated message—"Name" has retrieved a message

3. [I] am finished

4. Can you withdraw it

5. Scoundrel [Spanish]

6. Ha ha ha . . . [laughing]

7. [character for day, euphemism for F**k] + Smiley Face Emoji

8. [Picture: meaning unclear]

Figure 17.4 Scoundrel: Mixed Codes on Social Media

that the sender "has retrieved a message." Then in Turn 3, the initial poster wrote 完蛋, which can be translated as, "I am finished" or "I am dead." Apparently 1 belonged to a number of WeChat groups, and sent a message that was supposed to be sent to a different WeChat group. Turn 4 was a request to members of this WeChat group to withdraw the "wrong" message. Evidently there was a lag between the time the request was made to "withdraw" her message—using the WeChat messaging tool—and the time it was actually withdrawn. Following this sequence, in Turn 5 a second person replied, writing "*Sinvergüenzes*," Spanish for "Scoundrel." The members of this WeChat group worked at the same company, including one who was Spanish. Here this Spanish word functioned as a **"we-code,"** used among insiders and group members (Gumperz, 1982). It worked as an inside joke, intended to soften the mistake, and create the feeling that they were all inside members who could understand this Spanish language joke. Then in Turn 6, three took up the joke by "laughing." The exchange was closed with the character 日, a **euphemism** for the English swear word, "F**k," followed by a smiley face Emoji.

Here we see that WeChat afforded both the mistake and user-initiated repair. The mistake happened because WeChat allowed users to create "contact groups" for the sharing and reading of messages. Users often belong to multiple groups, and as happened in this instance, 1 mistakenly sent a message intended for another group, to this one. Such a mistake is less likely to occur in face-to-face communication, or in email discussion groups (although in the latter, email messages may be mistakenly sent to the wrong persons when the "reply to all" command is chosen). The **repair**, which involved both retrieving the message and openly acknowledging the mistake, was also more readily afforded by the technology. Thus, the exchange concluded with an "inside joke," laughter, and a swear word that worked interactionally and was intended to assuage 1's feelings of embarrassment.

Chapter Summary

Language can be understood in many ways. This chapter began with Saussure's definition of language as the ordered arrangement of signs. Meaning at the individual level is created when the outward symbol maps onto an inward mental image. Social understandings of meanings are possible because of the stability of speech genres, or recognizable forms. These in turn may form the basis of ritualized social interactions which are linked to specific cultures, and learned as children or novices in social situations. Problems of understanding can be due to categorical perception, or the ways speakers may not be aware of some objective sound differences, but subjectively construct others. Thus, words and/or categories of language can shape and impact human behavior. Language ideologies may also impact our understandings, and lead people to shift language practices, or make false assumptions about language and identity. Finally, we see that language forms are constantly changing, often led by youth, and afforded by new communication technologies. Thus, we see greater language mixing and new symbols found on social media and online environments.

Key Terms

Addressivity
Code-switch
Contextualization cues
Denotative
Euphemism
Indexical
Language identity
Language socialization
Phonemes
Ritual performance
Signifier
Social group
Social media
Syntax

Affordance
Computer mediated communication
Cultural discourse analysis
Dialect
Fordist methods
Interaction
Language ideology
Linguistic diversity
Referential
Sapir–Whorf hypothesis
Signs
Social information processing theory
Speech genres
Utterance

Arbitrary
Categorical perception
Connotative
Cultural practices
Dialogue
Grammar
Interactional resource
Language policies
Mixed codes
Repair
Signified
Situation-centered
Social interactions
Surplus of vision
We-code

Activities

1. In a group of 3–5 people, come up with a list of all the languages and/or dialects you know. If you were to think back several generations, to your parents and grandparents, what other languages would they know? Discuss how and why languages were passed down, or not passed down to your generation. How were you socialized to language as a child?
2. Do you believe that you can change society by changing language? If yes, are there words, vocabularies, codes, that you would want changed, in order to change society? If no, why do you think that language does not have the power to impact and change society? What do you see to be the link between language, identity, and society?
3. Look at your mobile phone. What "codes" do you see in your phone messages? Do you see any text that would be considered a "foreign" language or dialect? Are there new words, vocabularies, signs, (e.g., Emoji) on your phone messages? How and when did you learn these new codes and signs? Do you use different language with close friends and peers, than you would with strangers or older folk?

References

Alba, R., & Nee, V. (2003). *Remaking the American mainstream: Assimilation and contemporary immigration.* Cambridge, MA: Harvard University Press.

Bakhtin, M. (1981). *The dialogic imagination: Four essays by M. M. Bakhtin.* (M. Holquist, ed., C. Emerson, & M. Holquist, trans.) Austin, TX: University of Texas Press.

Carbaugh, D. (2005). *Cultures in conversation.* Mahwah, NJ: Lawrence Erlbaum.

Carbaugh, D. (2007). Cultural discourse analysis: Communication practices and intercultural encounters. *Journal of Intercultural Communication Research, 36,* 167–182. doi:10.1080/17475750701737090

De Saussure, F., & Baskin, W. (1959). *Course in general linguistics.* New York, NY: McGraw-Hill Paperbacks.

Diamond, J. (1992). *The third chimpanzee: The evolution and future of the human animal.* New York, NY: Harper Collins.

Eckert, P. (1989). *Jocks and burnouts: Social categories and identity in the high school.* New York, NY: Teachers College Press.

Fishman, J. A. (1991). *Reversing language shift.* Clevedon, UK: Multilingual Matters.

Gavrilos, D. (2010). Becoming "100% American": Negotiating ethnic identities through nativist discourse. *Critical Discourse Studies, 7*(2), 95–112. doi:10.1080/17405901003675398

Gumperz, J. (1982). *Discourse strategies.* New York, NY: Cambridge University Press.

Hall, E. T. (1959). *The silent language.* New York, NY: Anchor Books.

Holquist, M. (1990). *Dialogism: Bakhtin and his world.* New York, NY: Routledge.

Irvine, J. T., & Gal, S. (2000). Language ideology and linguistic differentiation. In P. V. Kroskrity (ed.), *Regimes of language: Ideologies, polities, and identities* (pp. 35–84). Santa Fe, NM: School of American Research Press.

Kroskrity, P. V. (2000). Regimenting languages: Language ideological perspectives. In P. V. Kroskrity (ed.), *Regimes of language: Ideologies, polities, and identities* (pp. 1–34). Santa Fe, NM: School of American Research Press.

Kulick, D. (1992). *Language shift and cultural reproduction: Socialization, self, and syncretism in a Papua New Guinean village*. New York, NY: Cambridge University Press.

Labov, W. (2012). *Dialect diversity in America: The politics of language change*. Charlottesville, VA: University of Virginia Press.

Morson, G. S., & Emerson, C. (1990). *Mikhail Bakhtin: Creation of a prosaics*. Stanford, CA: Stanford University Press.

Nuciforo, E. V. (2013). Russian toasting and drinking as communication ritual. *Russian Journal of Communication, 5*, 161–175. doi:10.1080/19409419.2013.805670

Ochs, E., & Schieffelin, B. B. (1995). Language acquisition and socialization: Three developmental stories and their implications. In B. B. Blount (ed.), *Language, culture, and society: A book of readings* (2nd ed., pp. 470–512). Prospect Heights, IL: Waveland Press.

O'Neill, S. (2015). Sapir-Whorf hypothesis. In K. Tracy, C. Ilie, & T. L. Sandel (eds.), *The International Encyclopedia of Language and Social Interaction* (pp. 1325–1334). Boston, MA: John Wiley & Sons. doi:10.1002/9781118611463.wbielsi086

Pennycook, A. (2007). Language, localization, and the real: Hip-hop and the global spread of authenticity. *Journal of Language, Identity & Education, 6*(2), 101–115. doi:10.1080/15348450701341246

Richtel, M. (2016, May 22). It's no accident: Advocates want to speak of car "crashes" instead. Retrieved May 23, 2016, from *The New York Times*: http://www.nytimes.com/2016/05/23/science/its-no-accident-advocates-want-to-speak-of-car-crashes-instead.html?hp&action=click&pgtype=Homepage&clickSource=story-heading&module=second-column-region&region=top-news&WT.nav=top-news

Sandel, T. L. (2003). Linguistic capital in Taiwan: The KMT's Mandarin language policy and its perceived impact upon the language practices of bilingual Mandarin and Tai-gi speakers. *Language in Society, 32*, 523–551. doi:10.1017/S0047404503324030

Sandel, T. L. (2014). "Oh, I'm here!" Social media's impact on the cross-cultural adaptation of students studying abroad. *Journal of Intercultural Communication Research, 43*, 1–29. doi:10.1080/17475759.2013.865662

Sandel, T. L. (2015). Dialects. In K. Tracy, T. L. Sandel, & C. Ilie (eds.), *The International Encyclopedia of Language and Social Interaction* (pp. 351–364). Boston, MA: John Wiley & Sons. doi:10.1002/9781118611463.wbielsi172

Sandel, T. L., & Ju, B. (2015). The code of WeChat: Chinese students' cell phone social media practices. In T. Milburn (ed.), *Communicating user experience: Applying local strategies to digital media design* (pp. 103–126). Lanham, MD: Lexington Books.

Schrock, A. R. (2015). Communicative affordances of mobile media: Portability, availability, locatability, and multimediality. *International Journal of Communication, 9*, 1229–1246.

Silverstein, M. (1995a). Language and the culture of gender. In B. G. Blount (ed.), *Language, culture, and society: A book of readings* (pp. 513–550). Prospect Heights, IL: Waveland Press.

Silverstein, M. (1995b). Shifters, linguistic categories, and cultural description. In B. Blount (ed.), *Language, culture, and society: A book of readings* (pp. 187–221). Prospect Heights, IL: Waveland Press.

Sperry, D. E., Sperry, L. L., & Miller, P. J. (2015). Language socialization. In K. Tracy, C. Ilie, & T. L. Sandel (eds.), *The International Encyclopedia of Language and Social Interaction* (pp. 931–947). Boston, MA: John Wiley & Sons. doi:10.1002/9781118611463.wbielsi114

Stack, L. (2016, May 17). College student is removed from flight after speaking Arabic on plane. Retrieved May 20, 2016, from *The New York Times*: http://www.nytimes.com/2016/04/17/us/student-speaking-arabic-removed-southwest-airlines-plane.html

Walther, J. B. (1992). Interpersonal effects in computer-mediated interaction: A relational perspective. *Communication Research, 19*(1), 52–90. doi:10.1177/009365092019001003

Walther, J. B. (2012). Interaction through technological lenses: Computer-mediated communication and language. *Journal of Language and Social Psychology, 31*, 397–414. doi:10.1177/0261927X12446610

Watson, J. L. (2006). *Golden Arches East: McDonald's in East Asia* (2nd ed.). Stanford, CA: Stanford University Press.

Whorf, B. L. (1956). *Language, thought, and reality: Selected writings of Benjamin Lee Whorf.* (J. B. Caroll, ed.) Cambridge, MA: The MIT Press.

Wolff, J. U. (1997). Peranakan Chinese speech and identity. *Indonesia, 64*, 29–44.

Student Paper

Vong Kuok U (Ida)

The Intercultural Usage of Emoticons: A Study of Gender, Closeness and Culture

When I first saw my friend using ":目", I could not get the exact meaning behind this emoticon. I was just amused by the variety of emoticons. Also I began to think how would a non-Chinese speaker interpret an emoticon like ":目", thus I began to be curious about the intercultural usage of emoticons in Computer-Mediated Communication (CMC). Thus, in the following I will discuss about the emoticons in CMC and highlight intercultural differences.

> Ida nicely motivates the paper with the use of a personal example.

As early as the 1980s, scholars observed a new symbol appearing in CMC, the "emoticon." This word was invented by blending the terms "emotion" and "icon" (Dresner & Herring, 2010). It described such symbols as :-) (smiley face) and :-((frown face). In more recent studies of CMC, it was claimed that emoticons could express emotion and replace the non-verbal communication forms of FtF

(Continued)

communication (Walther & D'Addario, 2001). Lo (2008) suggested that, based on the channel expansion theory, the communicative capability of CMC would not be weaker than FtF since the communicator had accumulated enough knowledge and skills to use this medium. E-mails with emoticons were also reported to give a more favorable impression towards the sender rather than the e-mail without emoticons (Yoo, 2007). Furthermore, expressing emotion is not the only function of emoticon; Derks, Bos and Von Grumbkow (2008a) suggested that emoticons could also strengthen the verbal meaning, express humor and regulate interaction.

Differences in Communication: North Americans and Chinese

There are many studies about different communication styles of Chinese and Americans. Distinctions are made in the name of collectivism and individualism or high-context culture and low-context culture. For example, Gao and Toomey (1998) mentioned that Chinese use the collective "we" pronoun more than the individual "I." Zakaria and Cogburn (2007) suggested that the CMC of a high context culture like Chinese is more indirect and ambiguous, while the CMC of low context culture like North Americans is more direct and succinct. Other studies suggested that based on individualism, North Americans would convey more pleasant feelings than East Asians (Inglehart, Foa, Peterson, & Welzel, 2008). Bazarova and Yuan (2013) suggested that compared to Americans; Chinese speakers were less confident and less influential in FtF communication. This difference, however, was not found in CMC. It suggested that technology has closed the gap between people in different cultures.

In addition to issues of culture, the use of emoticons may differ because of gender and friendship closeness. When talking with friends instead of strangers, emoticon usage goes up (Derks, et al., 2008b). Females were suggested to be more emotionally expressive and use more non-verbal cues

> *Ida sets up the paper well by showing how Emoticons have emerged and been studied in the literature. This is then linked to the three areas where differences have emerged: Culture, Gender, and relational Closeness.*

compared to males on the study of online messages in newsgroup (Witmer & Katzman, 1997). In Lee's (2003) study among college students, she suggested that males rarely use emoticons with those of the same gender, but use more when chatting with females. Females, however, would use the same amount of emoticons with both genders. Therefore, in this study I will examine the different uses of emoticons in terms of culture, gender, and relational closeness. The focus of this paper is the use of emoticons via Instant Messenger (IM). The IM chosen in current study is Facebook Messenger, called "Chat," and released in 2008 (Facebook, 2012).

Methodology

A Taiwanese female and an American male were recruited for the study. Both are 22 years old and studying in university. The Taiwanese female is "Annie" and the American male is "Peter" (pseudonyms). Both Annie and Peter are multilingual and have stayed in a different cultural context for no less than one month. Both have foreign friends and chat with them using Facebook messenger. Annie has used Facebook messenger for two years while Peter has used it for 4 years.

> *Ethical concerns were addressed. It is important when using Online data to receive permission from all participants.*

I contacted Annie and Peter through Facebook the beginning of October, 2012. Both were informed about the purpose of the current study. They were asked to provide eight, one-to-one dialogues, looking for examples that showed Gender, Culture, and relational Closeness. The languages included Chinese, English and French. Both Annie and Peter were also required to inform their interlocutors that their dialogues will be used in the current study.

The dialogues provided by Annie were longer than Peter's. The earliest time of the Annie's dialogues was July, 2011 while the earliest time of the Peter's dialogues was March, 2012. After collecting the Facebook IM dialogues, I interviewed Annie and Peter via Skype. I interviewed Annie twice, the first time 19 minutes and the second 6 minutes. I interviewed Peter once for 12 minutes.

(Continued)

Data analysis

Annie and Peter sent me a total of 16 dialogues, ranging from 36 to 700 lines. Lines are defined by the separation of punctuation and meanings. Dialogues were transcribed in the original languages. For the dialogues in French, Google Translator was used to find the meanings.

The emoticons analyzed in this study were those that can be typed directly on the keyboard. Upper- and lowercase letters were treated as the same, while emoticons used repeatedly were counted separately, that is to say ":))" counted as two smileys instead of one. The percentage of emoticons in dialogues were counted in Excel. This was calculated as the number of emoticons divided by the number of lines. So if in a dialogue of ten lines there were two emoticons, this would be 2/10, or 20 percent. Interviews were transcribed into Chinese (Annie) and English (Peter), yielding 9 single-spaced pages.

> The methods are clearly explained. Note the use of simple examples to explain what was done.

Results

Taiwanese female, Annie

Annie provided eight dialogues. When comparing the emoticon use (number of emoticons divided by number of lines in each dialogue), more (10.6%) were with people within the same culture, and less (5.7%) with people from a different culture.

Looking more closely at the kinds of emoticons Annie used, she said there are differences in the kinds of symbols used with "Foreigners" versus "Chinese" friends. For example, with her Chinese friends she types upper case XD, but foreigners, such as an Australian friend, used lower case xd. There were some other differences. Annie explained: "It seems that once my [foreign] friend asked me what is QQ, and I told him that meant to cry. And also for double A, and double T, my friend didn't understand these meanings." And she commented, "Most of the foreigners will use ☺, and for crying, they will mainly use :`

> A table showing the different kinds of emoticons, and who produced them, would help the reader better understand how this calculation was made.

Annie also saw differences in what kinds of emoticons are used by people from other countries in Asia. She said, "I got one Korean friend, and I don't quite understand the emoticons that he typed, maybe that is special for Koreans." She also commented on a Thai friend, "I think that people in Thailand like to use emoticons, like my best Thailand friend, she uses lots of emoticons that I have never seen before."

Yet what may better explain differences in the frequency and use of emoticons, is the closeness of a relationship. Annie said:

> I will use more emoticons with intimate friends. Maybe I will not talk that causally with friends that I do not know well, and to be more formal, less emoticons are used, or I will use some basic emoticons, like smileys. If I am chatting with my intimate friends, I will use emoticons in an exaggerated way, like many smileys, :)))))))))))))), or an exaggerated XOXOXO. I will not use == to express my speechless with someone I don't know well. I will only use this speechless emoticons or @@, which means to open eyes wide, with good friends.

British Male, Peter

When looking at Peter's eight dialogues, he used more (14.1%) emoticons, and less (12.0%) in dialogues with people of the same culture. He said that the first time he saw "QQ" (meaning to cry), it confused him. But then he figured it out and started to use it when chatting with Chinese friends.

But there was no significant intercultural difference in the variety of emoticons, whether they were with "foreign" or "local" friends. Peter usually used ":)" with friends, ":D" is the second most frequent emoticon he used. What was more important was the nature of the friendship. He used the most emoticons (30.8%) in messages with

Comments expressed by interview participants nicely illustrate how emoticons are interpreted. The final long interview quote nicely sums up the issue. However, it would be better if a summary of the key points followed the quote.

(Continued)

a close, local (Chinese) male friend. But with males who were only "acquaintances," he used fewer emoticons. Overall, he used more emoticons in messages with females. He commented on this in the interview, when he said that "men don't like to express their emotions, but it is acceptable for women to do so." And the emoticons used by males tend to be negative, which is different from the mostly positive ones used by females.

Discussion

People will use more emoticons with locals in their first language. However, we could not draw a conclusion that people will use fewer emoticons when chatting in a foreign language with foreigners. For example, Annie's French friend and Peter's Thai friend also used a high percentage of emoticons, but they also chatted in a foreign language. Thus, the percentage of emoticon may not be a strong indicator to show intercultural differences.

The overall use of emoticons shows that the emoticon use between Chinese and American are indeed different. Both of the interviewee suggested that they were aware of this difference. The differences were not closed by technology and can be seen by the frequency and varieties of emoticon use. Chinese character emoticons like "囧" were only seen in Chinese dialogues. Emoticons like "= =", "@@", "QQ" which are composed of symbol or alphabet were seldom seen in the western counterpart. The only exception was the "-__-" typed by Annie's French friend.

It seems that the ability to type the emoticon is not the issue; instead it is the Western and Eastern classification of emoticons as suggested by Dresner and Herring (2010). However, the reason for this regional expansion usage of emoticon is unknown, so does the ability or choices to adapt those different emoticons. Moreover, Chinese seemed to use more emoticons than Americans; however, it

> This section is shorter than the previous, making the findings appear unbalanced.

> These are interesting examples of "Chinese" emoticons. It would be better if this was presented and explained under Results, and not here in the Discussion.

(Continued)

is also biased to draw a conclusion like this in this small study.

However, there are still some findings correspond with previous ones. Wolf's (2000) study of newsgroup emoticons suggested that emoticons appeared more frequent in females, especially the smiling and laughing ones. In the current study, it seems that females had a higher percentage of emoticon use. Smiling and Laughing were also the most common ones, and were not limited to female. Furthermore, it seems that males used more emoticons with females, and this corresponds with previous studies (Lee, 2003). Besides, corresponding with Derks, Bos and Von Grumbkow's (2008b) study, positive emoticons were widely seen in the previous analysis, and neutral and negative one were used by close friends in conversation. Perhaps the topics of chat messages with close friends were more diverse, and were related to emotional support. This corresponds with Derks, et al.'s (2008b) finding, that people will use more emoticons with close friends.

Ida nicely shows how findings from her study relate to the literature.

Limitations and Future Directions

As this study is just a small study, no great cultural differences can be found. Also, the sampling includes one Taiwanese female and one American male, which is not representative enough. Besides, the dialogues that the researcher got in hand are not equal in length, and the Taiwanese female's dialogues were more than the American counterpart. These are the limitations of the current study.

I suggest that in the future, analysis should focus on the different emoticons used by people in different cultures, to learn how they adapt and interpret differences. Also, there are more than 20 kinds of emoticons appeared in the current study; however, no detailed analysis of them was made. Thus, it may be fruitful to analyse each of the emoticons in the future study, especially the neutral emoticons or the emoticons that can change in different situations. Besides, there are some

(Continued)

situations where the opposite emoticons are used. For example, there is a positive emoticon in a negative sentence. This contradiction is also worth studying in the future. Lastly, as most of the emoticons analyzed in the current studies are Western oriented, it is interesting to know accompanying with the widely learning of Chinese. Will the Chinese emoticons become universal? This is also a question that can be studied in the future.

> This section nicely shows future steps. One unexplored topic, however, is how emoticons may be studied as instances of "language." What theories of language could be used to study this form of communication?

References

Bazarova, N. N., & Yuan, Y. C. (2013). Expertise recognition and influence in intercultural groups: Differences between face-to-face and computer-mediated communication. *Journal of Computer-Mediated Communication*, 18(4), 437–453. doi:10.1111/jcc4.12018

Derks, D., Bos, A. E., & Von Grumbkow, J. (2008a). Emoticons and online message interpretation. *Social Science Computer Review*, 26(3), 379–388. doi:10.1177/0894439307311611

Derks, D., Bos, A. E., & Von Grumbkow, J. (2008b). Emoticons in computer-mediated communication: Social motives and social context. *CyberPsychology & Behavior*, 11(1), 99–101. doi:10.1089/cpb.2007.9926

Dresner, E., & Herring, S. C. (2010). Functions of the nonverbal in CMC: Emoticons and illocutionary force. *Communication Theory*, 20(3), 249–268. doi:10.1111/j.1468-2885.2010.01362.x

Facebook. (2012, December 7). Retrieved from Wikipedia, The Free Encyclopedia: http://en.wikipedia.org/wiki/Facebook

Gao, G., & Ting-Toomey, S. (1998). *Communicating effectively with the Chinese*. Thousand Oaks, CA: Sage.

Inglehart, R., Foa, R., Peterson, C., & Welzel, C. (2008). Development, freedom, and rising happiness: A global perspective (1981–2007). *Perspectives on Psychological Science–* 3(4), 264–285. doi:10.1111/j.1745-6924.2008.00078.x

Lee, C. (2003). *How does instant messaging affect interaction between the genders?* Retrieved September 12, 2012, from Stanford, CA: The Mercury Project for Instant Messaging Studies at Stanford University: http://web.stanford.edu/class/pwr3-25/group2/pdfs/IM_Genders.pdf

Lo, S.-K. (2008). The nonverbal communication functions of emoticons in computer-mediated communication. *CyberPsychology & Behavior*, 11(5), 595–597. doi:10.1089/cpb.2007.0132

Walther, J. B., & D'Addario, K. P. (2001). The impacts of emoticons on message interpretation in computer-mediated communication. *Social Science Computer Review*, 19(3), 324–347. doi:10.1177/089443930101900307

Witmer, D. F., & Katzman, S. L. (1997). On-line smiles: Does gender make a difference in the use of graphic accents? *Journal of Computer-Mediated Communication*, 2(4), 0–0. doi:10.1111/j.1083-6101.1997.tb00192.x

(Continued)

Wolf, A. (2000). Emotional expression online: Gender differences in emoticon use. *CyberPsychology & Behavior*, 3(5), 827–833. doi:10.1089/10949310050191809

Yoo, J. (2007). To smile or not to smile :) Defining the effects of emoticons on relational outcomes. *International Communication Association*, (pp. 1–27). San Francisco, CA. Retrieved from http://citation.allacademic.com/meta/p169395_index.htm

Zakaria, N., & Cogburn, D. (2007). Are we really different or simply unique? Understanding Online intercultural communication behaviors during globally distributed collaboration. *International Communication Association*, (pp. 1–13). San Francisco, CA. Retrieved from http://citation.allacademic.com/meta/p170026_index.html

18 INTERCULTURAL COMMUNICATION AND RELATIONSHIPS

Chia-Fang (Sandy) Hsu, University of Wyoming, USA

Chapter Outline

- Communication Challenges in Intercultural Relationships
  - Perceived Similarities
  - Communication Anxiety and Uncertainty
  - Ethnocentrism and Stereotypes
- Intercultural Relationships
  - Intercultural Friendships
  - Intercultural Dating and Marriages
  - Intercultural Relations at Work
- Conclusion
- Student Paper

The five students smiling and sitting on the university steps originally came from Africa, Asia, and Europe. One exciting aspect of university life is the opportunity to meet and interact with people from different cultures. As Dylan recalled on his first day of college in a freshman seminar, he was surprised to find out his professor originally came from China, and the student sitting next to him was from India. The professor's friendliness eased his anxiety quite a bit while trying to understand her accent. Such experiences are increasingly common among college students across the United States.

Due to the outcome of globalization, it is almost unavoidable to have neighbors, classmates, teachers, friends, and colleagues from a different country or culture than yours. Learning how to communicate and get along with culturally different others has become more important than ever. According to an

Ipsos Public Affairs poll (Pressley & Beall, 2013), nearly two-thirds (60%) of employers globally say intercultural skills, or the ability to work effectively with individuals and organizations from cultural backgrounds different from their own, are very important to their organization. In addition, census data (http://www.census.gov/) indicate that by 2050, there will be no racial or ethnic majority in the US. The likelihood for individuals to form relationships across cultural, ethnic, and/or national boundaries is increasing.

This chapter attempts to address how we can develop better relationships with people from different cultures. First, we will discuss benefits and challenges in forming intercultural relationships. The benefits often involve acquiring new knowledge and skills. The challenges may include overcoming barriers of **perceived similarities, anxiety, uncertainty, ethnocentrism,** and **stereotypes**. Second, we will discuss different types of intercultural relationships, including friendships, love and marriages, and relationships at work.

Intercultural relationships are generally defined as the interaction of people of different cultures (Gudykunst & Mody, 2002; Kim, 2001; Ting-Toomey, 1999). Although culture broadly refers to groups "inclusive of common ethnic, linguistic, racial, and historical backgrounds" (Kim, 2008, p. 360), this chapter focuses on the intercultural relationships of people representing different national and ethnic groups. In this chapter, we will discuss how friendships, romantic relationships, and work relationships are developed and maintained between persons with different nationalities or ethnicities.

There are many benefits of developing relationships with people from different cultures. First, we often learn about the partner's language, cultural patterns, and history. For example, John, married to a Chinese woman, went to China to visit her parents and relatives for the first time. To communicate with his wife's family, he learned to speak some Chinese used in greetings and conversation. Second, we often learn how to do new things, such as new recipes, new games, and new sports. For example, Emily made a Japanese friend while living in the dorm on campus. She learned how to make sushi from her Japanese friend. Third, we acquire new communication skills that may not be valued in our own culture. For example, Yifan learn that communicating clearly about what you want and need is very important while working with his colleagues in the US. But back in his hometown in Taiwan, people are more hesitant to make direct requests because they sound rude and impolite. Finally, building intercultural relationships provides information and experiences that may challenge previously held stereotypes. For example, Jennifer thought Asian students are very quiet and only interact with their own group of people. But the Japanese student sitting next to her is generous, sharing her notes and helps her complete the homework in a research method class.

If we can benefit from making intercultural friends, you may wonder what prevents people from forming relationships with people from another culture. That is, why do some people feel uncomfortable making friends with people from different countries even if such opportunities arise? What are some differences in verbal and nonverbal communication that might lead to misunderstandings between people of different cultures? How can we get along with people from different cultures despite differences? This chapter will attempt to address these questions by reviewing current research findings.

Communication Challenges in Intercultural Relationships

Perceived Similarities

As the ancient proverb says "birds of a feather flock together"; many people spend more time with others who share their own culture, race, and/or ethnicity. We tend to feel most comfortable and safe when we are with people similar to ourselves. It is easy to assume communicating with people from different cultures is difficult because of differences in languages, communication styles, and cultural values. As we form groups based on similarities, we may create barriers and exclude people who are different from us. The "different" others may feel like "outsiders" and hesitate to approach us.

For example, one American student observed that when international students got together speaking in their native language, it seemed that they wanted to be their own kind by excluding people who didn't speak their language. Indeed, researchers have found that both international and host American students tend to hang out with people of the same culture (Rienties, et al., 2012). International students have a tendency to develop relations with co-national students, due to the cultural shock they experience upon coming to America, as well as their eagerness to find support from people with similar cultural backgrounds (Neri & Ville, 2008). Furthermore, American students already have well-established friendship networks (Hendrickson, et al., 2011; Rienties, et al., 2012). International students might think negatively, such as "I am not welcome here." Such negative thoughts make it more difficult for them to initiate new friendships with American students.

Communication Anxiety and Uncertainty

During an intercultural encounter, many individuals experience **anxiety** and related negative affect (Neuliep & Ryan, 1998; Stephan & Stephan, 1985). Individuals may feel awkward and anxious when interacting with culturally different others partly because of communication obstacles (Spencer-Rodgers & McGovern, 2002). For example, they may fear being embarrassed or ridiculed by others while trying to speak in a foreign language (Lu & Hsu, 2008). Or they may experience feelings of impatience and frustration when communicating with non-native speakers of a language (Hsu, 2012). Non-native speakers are generally rated less favorably than native speakers on a wide range of attributes, including competence and trustworthiness (Dovidio & Gluszek, 2012). Although accented speech is sometimes viewed as socially attractive, processing accented speech is cognitively and emotionally taxing (Yook & Albert, 1999).

As a result, the discomfort or anxiety will lead people to avoid or leave the interaction as soon as possible.

Another factor strongly linked to anxiety is **uncertainty**—the inability to predict or explain the behavior of others (Neuliep & Ryan, 1998). Intolerance of uncertainty, where ambiguous situations are perceived as threatening, is regarded as a significant risk factor for generalized anxiety disorder (Boswell, et al., 2013). When the uncertainty associated with an intercultural communication increases, and the interaction partner is viewed as less predictable, anxiety is thought to increase (Duronto, et al., 2005).

Gudykunst (2005) developed the **anxiety uncertainty management theory**, postulating that managing levels of anxiety and uncertainty is central to the effectiveness of intercultural communication. If anxiety and uncertainty are either too high or low, effective communication will not occur. High levels of anxiety and uncertainty are thought to lead to avoidance of communication or aversive communication when avoidance is not possible. In contrast, low levels of anxiety and uncertainty may lead to a lack of motivation to communicate with the culturally different. Consistent with this theory, research findings indicate that anxiety provoked in an intercultural situation decreased willingness to engage in communication (Lin & Rancer, 2003; Logan, et al., 2015). Uncertainty was not directly related to willingness to interact, but reduced the likelihood of interaction indirectly through heightened anxiety levels (Logan, et al., 2015).

Ethnocentrism and Stereotypes

Research reveals that even when communication anxiety and uncertainty are low, people may still not want to engage in intercultural interactions due in part to ethnocentrism (Logan, et al., 2015). **Ethnocentrism** refers to the belief in the superiority of one's own culture. Neuliep (2012) explained that a person's own culture is the center of everything, thus judging others' cultures in reference to one's own. Ethnocentrism may lead to more misinterpretations and negative perceptions toward people of different cultures. It's not surprising that highly ethnocentric individuals are less willing to communicate with culturally different others. In a study on the **stereotypical beliefs** about international students, Spencer-Rodgers (2001) found that American students viewed international students as maladjusted, unsociable, and naïve/confused. Such negative stereotypes may contribute to unfavorable intercultural contacts between international and domestic students. The association of foreign students with difficult language and cultural barriers may also discourage host nationals from developing social relationships with members of the international community.

Moreover, ethnocentrism has been found to predict hostility toward international teaching assistants (ITA) (McCroskey, 2002). US students who have the most prejudiced expectations of internationals' English proficiency were least likely to engage in communication with those internationals (Lindemann, 2002). ITAs most often do possess sufficient language proficiency to accomplish their instructional assignments (Llurda, 2000). Students who hold negative stereotypes of ITAs appear to be exaggerating the incidence of language interference. In a series of studies, Rubin (2002) found students' comprehension of class lectures decreased when they were led to believe they were listening to a non-native speaking teacher (but in fact a native speaker).

In sum, several factors, including perceptions of cultural differences, anxiety and uncertainty experienced during interaction, and ethnocentric beliefs and stereotypes, might make people less willing to communicate and form a relationship with people from different cultures. Despite these challenges in intercultural relations, deep bonds between persons of diverse cultures are becoming more common in today's society than ever. Many people are still able to overcome these obstacles and develop meaningful intercultural relationships (Lee, 2006). In the next section, we discuss the intercultural relationships between friends, couples, and co-workers.

Intercultural Relationships

Intercultural Friendships

Friendship refers to a relationship where individuals voluntarily choose to come to know one another and develop a relationship (Wright & Scanlon, 1991). The developmental process of intercultural friendships is similar to friendships between people of the same cultures—communication gradually becomes broad, frequent, and intimate between friends (Sias & Cahill, 1998). However, intercultural friendships include some unique elements. Lee (2008) classified intercultural friendship development into three stages: initial encounters, interaction, and involvement. During the transition before moving to the interaction stage, partners develop needs or interests to explore each other's culture and clarify some cultural misunderstandings. During the transition to the involvement stage, usually a meaningful event takes place (e.g., providing emotional support, exchanging secrets), which confirms the relational closeness of their friendships. Also, there is the potential influence of a **third cultural context**, when neither partner is from the host culture. For example, the friendship between Gene (French Canadian) and Iris (Macedonian) who are both at the school swimming team is very much influenced by American sports culture.

Sias and colleagues (2008) also observed the influence of third culture on intercultural friends. Although perceived similarity is important to initial interaction, the similarity central to intercultural friendships is cultural similarity. For example, Chinese and Korean students perceived that they were both "Asian." The non-US students also constructed their cultural similarity by defining what they were not—US American. Their "non-American-ness" made them similar to one another, which enhanced the development of their friendships.

Unlike the same-cultural friends, perceived "difference" is important to the development of intercultural friendships (Sias, et al., 2008). The lack of fluency in a common language makes conversation difficult. However, those who overcome the challenges of language differences are able to proceed in developing rich and rewarding friendships. Chen (2002) also suggested that intercultural interactions are less perceptive and responsive than same-cultural interactions. Intercultural friends need explicit message inputs and adaptive verbal strategies to increase involvement and facilitate interaction. Interaction, once started, may lead to greater similarity or convergence of partners' behaviors.

Another factor that might influence intercultural friendships concerns different **expectations** about intimacy or feeling of closeness. For example, research indicates that Americans are more open and receptive to contact with strangers (Barnlund, 1989) and tend to have many friends of low intimacy (Triandis, 1995). One explanation is that Americans value freedom and independence, which makes them prefer broader relationships (Stewart & Bennett, 1991). In contrast, people from other nations, such as Germans, tend to value obligations and commitment, leading to deeper, more intimate relationships. Another explanation is that the meanings attached to the term "friend" differ across cultures. For example, in American English, "friend" includes relationships ranging from casual to long-standing and deeply committed (Matthews, 1986), but in other languages, such as German, it has a narrower connotation – close friend exclusively (Gareis, 2000). Therefore, Americans' friendliness at beginning may be falsely interpreted as a promise of friendship by Germans and other foreigners (Gareis, 2000).

One of the most important factors in the development of close relationships, including intercultural friendships, is **self-disclosure**—the process of revealing and sharing personal information about oneself to another (Barnlund, 1989; Kudo & Simkin, 2003). Kudo and Simkin (2003) found that among Japanese students in Australia, self-disclosure was the third major factor in intercultural friendship formation, next to similarity and frequency of contact.

Similar to the findings on higher intimacy in German friendships, self-disclosure tends to be more intimate among college students in Taiwan than Americans (Hsu 2007). Taiwanese mostly interact with family members and friends and relatively less with strangers; in contrast, social situations in the US often require individuals to have excellent "cocktail party" skills—to enter and leave groups of strangers with ease (Triandis, 1994).

Chen and Nakazawa (2012) also discovered that native-English speakers in Taiwan had significantly broader self-disclosure when talking with strangers in Taiwanese than Taiwanese students in the US talking with American strangers, whereas there were no differences talking with casual or good intercultural friends. Their findings suggest cultural dissimilarities influence early stages of relationship development more than later stages. That is, the effect of cultural backgrounds on self-disclosure depends on the degrees or stages of friendships.

Contrary to the findings on higher intimacy among native students in Taiwan, research reveals lower amount and depth of self-disclosure among Taiwanese and Japanese students in the US than American students (Chen, 1995; Kito, 2005). These inconsistencies could be explained by adaptation issues experienced by international students, such as cultural dissimilarities, English language competency, social difficulties, or discontentment with their American friendships as suggested by previous literature (Kudo & Simkin, 2003; Olaniran, 1996; Zimmermann, 1995).

In sum, while perceived similarity is important to the development of intercultural friendships, cultural dissimilarities influence early stages of relationship development more than later stages. Those who overcome the challenges of language differences and expectations of intimacy in friendships are able to proceed in developing rich and rewarding friendships.

Intercultural Dating and Marriages

With more opportunities for contact between people of different cultures, the probability of dating or marrying someone from different cultures also increases. According to the Pew Research Center (Wang, 2012), about 15% of all newlyweds married someone of a different race or ethnicity in the US, more than double the statistic (6.7%) in 1980. The trend toward more interracial marriages reflects a more open and accepting view of cross-cultural relationships. Thirty-seven percent of Americans said having more people of different races marrying each other was a good thing for society, up from 24% four years earlier (Wang, 2015).

The number of international marriages is also increasing worldwide. According to the Yearbook of Immigration Statistics (Department of Homeland Security, 2013), the number of spouses of US citizens admitted from other nations increased substantially to 273,429 in 2012 from 183,796 in 2003. Likewise, the statistics on immigrant spouses in Spain, Taiwan, and South Korea have also significantly increased from 2000 (SEOUL, 2011). Around one in five marriages in the US (Census Bureau, 2013) as well as in Sweden, Belgium and Austria (SEOUL, 2011) involves a foreign-born spouse.

Despite the growing number of **intercultural marriages**, several studies (Wang, 2012) using government data have found that overall divorce rates are higher for couples who married out than for those who married in. According to Hsu (2001), "Intercultural couples have a greater likelihood of encountering problems because they hold even more diverse values, beliefs, attitudes, and habits than couples who are of similar cultures" (p. 225). The potential for misunderstanding was significantly higher for intercultural couples among college students (Waldman & Rubalcava, 2005). Intercultural marriages may face higher levels of stress and conflict, and have less satisfying marital relationships compared to same-cultural marriages (Fu, et al., 2001).

What are major differences in values and beliefs between the intimate partners of intercultural relationships? Compared with Americans, Chinese tend to view romantic relationships as more serious and long-term, and regard searching for a mate as an obligation to their parents and family (Hsu, 1981). As opposed to the "hookup" culture in America (Paul, et al., 2000), Japanese culture emphasizes looking for a deeper love and appreciates investing in a partner more emotionally (Kanemasa, et al., 2004). Similarly, Asian Americans were less likely to engage in casual sexual behaviors than people with other ethnicities (Feldman, et al., 1999).

There are also some differences in beliefs about love in marriages. Gao (2001) found that American couples rated passion significantly higher than Chinese couples, but there were no differences between the two countries in terms of intimacy and commitment. Similarly, Kline, et al.'s (2008) study indicated that love in marriage was seen as important and unconditional for Americans, while East Asians (i.e., Chinese, Japanese and Koreans) were more likely to report caring as an important belief in marriage. In another study by Kline and colleagues (2012), on good marriage conceptions, US young adults reported love/caring, trust/honesty, fun, and faithfulness more than Asians (Chinese, Indians, and Koreans). On bad marriage conceptions, US adults mentioned abuse, dishonesty, and poor communication more than Asians did.

On the expression of love, both US and East Asian students expressed love to a friend through acts of support, open discussion, and sharing of common experiences, while they expressed love to a spouse through physical intimacy, acts of support, and expressions of love, such as "I love you" and "I miss you" (Kline, et al., 2008). However, for many international respondents and those with strong ethnic identities (e.g., first-generation immigrants), verbal expressions of love do not seem to be widely used in settings of family and friends. For example, Matsunaga and Imahori (2009) found Americans tended to endorse openly affectionate communication within family as ideal, whereas Japanese preferred more tacit and indirect ways of communication. For Germans, the locution "I love you" is traditionally reserved for private disclosure of a formal love, governed by a communal imperative for feelings of meaningfulness (Gareis & Wilkins, 2010). The only exception is in some Latino cultures, where the verbal expression of love seems to be more widespread than in the other cultures (Wilkins & Gareis, 2006). Interestingly, many non-native-speaking or bilingual respondents find it easier to say the words "I love you" in English than the translation in their native language (Wilkins & Gareis, 2006).

Americans not only are more open in expressing love, but also show more appreciation than Chinese. Regardless of relationship types, Americans relied about evenly on verbal and non-verbal methods of expressing appreciation, while Chinese favored non-verbal methods significantly over verbal ones (Bello, et al., 2010). People from collectivistic cultures might see a favor done for them by another as a normal and expected contribution to the group and therefore unremarkable. Appreciation is something that "goes without saying" for many collectivists.

According to Bustamante and colleagues (2011), **gender role expectations**, such as the expectation that women should take primary responsibility for childrearing and household chores, are also one source of conflict for immigrant spouses from traditionally male-dominated cultures (Persian, Mexican, Greek, and Colombian). People with spouses who speak a different native language may also have difficulties connecting with in-law families. For example, as an "outsider" spouse, they frequently experience marginalization from in-laws, particularly when family members converse in their native language rather than accommodate to the language of the in-law (Bustamante, et al., 2011).

Despite the culture-related difficulties, intercultural couples can have enriching interaction in which partners either learn from each other and blend or move beyond cultural differences through appreciation and humor (Heller & Wood, 2007). Some couples said they were able to find humor in their cultural differences and used humor to de-emphasize or "lighten up" differences, while others described being in an intercultural relationship as an opportunity to learn and grow in ways that one would not in a same-culture relationship (Heller & Wood, 2007). Intercultural couples appeared to explore and negotiate differences in ways that strengthened intimacy and led to greater mutual understanding than same-culture couples.

In sum, the major cultural differences between intercultural couples concern their beliefs or expectations about love and marriages, and expression of love and appreciation. Intercultural couples can offset cultural-related challenges through appreciation and humor and form satisfying and long-lasting relationships.

Intercultural Relations at Work

The workforce is undoubtedly becoming more diverse across the globe. According to the Bureau of Labor statistics in 2012, people of color (i.e., Hispanic, African and Asian) made up 36 percent of the labor force in the US (Burns, et al., 2012), while foreign-born workers steadily increased from 10.8 percent in 1996 to 16.1 percent in 2012 (Mosisa, 2013). In Europe, work-related migration increased considerably when mobility and employment restrictions were lifted for citizens of several East European states upon the EU expansion in 2004 and 2007 (Demireva, 2011).

There are both positive and negative sides of working in a culturally diverse environment. On the positive side, employees in two large multinational companies said they preferred current jobs with multi-cultural people than previous work with people of their own ethnicity (Umans, 2008). They explained that working in ethnically homogeneous environments was boring, while in diverse multi-ethnic environments there were more challenges and more vibrant interactions, including communication. In fact, research indicates culturally diverse groups perform better than homogeneous groups in identifying various perspectives on problems and generating alternate solutions (Watson, et al., 1993). **Cultural diversity** creates competitive and innovative management teams that contribute to the success of organizations (Bantel & Jackson, 1989; Hoffman & Hegarty, 1993).

On the negative side, cultural diversity in teams results in interpersonal problems and communication difficulties (Ruhe & Eatman, 1977), consequently leading to misunderstandings, weakened team cohesiveness (Elron, 1997; O'Reilly, et al., 1989), and competitive conflicts (Kirchmeyer & Cohen, 1992; Pelled, et al., 1999). Indeed, many managers are afraid that introducing people who may not agree with each other will hamper productivity. For example, one study (Taylor, 2006) surveyed expatriate manager-host national subordinate dyads in 29 countries and found expatriate managers overly concerned about dissimilarities, which made them likely to discriminate against culturally distant host nationals; in contrast, host national subordinates were more open and willing to invest in intercultural work relationships.

To overcome interpersonal problems associated with cultural diversity, building strong **organizational identity** among employees is the key. For example, higher levels of organizational identification among sales managers and sales representatives predicted subsequent team performance and higher sales turnover in two distinct organizational settings (Wieseke, et al., 2009). Morton and colleagues (2012) reviewed many articles on the importance of shared identity in organizations and concluded people worked and communicated most enthusiastically and effectively with others when they perceived those others shared their social identity and believed that cooperation was in the interest of their in-group.

Sawyer and Ehrlichman (2016) argue that diversity within a workplace presents a challenge to building trust among employees. To build the capacity to work together despite significant differences and disagreements, they recommend using approaches that allow employees to tell their life stories or share feelings on certain controversial issues in order to build common ground quickly. Self-disclosure is important to forming bonds and developing trust in organizations. Another study (Lahti & Valo, 2013) interviewed employees of a Finnish recruitment agency and Polish workers recruited by that agency, and found that not sharing a common language to exchange personal information was identified as the greatest obstacle in developing intercultural relationships at work. Learning a foreign language supports relational growth as it is an extra-organizational activity that the partners engage in together and enables the partners to self-disclose increasingly.

Employees working in multinational companies identified **shared aims and goals** as the primary factor leading to informal and open communication in ethnic diverse workplaces (Umans, 2008). They commented that open discussions were frequent and informal with ease and humor, there were no problems expressing their opinions, conflicts were all work-related and were always resolved by reaching consensus. The study concluded that good and open communication style was the result of cultural diversity, combined with orientation to shared goals and high professionalism.

ICC AND RELATIONSHIPS 165

In sum, the success of an organization depends on good intercultural relationships at work. Cultural diversity can increase employees' job satisfaction and work productivity only if the organizational culture facilitates open communication that leads to trust and shared identity among them.

Conclusion

As our society becomes more and more diverse, our ability to establish intercultural relationships has become more important than ever. Making friends with people of different cultures can open our mind, and helps us acquire new cultural knowledge and communication skills that we may have not learned from same-cultural friends. On the other hand, several communication-related challenges need to be overcome in order to build meaningful relationships. In particular, cultural differences in values, customs, expectations, and expressions might lead to misunderstandings and communication breakdown. Anxiety and uncertainty make us avoid interacting with culturally different others if possible. Moreover, stereotypical beliefs and ethnocentrism make us less willing to communicate with people of different cultures.

This chapter reviewed research findings on the intercultural relationships between friends, couples and co-workers. The literature suggests we are more likely to experience cultural and communication barriers in the early stages of intercultural relationships than later stages. During the initial encounter, we might feel discomfort or awkward due to uncertainty and negative stereotypes toward culturally different others. But once intercultural contact starts, the feeling of discomfort or awkwardness may dissipate gradually with time. Through self-disclosure and open communication, we may discover more similarities and realize that "we are not that different from each other." Establishing common grounds and shared interests allow us appreciating individual differences more and forming deeper trust toward each other. Furthermore, mutual adaptation to each other's culture, such as learning each other's languages, sharing each other's food preferences, and adopting forms of dress and social interactions that are characteristic of each group, should lead to more satisfying relationships and integrating societies.

Key Terms

Anxiety	Anxiety uncertainty management theory	Cultural diversity
Ethnocentrism		Gender role expectations
Intercultural friendship	Expectations	Intercultural relationships
Organizational identity	Intercultural marriage	Self-disclosure
Shared aims and goals	Perceived similarities	Third cultural context
Uncertainty	Stereotypes	Stereotypical beliefs

Activities

1. Think about your past experiences of interacting with people from different ethnic or cultural backgrounds. Answer the following questions, and discuss your answers with other classmates.

   a. What are your overall intercultural experiences? Are they more positive or negative? Describe specific instances that make you feel either positive or negative.

   b. Do you have close intercultural friends? If yes, how do you keep your relationships going? If not, what are your reasons for not forming intercultural friendships?

2. Carry out a separate conversation with an international student and a domestic student whom you have not met before. To make comparisons, the students you talk with should have the same gender. During each conversation, observe his or her nonverbal behaviors, such as facial expressions, eye contact, gestures, vocal cues etc. Answer the following questions, and discuss your answers with other classmates.

   a. What is your first impression of each student? Describe their verbal and nonverbal features that lead to your impression.

   b. Are you more comfortable talking with either student? What makes you feel that way?

3. Interview three students who all have the same ethnicity (e.g. Asian, African etc.), but their ethnicity is different from yours. Before the interview, prepare some questions to ask, such as what they expect most from close friends and family members, how they express love in the family, and show affection to their romantic partner. Answer the following questions, and discuss your answers with other classmates.

   a. What are the common expectations they hold toward their friends and loved ones? Are their expectations different from yours? Identify major expectations that are the same and different from yours.

   b. What are their common ways of expressing love to their friends and loved ones? Are their ways of showing affection different from yours? Identify the similarities and differences with yours.

   c. What factors lead to differences in their expectations and expression of love between you and them? Besides ethnicity, can you think of other factors explaining the differences?

References

Bantel, K. A. & Jackson, S. E. (1989). Top management and innovations in banking: Does the composition of the top team make a difference? *Strategic Management Journal*, 10, 107–24.

Barnlund, D. C. (1989). *Communicative styles of Japanese and Americans: Images and realities*. Belmont, CA: Wadsworth.

Bello, R. S., Brandau-Brown, F. E., Zhang, S., & Ragsdale, J. D. (2010). Verbal and nonverbal methods for expressing appreciation in friendships and romantic relationships: A cross-cultural comparison. *International Journal of Intercultural Relations*, 34, 294–302.

Boswell, J. F., Thompson-Hollands, J., Farchione, T. J., & Barlow, D. H. (2013). Intolerance of uncertainty: a common factor in the treatment of emotional disorders. *Journal of Clinical Psychology*, 69, 630–645. doi:10.1002/jclp.21965.

Burns, C., Barton, K., & Kerby, S. (2012). The state of diversity in today's workforce. Retrieved from, https://www.americanprogress.org/issues/labor/report/2012/07/12/11938/the-state-of-diversity-in-todays-workforce/

Bustamante, R. M., Nelson, J. A., Richard C., Henriksen, Jr., & Monakes, S. (2011). Intercultural couples: Coping with culture-related stressors. *The Family Journal: Counseling and Therapy for Couples and Families*, 19, 154–164.

Census Bureau (2013). Census Bureau reports 21 percent of married-couple households have at least one foreign-born spouse. Retrieved from: http://www.census.gov/newsroom/press-releases/2013/cb13-157.html

Chen, G.-M. (1995). Differences in self-disclosure patterns among Americans versus Chinese: A comparative study. *Journal of Cross-cultural Psychology*, 26, 84–91.

Chen, L. (2002). Communication in intercultural relationships. In W. B. Gudykunst & B. Mody (eds.), *Handbook of international and intercultural communication* (2nd ed., pp. 241–257). Thousand Oaks, CA: Sage.

Chen, Y.-W., & Nakazawa, M. (2012). Measuring patterns of self-disclosure in intercultural friendship: Adjusting differential item functioning using multiple-indicators, multiple-causes models. *Journal of Intercultural Communication Research*, 41, 131–151. doi:10.1080/17475759.2012.670862

Demireva, N. (2011). New migrants in the UK: Employment patterns and occupational attainment. *Journal of Ethnic and Migration Studies*, 37, 637–655.

Department of Homeland Security (2013). *Yearbook of immigration statistics: 2012*. Retrieved from: https://www.dhs.gov/sites/default/files/publications/Yearbook_Immigration_Statistics_2012.pdf

Dovidio, J. F., & Gluszek, A. (2012). Accents, nonverbal behavior, and intergroup bias. In H. Giles (ed.), *The handbook of intergroup communication* (pp. 87–99). New York, NY: Routledge.

Duronto, P. M., Nishida, T., & Nakayama, S. (2005). Uncertainty, anxiety, and avoidance in communication with strangers. *International Journal of Intercultural Relations*, 29, 549–560. doi:10.1016/j.ijintrel.2005.08.003

Elron, E. (1997). Top management teams within multinational corporations: Effects of cultural heterogeneity. *Leadership Quarterly*, 8, 393–412.

Feldman, S. S., Turner, R. A., & Araujo, K. (1999). Interpersonal context as an influence on sexual timetables of youths: Gender and ethnic effects. *Journal of Research on Adolescence*, 9, 25–52.

Fu, X., Tora, J., & Kendall, H. (2001). Marital happiness and interracial marriage: A study in a multi-ethnic community in Hawaii. *Journal of Comparative Family Studies*, 32, 47–60.

Gao, G. (2001). Intimacy, passion, and commitment in Chinese and US American romantic relationships. *International Journal of Intercultural Relations*, 25, 329–342.

Gareis, E. (2000). Intercultural friendship: Five case studies of German students in the USA. *Journal of Intercultural Studies*, 21, 67–91.

Gareis, E., & Wilkins, R. (2010). Love expression in the United States and Germany. *International Journal of Intercultural Relations*, 35, 307–319.

Gudykunst, W. B. (2005). An anxiety/uncertainty management (AUM) theory of effective communication: Making the mesh of the net finer. In W. B. Gudykunst (ed.), *Theorizing about intercultural communication* (pp. 281–322). Thousand Oaks, CA: Sage.

Gudykunst W. B., & Mody, B. (2002). *Handbook of international and intercultural communication*. Thousand Oaks, CA: Sage.

Heller, P. E., & Wood, B. (2007). The influence of religious and ethnic differences on marital intimacy: Intermarriage versus intramarriage. *Journal of Marital and Family Therapy*, 26, 241–252.

Hendrickson, B., Rosen, D., & Aune, R. K. (2011). An analysis of friendship networks, social connectedness, homesickness, and satisfaction levels of international students. *International Journal of Intercultural Relations*, 35, 281–295.

Hoffman, R. C., & Hegarty, W. H. (1993). Top management influence in innovations: Effects of executive characteristics and social culture. *Journal of Management*, 19, 549–574.

Hsu, C.-F. (2007) A cross-cultural comparison of communication orientations between Americans and Taiwanese. *Communication Quarterly*, 55, 359–374.

Hsu, C.-F. (2012). The influence of vocal qualities and confirmation of nonnative English-speaking teachers on student receiver apprehension, affective learning, and cognitive learning. *Communication Education*, 61, 4–16.

Hsu, F. L. (1981). *Americans and Chinese: Passages to differences*. Honolulu, HI: University of Hawaii Press.

Hsu, J. (2001). Marital therapy for intercultural couples. In W. S. Tseng, & J. Streltzer (eds.), *Culture and psychotherapy: A guide to clinical practice* (pp. 225–242). Washington, DC: American Psychiatric Press.

Kanemasa, Y., Taniguchi, J., Daibo, I., & Ishimori, M. (2004). Love styles and romantic love experiences in Japan. *Social Behavior and Personality*, 32, 265–282.

Kim, Y. Y. (2001). *Becoming intercultural: An integrative theory of communication and cross-cultural adaptation*. Thousand Oaks, CA: Sage.

Kim, Y. Y. (2008). Intercultural personhood: Globalization and a way of being. *International Journal of Intercultural Relations*, 32, 359–368.

Kirchmeyer, C., & Cohen, A. (1992). Multicultural groups: their performance and reactions with constructive conflict. *Group & Organization Management*, 2, 153–171.

Kito, M. (2005). Self-disclosure in romantic relationships and friendships among American and Japanese college students. *Journal of Social Psychology*, 145, 127–140.

Kline, S. L., Horton, B., & Zhang, S. (2008). Communicating love: Comparisons between American and East Asian university students. *International Journal of Intercultural Relations*, 32, 200–214.

Kline, S. L., Zhang, S., Manohar, U., Ryu, S., Suzuki, T., & Mustafa, H. (2012). The role of communication and cultural concepts in expectations about marriage: Comparisons between young adults from six countries. *International Journal of Intercultural Relations*, 36, 319–330.

Kudo, K., & Simkin, K. A. (2003). Intercultural friendship formation: The case of Japanese students at an Australian university. *Journal of Intercultural Studies*, 24, 91–114.

Lahti, M., & Valo, M. (2013). The development of intercultural relationships at work: Polish migrant workers in Finland. *Journal of Intercultural Communication, 31*. Retrieved from http://immi.se/intercultural/

Lee, P.-W. (2006). Bridging cultures: Understanding the construction of relational identity in intercultural friendship. *Journal of Intercultural Communication Research, 35*, 3–22. doi:10.1080/17475740600739156

Lee, P.-W. (2008). Stages and transitions of relational identity formation in intercultural friendship: Implications for identity management theory. *Journal of International and Intercultural Communication, 1*, 51–69.

Lin, Y., & Rancer, A. (2003). Ethnocentrism, intercultural communication apprehension, intercultural willingness-to-communicate, and intentions to participate in an intercultural dialogue program: Testing a proposed model. *Communication Research Reports, 20*, 62–72.

Lindemann, S. (2002). Listening with an attitude: A model of native-speaker comprehension of non-native speakers in the United States. *Language in Society, 31*, 419–441.

Llurda, E. (2000). Effects of intelligibility and speaking rate on judgments of non-native speakers' personalities. *International Review of Applied Linguistics, 38*, 288–299.

Logan, S., Steel, Z., & Hunt, C. (2015). Investigating the effect of anxiety, uncertainty and ethnocentrism on willingness to interact in an intercultural communication. *Journal of Cross-Cultural Psychology, 46*, 39–52.

Lu, Y., & Hsu, C.-F. (2008). Willingness to communicate in intercultural interactions between Chinese and Americans, *Journal of Intercultural Communication Research, 37*, 75–88.

Matsunaga, M., & Imahori, T.T. (2009). Profiling family communication standards: A U.S.-Japan comparison. *Communication Research, 36*, 3–31. doi:10.1177/0093650208326459.

Matthews, S.H. (1986). *Friendships through the life course: Oral biographies in old age*. Beverly Hills, CA: Sage.

McCroskey, L.L. (2002). An examination of factors influencing U.S. student perceptions of native and non-native U.S. teacher effectiveness. *Journal of Intercultural Communication Research, 31*, 63–83.

Morton, T.A., Wright, R.G., Peters, K., Reynolds K.J., & Haslam, S.A. (2012). Social identity and the dynamics of organization communication. In H. Giles, S. Reid, & J. Harwood (eds.), *The handbook of intergroup communication* (pp. 319–330). New York, NY: Peter Lang.

Mosisa, A.T. (2013). Foreign-born workers in the U.S. labor force. Retrieved from http://www.bls.gov/spotlight/2013/foreign-born/

Neri, F.V. & Ville, S. (2008). Social capital renewal and the academic performance of international students in Australia. *Journal of Socio-Economics, 37*, 1515–1538.

Neuliep, J.W. (2012). The relationship among intercultural communication apprehension, ethnocentrism, uncertainty reduction, and communication satisfaction during initial intercultural interaction: An extension of anxiety and uncertainty management (AUM) theory. *Journal of Intercultural Communication Research, 41*, 1–16. doi:10.1080/17475759.2011.623239

Neuliep, J.W., & Ryan, D.J. (1998). The influence of intercultural communication apprehension and socio-communicative orientation on uncertainty reduction during initial cross-cultural interaction. *Communication Quarterly, 46*, 88–99.

Olaniran, B. A. (1996). Social skills acquisition: A closer look at foreign students on college campuses and factors influencing their levels of social difficulty in social situations. *Communication Studies*, 47, 72–88.

O'Reilly, C. A. III, Caldwell, D., & Barnett, W. (1989). Work group demography, social integration, and turnover. *Administrative Science Quarterly*, 34, 21–37.

Paul, E., McManus, B., & Hayes, A. (2000). "Hookups": Characteristics and correlates of college students' spontaneous and anonymous sexual experiences. *Journal of Sex Research*, 37, 76–88. doi:10.1080/00224490009552023.

Pelled, L. H., Eisenhardt, K. M., & Xin, K. R. (1999). Exploring the black box: an analysis of work group diversity, conflict, and performance. *Administrative Science Quarterly*, 44, 1–28.

Pressley, D. L., & Beall, J. (2013). Culture at work: The value of intercultural skills in the workplace. https://www.britishcouncil.org/sites/default/files/culture-at-work-report-v2.pdf

Rienties, B., Beausaert, S., Grohnert, T., Niemantsverdriet, S., & Kommers, P. (2012). Understanding academic performance of international students: The role of ethnicity, academic and social integration. *Higher Education*, 63, 685–700.

Rubin, D. L. (2002). Help! My professor (or doctor or boss) doesn't talk English! In J. Martin, T. Nakayama, and L. Flores (eds.), *Readings in intercultural communication: Experiences and contexts* (pp. 127–137). Boston, MA: McGraw Hill.

Ruhe, J., & Eatman, J. (1977). Effects of racial composition on small work groups. *Small Group Behavior*, 8, 479–486.

Sawyer, D., & Ehrlichman, D. (2016). *Stanford Social Innovation Review*, 14, 61–62.

SEOUL (2011, November). International marriage: Herr and madame, señor and mrs. *The Economist*. Retrieved from http://www.economist.com/node/21538103

Sias, P. M., & Cahill, D. J. (1998). From coworkers to friends: The development of peer friendships in the workplace. *Western Journal of Communication*, 62, 273–299.

Sias, P. M., Drzewiecka, J. A., Mears, M., Rhiannon, B., Konomi, Y., Ortega, M., & White, C. (2008). Intercultural friendship development, *Communication Reports*, 21, 1–13. doi:10.1080/08934210701643750.

Spencer-Rodgers, J. (2001). Consensual and individual stereotypic beliefs about international students among American host nationals. *International Journal of Intercultural Relations*, 25, 639–657.

Spencer-Rodgers, J., & McGovern, T. (2002). Attitudes toward the culturally different: The role of intercultural communication barriers, affective responses, consensual stereotypes, and perceived threat. *International Journal of Intercultural Relations*, 26, 609–631

Stephan, W. G., & Stephan, C. W. (1985). Intergroup anxiety. *Journal of Social Issues*, 41, 157–176.

Stewart, E. C., & Bennett, M. J. (1991). *American cultural patterns: A cross-cultural perspective*. Yarmouth, ME: Intercultural Press.

Taylor, M. S. (2006). Leveraging intercultural work relationships: A study of cultural diversity, perceptions and leader-member exchange between expatriate managers and host national subordinates (Unpublished doctoral dissertation). Cornell University, Ithaca, NY. Retrieved from https://ecommons.cornell.edu/handle/1813/3233

Ting-Toomey, S. (1999). *Communicating across cultures*. New York, NY: Guilford Press.

Triandis, H. C. (1994). Major cultural syndromes and emotion. In S. Kitayam & H. R. Markus (eds.), *Emotion and culture* (pp. 185–306). Washington, DC: American Psychological Association.

Triandis, H. C. (1995). *Individualism and collectivism.* Boston, MA: Westview.

Umans, T. (2008). Ethnic identity, power, and communication in top management teams. *Baltic Journal of Management*, 3, 159–173. Retrieved from www.emeraldinsight.com/1746-5265.htm.

Waldman, K., & Rubalcava, L. (2005). Psychotherapy with intercultural couples: A contemporary psychodynamic approach. *American Journal of Psychotherapy*, 59, 227–245.

Wang, W. (2012). The rise of intermarriage rates, characteristics vary by race and gender. Retrieved from http://www.pewsocialtrends.org/2012/02/16/the-rise-of-intermarriage/

Wang, W. (2015). Interracial marriage: Who is "marrying out"? Retrieved from http://www.pewresearch.org/fact-tank/2015/06/12/interracial-marriage-who-is-marrying out/

Watson, W. E., Kumar, K., & Michaelsen, L. K. (1993). Cultural diversity's impact on interaction process and performance: comparing homogeneous and diverse task groups. *Academy of Management Journal*, 36, 590–602.

Wieseke, J., Ahearne, M., Lam, S. K., & van Dick, R. (2009). The role of leaders in internal marketing. *Journal of Marketing*, 73, 123–145.

Wilkins, R., & Gareis, E. (2006). Emotion expression and the locution "I love you": A cross-cultural study. *International Journal of Intercultural Relations*, 30, 51–75.

Wright, P. H., & Scanlon, M. B. (1991). Gender role orientations and friendship: Some attenuation but gender differences abound. *Sex Roles*, 24, 551–566.

Yook, L. E., & Albert, R. D. (1999). Perceptions of international teaching assistants: The interrelatedness of intercultural training, cognition, and emotion. *Communication Education*, 48, 1–17.

Zimmermann, S. (1995). Perceptions of intercultural communication competence and international student adaptation to an American campus. *Communication Education*, 44, 321–335.

Student Paper

Assignment: In this paper, you will choose a topic related to intercultural relationships, such as anxiety management in initial interaction; self-disclosure and intimacy between intercultural friends, relational satisfaction among intercultural couples. You will review articles relevant to your topic, make your own arguments based on the literature review, and pose research questions and/or hypotheses at the end. The paper should consist of three sections: Introduction, literature review and references. In the introduction, you should identify the problem you want to investigate,

(Continued)

specify research objectives and provide a rationale of why your study is important based on the limitations of previous research. The literature review should synthesize the *most relevant* theories and findings of previous research to your topic. Following the literature review, you will pose hypotheses or research questions. That is, the literature review should serve as a rationale to support your hypotheses or research questions. All paper must be typed, double-spaced, and follow the 6th edition of APA Style Manual. You must include a thorough reference list in proper APA format at the end of the paper.

Cassandra Craddock

Ethnocentrism as it Relates to Willingness to Communicate and Animosity

Introduction

Almost every country in the world is dependent on another in our global economy and global networking system. This makes it crucial for people from different ethnic and cultural backgrounds to be able to communicate and work towards a common goal.

> Good comments at beginning.

Ethnocentrism, or the beliefs in the superiority of one's own ethnic group/culture, leads to conflict in a world that relies on intercultural networking. The main problem with ethnocentrism is that it creates rigid attitudes and behaviors that tend to be negative towards the perceived "others" or other cultures (Schwarz & Fritsch, 2014). Past investigations about ethnocentrism have been focused on the idea of consumer ethnocentrism and global marketing. However, few research findings are available about its effect on intercultural communication and increased animosity during verbal communication.

> Cite the original definition and author.

> Define animosity.

Intercultural communication is the way people who do not share a common cultural upbringing communicate (Bennett, 1998). Intercultural verbal

(Continued)

communication is defined as any verbal communication in either the majority or minority language between two people from different countries by the author of this study. Due to the globalization of the world and the interdependence of countries and their economy, intercultural communication is a vital skill for the success and cooperation of all nations. The idea that this can be affected by something as common as ethnocentrism is important and cannot be ignored if we want to improve inter-nation relationships.

Animosity due to ethnocentrism has been heavily researched in the areas of consumer behaviors and media advertising. The motivation behind these studies has often been related to money and how to market to various target audiences. In a study conducted by Lwin, Stanaland and Williams in 2010, the relationship between animosity and ethnocentrism on consumer attitudes led to inconclusive results. Animosity and ethnocentrism were not significantly related to each other. Outside of studies like this, very little has been done in terms of researching verbal communication patterns and how animosity is affected by ethnocentrism during intercultural communication. It is important to understand the relationship between ethnocentrism, intercultural communication and animosity in order to increase successful intercultural communication in the world. Therefore, this study will investigate how ethnocentrism relates to the likelihood of verbal intercultural communication and the level of country-specific animosity among college students.

Literature Review

Intercultural Willingness to Communicate

Intercultural communication is vital in the current age of global networking and the interdependent global economy. The study of this type of communication tries to answer the question: "How

---

Ok to define it yourself. Would be better to find a definition by a scholar.

What skills are involved for successful intercultural communication?

Explain a bit why ethnocentrism impacts intercultural communication.

Approximately how many studies on this subject? Cite scholars to support this.

Good justification on the importance of the study.

(Continued)

> Insert a page number for all direct quotes.

do people understand one another when they do not share a common cultural experience" (Bennett, 1998, p.#). People participating in intercultural communication come from different ethnic and/or cultural backgrounds and their communication can be described as cross-cultural (Kuo, 1999). This type of communication is the opposite of monocultural communication which is defined by Bennett as "similarity based" with "common language, behavior patterns and values" (p.#). These intercultural people have differences due to different cultural upbringing and country of origin (Kuo, 1999).

> What is the definition?

Willingness to communicate has a self-explanatory definition. Kassing (1997) developed the intercultural willingness to communicate scale (IWTC) to measure the likelihood that one would engage in communications with someone from a different culture if the opportunity presented itself. The questions start with "a very close friend" and continue to "someone of a different race than mine" and "talk with someone that speaks English as a second language." Research participants were asked to choose an answer on a scale from 0% to 100%. The evidence from the study by Kassing reported that people with higher scores in IWTC tend to have more friends in foreign countries and that people who would readily communicate with others from their own culture may not interact with the same enthusiasm or consistency with those of other cultures (Kassing, 1997).

> Explain why people may be less enthusiastic interacting with different others? ethnocentrism?

The above research findings suggest that success in intercultural communication relies on ethnic attitudes. An ethnic attitude, according to Aboud and Skerry (1977) in a critical review on the development of ethnic attitudes, is "a predisposition to respond in a favorable or unfavorable manner toward people from different ethnic groups"(p.#) with the basis of this being different race, nationality and religion. Ethnocentrism is prevalent in all cultures and societies in the world. People have a tendency to favor others with same-ethnic backgrounds than "different" others.

> Explain why?

(Continued)

> The idea that one's own culture is superior to another's culture is a popular belief that stems from being brought up within a certain culture. Another equal part of ethnocentrism is the idea that one's own culture is the center of everything, thus judging others' cultures in reference to one's own (Neuliep, 2012). Things that fuel ethnocentrism include patriotism and country-specific animosity (Schwarz & Fritsch, 2014; Neuliep, 2012). Ethnocentrism has become a prevalent topic since the term was introduced to the vocabulary of social scientists by William Sumner in 1906. It encompasses many ideas and is on the same continuum as patriotism (which can be positive when looking from a collectivist perspective). As cited by Neuliep (2012), Sumner (1906) defined ethnocentrism as "the technical name for this view of things in which one's own group is the center of everything, and all others are scaled and rated with reference to it" (p. 13).
>
> In sum, ethnocentrism may lead to more negative perceptions toward people of different cultures. It can be expected that highly ethnocentric individuals are less willing to communicate with the culturally different others. Therefore, the following hypotheses were advanced:
>
> H1: Ethnocentrism is negatively associated with one's willingness to communicate with someone who has a different ethnicity.
>
> H2: Ethnocentrism is negatively associated with one's willingness to communicate with someone who does not speak English as a first language (when their country of origin is the USA).
>
> ### *Country-specific Animosity*
>
> Country-animosity was discussed in the study conducted by Khan and Farhat in 2014. Its definition in the terms of country-specific animosity as it relates to consumers is a "consumer's dislike towards a foreign nation stemming from past and

Margin comments:
- Cite and explain more.
- Any previous research findings to support this? Explain why they may have lower WTC?

present military, political or economic events and is positioned negatively affect the consumers' purchase intention of goods associated with that country" (p. 4). This idea has led to increased efforts by public relations teams of global businesses and increased interest in how to combat these attitudes in people, specifically consumers.

With the growing international nongovernmental organizations (INGOs), the importance of understanding ethnocentrism and its connection to country-specific animosity is relevant (Schwarz & Fritsch, 2014). Ethnocentrism, especially in consumers, has been investigated in relation to animosity towards members of perceived "outgroups" in consumers. INGOs have become very influential in global awareness and they use communication (mass and interpersonal) in order to achieve their goals. INGOs manage their international communication in many different ways and these messages directly reflect on the public relations department for these countries. The ethnocentrism and country-specific animosity levels must be measured and understood by the departments generating the messages for the IGNOs in order for the global society to be successful and the messages to be well received.

> Combine the definition of ethnocentrism here with the earlier section. Cite some of the social scientists' names.

The basic definition of ethnocentrism has been expanded on by other social scientists to include persons holding "rigid attitudes and behaviors toward outgroups" which are biased in favor of the "ingroup" and incorporates people's tendencies to see their cultures' systems of doing things as the only correct way. This behavior can result in prejudice, discrimination, and even ethnic cleansing, which are dangerous to society and the integrated society that many Americans live in. Lwin and colleagues (2010) explain that consumer ethnocentrism focuses on the study of a specific consumer's national/cultural background and ingroup preferences or hostility towards outgroup messages. The effect of ethnocentrism on the bank accounts

(Continued)

of global businesses piqued the interest of marketing departments and has inspired research in studies like those above. Animosity stemmed from ethnocentrism in messages is important to global companies who need to communicate to a variety of audiences from very different cultural backgrounds.

When considering the cultural differences that are prevalent, even within a single country, it is expected that there is a hesitancy in discussing race and cultural differences.

According to Stringer (2015), in an open response to an article in "HR News," there are many factors that stop conversations about race including being politically correct. Stringer recommends three key factors to successful conversations about race: "a willingness to achieve self-awareness and offer self-disclosure; establishing guidelines for safety and trust within conversations; and specific communication skills"(p. 34). In every culture there are levels of abstraction and groups, such as Mexican, US American and pan-national ethnic groups, such as Arab or Zulu demonstrate qualities that "adhere to must member (but not all) members of the culture are very general and the group includes a lot of diversity" (Bennett, 1998, p. #).

With these ideas in mind, it can be expected that the more superior a person thinks his or her country is, the more dislike he or she might have toward other countries. Thus, the following hypothesis was advanced:

H3: Ethnocentrism is positively associated with animosity towards other countries.

> How does this relate to animosity, IWTC and ethnocentrism?

> This paragraph doesn't follow logically. Need to articulate the ideas here. What leads to this conclusion?

References

Aboud, F. E. & Skerry, S., A. (1977). The development of ethnic attitudes: A critical review. McGill University. http://jcc.sagepub.com/content/15/1/3.full.pdf+html

Bennett, M. J. (1998). Intercultural communication: A current perspective. In M. J. Bennett (ed.), *Basic concepts of intercultural communication: Selected readings*. Yarmouth, ME: Intercultural Press.

(Continued)

Kassing, J. W. (1997). Development of the intercultural willingness to communicate scale. *Communication Research Reports, 14,* 399–407.

Khan, B. M., & Farhat, R. (2014). Impact of ethnocentrism and animosity on consumer's attitude towards foreign product: A conceptual framework. *International Journal of Retailing & Rural Business Perspectives, 3,* 793–803. Retrieved from http://search.proquest.com/docview/1648715764?accountid=14793

Kuo, C. (1999, Jun 30). The biggest challenges intercultural couples face: The lessons learned about intercultural communication. *Interrace, 10.* Retrieved from http://search.proquest.com/docview/218809844?accountid=14793

Lwin, M. O., Stanaland, A. S., & Williams, J. D. (2010). American symbolism in intercultural communication: An animosity/ethnocentrism perspective on intergroup relations and consumer attitudes. *Journal of Communication, 60,* 491–514. doi:10.1111/j.1460-2466.2010.01494.x

Neuliep, J. W. (2012). The relationship among intercultural communication apprehension, ethnocentrism, uncertainty reduction, and communication satisfaction during initial intercultural interaction: An extension of anxiety and uncertainty management (AUM) theory. *Journal of Intercultural Communication Research, 41,* 1–16. doi:10.1080/17475759.2011.623239

Schwarz, A., & Fritsch, A. (2014). Communicating on behalf of global civil society: Management and coordination of public relations in international nongovernmental organizations. *Journal of Public Relations Research, 26,* 161–183. doi:10.1080/1062726X.2013.864242

Stringer, D. M. (2009, August). Three factors aid Intercultural communication. *HR Magazine, 54*(8), 10. Retrieved from http://go.galegroup.com/ps/i.do?id=GALE%7CA206692984&v=2.1&u=wylrc_uwyoming&it=r&p=ITOF&asid=e204590ce2eb5355856ebc11befb5017

Sumner, W. G. (1906). *Folkways.* Boston, MA: Ginn.

19 CULTURE AND CONFLICT

Dale Hample and Mengqi Zhan, University of Maryland, USA

Chapter Outline

- Interpersonal Conflict
- Culture
- Culture Can Cause or Contribute to Conflict
- Values
- Face
- Conflict Styles
- Conclusions
- Student Paper

The two business people in the picture above are arguing about how a conflict with clients should be resolved. The company they work for is trying to sign a deal with a client, but the client requested some contingencies for the deal. The Asian woman thinks that they should satisfy the client's needs and make compromises, while the Caucasian man thinks that they should prioritize their own company's needs. The two persons are both well-educated and trained, and are good at their jobs. However, because of their different cultural backgrounds, their values and beliefs differ, which leads to their different perspectives on conflict resolution.

As we work through these sorts of possibilities in this chapter, we will do a few things. We will begin by noticing that interpersonal conflicts are unavoidable, and in fact give spice and flavor to our social lives. Then we will go on to explore what culture has to do with the nature of our conflicts: how it shapes our conflicts, how it affects our values and self-definitions, and how it even influences our understandings of how to proceed with disagreements. We end the chapter with a summary of advice and an example of how one student combined the ideas of culture and conflict to analyze a particular historical episode.

People have **agency**. That is, they are agents: they can do things by themselves, they can think and say individualized things, and they construct, reconstruct, and reinforce their personal lives. No government or prison has ever been so repressive as to erase human agency completely (excepting executions, of course). But the freedom that agency implies also gives rise to the inherency of conflict between people. I am sometimes in the way of your agency, and you are sometimes in the way of mine. If we were all identical in every respect—values, thoughts, intentions, capabilities, full commitment to the other's needs—it wouldn't be at all clear that any of us had agency because we would all act indistinguishably. Difference should be celebrated, even if it is inconvenient in the moment.

Interpersonal Conflict

Interpersonal conflict is therefore inevitable due to the complexity and interdependence of people's everyday lives. You may have had the experience of having a fight with your romantic partner over small issues such as where to have dinner, or larger issues such as how to proceed in your careers. These discussions can be quietly reasonable or emotionally explosive. For many people, "conflict" means hostile exchanges instigated by some disagreement.

However, interpersonal conflict researchers have a different view. **Interpersonal conflict** is the social experience and expression of differences in values, beliefs, goals, desires, or expectations, and it induces "complex, goal-directed reactions" that lead to costs and benefits for the parties involved (Barki & Hartwick, 2004; Van de Vliert, 2013, p. 4). Among the implications of this understanding are that non-confrontational disagreements are also interpersonal conflicts (e.g., cooperative business negotiations) and that conflicts are fundamentally social. Furthermore, some conflicts do not find public expression, either because they are internal to one person (e.g., feeling conflicted between family loyalty and an attractive out-of-town job offer) or because a person can feel upset about what someone else has said or done, but swallow the annoyance and never act it out.

Notice, too, the importance of goals and values in this understanding of conflict. Facts do not speak for themselves—they are interpreted, and people (re)construct them mentally as part of a process of **sense-making**. Suppose, for example, a woman was passed over for promotion in favor of a somewhat less qualified man. Applying modern feminist values, one person could say this was objectionable, sexist, and dishonest. Applying traditional values characteristic of societies that are not yet very committed to women's equality, another person could say the supervisor was doing the woman a kindness, helping her make more room in her life for her family. We can easily imagine a conflictive exchange between these two people, but it would be due to different values, different goals, and different sense-making; it would not be due to different objective circumstances.

Conflict results from some general elements of human experience, and it is very rare for only one of these to be involved in causing a disagreement to appear. Some people have *personal* characteristics that lead them to seek conflict, to enjoy it, to persist in it beyond reason, and other people are the opposite. Sometimes a person might find him/herself in a *situation* that requires self-defense or that suggests an opportunity to make real progress on some valued matter. Many of these situationally dominated cases of conflict involve one person just *responding* to strong demands made by another person or a particular event. We say in those cases that someone was simply drawn into a disagreement, and acted as almost anyone would. In other situation-influenced matters, a person might disagree *opportunistically*, which we might characterize critically as "picking a fight." For example, a spouse who is generally unhappy about the distribution of household responsibilities might notice a towel on the table and seize on that as a chance to start what he or she probably understands will be a conversation that the other spouse is going to find unwelcome. This last example helps illustrate again that values color the facts to control the sense-making that is critical in realizing you have a conflict with someone.

Culture

These personal and situational conflict elements come from somewhere. Our personalities are strongly influenced by our genetic inheritance from our parents (Bouchard, 2004), but biology is not destiny. Just as a right-handed person who suffers an injury can eventually become left-handed, an aggressive child can learn manners and a child whom biology aimed at being passive can learn to be assertive. This shaping of children and adults occurs in the home, at school, in church, in the workplace, on the sports field, and in many other particular places, all of which we can summarize as being contained and defined within a culture. In our lives, we find these structural systems already waiting for us, making certain demands and creating certain affordances.

A **culture** is something that stands outside an individual person. Culture surrounds each of us with religion, language, an economic organization, an approach to government and collective life, and values about self and others. People come into contact with this system of meanings in predictable ways: through the family, through a school system, through organized religion, through the media, and through direct contact with grandmothers, stores, clinics, voting places, police officers, and so forth. Not everyone participates enthusiastically in his or her culture, but it is not quite right to think that we choose our own culture. The circumstances of our birth and upbringing restrict our choices and limit the inventory of interpretations available to us and the values we can apply. Sometimes a person completely escapes his or her home culture, but this is rare. Most of us remain small town Christian, cosmopolitan Parisian, or quiet Buddhist in some measure throughout our lives.

Culture is passed on (reproduced) in two main ways (Buss, 1995). It is *evoked* or *transmitted*. All humans share a considerable amount of genetic similarity and capability. One set of circumstances may evoke (or call out) one element of people's possibilities and another set might call out the opposite. In spite of otherwise distinct cultural contexts, it would not be surprising to learn African farmers have a lot of values in common with South American farmers, or residents of Beijing act similarly in some respects to New Yorkers, or Buddhist monks have outlooks familiar in some ways to rabbis. The immediate environment (farm, city, poverty, wealth, etc.) evokes (that is, energizes and cements) certain of our human possibilities. If the key environmental characteristics are enduring, people in that environment will continue to have similar characteristics for many generations (Nisbett, 2003). Culture can also be transmitted in the home or other common settings. Children are taught to repeat proverbs, the same little stories are told to most young children living in a particular region, children's cooperative/competitive play is regulated and supervised, and televised cartoons deliver various messages about courage, friendship, and whether good triumphs over evil. These are all methods of cultural transmission.

Conflict is inherent to human social life, so it is unsurprising that cultures address the nature of difference and competition. Everyone has the ability to disagree and to participate in conflict. One's culture sketches out rules about when open disagreement is allowed, and how a person should act. However, because cultures are complex and because everyone is not a perfect instantiation of any culture, it is important to recognize that a specific thing that seems to be generally true of a culture does not always express itself within individuals. Here is a cautionary story of that kind of mistake.

For quite a long time, scholars thought Chinese and other Asian people were argument-averse, that is, that they would insist on avoiding confrontation rather than engaging in open disagreement that might settle the problem. A common reference given to support this judgment was Becker (1986). Becker analyzed the various philosophical and religious traditions in China and Japan, and noticed they prize harmony and discourage contradiction. These elements do point away from explicit conflict. However, he did not take the next step, to examine how and whether these principles appeared in individuals' lives. He simply drew conclusions about China as a whole and Japan as a whole. On the face of it, it would be odd to find a human culture that could not deal with disagreement openly, because as we noticed earlier, disagreement is inherent to our natural agency. Several of us did look at individuals (Xie, et al., 2015). We surveyed Chinese undergraduates on some measures for which we already had US data, and we found the Chinese respondents were actually *less* avoidant of interpersonal arguing than the US undergraduates, and the Chinese also had a *greater* predisposition to engage in arguing than the Americans did. This doesn't invalidate Becker's understanding of Chinese and Japanese culture generally (Morris, et al., 1998, even have some individual-level evidence to support it), but it does serve as a warning against expecting one cultural feature to control individual views and behavior. Harmony is valorized in those cultures, but apparently so too are self-expression, justified assertiveness, and competition. These other values might be especially growing in importance for younger generations of Chinese, and the Xie et al. study used undergraduate data. It is well to study a culture broadly, examining religions, vocabularies, and child-rearing practices, but it is a delicate step to transfer those findings to the level of interpersonal actions. Something generally characteristic of millions of people living together might not precisely describe particular individuals. A "culture" doesn't really do anything—only people do. Culture's influence is always and only expressed in individual lives.

This point is evident when one notices a sharp division in how scholars study intercultural matters. Some characterize a culture or nation generally, noting its prevalent values. An especially prominent exponent of this approach is Hofstede (2001; Hofstede, et al., 2010). He typifies nations on various orientations that we will discuss momentarily, and is able to show which nations are similar and which have quite different world views. The other point of view, sharply distinct, concentrates on individuals and how (whether) their surrounding culture is expressed in them. For example, Hofstede distinguishes between collectivist and individualist nations, but this second group of scholars does not assume that everyone in a collectivist culture has actually taken on collectivist values. So individuals are studied independent of their nationality, and values that seem to be culturally relevant are assessed more or less as personality traits (e.g., Singelis, 1984). Fortunately, the variables get renamed in this process, so that Hofstede's collectivism is conceptually related to Singelis' interdependent self-construal, for instance, and Hofstede's individualism is similar to Singelis' independent self-construal.

Nations and people are different logical types, and something true at one level of analysis may not be true at the other. In fact, research identifying individual nations with particular values has been criticized for not being able to explain why people within a culture vary from one another on their world views (Hong, et al., 2000). For example, whether people from collectivist cultures have interdependent self-construals is an empirical question, not one that can be answered with arguments from definition. Findings about nations do not dictate what will be the findings about people, and therefore the relevant literature has to be read carefully, respecting this distinction. Readers should also note that "nation" and "culture" do not cover the same ground, because many nations contain distinct cultures. The study of the cultures within one country is sometimes called **intergroup communication**.

We need to make one final point about studying culture, and this is a simple one. Scholarship can be **cross-cultural** or **intercultural**. Cross-cultural studies collect data in two (or more) cultures and compare them. The respondents from the first culture do not meet or interact with the people in the other culture. In intercultural research, the participants do meet and interact. So the researcher might induce Germans to argue with Koreans, and examine how (whether) their distinct cultural backgrounds affect their interaction. The second sort of study is far less common because it is complicated to bring together people from different cultures.

Culture Can Cause or Contribute to Conflict

Conflicts are about topics: What should be the price of the materials we wish to import? Are you aware that you have insulted my wife? Who should type our group paper and who should do the library research? Normally it is the topic—and people's conflicting goals on that matter—that directly instigate the conflict. The disagreement can take on an additional layer of complication if the participants come from different cultures and therefore have different understandings of how people should act while disagreeing. In addition, they might also have unanticipated value orientations to the matter at issue (e.g., how important are a woman's feelings, anyway?). This could make the conflict more difficult to navigate, and we would say culture contributed to the participants' challenges.

Sometimes, however, cultural differences themselves can stimulate a conflict. People with different cultural backgrounds usually speak different native languages, so in intercultural interactions one or more parties need to accommodate to others and communicate in their second language. The use of non-native languages and possible accents associated with them may lead to miscommunication or prejudice, which could result in conflicts.

People raised in different cultures may also have different belief structures based on their life experiences and training (Pelled, et al., 1999). They might have different assumptions and understandings of the world, and expectations about the future events. Therefore, people may have quite divergent views about some simple event. For no reason apparent to a person from one culture, a member of another culture might become upset about a casual remark and express an objection.

As we mentioned earlier, many nations contain distinct cultural groupings. According to **social identity theory** (Tajfel, 1982; Tajfel & Turner, 1979), people can take part of their personal identity from their group membership. For example, one person may consider his identity as an African-American is very important, and another person may feel her group identity as a French Muslim is at the core of her person. People naturally tend to look out at the world from the viewpoint of the group they feel they live within. Therefore, they may have biased perceptions about in-group favoritism and out-group discrimination when they are interacting with someone from another group. These effects are particularly marked when a person's identity group is a minority within the larger society. Generally speaking, when people from different cultural backgrounds interact with each other, they could all tend to feel out-group discrimination in regard to the other people. This may lead to interpersonal conflicts about many things that would otherwise be seen as minor and not worth the energy needed for explicit conflict.

Values

We can point to several things that distinguish one culture from another—its most common language, its religious traditions, its form of government, how its families work—but a particularly important (and summarizing) difference is its values. **Values** are abstract psychological elements that attach meaning and valence to various things or patterns. For example, you probably value honesty over dishonesty and equality over racism. You can apply a value to a very specific case, such as a person who stole a waitress's tip, but the value itself is an entirely general way of orienting to the world and making evaluative sense of it. The thing or pattern to which the value applies is a fact perceived to be part of an immediate situation (e.g., the theft). You apply the value to fill out your understanding of the circumstances. We have already commented at several points that values can direct a person's position and behavior in a conflict. Conflicts are only about things you care about, and your values summarize your carings.

Cultures could show value differences in two ways. First, the cultures could actually have distinct values. One culture might prize aggression and the other might have no such orientation at all. When international conflicts cause nationalistic rhetoric to heat up, one can sometimes hear claims such as those. The other way cultures could differ is they could have the same values, but in a different priority order. So two cultures could both be committed to the idea that equality is good, but it might be the first or second most important value for one culture and the fifteenth for the other. In complex situations, it is common for several values to be potentially relevant, and each participant will trade values off for one another. A person's value hierarchy will be a guide as to what values will be subordinated to others (Perelman & Olbrechts-Tyteca, 1969).

Research shows neither thing happens starkly, at least at the most abstract level. Certainly there are cultural value differences, but these are differences of degree, not of kind. Schwartz and Bardi (2001) collected data from more than 50 nations and summarized how students and teachers rated each value. The researchers were able to summarize various nations' priority orderings for ten values they had earlier found to be present throughout the world (e.g., Schwartz, 1994). Those values are power, achievement, hedonism, stimulation, self-direction, universalism, benevolence, tradition, conformity, and security. They obtained something like a world priority average by summing across the ratings from all the nations, and then compared each nation's priority set to that of the rest of the world. Some nations (Finland, Israel, and Italy, for example) were very typical and correlated with the world average at $r = .90$ or more. Other countries' value priorities did not match the rest of the world as well, with $r = .75$ or less (India, Philippines, Ghana, Nigeria, Fiji, and Uganda). All the nations' correspondences are in the Schwartz and Bardi paper (p. 277), and you might wish to browse their results for nations you are interested in. Some nations are more immediately aligned with one another than others in terms of their value hierarchies, but even the lower correlations indicate a recognizable level of similarity.

These results are quite encouraging for the prospect of conversation and constructive conflict with people from another culture, but it must be admitted that these values are pretty general. The top-ranked value, for instance, is benevolence, which is defined as "preservation and enhancement of the welfare of people with whom one is in frequent personal contact (helpful, honest, forgiving, loyal, responsible)" (Schartz & Bardi, 2001, p. 270). It is frankly pretty difficult to imagine a functional human society that largely lacked these kinds of social commitments, but those ideas can still be implemented in quite different ways. For instance, suppose you were coaching a youth baseball team and had a player who couldn't field a ground ball. Would it be kinder just to be encouraging ("Great try!"), or kinder to teach the child how to do things differently ("No, start with your glove on the ground")? In English, we navigate among some proverbs that might be difficult to reconcile. On one hand, we have "kill him with kindness" and "sometimes you have to be cruel to be kind." On the other hand, you may have been taught "kind words are worth much and they cost little" or Mark Twain's "kindness is the language which the deaf can hear and the blind can see." So how should you *kindly* coach your third baseman? Would you be surprised if a coach from another culture made a different choice? And would you be surprised if the third baseman's parent got upset with one or the other of you and started a conflict? Yet you are all committed to kindness.

Two other large-scale culture-and-value projects aimed at somewhat more specific values. One of these is Hofstede's (2001; Hofstede, et al., 2010). **Hofstede** was hired by IBM to analyze an enormous amount of survey data the company had already collected from IBM employees around the world. We are all fortunate that after some sophisticated data analysis, Hofstede was able to find some value orientations that distinguished the workers in one nation from those in others.

He began with his discovery of four such dimensions, but over the years has added two more. **Power distance** reflects the degree to which people who are more or less at the bottom of a nation's social and economic system are accepting of the differences in power that separate them from people on top. Those nations that are culturally committed to clear social hierarchies have high scores on this measure. **Individualism versus collectivism** refers to whether people are expected to be self-determining or whether they are entitled to depend on their networks (e.g., family, friends, coworkers) to help them. Loyalty to your groups is part of the bargain for collectivist societies. **Masculinity versus femininity** now seems somewhat misnamed. Hofstede had a notion as to what characterized masculinity (achievement, ambition, heroism, assertiveness) and he measured whether nations were more oriented to that pole or what he regarded as its opposite (nurturing, caring, modest). **Uncertainty avoidance** indicates whether a culture is comfortable with uncertainty, ambivalence, and ambiguity. Does a culture try to control the future to make it more predictable or just let it unfold? **Long-term orientation versus short-term normative orientation** contrasts cultures that prize tradition (the short-term norms) with those that are willing to create changes in a pragmatic effort to change the future (long-term orientation). Finally, Hofstede studied

indulgence versus restraint. This contrasts instant gratification societies with those that restrain indulgence with norms and regulations. All these are a matter of degree.

Readers might enjoy poking around Hofstede's website (http://geert-hofstede.com/countries.html) and comparing various nations to one another. Here are a few examples. The United States is low on power distance, very high on individualism, high on masculinity, a little low on uncertainty avoidance, low on long-term orientation (i.e., the US is more characterized by short-term norms), and is high on indulgence. China shows some points of contrast with the US. China is high on power distance, low on individualism (i.e., highly collectivist), high on masculinity, low on uncertainty avoidance, high on long-term orientation, and low on indulgence. Finland is low on power distance, high on individualism, low on masculinity (i.e., high on femininity), high on uncertainty avoidance, low on long-term orientation (i.e., characterized by its embrace of traditional norms), and high on indulgence.

How might these differences be manifest in a face-to-face conflict? Suppose a representative from a small company in one nation were negotiating with a high-ranking manager from a giant global firm in another country. If the negotiators were from China and the US, the Chinese negotiator would naturally expect deference to the larger company's manager and accept some condescension from that person to the other. The American would expect both negotiators to treat one another as equals. If both negotiators conducted themselves ordinarily (based on their national scores), the American would see the Chinese businessperson as either arrogant or passive (depending on which company was which) and the Chinese person would be offended by the American's arrogant disregard for the obvious social and power differences between the two of them. Now suppose the negotiators were from China and Finland. The Chinese are highly "masculine"—that is, they are aggressive, they strive, and they insist on victory. The Finnish manager, if he or she is typical of Finland, is more cooperative and conciliatory. In this contest (for that is how the Chinese negotiator would see it), the Chinese businessperson has a clear advantage, because all the impulse for cooperation and compromise will be coming from the Finnish negotiator. You can work out many more possibilities like these by choosing a pair of nations and thinking through how those different orientations would express themselves during an interpersonal disagreement.

Besides Hofstede's work, another large project that studies values across the world is the **World Values Survey** (WVS; e.g., Inglehart & Baker, 2000; Welzel, 2013). They have survey data from about 100 nations, and for many of them the WVS also has chronological data because they began the work in the early 1980s and repeat their surveys every few years. This project deals with a different set of values than either Hofstede or Schwartz, although their huge survey includes items relevant to those other value theories. The two main value systems for WVS are **secular** and **emancipative.** Each of these is a term that covers more specific matters. Secular values include defiance, disbelief, relativism, and skepticism, all of which are measured separately and then combined into the summarizing "secular" construct. Highly secular societies permit defiance, skepticism, and similar resistance to tradition, especially religious tradition. They do not reflexively respect the establishment as much as the establishment might wish. Emancipative subscales include autonomy, equality, choice, and voice. Highly emancipative cultures believe in personal autonomy and equality, and grant voice to many kinds of people.

Although their website is somewhat more difficult to use than Hofstede's, the WVS also has an online interface that allows people to compare nations to one another (http://www.worldvaluessurvey.org/WVSOnline.jsp; the overall values for secular and emancipative values are almost at the end of the variable lists). Let us examine the scores for Mexico, Japan, and Sweden. For secular values (on a 0 to 1 scale, using the data from 2010–2014), Mexico is lowest (.34), compared to Japan (.44) and Sweden (.50). Emancipative values result in the same order: Mexico (.46) is lowest again, followed by Japan (.51), and Sweden (.72) is highest.

To see how these differences might play out in an intercultural conflict, imagine the same negotiating scenario that we used before, but this time add in the complication that one of the negotiators is a man in his 60s and the other is a woman in her 30s. In traditional societies, the woman would be supposed to defer to the man but in a secular emancipatory society she would have voice and autonomy, and would be entitled to insist on equality. A Mexican negotiator (either male or female) would likely have some trouble with this more modern view of women, while the Swede would perhaps be most comfortable. It is hard to have a comfortable or constructive conflict if the man thinks the woman is trying to act "above her station" or if the woman thinks the man is being an unevolved male sexist. It is just as hard to disagree productively if the woman is being asked to be more aggressive than her culture permits, or if the man is supposed to be more egalitarian than he has been raised to think is right. The internal psychological conflicts implied in these strains can easily restrict the levels of trust, respect, and cooperation that the negotiators find to be natural.

Face

Across the globe, all people have "face" needs (Brown & Levinson, 1987). In fact, face has two elements, **positive face** and **negative face**. Positive face refers to the identity you want to project affirmatively. Most college students want to be seen as friendly and intelligent. But members of a drug ring might want to be regarded as ruthless and unsympathetic. Regardless, positive face is what you try to project, and you need other people to cooperate with you in the projection. Negative face is your wish to be unimpeded in thought or action. Telling someone what to do or think is an imposition on his or her negative face. Even though both kinds of face needs seem to be pan-cultural, once we move to the details they can become culture-specific. A modern Englishwoman might want to be regarded as independent and capable, but a traditional Asian woman might want to project modesty and quiet acquiescence. Both are positive faces, but what is a desired identity can obviously be influenced by a person's culture or group affiliations (Kim, 2013). All cultures studied to date have something like a social contract about face: I will cooperate in doing facework for you, and I expect you to help me, too. Obviously, face needs are a subset of one's values, but they are especially important because they are involved in every interaction.

Face negotiation theory, developed primarily by Ting-Toomey (e.g., Ting-Toomey & Kurogi, 1998) uses the concept of face to explain the underlying mechanisms of conflict behaviors in different cultures and to understand how people can act competently during intercultural conflicts. In this theory, the concept of **face** refers to "a claimed sense of favorable social self-worth that a person wants others to have of her or him" (Ting-Toomey & Kurogi, 1998, p. 187). In other words, face is the positive self-image one wants to retain during social episodes, what we identified as positive face just above. Face is thus a precious social identity resource that can be threatened, maintained, damaged, or negotiated (Ting-Toomey, 2005). When people's identity claims are challenged or identity expectancy is violated, they are said to be engaged in a face-threatening episode. For example, if you are called on by your professor but you do not have the answer ready, you probably will feel your internalized identity of "a good student" is challenged in that social episode, and you may feel embarrassed. In this scenario, you are experiencing face loss, and you may want to restore your face. "Facework" refers to the communicative behaviors (i.e., both verbal and non-verbal) people use to manage face-threatening scenarios, such as restoring or upholding their face or that of the other person. In the classroom scenario described above, you might make an excuse to repair your face and the professor might accept it publicly. Face negotiation theory assumes people negotiate and maintain face regardless of the culture they come from, but their cultural values (e.g., individualism–collectivism, emancipatory, and so forth), together with individual, relational, and situational factors, influence their use of facework behaviors in conflict situations (Ting-Toomey, 2005).

Some of this research has been informed by Hofstede's analyses of values as well as the person-based parallels to his national values (e.g., Singelis, 1984). Specifically, face negotiation theory predicts people from collectivistic cultures with large power distance tend to express a greater degree of other-face and mutual-face concern, and thus are more likely to use avoidance or conflict styles that respect the other person's goals. In contrast, people from individualistic cultures with small power distance tend to focus on self-face maintenance concerns, and thus are more likely to use dominating conflict styles. Parallel predictions were made when the researchers moved from the level of culture to that of the person. On the individual level, similar predictions were made, except that independent self-construal and interdependent self-construal were used as the individual-level counterparts of individualism–collectivism.

Those predictions are generally supported by empirical tests of the model (Ting-Toomey, 2005). For example, researchers found cultural individualism–collectivism influences conflict styles partially through self- or other-face concern. Specifically, they found self-face concern predicted dominating style, and other-face concern predicted avoiding and integrating conflict styles (Oetzel, et al., 2001; Oetzel & Ting-Toomey, 2003). In individualistic cultures, conflict was addressed in a fairly direct manner, but in collectivistic cultures, because of the high levels of other-face concerns, smoothing over or avoidance of conflict were preferred tactics for conflict management (Oetzel, et al., 2001).

Conflict Styles

The work just reported involved what are called "**conflict styles**," and so it is time to consider this idea in more detail. It originated with Blake and Mouton (1964), who created a **dual concern model** of the concerns of conflict participants. The dual concerns were concern for people and concern for task. (Later writers have sometimes changed this vocabulary, as well as the labels for tactics.) These concerns are independent, so that a person can be high or low on one of them, both of them, or moderate on both. People high on concern for people but low on concern for task prefer a *smoothing* (or obliging) conflict style, in which they essentially concede. People low on concern for people and also low on concern for task prefer a *withdrawing* (avoiding) style. They have no real commitment to the conflict, so they just leave if they can. People with low concern for people and high concern for task prefer a *forcing* (competing, dominating) style, in which they press hard to "win" the conflict. People moderate on both concerns try to *compromise*, or work things out in the middle. Finally, people high on both concerns want to use a *problem-solving* (integrating, collaborative) style, in which they are equally committed to their own and other's goals. This last style is held to be the ideal on normative grounds. Sometimes a few other conflict tactics are added to the list, such as appeal to a third party for help, emotional expression (relying on one's intuitive feelings), and neglect (essentially verbal aggressiveness aimed at the other person). And sometimes various conflict styles are combined into one term.

A great deal of research, mainly cross-cultural, has attempted to connect cultural orientations to preferred conflict styles. Common hypotheses are that collectivist cultures will prefer avoidant styles and that independent cultures will prefer aggressive tactics. Let us give you a sample of the findings from across the world.

Holt and DeVore (2005) have summarized 36 separate studies into one meta-analysis. They found that, throughout the globe, cultures classified as highly independent preferred forcing tactics (i.e., domination, competitiveness). Clearly collectivistic cultures, in contrast, showed preferences for withdrawal, compromise, and problem-solving. (Holt and DeVore also found continuing distinctions between men and women, but that would take us off track in this chapter.) These are as close to defensible generalizations as the literature presently permits. Nonetheless, we should point out that when cultural values were measured at the individual level rather than the national level, a study of people from 31 countries but all residing in the US (Cai & Fink, 2002) found individualists were the ones who preferred to avoid (but the collectivists were still higher on compromising and integrating). Forcing was unrelated to individualism/collectivism. So reading the literature hoping for a simple answer to questions about how different cultures prefer to manage conflicts is very challenging.

A number of studies have focused on conflict styles in East Asia, and compared them to the preferences of various nations. T.-Y. Kim, et al. (2007) asked employees in China, Japan, and Korea to say how they would conduct themselves in a conflict with their superior. When all three nations were compared, it was Korea and Japan that stood out. The Koreans notably preferred to compromise, whereas the Japanese were highest on obliging and clearly low on forcing. Both the obliging and avoiding conflict styles were associated with high power distance and high collectivism, across all three nations. The forcing style was predicted by a high level of concern for own face. Brew and Cairns (2004) compared East Asians with Australians, all working in Singapore or Bangkok. They found the East Asians (compared to the Australians) would mainly be indirect with their superiors, but this did not carry over to their conflicts with subordinates. Besides the rank of the other conflict person, these researchers found another situational feature, urgency, also affected tactic preference. Both cultural groups became more direct when the matter was urgent. S.-Y. Kim, et al. (2013) compared Korean and American workers. They discovered the US respondents were comparatively more likely to want to compete or avoid, whereas the Koreans preferred collaboration or obliging. The Morris et al. (1998) study mentioned earlier in this chapter compared MBA students in the US, China, the Philippines, and India, reporting Chinese were more avoidant and the US students were more competitive. Boonsathorn (2007) studied the employees of multinational corporations in Thailand. She compared the Thai employees to those from the US. The Thais were more avoidant and obliging than the Americans. Interestingly, she found that the more time the Thai employees had spent in other countries, the less they preferred those two passive tactics, and the more forcing they wanted to be.

We found two studies relevant to the Middle East. Khakimova, et al. (2012) compared Arab and US men, all of whom were studying in the US. Compared to the Americans, Arabs more strongly preferred integrating, avoiding, and appealing for the assistance of third parties. The US men had higher scores for emotional expression (trusting their intuition), forcing, and neglect (which amounts to being verbally aggressive toward the other person). For both samples, having an independent orientation led to preference for the forcing style, and being interdependent was associated with obliging and appeals to a third party. Cingöz-Ulu and Lalonde (2007) compared Canadian and Turkish students, both studying in their home countries. Readers should notice Turkey stands between Europe and the Middle East in several respects, not merely geographically. At any rate, compared to Canadians, the Turks preferred to avoid or postpone conflicts and to take a persuasive stance. The Canadians had more interest in compromise, appeals to a third party, and deference to the other person.

To say these results do not congeal into straightforward conclusions would be an understatement, but there are even some further problems. First of all, whole continents seem to be quite under-researched. We did not find research on South/Central America or Africa, for instance, much less the various specific cultures to be found within those continents. Furthermore, the nation-to-nation comparisons we have are inconsistent. Comparison to the US is fairly common, but we do not think the instrumentation or sampling in this body of studies is consistent enough to assume relationships are going to be transitive: that is, if country A prefers some conflict style more than country B, and country B prefers it more than country C, we would not accept the conclusion that country A will be higher than country C without direct evidence.

A second issue is people's reports about their preferred conflict styles do not necessarily indicate how they will actually behave in a conflict. There are two reasons for this. First, people have self-serving biases in their reports of how they would act. Long ago, Thomas and Kilmann (1975) documented people's choices for conflict styles were highly correlated with the styles' social desirability. Most people can see that problem-solving (integrating) is the "nicest" style, so they honestly over-estimate the degree to which they use it.

The second reason for mistrusting the preference–behavior link for conflict tactics is perhaps related to the first. When conflict style preferences are held up against actual conflict behavior, the correspondences can be modest. A study in the Netherlands (de Dreu, et al., 2001) asked students to rate the strategies they had just used in a negotiation task. They also rated each other. And third, independent observers went through the actual negotiations to code what had actually happened. Results were not encouraging. The self and other ratings were mostly correlated in the range of $r = .20$ to $.40$. This was also the approximate range of agreement between self-ratings and observers' codings. These correlations are not high enough to justify the assumption that anyone (or any national group) that says they prefer one style actually enact it (although the correlations are high enough to make that one's best guess).

An explanation for this mismatch between preference and behavior is that the conflict style preferences are just that—preferences. When one is anticipating a conflict or reporting on conflicts in general, these preferences are reflective of what the person intends to do. But once the conflict begins, things become concrete, another person is there disagreeing with you, you may have to defend yourself, you have face needs to manage, and so forth. The de Dreu, et al. (2001) study discovered that in the actual negotiations, people tended to reciprocate the other person's moves, with correlations ranging from $r = .15$ to $.40$. Another line of research supports this sort of result. People who take conflict personally want to avoid it. But when they find themselves engaged in a conflict, they are just as aggressive as people who do not personalize disagreement (summaries are in Hample, 1999, and Hample & Cionea, 2010).

In fact, the best predictor of someone's aggressiveness was not his/her degree of personalization, but was the aggressiveness of the other person. Similarly, Stamp, et al. (1992) found one person's defensiveness was highly correlated ($r = .60$) with his or her partner's defensiveness.

Research on conflict styles is perhaps the most common way of directly approaching the connections between culture and conflict management. Because of the number of cultures in the world, the number of ways of assessing culture, and even the number of conflict style instruments, we are some years away from any steady conclusions about how people from one culture disagree compared to people from another culture. Research that examines actual conflict behavior certainly needs to be done more often. And we need intercultural studies, not merely cross-cultural ones.

Conclusions

So what advice can we offer to someone on the verge of an intercultural conflict interaction? We simply cannot justify advising someone to adopt a particular tactical orientation or to act in a specific way. These things are going to depend on what happens between the two of you. You need to pursue your own goals effectively. If the interaction is part of a long-term relationship with the other party, it makes practical sense to make sure that you are protecting the other party's interests as well. We do have some other general suggestions as well.

First, interrogate yourself. As an individual, and as a member of your own culture and special groups, you have certain values and particular priorities among them. You may have been able to take these for granted throughout your life among similar others. You should also realize what your own face needs are, and how these compare in importance to the actual issues that create the conflict's topic.

Second, try to anticipate the values and face needs of the other person. You can start with the various websites we have suggested, but you will do well to supplement these findings with some reading or conversation about the general culture you will be encountering: What are its religious traditions? How competitive are its economic relationships? How are interpersonal relationships conducted? What sort of government has emerged from this society? How do families work? What expectations are there about proper roles for men and women, natives and foreigners, and people of different ages? Perhaps you can find research about their generally preferred conflict styles. Take this information as no more than a background briefing, whose details are hypotheses but not conclusions. Your preparation should tell you what to be alert for, but it will not tell you what is going to happen in a concrete interaction with a particular individual. If you have social opportunities with the other party prior to the conflict, try to find out these sorts of things about him or her without being pushy about it. Share your own background, too.

When engaged in conflict with a person from another culture, your most important communication attributes will probably be self-awareness, perceptiveness, and flexibility. You should be prepared to register and think about behaviors and remarks that strike you as a bit odd and be careful about over-interpreting other behaviors as being normal in your terms. You should be able to modify your own preferred behavior, perhaps learning to be either more forceful or more cooperative than is natural to you. If you are fortunate, the other person will be trying to do all this as well.

Key Terms

Agency
Conflict styles
Dual concern model
Face
Hofstede
Individualism v. collectivism
Intercultural
Interpersonal conflict
Long-term orientation v. short-term normative orientation
Positive and negative face
Secular v. emancipative values
Social identity theory
Values

Conflict
Cross-cultural
Culture
Evoked and transmitted culture
Face negotiation theory
Independence v. interdependence
Indulgence v. restraint
Intergroup communication
Masculinity v. femininity

Power distance
Sense-making
Uncertainty avoidance
World values survey

Activities

1. Outside of class, each student will interview someone from a culture different from the local majority culture and ask that person to share an experience of a conflict with members of another culture. After each student summarizes his/her interview in class, discuss the following questions: a) Which cultures did the people come from? What have researchers found about values of these cultures? b) Did cultural differences contribute to the conflict? If so, how? For example, was it because of language barriers and misunderstandings, or cultural values differences, or something else? c) Now that you have learned about cultural differences and conflict, how would you have handled the conflict?
2. Form groups based on students' cultural backgrounds (or if the class is culturally homogenous, students can interview someone from another culture outside of class to get information). Each group needs to prepare a skit showing how conflicts are resolved typically within the other cultures. It is okay if the skit exaggerates a little bit, but avoid negative stereotypes. The conflicts could be from different situations, such as between romantic partners, colleagues, citizens and officials, or friends. Perform the skit in front of the class. The rest of the class should discuss the following questions: a) Which conflict management style did participants illustrate in the skit?

Is it consistent with relevant research findings? b) Did the skit's conflict management style differ from the majority culture of the class? Did any difference illustrate cultural value differences? If so, how?

3. Form small groups of people who have some knowledge (or just interest) about social life in particular cultures. Use one or more of the websites mentioned in the chapter to look up average values for the different cultures mentioned in your group. The websites are http://geert-hofstede.com/countries.html and http://www.worldvaluessurvey.org/WVSOnline.jsp. You can also look at the tables in the Schwartz and Bardi (2001) article or some similar resource. Ask group members how those value scores might affect how people deal with disagreements or contradictory impulses in the different cultures.

4. Form groups of people who are all from the same nation. Ask them what other groups they identify with, but within the nation. These might be social groups, religions, demographic identities (e.g., woman, second generation immigrant), political affiliations, or anything else that a person supplies as representing part of his or her personal identity. Discuss how those different values might express themselves on these sorts of conflict topics: (a) a teenager who disobeys parents; (b) a young person being questioned by a police officer; (c) two co-workers trying to decide who needs to work extra hours during a busy week. Be tolerant and non-judgmental as you work through this material with one another.

References

Barki, H., & Hartwick, J. (2004). Conceptualizing the construct of interpersonal conflict. *International Journal of Conflict Management, 15*, 216–244.

Becker, C.B. (1986). Reasons for the lack of argument and debate in the Far East. *International Journal of Intercultural Relations, 10*, 75–92.

Blake, R.R., & Mouton, J.S. (1964). *The managerial grid*. Houston, TX: Gulf.

Boonsathorn, W. (2007). Understanding conflict management styles of Thais and Americans in multinational corporations in Thailand. *International Journal of Conflict Management, 18*, 196–221.

Bouchard, T.J., Jr. (2004). Genetic influence on human psychological traits: A survey. *Current Directions in Psychological Science, 13*, 148–151.

Brew, F.P., & Cairns, D.R. (2004). Do culture or situational constraints determine choice of direct or indirect styles in intercultural workplace conflicts? *International Journal of Intercultural Relations, 28*, 331–352.

Brown, P., & Levinson, S.C. (1987). *Politeness: Some universals in language usage*. Cambridge, UK: Cambridge University Press.

Buss, D.M. (1995). Evolutionary psychology: A new paradigm. *Psychological Inquiry, 6*, 1–30.

Cai, D., & Fink, E. (2002). Conflict style differences between individualists and collectivists. *Communication Monographs, 69*, 67–87.

Cingöz-Ulu, B., & Lalonde, R.N. (2007). The role of culture and relational context in interpersonal conflict: Do Turks and Canadians use different conflict management strategies? *International Journal of Intercultural Relations, 31*, 443–458.

de Dreu, C. K. W., Evers, A., Beersma, B., Kluwer, E. S., & Nauta, A. (2001). A theory-based measure of conflict management strategies in the workplace. *Journal of Organizational Behavior, 22,* 645–668.

Hample, D. (1999). The life space of personalized conflicts. *Communication Yearbook, 22,* 171–208.

Hample, D., & Cionea, I. A. (2010). Taking conflict personally and its connections with aggressiveness. In T. A. Avtgis & A. S. Rancer (eds.), *Arguments, aggression, and conflict: New directions in theory and research* (pp. 372–387). New York, NY: Routledge, Taylor, and Francis.

Hofstede, G. (2001). *Culture's consequences: Comparing values, behaviors, institutions and organizations across nations.* 2nd. ed. Thousand Oaks, CA: Sage.

Hofstede, G., Hofstede, G. J., & Minkov, M. (2010). *Cultures and organizations: Software of the mind: Intercultural cooperation and its importance for survival.* 3rd. ed. New York, NY: McGraw Hill.

Holt, J. L., & DeVore, C. J. (2005). Culture, gender, organizational role, and styles of conflict resolution: A meta-analysis. *International Journal of Intercultural Relations, 298,* 165–196.

Hong, Y.-Y., Morris, M. W., Chiu, C.-Y., & Benet-Martinez, V. (2000). Multicultural minds: A dynamic constructive approach to culture and cognition. *American Psychologist, 55,* 709–720.

Inglehart, R., & Baker, W. E. (2000). Modernization, cultural change, and the persistence of traditional values. *American Sociological Review, 65,* 19–51.

Khakimova, L., Zhang, Y. B., & Hall, J. A. (2012). Conflict management styles: The role of ethnic identity and self-construal among young male Arabs and Americans. *Journal of Intercultural Communication Research, 41,* 37–57.

Kim, S.-Y., Kim, J., & Lim, T.-S. (2013). The impact of relational holism on conflict management styles in colleagueship and friendship: A cross-cultural study. *Studies in Communication Sciences, 13,* 58–66.

Kim, T.-Y., Wang, C., Kondo, M., & Kim, T.-H. (2007). Conflict management styles: The differences among the Chinese, Japanese and Koreans. *International Journal of Conflict Management, 18,* 23–41.

Kim, Y. Y. (2013). The identity factor in intercultural conflict. In J. G. Oetzel, & S. Ting-Toomey (eds.), *The SAGE handbook of conflict communication: Integrating theory, research, and practice* (pp. 639–660). Los Angeles, CA: Sage.

Morris, M. W., Williams, K. Y., Leung, K., Larrick, R., Mendoza, M. T., Bhatnagar, D., Li, J., Kondo, M., Luo, J.-L. & Hu, J. C. (1998). Conflict management style: Accounting for cross-national differences. *Journal of International Business Studies, 29,* 729–747.

Nisbett, R. E. (2003). *The geography of thought.* New York, NY: Free Press.

Oetzel, J., Ting-Toomey, S., Masumoto, T., Yokochi, Y., Pan, X., Takai, J., & Wilcox, R. (2001). Face and facework in conflict: A cross-cultural comparison of China, Germany, Japan, and the United States. *Communication Monographs, 68,* 235–258.

Oetzel, J. G., & Ting-Toomey, S. (2003). Face concerns in interpersonal conflict a cross-cultural empirical test of the face negotiation theory. *Communication Research, 30,* 599–624.

Pelled, L. H., Eisenhardt, K. M., & Xin, K. R. (1999). Exploring the black box: An analysis of work group diversity, conflict, and performance. *Administrative Science Quarterly, 44,* 1–28.

Perelman, C., & Olbrechts-Tyteca, L. (1969). *The new rhetoric: A treatise on argumentation.* J. Wilkinson & P. Weaver (trans.). Notre Dame, IN: University of Notre Dame Press.

Schwartz, S. H. (1994). Are there universal aspects in the structure and contents of human values? *Journal of Social Issues*, *50*, 19–45.

Schwartz, S. H., & Bardi, A. (2001). Value hierarchies across cultures: Taking a similarities perspective. *Journal of Cross-Cultural Psychology*, *32*, 268–290.

Singelis, T. M. (1984). The measurement of independent and interdependent self-construals. *Personality and Social Psychology Bulletin*, *20*, 580–591.

Stamp, G. H., Vangelisti, A. L., & Daly, J. A. (1992). The creation of defensiveness in social interaction. *Communication Quarterly*, *40*, 177–190.

Thomas, K. W., & Kilmann, R. H. (1975). The social desirability variable in organizational research: An alternative explanation for reported findings. *Academy of Management Journal*, *18*, 741–752.

Tajfel, H. (1982). Social psychology of intergroup relations. *Annual Review of Psychology*, *33*, 1–39.

Tajfel, H., & Turner, J. C. (1979). An integrative theory of intergroup conflict. *The Social Psychology of Intergroup Relations*, *33*(47), 74.

Ting-Toomey, S. (2005). The matrix of face: An updated face-negotiation theory. In W. B. Gudykunst (ed.), *Theorizing about intercultural communication* (pp. 71–92). Los Angeles CA: Sage.

Ting-Toomey, S., & Kurogi, A. (1998). Facework competence in intercultural conflict: An updated face-negotiation theory. *International Journal of Intercultural Relations*, *22*, 187–225.

Van de Vliert, E. (2013). *Complex interpersonal conflict behaviour: Theoretical frontiers*. New York, NY: Psychology Press.

Welzel, C. (2013). *Freedom rising: Human empowerment and the quest for emancipation*. New York, NY: Cambridge University Press.

Xie, Y., Hample, D., & Wang, X. (2015). A cross-cultural analysis of argument predispositions in China: Argumentativeness, verbal aggressiveness, argument frames, and personalization of conflict. *Argumentation*, *29*, 265–284.

Student Paper

Assignment: This paper will challenge you to apply your knowledge about intercultural communication to an intercultural exchange. In regards to both the communication and your analysis this assignment is very open and can be made into whatever you are interested in writing about. While the communication does need to be INTERcultural (involving members of at least two different groups) it is up to you to decide which cultures you are interested in, as well as the medium of the communication (e.g. interpersonal, small group, social, business, text, Skype, media, vicarious, participatory, observation, etc.). Regarding your analysis it is also up to you to decide on a topic, as there are many ways to analyze the same

(Continued)

> topic. For example, three students might look at the same intercultural argument. One might ask how each of the members of the argument embraced or rejected their cultural traits and how this was responsible for the argument. A second might ask what accommodations or shifts in communication occurred as a result of the intercultural nature of the conversation. A third might ask what the ultimate outcome of the intercultural communication would be for the participants involved.
>
> Julianna Himelstein
>
> ### Ehime Maru Apology Incident
>
> It is important to recognize that each culture has a unique way of dealing with apologizes due to differences in cultural roots and norms. Japan and America contrast in many sectors of apology behavior and norms, which is important to realize when facing sensitive situations such as the Ehime Maru incident. Japans collectivist ideals encompass concepts of amae, sunao and facework which is a salient component as to why they expected the United States to react differently when the Ehime Maru incident occurred. It is important to be aware of differences in apology behaviors and norms between cultures in order to be culturally sensitive and avoid negative cultural interactions such as the Ehime Maru incident, which could have been handled in alternative ways to appear more genuine to the Japanese.
>
> On Feburary 9, 2001 the USS Greenville a United States Navy nuclear submarine was executing a rapid surfacing maneuver off the coast of Oahu, Hawaii. In the process it rammed and sunk a Japanese fishery training vessel, three crew members and six student trainees and instructors from Uwajima fishery school perished due to the negligence (Martin). United States officials under Bush promptly apologized to Japanese officials and the affected families following the accident but this did not suffice as a genuine apology from the Japanese perspective.

Margin note: This is an interesting point. Different cultural orientations on individualism/collectivism render the Japanese people and American people distinct expectations of how conflicts should be handled. Japan scored 46 on the individualism dimension while the United States scored 91 (Hofstede, 2015). Comparatively speaking, Japanese people concerns interpersonal relationship harmony more than the US people. http://geert-hofstede.com/japan.html

(Continued)

> The Japanese wanted a direct apology from Scott Waddle the Navy commander, but did not receive one until a month after the incident when Waddle traveled to Hawaii to personally apologize to the affected families. Waddle was found guilty of dereliction of duty by the Navy Board of Inquiry and was reprimanded and compelled to retire, which he did (Battistella). The United States gave Japan millions of dollars for costs that included compensation to victims' families, costs to raise the Ehime Maru from the sea and the costs to build a replacement Ehime Maru. A lack of information on Japanese apology behaviors and norms caused a negative cultural interaction and should be analyzed in-depth in order to avoid similar situations in the future.
>
> The Japanese believe that Commander Waddle did not apologize adequately, the apology was important to Japan especially due to their sensitivity to inequality and vulnerability in its relations with the United States at the time (Battistella). The Japanese considered the apology from Commander Waddle to be most important but Commander Waddle's legal counsel required him to remain silent for several weeks about the incident which strained the ability for him to apologize effectively. During this time President George Bush spoke about the instance and stated "I know this fine American patriot feels terrible about what took place. It was a terrible accident and like any good commander he's taking the heat" (Battistella). When President Bush said this the Japanese were outraged by Bush's praise of Commander Waddle at a time when the subject was so sensitive for the Japanese. The Japanese noted that if this situation occurred the other way around the Japanese captain would have been taken to trial and punished based off of their strong belief in Amae.
>
> Amae in the Japanese culture is a trustful dependence that two or more parties have towards each other, it is a concept used to describe behavior when you desire to be loved, taken care of, and choose to depend on another entity somewhat

The political context or situation plays an important role when handling international conflicts at the country level.

Japanese culture values politeness, as Ruth Benedict pointed out. Therefore, an apology that comes from Commander Waddle, who was the person that made the mistake, was considered to be a very important ritual to maintain harmonious international relationships here.

Why Amae of Japanese culture is appropriate to be applied here? We probably need more background information about why there was a trustful and dependent relationship between Japan and U.S. at that time.	submissively (Sugimoto). This was the relationship that the US and Japan had at the time, the U.S. was the more powerful ally and was expected to look out for Japans interests and rights. The Japanese willingness to accept the U.S. as a protector included the faith the Japanese had bestowed in the U.S. military, that it could be trusted and would not harm those under its protection. The Ehime Maru incident caused Japan to feel betrayed by the United States. Amae principles infer the stronger partner is the one to show sincere remorse, which did not happen correctly through apology after the incident and further strained relations. Although, Americas willingness to undertake the costs of compensating the perished ones family, retrieving valuables underwater from the Ehime Maru, building a replacement Ehime Maru and bringing it to the ocean's surface all helped the United States creditability. When attempting to reconstruct how the apology should have occurred it is important to understand the differences in Japans collectivist society compared to the United States individualist society.
Feel betrayed by Japan's "indulgent dependence" on the U.S.	
Why those behaviors were not considered to be "sincere remorse"?	
Apology is especially important for existing interpersonal relationships in Japan.	Collectivist and individualists societies differ in many aspects including their apology behaviors and norms. Sugimoto gathered the cultural norms of American and Japanese culture based on both nations conduct manuals, which describe when and how to apologize in situations. In the apology sector of the Japanese etiquette manual apology situations involving individuals who know each other are emphasized, which makes sense due to their emphasis on collectivist culture and the in-group. Those immersed in Japanese culture are expected to apologize for more people including those in their in-group and in more situations than their American counterparts (Sugimoto). American conduct manuals contain more information about apologizes exchanged in public places with strangers (Sugimoto). It is stated that in the United States individuals are most likely to apologize for their own mistakes, with the exception of apologizing for a spouse or child (Sugimoto).
In the Ehime Maru incident, is it because Japan considers the U.S. as a dependable and trustworthy partner, so that Japan expected U.S. to apologize sincerely?	

(Continued)

> Although these cultures contrast in many ways, it is important to notice that individuals in both cultures are expected to apologize for the misconduct of themselves and those who belong to their close knit group.
>
> A Japanese speaker is always expected to apologize in awkward situations, regardless of the degree of actual responsibly (Battistella). This contrasts with the American apology style which is seen as individualistic and connected to personal responsibility. Shared responsibility might be a reason why the Ehime Maru victims apologized to the civilians of Hawaii and America:
>
>> "The resentment with regard to this accident is definitely not something which is aimed toward the people of Hawaii and the American people. We are worried that, in our grief, we might have been somewhat thoughtless and impolite. If that is the case, we would like to deeply apologize".
>>
>> (Battistella)
>
> After the Ehime Maru incident occurred, Japan had many apology expectations that the United States did not adhere to which caused the United States to appear as insensitive. Unlike Japans emphasis on sunao the United States stresses sincerity when apologizing, this difference is important when deciding how post-Ehime Maru should have been handled.
>
> A major difference that can be observed in Japanese and American perspectives pertaining to apologies can be seen with the Japanese emphasis on sunao and the American emphasis on sincerity. Sunao is translated into English as "gentle, submissive, compliant, yielding, meek, obedient, pliable and with good grace", with submission to order and return to harmonious relationship as the most distinct quality (Sugimoto). Sincerity can be defined as suggesting purity and truthfulness or lack of vicious intent, with wholeheartedness as the most distinct quality.

Side note 1: This illustrates the Japanese tendency to apologize for something that they are responsible for at a very low level.

Side note 2: What are the expectations? And how do the expectations illustrate characteristics of Japanese culture?

What is relational truthfulness?	(Continued)
	In Sunao, relational truthfulness is cherished more than the physical reality and evidence Americans cherish when apologizing. Sunao emphasizes the relational truthfulness in which the apologizer stays true to the recipient's perception of the situation (Sugimoto). This can cause the apologizer to describe damage as more severe than they think in order to submit to the victims perception of the damage, or beg for forgiveness to humble themselves. Sunao explains why a father of a deceased member of the Ehime Maru said "if you're a man you should fall to your knees and ask for our pardon", when talking about Waddle's delayed apology (Battistella). On the other hand, U.S. Americans are expected to be truthful to what they know about the situation or present themselves in that way, in order for an apology to be considered sincere. To Americans, sunao can be seen as insincere since it includes adjusting to the victim's feelings and perceptions, sometimes against one's own belief or physical reality (Sugimoto). These differences in apologetic ideals can cause intercultural confusion, which is why it is important for individuals and government institutions to learn how to be culturally sensitive. Sunao stresses the importance of "saving face" among the Japanese culture.
In Japanese eyes, falling to knees and asking for pardon is the appropriate way to apologize in such context. The apologizer should show submissiveness, obedience, and focus on remedying relationship in order to apologize sincerely.	
Americans, as individualists, value objective truth.	
Japanese people expected Americans to focus on restoring the relationships between them, which may include understand their emotions and apologize in order to save face of Japanese people. Japanese people are high in other concern, so that they expected American people to be so as well. American people are high in own concern, so that they focused more on saving	In societies like Japan group membership is the primary source of identity and status, and considerable value is placed on maintaining harmonious relationships with others. To the Japanese face involves "honor, appearance of propriety, presence and the impact on others" (Samovar, Porter, McDaniel, Roy). Pertaining to sunao, it is safer for Japanese apologizers to emphasize their violation of the victim in order to help save face which ultimately ends in the harmonious relationship being restored (Sugimoto). American individualistic culture is more concerned with maintaining one's own face and place more value on candid communication where harmonious interpersonal relationships can become secondary. Apologizing between cultures is a difficult task so it

(Continued)

is important to be aware of these differences when handling situations such as the Ehime Maru.

Looking back on how the United States handled the Ehime Maru incident it is salient that different measures could have been implemented in order to insure the situation was dealt with more sensitively. The United States should have taken into account the Japanese principle of amae and understood that the Japanese invested trust in the United States and the Ehime Maru incident was fragile and needed to be treated as such. When the highly advanced USS Greenville collided with the fishery vessel it did not make sense how something so negligent happened in the first place and once it did happen the United States being the stronger ally was expected to show remorse but without Captain Waddles apology the state level apology was not complete.

Waddle was unable to have a face-to-face apology with the families of the perished directly after the incident based off of his attorney's wishes. Instead he released a statement that was viewed as insincere and impersonal by the Japanese. Waddle's attorneys' most important job should have been to make sure Waddle met with the families in person before the situation got out of hand. Instead Waddle had to wait a month and eventually went against his attorneys wishes in order to apologize to the families of perished (Martin). Although the Japanese were appreciative of the promptness, sincerity and frequency that the United States officials showed when apologizing to the Japanese officials, citizens, and families of the perished, Waddles apology was seen as the most important (Martin).

Acquiring a better understanding for Japans collectivist ideals that encompass concepts of amae, sunao and face is important in realizing why they expected the United States to react differently when the Ehime Maru incident occurred. It is also important in understanding how these situations should be dealt with in the future. Different cultures commonly differ strongly in their basic value dimensions, in order to ensure intercultural

---

Margin comments:

their own face by emphasizing the commander is a good person, and put less focus on restoring the relationship with Japan.

Japanese people value interpersonal relationship, so that it is important for Japanese people to have the personal apology from the commander.

This is a good paper, and I was very interested to read it. There are some minor issues with this paper (mostly writing and grammar related), and in the end I want to buy your argument that things would have been better if people only knew how to apologize to others in a way that seemed sincere and appropriate to them. HOWEVER, there is a counter-argument that kept coming to me as I read this. Which is worse, the fallout over not apologizing correctly, or the fallout for actually apologizing correctly. How would a Japanese style apology impact the captain's court case, perceptions of G.W. Bush, etc.? There are things like Obama bowing to the Japanese emperor that create reactions amongst the American populace that are as predictable as the dissatisfaction of the Japanese if he did not bow. In the end I think it would have made an extraordinary paper to really tackle this question from both sides and ultimately ask if communication competence on the public stage is ultimately much differently conceived of than the interpersonal variety we tended to learn about this semester.

(Continued)

communication competence and avoid negative cultural interactions such as the Ehime Maru it is important to examine each cultures unique traits.

References

Battistella, Edwin L. "Come to Japan and Apologize." *Sorry about That the Language of Public Apology*. New York, NY: Oxford UP, 2014. 136–41. Print.

"Divers Find Body from Sub Collision." *Chicago Tribune*. N.p., 18 Oct. 2001. Web. 25 Nov. 2014. <http%3A%2F%2Farticles.chicagotribune.com%2F2001-10-18%2Fnews%2F0110180331_1_ehime-maru-rapid-surfacing-drill-hirotaka-segawa>.

Martin, Curtis H. "The Sinking of the Ehime Maru: The Interaction of Culture, Security Interests and Domestic Politics in an Alliance Crisis." *Japanese Journal of Political Science* 5.2 (2004): 287–307. Print.

Samovar, Larry A., Richard E. Porter, Edwin R. McDaniel, and Carolyn S. Roy. *Communication between Cultures*. 8th ed. Belmont, CA: Wadsworth Pub., 1991. Print.

Sugimoto, Naomi. "Norms of Apology Depicted in U.S. American and Japanese Literature on Manners and Etiquette." *International Journal of Intercultural Relations* 22.3 (1998): 251–76. Print.

20 INTERCULTURAL COMMUNICATION AND ADAPTATION

Gina Barker, Liberty University, USA

Chapter Outline

- Cultural Orientation and Culture Shock
  - Culture Shock Theories and Models
  - Stress–Adaptation–Growth Dynamic
- One-Dimensional Perspectives on Acculturation
- Two-Dimensional Perspectives on Acculturation
  - Assimilation
  - Separation
  - Marginalization
- Integration
- Complex Perspectives on Acculturation
  - Acculturation Differences across Cultural Domains
  - Selective Acculturation Processes
- Third-Culture Perspectives
  - Third-Culture Building
  - Third-Culture Individuals
- Chapter Summary
- Student Paper

The woman above appears to be fairly comfortable in her environment. She may have stopped for her usual coffee and muffin on her way to college in the neighborhood where she grew up with her expatriate parents. She may be meeting the study partners she teamed up with during her semester abroad. She may be waiting on her husband-to-be, for whom she moved to a country that is still foreign to her. Culturally, she may be very similar to the people in the background. Or she may act similarly and speak the local language without an accent, while maintaining core values that are quite different from theirs. To learn more about her intercultural adaptation, we would need to get to know her.

Intercultural adaptation is the context in which intercultural communication takes place. In other words, when studying intercultural adaptation, you consider the circumstances and the reasons why people interact with others who are culturally different. A student of mine asked me once, "Who adapts to whom?" My answer was, "Whoever wants the relationship more or has the least power in the relationship." That said, in order for intercultural communication to be effective and intercultural relationships to be meaningful, both parties have to adapt to one another to a greater or lesser extent.

When visiting a foreign country as a tourist, as a student enrolled in a short-term study-abroad program, or while on an international business trip, your adaptation is usually pretty minimal. You ensure you will be able to get by linguistically, you familiarize yourself with the most significant cross-cultural differences by reading a travel guide or talking to people who have been there, and you educate yourself on behavioral norms and laws that would be uncomfortable to violate. It is useful, for example, to know it is illegal to chew gum in Singapore, that people drive on the left side of the road in New Zealand, and that eating involves only the right hand—and never the left—in India.

International travelers who live abroad for a short period of time are referred to as **sojourners**. Communication researchers are typically interested in factors that inhibit or promote sojourners' intercultural interactions with host nationals, including language proficiency, attitudes, level of contact, and host receptivity (Ward, et al., 2001). Since the intercultural adaptation of tourists is usually pretty limited, those who live in places that are popular tourist destinations may get tired of dealing with a steady stream of culturally insensitive visitors and even begin to resent their community's economic dependence on them. Negative attitudes toward visitors may lead to unwillingness to speak English, deliberately sending sightseers in the wrong direction, over-charging for merchandise, ridiculing, insulting, or even threatening them. Recently, researchers have begun to focus more on the impact of sojourners on host nationals and their culture (Jack & Phipps, 2005).

Most intercultural adaptation research, however, focuses on people who actually live outside of their country of origin, which is over 230 million people, according to the United Nations Population Fund. People who relocate abroad for longer periods of time for the purpose of employment, deployment, volunteer work, study abroad, pursuit of adventure, culture learning, language study, etc. are called **expatriates**. In general, the cultural adaptation of expatriates is deeper than that of sojourners; however, level of immersion and degree of cultural change depend more on his or her attitude toward the host culture than length of stay. The term **host culture** is used throughout this chapter to describe the foreign culture one moves to, whereas the term **home culture** is used to identify the culture one grew up in and moved away from. For people who move at a young age, that distinction is not always clear-cut; therefore, we will return to a more in-depth discussion on home- and host-culture integration later. Some people approach their short-term experience with interest in and openness toward their host culture. They form relationships with host-culture members and develop language and communication skills that allow them to function like cultural "insiders." Others limit their host-culture involvement. Their strategic purpose for being there may not necessitate forming relationships or they may not feel comfortable in the host culture. Alternatively, their employer or sponsoring organization may expect a certain distance to be maintained; thus "going native" would violate policies or expectations governing the intercultural encounter.

The third group is made up of long-term or permanent **immigrants**, which includes **refugees** as well. Refugees may live in their host culture for the rest of their lives while hoping to one day be able to return "home." Immigrants with a greater range of options may intend to live in the host country only for a few years, but end up settling for good. Alternatively, they may set out to relocate permanently, but end up going back after a period of time. When examining how different people adapt interculturally, it is important to remember that the degrees of voluntariness, mobility, and permanence influence attitudes and approaches. Another main factor to keep in mind is the degree of similarity between home and host cultures.

The process of adapting to a new culture or to culturally different others is called **acculturation**. Acculturation theory has its historic roots in the field of social anthropology, where one of the earliest, still popular, definitions was coined in 1936: "Those phenomena which result when groups of individuals having different cultures come into continuous first-hand contact with subsequent changes in the original culture patterns of either or both groups" (Redfield, Linton, & Herskovits, 1936, p. 149). In this chapter we will review several acculturation theories. First, we will address theories about the initial cultural orientation phase. Next, we will review theories about longer-term acculturation. Finally, we will address some less theorized areas of intercultural adaptation, including third-culture perspectives. These different theories are all derived from research among acculturating individuals. I use the term **acculturating individuals** inclusively of immigrants, refugees, and sojourners. However, since different people acculturate differently depending on a number of different factors—some of which we have already briefly touched upon—researchers sometimes end up with different, and even contradictory, results. This leads them to draw different conclusions, which explains why some of the theories and perspectives discussed in this chapter vary quite a bit from one other.

Cultural Orientation and Culture Shock

People who relocate to a different country obviously expect to adapt to their new environment and may, to a greater or lesser degree, welcome the adventure and opportunity associated with experiencing a new culture. The initial adaptation process usually involves adopting behaviors that allow them to greet people, get around, get situated, and interact without offending anyone. My Canadian colleague was quite surprised when her Japanese students stood up and started walking towards her after she waved "hello" to them. She learned quickly that the gesture used for "hi" in Canada meant "come" in Japan. Other initial learning lessons involved using chopsticks in an appropriate and polite manner. Similarly, people moving to Stockholm quickly learn that there are strict, unwritten rules for how to enter and exit trains and using escalators in the subway.

A person who is open and flexible is better equipped to deal with intercultural change than a person who is **ethnocentric**, but even people who are identified as poised to handle the transitions well will usually experience some emotional stress commonly referred to as **culture shock**. The reason for such inner conflict is that the human psyche tends to question ideas that are interpreted as inaccurate, react to values that contradict currently held ones, and to resist behaviors that are perceived as inappropriate or just simply wrong. The knowledge, beliefs, values, attitudes, experiences, habits, tastes, preferences, and skills that we possess are acquired within the context of our home culture and are largely shared with others who belong to our culture. At the same time, the unique combination of these elements is what gives each of us an internal structure and an individual identity. When intercultural encounters challenge us to question and ultimately change one or several of the components of our home culture, it may feel as though our very identity is being threatened.

Culture Shock Theories and Models

The term "culture shock" was coined by anthropologist Kalervo Oberg (1960), who described feelings of anxiety, tension, and stress arising from trying to meet the demands of the host culture, combined with feelings of loss, confusion, and powerlessness associated with being removed from the home culture. He identified four distinct stages of this initial intercultural adaptation process. The four stages are characterized by excitement, crisis, recovery, and adjustment, respectively. Variations of these four stages have been proposed by several researchers (e.g. Smalley, 1963; Richardson, 1974). Noting that the level of emotional satisfaction people feel when completing these stages follows a U-shape, sociologist Sverre Lysgaard (1955) introduced the U-Curve Theory. The initial optimism gives way to frustration that necessitates adaptation, which eventually leads to a newfound positivity. The middle stages at the bottom of the "U" typically occur around one year after moving abroad.

The crisis stage is experienced in a number of ways and may include a range of psychological and psychosomatic symptoms, such as anger, worry, confusion, irritability, fatigue, depression, loss of appetite, and paranoia. Feelings of extreme homesickness and perceptions of being "trapped" in the host culture may cause people to return to their home country rather than put themselves through the adaptation process. My nephew described his culture shock in Syria as experiencing a profound lack of control, being unable to "get anything done" or to get needed information in a society that—unlike his native Sweden—is neither results- nor information-oriented.

The severity of the culture shock that acculturating individuals experience depends on a number of factors, including age, personality, prior intercultural experiences, level of preparation, expectations, and interpersonal/social context. Other obvious variables are degree of home- and host-culture similarity, attitudes toward the host culture, level of host-culture immersion, and time frame. A fashion designer from New York, who had spent significant time in India and China and been able to adapt to these cultures with seeming ease, shared about the severe culture shock she experienced when she left the United States for good and moved to Sweden: "All of a sudden, I realized: 'Wow, I'm not going back so fast. I'm not going back. This is it! My whole life.' . . . It was a big culture shock. I think permanently was key. It was permanent. In India I could survive for a year because I knew that eventually I would be going back."

Although the prospect of eventually returning to one's home culture may reduce the severity of the initial culture shock, the re-adaptation to one's home culture—sometimes referred to as "reverse culture shock" or the "W-curve"—has been considered and studied as well. John and Jeanne Gullahorn (1963) developed the Extended U-Curve Model of Intercultural Adjustment, depicted in Figure 20.1. This model takes into account the experience of home-culture readjustment. They proposed that intercultural adaptation takes place in several stages. First, in the *honeymoon stage*, the novelty of being in the host culture is perceived as highly enjoyable. This positive experience rapidly turns negative as the acculturating individual is confronted by cross-cultural differences and enters the *hostility stage*. During the process of gaining understanding of these differences, he or she learns to laugh at cultural faux-pas and cultural differences that are deemed absurd or bizarre. Upon further adaptation, he or she enters the *in-sync stage*, and begins to feel comfortable. As the individual faces the prospect of returning home after having settled into a level of functionality in the host culture, he or she enters the *ambivalence stage*. Upon returning and realizing the full extent of the intercultural adaptation that has taken place while living abroad, the individual finds himself or herself in a *reentry culture shock stage*, which necessitates further adaptation to the home culture which, in turn, eventually ushers in the *resocialization stage*.

People sometimes fail to prepare themselves for reentry, because they don't realize how much they have changed culturally while in the host culture. The resocialization process is generally faster than the host-culture adaptation process, since reacquiring language fluency and cultural competence is easier than acquiring it for the first time. However, something else that may catch them by surprise is that in their absence, life in their home culture has gone on, home-culture features may have shifted, and new words and practices may have come

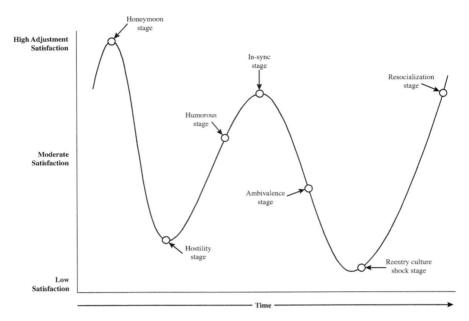

Figure 20.1 Extended U-Curve Model of Intercultural Adjustment
(Source: Spitzberg & Changnon, 2009, p. 23. Adapted visualization from Gullahorn & Gullahorn, 1963.)

into common use. For example, my American husband, who returned after several years in Sweden, had to familiarize himself with the term and concept "24/7." In addition, the inability to share the experience of being transformed culturally while living abroad with family members and friends may lead to a sense of alienation, even after successful resocialization.

Researchers have spent a great deal of effort studying personality characteristics and attitudes that predict successful intercultural transition (Van der Zee & Van Oudenhoven, 2013). Companies or nonprofit organizations that regularly send people out to work abroad have a financial incentive to screen candidates based on such research findings. Scholars have also examined whether the experience of culture shock is affected by level of control over the decision to move abroad, the geography of the host country, prior knowledge about the host culture, and the degree of similarity between home and host cultures. Many people worldwide are more exposed to cultural diversity now than when the term "culture shock" was introduced in the 1960s because of increased immigration, globalization, and international tourism. As a result, some think the concept is outdated and that the term "culture confusion" better captures the experiences of adapting to new cultures through communication online, abroad, and in increasingly diverse local communities (Hottola, 2004). In addition, several studies have shown that the level of stress sojourners experience is actually greatest upon arrival to a new country and does not follow a U-curve (Ward, et al., 1998).

The Stress–Adaptation–Growth Dynamic

In order to show how the stress of the intercultural adaptation process is managed internally, Kim (2001) proposed a three-dimensional Stress–Adaptation–Growth Dynamic Model, illustrated in Figure 20.2. She explained that *stress* "occurs whenever the capabilities of the individual are not adequate to the demands of the environment. Stress is a direct function of the lack of fitness between the stranger's subjective experiences and the prevailing modes of experience among the natives" (p. 55). The stress, which may be experienced as anxiety, confusion, uncertainty, or depression, is difficult to face. In order to reduce the stress, individuals assess and reflect on their experience and employ some type of coping strategy, which allows them to *adapt* to their situation. The learning that occurs in the process causes *growth*.

When my Canadian colleague moved to Japan to teach for a year, the cross-cultural differences in both verbal and nonverbal communication made it extremely difficult for her to get to know people and to form close friendships. She found herself drinking increasing amounts of saké to cope with the resulting stress and frustration. She recalled thinking, "This is not why I'm here" and started instead to take mini-vacations to bigger cities on the weekends, where she was able to connect with other foreigners and English-speaking Japanese. Although she did not fall in love with the culture, the personal growth she experienced as she was adapting to life in Japan made her feel more independent, accomplished, confident, and "a better person."

The stress–adaptation–growth process continues in a cyclical fashion while propelling the individual forward toward increased growth and upward to where the stress is lesser and the adaptation greater with each encounter. Over time, the

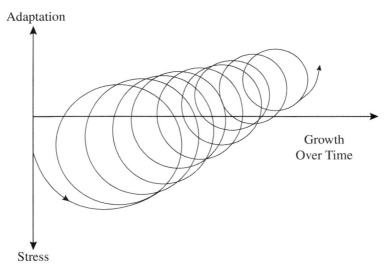

Figure 20.2 Stress–Adaptation–Growth Dynamic
(Source: Kim, 2001, p. 59)

tension between stress and adaptation diminishes to a point where it resembles the growth process that most people experience when dealing with change.

The Stress–Adaptation–Growth Dynamic has been applied in a large number of studies across various acculturating groups in different nations. For example, Pitts (2009) identified nine areas of communication used by Americans while studying short-term in Paris to cope with acculturative stress and adapt, i.e., advice, superficial introductory talk, information sharing, comparison, humor, storytelling, gossip, complaint, and supportive talk. Studies have revealed that younger people experience less acculturative stress and that social support is an important aspect of reducing stress through adaptation (Cuadrado, et al., 2014). When studying acculturative stress, researchers in the field of psychology have pointed out that the stress experienced during intercultural adaptation is not detrimental to an individual's wellbeing as long as it does not lead to unresolved conflict (Riedel, et al., 2011).

One-Dimensional Perspectives on Acculturation

Early theories of immigrants' intercultural adaptation treated the process as one-dimensional. It was assumed immigrants would have to choose between keeping their home culture and adopting their host culture, but would not be able to do both. The origin of the one-dimensional acculturation model is generally attributed to sociologist Milton Gordon, who proposed immigrants had to transition from home-culture maintenance to host-culture adoption and necessarily become assimilated in order to function successfully in their host society (Gordon, 1964). This view is sometimes illustrated by the analogy of a melting pot.

The most comprehensive intercultural adaptation theory originating in the communication field is the Integrative Theory of Intercultural Adaptation developed by Young Kim. In this theory, acculturation is defined as new culture acquisition. The process is illustrated in Figure 20.3. Kim (2001) reasoned that acculturation takes place in the same manner that each of us is socialized into our home culture, a process labeled **enculturation.** When making the home- to host-culture transition, **deculturation** is also required. Kim explained,

> Adaptation in the new environment is not a process in which new cultural elements are simply added to prior internal conditions. As new learning occurs, deculturation (or unlearning) of at least some of the old cultural elements has to occur, in the sense that new responses are adopted in situations that previously would have evoked old ones.
>
> (p. 51)

In this model, the goal of the process is **assimilation,** which Kim (2001) defined as, "a state of the highest degree of acculturation into the host milieu and deculturation of the original cultural habits that is theoretically possible" (p. 52). A friend of mine, who lived in Belarus and the Ukraine for 14 years, explained that she learned to avoid eye contact with strangers in public places. Even though

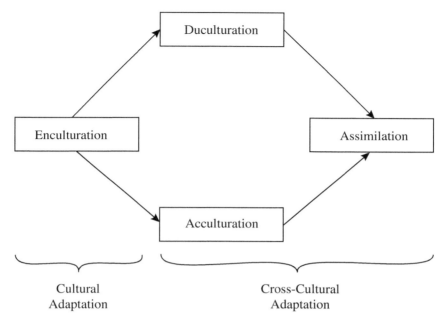

Figure 20.3 Relationships among Components of Acculturation
(Source: Kim, 2001, p. 53)

she visited the US every year, this nonverbal communication behavior became reflexive and automatic for her. When she moved back to the US, she became aware of the **deculturation** that had occurred, as it no longer felt normal or appropriate to greet strangers by making eye contact and nodding or smiling.

Communication is central to intercultural adaptation. Specifically, it is achieved through both personal communication—including language learning and host-culture competence acquisition—and social communication—including interpersonal communication with members of the host culture and mass communication. Watching news and reading newspapers is not only a great way for acculturating individuals to build their vocabulary, but is also helpful for familiarizing oneself with the political system and social institutions of the host country. For example, the world of sports and the role sports play in casual conversations in the US is difficult for immigrants to understand, but watching televised games and commentary on a regular basis can be a discreet way to become a cultural insider. Similarly, a Swede who lives in the US shared with me how watching *Will and Grace* helped him gain cultural fluency in American popular culture, because the dialogue within the series contained a plethora of pop culture references.

Ethnic (i.e. home-culture) interpersonal and mass communication is also included in this theory. Kim (2005) regarded close contact with others from one's home culture as helpful early in the adaptation process, but counterproductive later on. She explained,

Whether by choice or circumstance, strangers' heavy and prolonged reliance on co-ethnics sustains their original cultural identity and limits their opportunities to participate in the social communication activities of the host society. Implied in this observation is that strangers cannot remain exclusively ethnic in their communication activities and, at the same time, become highly adapted to the host environment.

(p. 387)

The Integrative Theory of Intercultural Adaptation, illustrated in Figure 20.4, addresses several additional factors that influence the process. The opportunity for individuals to adapt depends largely on the *environment*, which includes host-culture receptivity, host-culture conformity pressure, and ethnic group strength (i.e. the presence and organization of other home-culture members). These three factors will be discussed in greater detail later in this chapter. **Predisposition** refers to individual factors that impact the process. These include preparedness for change, ethnic proximity (i.e. degree of similarity between home and host cultures), and adaptive personality. Individuals who possess a highly adaptive personality are able to be open to the host culture because they have a secure sense of self.

The outcome of this process is intercultural transformation, which is characterized by functional fitness (i.e. ability to carry out day-to-day activities with ease), psychological health, and **intercultural identity**. Intercultural researchers in the field of psychology generally examine the outcomes of the adaptation process in terms of sociocultural adjustment—i.e. competence to interact appropriately and effectively—and psychological adjustment—i.e. experience of well-being and satisfaction (Ward & Kennedy, 1994). During my nephew's two-year

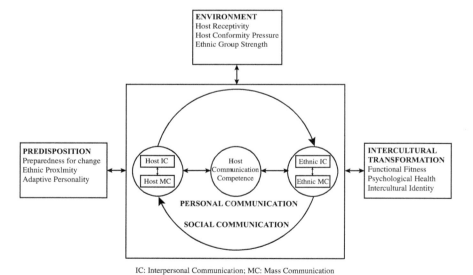

Figure 20.4 Integrative Theory of Intercultural Adaptation
(Source: Kim, 2001, p. 87)

stay in Syria, achieving functional fitness and psychological wellbeing required not only learning Arabic and the subtle, high-context cues that guide social interactions, but also gaining an insider's understanding about how to act in a society that is fundamentally oriented toward upholding and affirming honor.

In a survey of intercultural communication articles, intercultural adaptation and training emerged as the most popular topics (Hu & Fan 2011). Research based on Kim's (2001) Integrative Theory of Intercultural Adaptation model has been conducted in different national contexts. One study examined the adaptation of American expatriates in South Korea (Kim, 2007) and another study investigated the adaptation of Hispanic adolescents in the US (McKay-Semmler & Kim, 2014), both closely following the model. Researchers have examined how adaptation is influenced by the host country's socioeconomic conditions as well as attitudes toward immigrants and cultural diversity among host-country members, noting that a preference for assimilation versus cultural pluralism translates into different immigration policies. Studies have shown that motivation for moving abroad has a great impact on adaptation (Ward, et al., 2001). Some researchers have also studied the importance of various demographic variables, including age, gender, and educational level. Others have focused more on how social contact with home- versus host-culture members and use of home- versus host-culture media affect the process. Recently, researchers have begun examining the role of social media use in the adaptation process (Kim & McKay-Semmler, 2013).

Two-Dimensional Perspectives on Acculturation

Unlike the one-dimensional view of acculturation, in which acculturation requires deculturation, the two-dimensional view is based on a notion that home-culture maintenance and host-culture participation are actually two independent processes. In recent years, most acculturation research has relied on an Acculturation Strategies Theory introduced by psychologist John Berry (1980). He theorized that if these two simultaneous processes are not mutually exclusive, their intersection creates four distinct approaches to acculturation: assimilation, separation, marginalization, and integration. These are illustrated in Figure 20.5 and were described by Berry and Sabatier (2011) as follows:

> When individuals express a preference for not maintaining their heritage culture and to participate in the larger society, the assimilation orientation to acculturation is defined. In contrast, when there is a desire to maintain heritage culture and not to participate in the larger society, the separation orientation is defined. When there is both a wish to maintain one's heritage culture, and also to participate in the larger society, the integration orientation is defined. When there is both little desire to maintain one's heritage culture nor to have relations with the larger society, then marginalization is defined.
>
> (p. 659)

	Home-culture maintenance	
	Yes	No
Host-culture participation — Yes	Integration	Assimilation
Host-culture participation — No	Separation	Marginalization

Figure 20.5 Acculturation Strategies
(Source: Adapted visualization from Berry, 1980)

Assimilation

Kim (2001) viewed assimilation as a natural, gradual, and inevitable outcome of intercultural adaptation. Having defined **assimilation** as "an ideal state characterized by the maximum possible convergence of strangers' internal conditions to those of the natives" (p. 52), she described highly assimilated individuals as "functionally fit" in the host culture. However, she also recognized that the ideal of assimilation is not realistically achievable, especially for individuals who move abroad as adults. Rather than expecting these individuals to completely trade their home-culture identity for a host-culture one, she proposed an intercultural identity. She said, "Having internalized an increasing level of host communication competence and integration into the host social communication process, strangers are better able to manage the dynamic and dialogical interaction between the original culture and the new culture" (p. 192).

Most host societies prefer that refugees and other immigrants assimilate into the mainstream culture. Whether this expectation is perceived positively or negatively, those who acculturate in small numbers often see this strategy as their best option. By reducing communication barriers associated with cross-cultural differences, they are able to make themselves feel at home in their new environment. That said, members of a host culture that is highly traditional and homogeneous may not view assimilation by foreigners as acceptable or appropriate. While working as a volunteer on the island of Yap, Micronesia, I had to wrestle with the question of whether adopting the local practice of chewing betel nut would reduce or erect barriers to communication, especially since my skin color left little hope of blending in.

Separation

People may seek the benefits of living in a foreign country without having a particularly strong desire to associate with host-culture members beyond what is necessary for daily functioning. Expatriates, international students, and sojourners who acculturate for a limited period of time with the intention of returning to their home country may not wish to change culturally. Historically, during times of colonization, colonizers often viewed host cultures as primitive and inferior and saw little merit in the beliefs, values and practices of such cultures. This attitude of cultural imperialism still prevails in certain situations, particularly in developing countries.

Immigrant groups who are present in large numbers may form what Portes (1997) referred to as transnational communities. These provide social support that mitigates the need for host-culture immersion and allows community members to advance politically and economically without giving up their native cultural heritage. Examples of such communities include Chinatown, Little Italy, and Amish areas. This acculturation strategy of separation may be preferable for immigrants who want to preserve their ethnic and religious distinction, maintain their group vitality and identity, and pass on their culture to the next generation (Croucher, 2011). A lack of resources, education, language skills and—in some cases—citizenship may explain less intentional acculturation by way of separation, which appears to be the case with some Latino immigrants in the US (Christmas & Barker, 2014).

Acculturation is also affected by how receptive the host society is. When immigrants do not feel welcome but, rather, experience discrimination or pressure to assimilate, they are likely to react by using a strategy of **separation**, i.e. preserving their home-culture while resisting adaptation (Padilla & Perez, 2003; van Oudenhoven, et al., 2006). Berry (2009) said, "When cultural incompatibility or conflict is present, then integration is not likely or even possible; instead other strategies (particularly separation and marginalization) are the most common ways of acculturating" (p. 369).

Marginalization

Marginalization emerges as the least preferred acculturation strategy in most acculturation research. It is usually considered more as a theoretical possibility than as an actually viable option. However, some people who move abroad report that they never felt like they fit in their home culture in the first place; therefore, they have little desire to hold on to it. For such people, acculturation may be an opportunity to "start over" and reinvent themselves in a new cultural context. If they are simultaneously unable or unwilling to embrace the host culture, perhaps for reasons discussed above, they may find themselves in a cultural "no man's land," lacking a clear sense of belonging to either the home or host culture. Gillespie, McBride, and Riddle (2010) suggested acculturating individuals choosing a marginalization strategy be re-defined as culturally independent or cosmopolitan to avoid a negative connotation with the idea of being marginalized. They argued that such individuals are not without culture, but rather transcend any two cultures. They said, "Cultural independents are likely to possess qualities of self-motivation, self-efficacy, independent thought, and effective management" (p. 41).

Integration

Integration has been identified as the most popular and beneficial acculturation strategy for immigrants, because it allows them to acquire a new culture without giving up their native culture (Ward, 2008). The research that *Acculturation Strategies* was based on originally measured attitudes toward the two cultures, but was later changed to also incorporate identity, language, social behavior, and motivations (Berry, et al., 2006). There turns out to be a pretty big difference between participating in the host culture and actually adopting it as your own. When studies emphasize cultural identity and adoption of host-culture beliefs and values for the host-culture dimension, the use of the integration strategy is reported less often (Ward & Kus, 2012). Berry and Sabatier (2011) showed that participants classified as using an integration strategy varied from a high of 61% when emphasizing cultural contact, to 46% when emphasizing adoption of culture, to 39% when emphasizing cultural identity. They also cited research showing a decrease from 82% to 10%, depending on how the host-culture dimension was measured. They concluded, "it appears that this more internal way of becoming linked to the national society (identification with it) is somehow more difficult or less salient than the more external or behavioural ways" (p. 667).

Individuals who have fully integrated two cultures are considered **bicultural**. Compared to people who acculturate as adults, it is easier for second-generation immigrants or third-culture individuals (see below) to become truly bicultural, because their acculturation takes place at an earlier age. A bicultural person possesses intimate knowledge of the beliefs and values of two cultures, communication competence in both cultures, and a positive attitude toward both cultures (Phinney, et al., 2001).

The Acculturation Strategies Theory does not explain how the two cultures are integrated, only that the home culture is maintained alongside the acquired host culture. Other scholars have discovered different ways that bicultural people manage and integrate their two cultures. Phinney and Devich-Navarro (1997) theorized a bicultural individual may *fuse* his or her two cultures together completely, keep them more or less separate and *alternate* between the two, or *blend* the two by allowing them to partially overlap while existing somewhere in their intersection. When bicultural people fuse their cultures, the origins of their cultural make-up are not salient or relevant; thus, trying to distinguish between the two can be problematic. Kim (2008) used the term "intercultural personhood" to describe this phenomenon. When biculturals feel "at home" in two cultures but don't blend them into a coherent one, they instead alternate between them by enacting one cultural framework or the other, depending on the context (LaFromboise, et al., 1993). This phenomenon is also referred to as **cultural frame-switching**. Research in this area shows how biculturals shift between their different cultures in response to cultural cues while keeping their cultural systems distinct, separate, or even dissociated (Benet-Martínez, et al., 2006).

The two-dimensional view of acculturation and the associated model containing four acculturation strategies introduced by Berry (1980) have come to dominate recent acculturation research with over 800 studies published across disciplines (Ward, 2008). Many researchers, particularly in the field of cross-cultural psychology, are interested in examining the relationship between acculturation strategy and social and psychological adjustment in the host society (Nguyen & Benet-Martínez, 2013). While some findings generated among a large number of studies are inconclusive, a common theme is that biculturals who integrate their home and host cultures are more adjusted than people who chose the other three strategies. However, scholars have recently begun to examine more closely how cultural integration is actually measured (Ward & Kus, 2012) in addition to ethno-cultural conflicts associated with acculturation and strategies employed by host-country members, particularly in immigrant-receiving nations (Berry, 2009).

Complex Perspectives on Acculturation

As mentioned above, the Acculturation Strategies Theory is extremely popular. As might be expected, the theory has received its fair share of critique as well, from scholars voicing concerns about political motives (Rudmin, 2003), over-simplification (Chirkov, 2009), and failure to account for the actual process (Ward, 2008). As a result, new models and perspectives have surfaced, as scholars are trying to understand and explain the complexity of the acculturation process and the various factors influencing acculturating individuals.

Acculturation Differences across Cultural Domains

In order to explain and illustrate how acculturating individuals use different strategies in different sociocultural domains, Marisol Navas and her colleagues developed the Relative Acculturation Extended Model (RAEM), which is depicted in Figure 20.6. Navas, et al. (2005) said, "The same strategies are not applied in all of the domains, and interaction with other cultures in the workplace is not the same as when it affects the complex world of religious experience or family relationships" (pp. 31–32). The model includes seven domains, ranging from the most material to the most symbolic: 1) political and government systems; 2) work and occupations; 3) consumer economics; 4) family relationships; 5) social relationships; 6) ways of thinking; and 7) religious

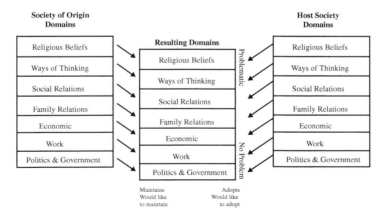

Figure 20.6 Relative Acculturation Extended Model
(Source: Navas, et al., 2005, p. 28)

beliefs and customs. When testing the theory, Navas, et al. (2007) found immigrants are more likely to assimilate in public or peripheral areas, where change is also more likely to be imposed upon them, and less likely to do so in the more private, or central, aspects of culture.

A Swedish couple who lived a very American lifestyle as expatriates for nine years shared with me how comfortable they felt in the US and how much they enjoyed social interaction with friends and neighbors, as long as they were able to avoid discussions about social issues. The wife explained, "We don't want to stand out too much but, rather, feel that we are welcome... We keep a low profile. We don't want to provoke anyone, but feel accepted for who we are." Although they had become quite "Americanized" on the surface, their core beliefs and values remained unchanged.

The *RAEM* model takes into consideration that acculturation attitudes across the seven domains vary between immigrants and their hosts. Host-culture members generally expect immigrants to acculturate by way of assimilation (Navas, et al., 2005). There are also differences between (actual or perceived) practices and preferences. Navas, et al. (2007) explained:

> The model differentiates between acculturation strategies and attitudes. That is, between the real plane, those acculturation options, which immigrants say they have put into practice in their new society, and those the natives perceive that the immigrants have adopted, and the ideal plane, those options that the immigrants would use if they could choose, and those natives would prefer for the immigrants.
>
> (p. 70)

Immigration affects not only the immigrants, but the host society as well. Conversely, immigrant acculturation is profoundly impacted by the host society's attitudes, which Navas was able to demonstrate with her research and theory development. Her *RAEM* model has been recognized by acculturation scholars (van Oudenhoven & Ward, 2013; Ward & Kus, 2012), tested and validated among various immigrant groups (Moreno, et al., 2014), and used to gauge host-member attitudes and prejudice toward immigrants (López-Rodríguez, et al., 2014; Montaruli, et al., 2011). One study conducted in Italy showed the Italians want immigrants to assimilate in all cultural domains but perceive they separate themselves, especially in central areas. Conversely, the adolescent immigrants in the study reported that they use a strategy of integration, even though they actually prefer to maintain central aspects of their home culture in favor of the host culture (Mancini & Bottura, 2014).

Selective Acculturation Processes

As you have probably realized at this point, the process of intercultural adaptation is neither uniform nor easily predictable. Influenced by a large number of different factors, it is actually rather complex. As individuals navigate this process, they first identify and familiarize themselves with cross-cultural differences that they encounter in various domains of society. They then evaluate and compare salient aspects of their host and home cultures. In doing so, they assess whether specific cultural features are complementary, superior or inferior compared to home-culture ones (Barker, 2015). Complementary aspects can easily be added to one's cultural repertoire, thus using a strategy of integration with no deculturation necessary. For example, one can learn how to be polite, show respect and appreciation, and cultivate friendships in a host culture, and still be equally able to do so in one's home culture, albeit in a different manner. Some home- and host-culture features may be integrated by combining the two. In other situations, acculturating individuals "pick and choose" the cultural features that they like the best, thus adopting host-culture features that are deemed desirable and beneficial, opposing those deemed negative and contrary to deeply held beliefs or values, retaining home-culture features deemed preferable to host-culture ones, and discarding those deemed inferior.

For people who relocate as adults, retention of a home-culture identity often feels inevitable, expressed in sentiments such as, "You can take the boy out of America, but you can't take America out of the boy." Core values and associated beliefs are likewise instilled through socialization in the home culture (i.e. enculturation) and are not easily replaced with host-culture ones. These include not only religious beliefs and worldviews in general, but also beliefs about the ideal relationship between society and the individual. For example, Swedish culture, while similar to mainstream American culture in many ways, emphasizes a shared responsibility for the welfare of all citizens that is carried out by the government and social institutions—a tendency that was termed institutional collectivism in one large-scale, cross-cultural, multi-nation comparison (House, et al. 2004). As a result, Swedes living in the US have a difficult time accepting the value of independence that has strong support among Americans, i.e. the idea that each individual is responsible for himself/herself (Barker, 2015). There are certain components of culture that are "competing, conflicting, and irreconcilable" (Ward, 2008, p. 109) when home and host cultures are compared. Another example of this that many Swedish Americans and American Swedes encounter is that Swedish culture fosters a greater demand for conformity that causes Swedes to strive for sameness, whereas American culture fosters a greater tolerance for diversity that causes Americans to strive for differentiation.

The acculturation process thus selectively incorporates each of the four strategies proposed by Berry (1980), i.e. assimilation, separation, marginalization, and integration. Choice of strategy is influenced by attitudes toward both home and host cultures, home-culture contact, and host-culture interaction. In order for acculturating individuals to experience social acceptance, host-culture receptivity is required. While the US is known as a culture of immigrants, more traditional and tight-knit cultures may not allow immigrants to be accepted as cultural "insiders," but, rather, assigned "foreigner" status. It's important to realize that cultural diversity exists in every country to a greater or lesser degree through the practice of multiple cultures and **microcultures**, also referred to as subcultures. In general, larger cities are more diverse and tolerant toward newcomers than smaller towns in rural areas. An emerging area of research, the selective acculturation model, needs further testing and examination across different cultures and intercultural contexts.

Third-Culture Perspectives

So far, we have discussed how bicultural individuals integrate two distinct cultures. Of course, it is possible to become tricultural or multicultural as well. However, when biculturalism or multiculturalism is discussed, it is usually assumed that each culture is somehow kept contained and intact. Several scholars have questioned this assumption and theorized that the reality of intercultural communication and adaptation is messier, because not only do acculturating individuals change, but the culture(s) they share with others change(s) as well (Berry, 2009). However, this aspect of intercultural adaptation has received much less attention. We have already seen that the Relative Acculturation Extended Model (Navas, et al., 2005) takes host-society acculturation attitudes into account. Another acculturation model, the **Interactive Acculturation Model**, introduced by Bourhis and colleagues (1997), also provides a framework for showing how the intercultural adaptation of immigrants and host-society members is interdependent and influenced by the ethnocultural origin of the immigrants.

One factor that must be taken into account when examining the interaction and adaptation between acculturating individuals and host-society members is that of power. Kim (2001) said, "The power of individual strangers to change the dominant culture is minuscule, at least in the short run, when compared to the pervasive influence of the host culture on them" (p. 54). In contexts where the power of the culturally different individuals or groups is fairly equal, the term **third culture** has been coined to articulate how a new culture may emerge from intercultural communication. Two different perspectives on this will be discussed next, i.e. third-culture building and third-culture individuals.

Third-Culture Building

Communication scholar Fred Casmir (1999) developed a theory labeled Third-Culture Building to explain how new cultures are created when individuals from two different cultural backgrounds interact over time in a manner characterized by equality, mutual respect, and dialogue. Emphasizing the dynamic, interactive, and evolving nature of culture, he outlined five phases of the third-culture building process, illustrated in Figure 20.7: 1) contact, 2) need, 3) interaction, 4) dependence, and third-culture interdependence. Basically, when intercultural contact produces a mutual need for companionship or cooperation, those involved begin to interact while gathering information about one another and subsequently forming a relationship that is characterized by dependence. The development, negotiation, and maintenance of this

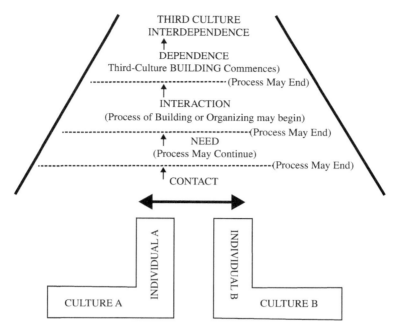

Figure 20.7 Third-Culture Building
(Source: Casmir, 1999, p. 109)

relationship through ongoing dialogic communication eventually results in the creation of an interdependent, shared third culture.

Casmir (1999) described this culture-building as an organic process rather than as an outcome; however, his model nevertheless predicted that a negotiated and shared system of standards and values would result. Because he focused more on the process than on the specific "content" of the emerging third culture, he did not stipulate whether the resulting third culture is a hybridization, or fusion, of the cultures originally represented, or whether it is made up of new features emerging from the encounter. Other scholars have taken these ideas further and theorized that the original cultures serve as a point of departure but the third culture also incorporates "additional potentially evolving cultures" (Sackmann & Phillips, 2004, p. 377). It is initially anchored in the original two cultures, but their influence diminishes over time as the third culture develops and takes on a life of its own (Rodríguez, 2005).

Although this theory has not yet been tested extensively through empirical research, the third-culture building perspective has been applied in a variety of fields, including public relations (Casmir & Muir-Packman, 1999), identity management (P.-W. Lee, 2006), and intercultural marriages (S. Lee, 2006). Casmir's work has been praised for its philosophical and methodological contribution to mainstream intercultural communication research, and some scholars even describe it as having caused a "paradigm shift" (Hopson, et al., 2012, p. 794). Several studies have confirmed the validity of the perspective and basic components of this theory, including the creation of unique third-culture features (McEwan & Sobre-Denton, 2011), the premise that transcending the original cultures requires both equality and commonality between the parties involved (S. Lee, 2006), and the negotiation of a hybrid culture as a middle ground for international work teams (Clausen, 2007; Larsson & Lubatkin, 2001), or intercultural friendships (P.-W. Lee, 2006). My cousin, who works for a Swedish company in the US described the third-culture building taking place as they sought to incorporate key aspects of both cultures. He said, "They try to let the team decide instead of the boss just saying, 'This is the way we are going to do it,' which is supposedly the American way. Some of my colleagues are more used to the boss making the decisions and team following along." He also shared about how expectations regarding productivity that he identified as more American were incorporated in this organizational third culture as well. Since the process of third-culture building requires openness from all involved, it is unlikely to happen in situations where one culture dominates over the other or among individuals who purposely are assimilating into a host-culture environment.

Third-Culture Individuals

When adults move abroad, they already have a cultural identity, which means that their view of themselves and their place in the world is more or less established. But what happens to children of expatriate parents when they become socialized into their home culture and host culture(s) simultaneously and develop their identity while influenced by several different cultural frameworks? Unlike second-generation immigrants, who typically settle into the cultural environment that their parents brought them to, third-culture individuals have every intention of returning "home" at some point. In addition, these expatriate families are often quite mobile and do not necessarily stay in one place for very long. Since their cultural identity is derived largely from their atypical childhood involving multiple intercultural transitions and adaptation experiences, people with this particular background generally refer to themselves as Third Culture Kids or TCKs.

The term third culture was coined by sociologists John and Ruth Useem to describe the blend of home and host cultures that form within expatriate communities (Useem, et al., 1963; Useem & Useem, 1967). Later, the meaning of the term shifted to signify the unique and shared experience of these individuals who grow up between cultures, explained as follows: "Our family, our homeland is in the company of others with similar experience. Our heritage was not formed by a national tradition but by a particular situation" (Seaman, 1996, p. 54). The most comprehensive overview on the topic has been provided by David Pollock and Ruth Van Reken (2009) who defined a TCK as:

> a person who has spent a significant part of his or her developmental years outside the parents' culture. The TCK frequently builds relationships to all of the cultures, while not having full ownership in any. Although elements

from each culture may be assimilated into the TCK's life experience, the sense of belonging is in relationship to others of similar background.

(p. 13)

Differentiated from others by their unusual background and extraordinary intercultural skills, third-culture individuals are also described as **cultural hybrids** (Bhabha, 1994), **global nomads** (McCaig, 1996), and **cultural chameleons** (Smith, 1996). Although a formal theory of third-culture individuals has yet to emerge, researchers have recently begun to produce evidence that the unique intercultural adaptation of third-culture individuals allows them to acquire specialized intercultural communication skills. Many of these have previously been identified in popular and professional literature. Since third-culture individuals' intercultural adaptation takes place during their developmental stage, i.e. age 6–18, they may become linguistically and culturally fluent in as little as one year, depending on their age and level of host-culture immersion. For example, a military brat who lives on base is probably less involved with local children than a missionary kid who lives in a village. At the same time, these children and adolescents may be reluctant to develop deep relationships, knowing they will likely not last for very long. "A child raised abroad cannot form permanent roots in the host culture, and this can feel both liberating and isolating" (Eidse & Sichel, 2004, p. 3).

Compared to the general population or other interculturals, third-culture individuals possess enhanced abilities to adapt even as adults because of their enhanced social sensitivity (Lyttle, et al., 2011). They are also recognized for their open-mindedness and appreciation for different people and perspectives (Dewaele & van Oudenhoven, 2009). Their identity is a bicultural or **multicultural** blend of the cultures they have experienced first-hand. They are also known for their ability to alternate among these different cultures and to blend into any of them with little conscious effort (Moore & Barker, 2012). One third-culture individual explained,

> I can function in both cultures. So I can go to Brazil and nobody would ever notice that I've been living in the U.S. for my whole [adult] life, and a lot of times here in the U.S. people are surprised when I tell them that I was born and raised in Brazil.
>
> (Moore & Barker, 2012, p. 557)

Research on third-culture individuals has shown this extraordinary intercultural ability comes at a price. Sometimes referred to as "hidden immigrants," they often feel out of touch with their home culture. While relying on relationships with people like them and strong ties to their immediate families, many continue their international, mobile lifestyle.

Lacking a sense of belonging, they feel at home "everywhere and nowhere," and answering the simple question "Where are you from?" is highly problematic (Fail, et al., 2004; Hoersting & Jenkins, 2011). One third-culture individual said,

> I don't feel like I belong, I feel like a tourist when I go to my home country. Yet, I feel like I can fit in and adapt easily without having that sense of belonging or attachment to that culture. That's what's incredible about this lifestyle.
>
> (Moore & Barker, 2012, p. 558)

Intercultural scholars, who have taken an interest in third-culture individuals since the early 2000s, continue to study the difficulties associated with growing up internationally mobile and culturally diverse (Purnell & Hoban, 2014), but have also begun to examine third-culture individuals' multicultural identity, global worldview, intercultural competence, and social sensitivity. The bulk of this research is generated within the fields of international education, cross-cultural psychology, cross-cultural management, and intercultural communication. Some researchers have examined the internationally mobile tendencies of third-culture individuals, trying to predict their suitability for expatriate employment (Lam & Selmer, 2004). Others focus on testing assertions made in popular and professional literature about third-culture individuals being less ethnocentric, and more globally aware, open-minded, flexible, and adept at intercultural adaptation (Dewaele & van Oudenhoven, 2009; Tarique & Weisbord, 2013).

Chapter Summary

This chapter has provided an overview of some of the most popular and significant theories, models, research and perspectives on short-term as well as long-term intercultural adaptation. By reading it, you will have gained knowledge of these different approaches to the topic, insights into your own intercultural adaptation experiences, and perspectives that will guide your future intercultural encounters. With over two million people crossing international borders daily (Omelaniuk, 2005) and the world's societies becoming increasingly culturally diverse through immigration, one does not have to travel far to engage in intercultural communication and to experience intercultural adaptation.

Key Terms

Acculturating individuals	Acculturation	Assimilation
Bicultural	Cultural chameleon	Cultural frame-switching
Cultural hybrid	Culture shock	Deculturation
Enculturation	Ethnocentric	Expatriate
Global nomad	Home culture	Host culture
Immigrant	Integration	Intercultural identity
Marginalization	Microculture	Multicultural
Predisposition	Refugee	Separation
Sojourner		

Activities

1. Divide the class into pairs. Instruct the students to interview each other about an intercultural adaptation experience. (Students who have not lived abroad may share about moving to a different state or a similar encounter with an unfamiliar culture.) The students will then briefly recap their interviewees' experience, including: a) the intercultural context; b) the most salient cultural differences encountered; c) the extent to which he/she experienced culture shock, and d) how they adapted to the new culture.
2. Form groups based on some type of cultural categorization. Ideally, each group should share some type of cultural feature that distinguishes them from the rest of the class. Instruct each group to choose a cultural practice that is important to group members (a way to convey respect, show hospitality, celebrate a holiday, dress, carry out a ritual, etc.) that would be important for someone acculturating to understand and adopt. Each group will prepare a brief presentation for the class in which they: a) describe/demonstrate the practice, and b) explain the beliefs and values that undergird this practice.
3. Find out if any of the students in the class are: a) third-culture individuals; b) have been involved in a longer-term intercultural dialogue resulting in third-culture building, and/or: c) have been in close contact with acculturating individuals as a host-culture member. Ask these students to form a panel, give an opening statement reflecting and expanding upon what this chapter says about their special intercultural circumstance, then respond to questions from the class.

References

Barker, G. G. (2015). Choosing the best of both worlds: The acculturation process revisited. *International Journal of Intercultural Relations, 45*(1), 56–69.

Benet-Martínez, V., Lee, F., & Leu, J. (2006). Biculturalism and cognitive complexity: Expertise in cultural representations. *Journal of Cross Cultural Psychology, 37,* 386–407.

Berry, J. W. (1980). Acculturation as varieties of adaptation. In A. Padilla (ed.), *Acculturation: Theory, models and findings* (pp. 9–25). Boulder, CO: Westview.

Berry, J. W. (2009). A critique of critical acculturation. *International Journal of Intercultural Relations, 33,* 361–371.

Berry, J. W., & Sabatier, C. (2011). Variations in the assessment of acculturation attitudes. *International Journal of Intercultural Relations, 35,* 658–669.

Berry, J. W., Phinney, J. S., Sam, D. L., & Vedder, P. (2006). *Immigrant youth in cultural transition: Acculturation, identity, and adaptation across nations.* Mahwah, NJ: Lawrence Erlbaum.

Bhabha, H. K. (1994). *The location of culture.* London, UK: Routledge.

Bourhis, R. Y., Moïse, L. C., Perreault, S., & Senécal, S. (1997). Towards an interactive acculturation model: A social psychological approach. *International Journal of Psychology, 32,* 369–386.

Casmir, F. L. (1999). Foundations for the study of intercultural communication based on a third-culture building model. *International Journal of Intercultural Relations, 23*, 91–116.

Casmir, F. L., & Muir-Packman, H. (1999). Learning from the Euro Disney experience: A case study in international/intercultural communication. *Gazette: The International Journal for Communication Studies, 61*, 473–489.

Chirkov, V. (2009). Critical psychology of acculturation: What do we study and how do we study it, when we investigate acculturation? *International Journal of Intercultural Relations, 33*, 94–105.

Christmas, C. N., & Barker, G. G. (2014). Assessing intercultural experience: Differences in acculturation, intercultural sensitivity, and cognitive flexibility between the first and second generation of Latino immigrants. *Journal of International and Intercultural Communication, 7*, 238–257.

Clausen, L. (2007). Corporate communication challenges: A 'negotiated' culture perspective. *Journal of Cross Cultural Management, 7*, 317–332.

Croucher, S. M. (2011). Social networking and cultural adaptation: A theoretical model. *Journal of International and Intercultural Communication, 4*, 259–264.

Cuadrado, E., Tabernero, C., & Briones, E. (2014). Dispositional and psychosocial variables as longitudinal predictors of acculturative stress. *Applied Psychology: An International Review, 63*, 441–479.

Dewaele, J.M., & Van Oudenhoven, J.P. (2009). The effect of multilingualism/multiculturalism on personality: No gain without pain for third culture kids? *International Journal of Multilingualism, 6*, 443–459.

Eidse, F. & Sichel, N. (2004). *Unrooted childhood*. Yarmouth, ME: Intercultural Press.

Fail, H., Thompson, J., and Walker G. (2004). Belonging, identity and Third Culture Kids: Life histories of former international school students. *Journal of Research in International Education, 3*, 319–338.

Gillespie, K., McBride, J. B., & Riddle, L. (2010) Globalization, biculturalism and cosmopolitanism: The acculturation status of Mexicans in upper management. *International Journal of Cross Cultural Management, 10*, 37–53.

Gordon, M. M. (1964). *Assimilation in American life*. New York, NY: Oxford University Press.

Gullahorn, J. T. & Gullahorn, J. E. (1963). An extension of the U-curve hypothesis. *Journal of Social Issues, 19*, 33–47.

Hoersting, R. C., & Jenkins, S. R. (2011). No place to call home: Cultural homelessness, self-esteem and cross-cultural identities. *International Journal of Intercultural Relations, 35*, 17–30.

Hopson, M. C., Hart, T., & Bell, G. C. (2012). Meeting in the middle: Fred L. Casmir's contributions to the field of intercultural communication. *International Journal of Intercultural Relations, 36*, 789–797.

Hottola, P. (2004). Culture confusion: Intercultural adaptation in tourism. *Annals of Tourism Research, 31*, 447–466.

House, R. J., Hanges, P. J., Javidan, M., Dorfman, P. W., and Gupta, V. (2004) *Culture, leadership, and organizations: The GLOBE study of 62 societies*. Thousand Oaks, CA: Sage.

Hu, Y. & Fan, W. (2011). An exploratory study on intercultural communication research contents and methods: A survey based on the international and domestic journal papers published from 2001 to 2005. *International Journal of Intercultural Relations, 35*, 554–566.

Jack, G., & Phipps, A. (2005). *Tourism and intercultural exchange*. Clevedon, U.K.: Multilingual Matters.

Kim, Y.-S. (2007). Communication experiences of American expatriates in South Korea: A study of cross-cultural adaptation. *Human Communication*, 11, 511–528.

Kim, Y.Y. (2001). *Becoming intercultural: An integrative theory of communication and cross-cultural adaptation*. Thousand Oaks, CA: Sage.

Kim, Y.Y. (2005). Adapting to a new culture: An integrative communication theory. In W.B. Gudykunst (ed.), *Theorizing about intercultural communication* (pp. 375–400). Thousand Oaks, CA: Sage.

Kim, Y.Y. (2008). Intercultural personhood: Globalization and a way of being. *International Journal of Intercultural Relations*, 32, 359–368.

Kim, Y.Y., & McKay-Semmler, K. (2013). Social engagement and cross-cultural adaptation: An examination of direct- and mediated interpersonal communication activities of educated non-natives in the United States. *International Journal of Intercultural Relations*, 37, 99–112.

LaFromboise, T., Coleman, H., & Gerton, J. (1993). Psychological impact of biculturalism: Evidence and theory. *Psychological Bulletin*, 114, 395–412.

Lam, H. & Selmer, J. (2004). Are former "third culture kids" the ideal business expatriates? *Career Development International*, 9, 109–122.

Larsson, R. & Lubatkin, M. (2001). Achieving acculturation in mergers and acquisitions: An international case survey. *Human Relations*, 54, 1573–1607.

Lee, P.-W. (2006). Bridging cultures: Understanding the construction of relational identity in intercultural friendship. *Journal of Intercultural Communication Research*, 35, 3–22.

Lee, S. (2006). Somewhere in the middle: The measurement of third culture. *Journal of Intercultural Communication Research*, 35, 253–264.

López-Rodríguez, L., Zagefka, H., Navas, M., & Cuadrado, I. (2014). Explaining majority members' acculturation preferences for minority members: A mediation model. *International Journal of Intercultural Relations*, 38, 36–46.

Lysgaard, S. (1955). Adjustment in a foreign society: Norwegian Fulbright grantees visiting the United States. *International Social Science Bulletin*, 7, 45–51.

Lyttle, A., Barker, G.G., & Cornwell, T. (2011). Adept through adaptation: Third culture individuals' interpersonal sensitivity. *International Journal of Intercultural Relations*, 35, 686–694.

Mancini, T. & Bottura, B. (2014). Acculturation processes and intercultural relations in peripheral and central domains among native Italian and migrant adolescents. An application of the Relative Acculturation Extended Model (RAEM). *International Journal of Intercultural Relations*, 40, 49–63.

McCaig, N.M. (1996). Understanding global nomads. In C.D. Smith (ed.), *Strangers at home: Essays on the effects of living overseas and coming 'home' to a strange land* (pp. 99–120). Bayside, NY: Aletheia Publications.

McEwan, B., & Sobre-Denton, M. (2011). Virtual cosmopolitanism: Constructing third cultures and transmitting social and cultural capital through social media. *Journal of International and Intercultural Communication*, 4, 252–258.

McKay-Semmler, K., & Kim, Y.Y. (2014). Cross-cultural adaptation of Hispanic youth: A study of communication patterns, functional fitness, and psychological health. *Communication Monographs*, 81, 133–156.

Montaruli, E., Bourhis, R.Y., Azurmend, M-J., & Larrañaga, N. (2011). Social identification and acculturation in the Basque Autonomous Community. *International Journal of Intercultural Relations*, 35, 425–439.

Moore, A. M., & Barker, G. G. (2012). Confused or multicultural: Third culture individuals' cultural identity. *International Journal of Intercultural Relations*, 36, 553–562.

Moreno, P. P. J., Rojas Tejada, A. J., Navas Luque, M., & Lozano Rojas, O. M. (2014). Structural model of acculturation attitudes and related psychosocial variables: Empirical evidence in native Spaniards. *International Journal of Psychology*, 49, 175–182.

Navas, M., García, M. C., Sánchez, J., Rojas, A. J., Pumares, P., & Fernández, J. S. (2005). Relative Acculturation Extended Model: New contributions with regard to the study of acculturation. *International Journal of Intercultural Relations*, 29, 21–37.

Navas, M., Rojas, A. J., García, M., & Pumares, P. (2007). Acculturation strategies and attitudes according to the Relative Acculturation Extended Model (RAEM): The perspectives of natives versus immigrants. *International Journal of Intercultural Relations*, 31, 67–86.

Nguyen, A. D., & Benet-Martínez, V. (2013). Biculturalism and adjustment: A meta-analysis. *Journal of Cross-Cultural Psychology*, 44, 122–159.

Oberg, K. (1960). Culture shock: Adjustments to new cultural environments. *Practical Anthropology*, 4, 177–182.

Omelaniuk, I. (2005). *World migration 2005: Costs and benefits of international migration*. Geneva, Switzerland: International Organization for Migration.

Padilla, A. M., & Perez, W. (2003). Acculturation, social identity, and social cognition: A new perspective. *Hispanic Journal of Behavioral Sciences*, 25(1), 35–55.

Phinney, J. S., & Devich-Navarro, M. (1997). Variations in bicultural identification among African American and Mexican American adolescents. *Journal of Research on Adolescence*, 7(1), 3–32.

Phinney, J. S., Horenczyk, G., Liebkind, K., & Vedder, P. (2001). Ethnic identity, immigration, and well-being: An interactional perspective. *Journal of Social Issues*, 57(3), 493–510.

Pitts, M. J. (2009). Identity and the role of expectations, stress, and talk in short-term student sojourner adjustment: An application of the integrative theory of communication and cross-cultural adaptation. *International Journal of Intercultural Relations*, 36, 450–462.

Pollock, D. C., & van Reken, R. E. (2009). *Third culture kids: The experience of growing up among worlds*. Boston, MA: Nicholas Brealey.

Portes, A. (1997). Immigration theory for a new century: some problems and opportunities. *International Migration Review*, 31, 799–825.

Purnell, L. & Hoban, E. (2014). The lived experiences of Third Culture Kids transitioning into university life in Australia. *International Journal of Intercultural Relations*, 41, 80–90.

Redfield, R., Linton, R., & Herskovits, M. J. (1936). Memorandum on the study of acculturation. *American Anthropology*, 38, 149–152.

Richardson, A. (1974). *British immigrants and Australia: A psychological inquiry*. Canberra, Australia: Australian National University Press.

Riedel, J., Wiesmann, U., & Hannich, H.-J. (2011). An integrative theoretical framework of acculturation and salutogenesis. *International Review of Psychiatry*, 23, 555–564.

Rodríguez, C. M. (2005). Emergence of a third culture: Shared leadership in international strategic alliances. *International Marketing Review*, 22(1), 67–95.

Rudmin, F. W. (2003). Critical history of the acculturation psychology of assimilation, separation, integration, and marginalization. *Review of General Psychology*, 7, 3–37.

Sackmann, S. A., & Phillips, M. E. (2004). Contextual influences on culture research: Shifting assumptions for new workplace realities. *International Journal of Cross Cultural Management*, 4, 370–390.

Seaman, P. A. (1996). Rediscovering a sense of place. In C. D. Smith (ed.), *Strangers at home: Essays on the effects of living overseas and coming 'home' to a strange land* (pp. 36–56). Bayside, NY: Aletheia Publications.

Smalley, W. A. (1963). Culture shock, language shock, and the shock of self-discovery. *Practical Anthropology*, 10, 49–56.

Smith, C. D. (1996). *Strangers at home: Essays on the effects of living overseas and coming 'home' to a strange land* (pp. 189–201). Bayside, NY: Aletheia Publications.

Spitzberg, B. H., & Changnon, G. (2009). Conceptualizing intercultural competence. In D. K. Deardorff (ed.), *The Sage handbook of intercultural competence* (pp. 2–52). Thousand Oaks, CA: Sage.

Tarique, I., & Weisbord, E. (2013). Antecedents of dynamic cross-cultural competence in adult third culture kids (ATCKs). *Journal of Global Mobility*, 1, 139–160.

Useem, J., Donoghue, J. D., & Useem, R. H. (1963). Men in the middle of the third culture: The roles of American and non-western people in cross-cultural administration. *Human Organization*, 22(3), 169–179.

Useem, J., & Useem, R. (1967). The interfaces of a binational third culture: A study of the American community in India. *Journal of Social Issues*, 23, 130–143.

Van der Zee, K., & van Oudenhoven, J. P. (2013). Culture shock or challenge? The role of personality as a determinant of intercultural competence. *Journal of Cross-Cultural Psychology*, 44, 928–940.

van Oudenhoven, J. P., & Ward, C. (2013). Fading majority cultures: The implications of transnationalism and demographic changes for immigrant acculturation. *Journal of Community & Applied Social Psychology*, 23, 81–97.

van Oudenhoven, J. P., Ward, C., & Masgoret, A. (2006). Patterns of relations between immigrants and host societies. *International Journal of Intercultural Relations*, 30, 637–651.

Ward, C. (2008). Thinking outside the Berry boxes: New perspectives on identity, acculturation and intercultural relations. *International Journal of Intercultural Relations*, 32, 105–114.

Ward, C., Bochner, S., & Furnham, A. (2001). *The psychology of culture shock*. London: Routledge.

Ward, C., & Kennedy, A. (1994). Acculturation strategies, psychological adjustment and socio-cultural competence during cross-cultural transitions. *International Journal of Intercultural Relations*, 18, 329–343.

Ward, C., & Kus, L. (2012). Back to and beyond Berry's basics: The conceptualization, operationalization and classification of acculturation. *International Journal of Intercultural Relations*, 36, 472–485.

Ward, C., Okura, Y., Kennedy, A., & Kojima, T. (1998). The U-curve on trial: A longitudinal study of psychological and sociocultural adjustment during cross-cultural transition. *International Journal of Intercultural Relations*, 22, 277–291.

Student Paper

Marie Ontermaa

Third Culture Kid Identity Formation and its Effects

What is a Third Culture Kid?

Third culture kids are a world of their own, and many times, their feelings of displacement reflect this. A third culture kid refers to the group of individuals that, for various reasons, including their parents being in business, missions, diplomacy, etc, grow up in a country or countries outside of the country of their parent's origin, especially during their developmental years (birth to 18). A person cannot be identified as a Third Culture Kid if they have only been out of their passport country for six months or another comparable time frame—they must have spent a significant amount time in the host culture. This combination of cultures that the children grow up in—the home culture (passport country) and the "outside" culture (host country) then, in turn, gives way to a third, new culture, unique to them, and thus these children are called Third Culture Kids, or TCKs (Pollock & Van Reken, 2009).

What do Third Culture Kids do?

Upon the initial move into the host culture, there are a few typical stages that most families and the individuals in the families undergo. The cycle is represented by Lysgaard's U curve; the first stage is the honeymoon stage, in which the individual is enthusiastic about all of the new sights and ways of life. Things are easy and exciting. After this is the crisis period, where the person might begin to notice the glaring differences between his or her own passport country/culture and of the host culture, many of them perhaps incompatible, or at least they might feel incompatible at the moment. This will result in feelings of stress and anxiety,

---

> Because of their atypical cultural identity, third-culture individuals often struggle to develop a sense of belonging.

> Some researchers set a minimum age of 6. This is when children begin to form a rudimentary identity.

> Depending on age and degree of host-culture immersion, one year may be a sufficient amount of time to become a third-culture individual.

> It would have been good to include a brief discussion on how the adaptation process of TCKs differ from that of adults. Research shows that they adapt easier, faster, and more fully.

(Continued)

possibly depression and frustration and a desire to leave the country to return home. However, in most cases this stage leads slowly upward to the adjustment period, where the person, depending on their personality, feelings of identification with their passport country, and experiences in and desire to integrate into the host culture, will begin to resolve this internal conflict. Once the conflict is resolved, they will arrive at the fourth stage, where they will either, A) integrate, meaning that they will become bi-cultural, identifying with both their passport countries and host countries, B) assimilate, meaning that they will reject their passport country's culture to identify more with their host culture, C) separate, in that they would reject the host culture and maintain their identification with their passport country, or D) marginalize, meaning that they would reject both the host culture and the passport country's culture (Ward, et al. 1998; Zhou, et al. 2008).

This process of re-entry has been called by many names, but the most generally used and favored is "repatriation." A person might think that repatriation would be simple in and of itself, just re-establishing oneself at in the familiar environment of home, but research shows "high levels of repatriate distress on returning" (Sussman, 2002, 360).

Sussman (2000) found those who assimilate/integrate most fully into their host culture have the hardest time readjusting to their old, yet new, environment when once again in their passport culture. Pollock and Van Reken (2009) said that while the TCKs, who grew up in a host country, may think that they know what life in their passport culture is like, many times the picture is deceptive because going "home" on vacation from the host country is very different than actually living at home in the passport country. The vacations may have painted a picture of exciting events and family reunions, and when the TCK finds that life at home is just as unremarkable as life anywhere else, it may result in disappointment. Not only that, but again, their experiences in other cultures have created within

---

Margin notes:

Lysgaard (1955) introduced the U-Curve Theory and described three phases of adjustment without assigning specific labels. The terminology used here is supplied by researchers expanding his work.

I would recommend citing a primary source for the Acculturation Strategies model, e.g. Berry (1980).

234 GINA BARKER

(Continued)

them a new identity which may or may not be compatible with their passport culture.

Pollock and Van Reken (2009) created a model of transition with five stages that repatriating TCKs usually go through which has gained quite a bit of popularity among sojourners of all kinds. A blogger on blogspot.com even listed the traits that went along with the five stages:

> Reference for blogger?

1) Involvement: the active and comfortable life of the TCK in their host culture. This stage is characterized by belonging, inclusion in group, reputation, position, known (friends: confide, listen), commitment, responsiveness, responsibility, friendship, intimacy, affirmation, security, safety.
2) Leaving: The anticipation or perhaps even dread of knowing that they will be exiting their host culture soon in order to return to their passport country. This stage is characterized by feelings of separation, closure, recognition, farewells (celebration), withdrawal/exclusion, betrayal, disengagement, role relinquishment, distance, criticism, loosening of ties/conflicts, new relationships, denial, rejection, resentment, grief and sadness, postponement of goodbyes, emphasizing on the future, idealization, expectation.

> Because of their mobile childhood, third-culture individuals may be reluctant to form deep relationships as adults.

3) Transition: These are the feelings of stress, anxiety, and chaos that the TCK might experience once the transition to the passport country has been made. This is a crucial portion of time in which the TCK may feel uprooted and dislodged from their social norms, but is also a time in which they have the opportunity to "start afresh and reinvent" themselves (Purnell, Hoban, 2014, 81) Some ideas associated with it might be as follows: unknown, no status, no structure, clueless, chaos, exaggeration of problems and behavior, misunderstanding, ambiguity, self-centeredness, isolation, anxiety, fear, uncertainty, dreams, emotional instability, grief, disappointment.

> It is not uncommon for TCKs to experience multiple transitions, including several from and to their home culture.

(Continued)

> 4) Entering: This is a time in which the TCK is beginning to familiarize themselves with the "new" culture, but is yet unstable and uncertain in their social and emotional life. They may feel alone and open to attack as a result of this. This is characterized by the following: marginalization, superficiality, tentative acceptance, uncertainty of placement and use, misinterpretations, behaviors/signals, searching for mentors, introductions, observations, taking risks, unusable special knowledge, uncertainty of knowledge, initiation of relationships, issues with trust, vulnerability, loss of self-esteem, loss of continuity with the past, loss of identity, ambivalence, psychosomatic problems, grief processing, depression.
>
> 5) Reinvolvement: this is when the TCK has found their "feet" and is finally able to feel themselves at home in the new/old environment. This final phase is characterized by belonging, inclusion in the group, reputation, position, being known (friends: confide, listen), being an outsider and a newcomer, commitment, responsiveness, responsibility, friendships, adjustments—even surprise ones, intimacy, affirmation, security, safety, and alien-ness. (Purnell, Hoban, 2014; blogspot.com).
>
> Adler (1981) suggests that repatriation follows a "flattened" U-shaped curve, in which the person in the repatriation process would feel first the feelings of euphoria that came with entering a new country, then a crisis period, followed by adjustment and feelings of well-being, albeit not as maniac as the initial stage.
>
> ### Third Culture Kid Identity
>
> These children (and adults) are curiosities because they create a norm of their own. Although they individually do not have any background in common,

Margin notes:

Third-culture individuals have been quoted describing themselves as "terminally unique," i.e. culturally fundamentally different from their home-culture peers.

It would have been good to compare Pollock & Van Reken's (2009) and Purnell & Hoban's (2014) transition models.

The reverse culture shock is also illustrated in the W-curve model (Gullahorn & Gullahorn, 1963).

Rather, a culture (which also involves norms).

(Continued)

they collectively have a lot in common. Pollock, in his book "Third Culture Kids: The Experience of Growing up Among Worlds," describes a convention in which these global nomads gather. None of them had any background in common and yet, looking at them, this lack of commonalities would never have been noticed because they acted like long-lost friends. Therefore, a life that is very mobile must ingrain into the mind certain characteristics different from characteristics that a non-mobile person would have (Pollock & Van Reken, 2009).

Sussman (2000) said that the creation of a person's identity, "self-clarity"—or the ability to understand ones' self—and self-esteem are intricately linked. This includes not only one's own perception of self, but also of the "meaningful social groups to which we belong" (Sussman, 2000, 358). These social groups usually point to the individual countries in which people were born, but in the case of TCKs, they cannot identify with any one particular country because of their transient history globally. Immigrants will many times assimilate into their new culture and thus, take on two cultural identities and even names, ie, if they are Irish and have moved to Canada, Irish Canadians, or if they are perhaps Korean, Japanese, Thai, or any such country in Asia, and have moved to the US, they might be called Asian Americans.

However, with the TCK, the assimilation into the new culture is not the final step as is with the immigrant, because many times, after assimilating in their youth, they will then return to their country of origin, perhaps for university, perhaps for other purposes. Thus, they do not belong to any particular country—having been born in one, raised and assimilated into another, and then returned to their country of birth. For this reason, many times, Third Culture Kids do not feel at home in any particular country, always referring and identifying themselves with the "other;" with their parent's passport country while in their host

> Third-culture individuals are sometimes referred to as cultural hybrids.

(Continued)

country, and with the host country while in the passport country (as cited in Fail et al. 2004).

Because of this feeling of not belonging, and especially in their formative years, TCKs begin to find their identity with people and ethnic groups, ideas, goals and aspirations, rather than with strictly geographical areas, as would many other adolescents or children of their own age (Gillies, 1998; Sussman, 2000; Fail, et al. 2004). Research among military children indicates that a feeling of rootlessness, which other authors have contended TCKs possess, is not an issue for this very reason. Their strong family togetherness and bondedness, as well as often spiritual roots, helped alleviate any feelings of lack in the sense of a geographical home (Finley, 2014). However, the parents of TCKs, albeit supportive, may many times worry that the children will have problems feeling like they belong upon return to the passport culture (Gillies, 1998).

A TCK's cultural identity begins to morph immediately upon moving to the new culture. They must adapt and find ways to fit in with then unfamiliar surroundings. Little by little they more or less "find themselves" and, like the Irish that became Irish Canadians, they take on characteristics, mannerisms, and values found in the new host environment. They assimilate. However, then comes the day of return to their old country, their passport country, and all of a sudden they find that there, among old friends and colleagues, they once again do not fit in. They are again part of the "other," even where they were not before. Because of their abundance of cultural experiences different from the average Joe or Jill, many times TCKs feel that they do not necessarily identify with the mainstream culture of their passport country upon return (Purnell, Hoban, 2012). They do not recognize the popular music or television shows their peers are interested in, may have a different idea of what is "humorous, appropriate, morally acceptable, and offensive," and may also try to avoid

For example Eidse & Sichel (2004) and McCaig (1996).

calling attention to their experiences abroad, as this might cause even greater separation from the ingroup, being "dismissed as attention seeking" or merely misunderstood (Finley, 2014, 23, 25; Gillies, 1998). This is a difficult realization to face, as expressed by Dormer in his article "We are the Rootless Ones:"

> But they are all things that you expect may happen when you travel to a foreign country, and because they are expected then, they do not come as a shock. It is perfectly normal to feel foreign in a foreign country. What is not normal is to feel foreign in your own country. This is the essential feature of the conflict: you do not feel that you belong there, but you feel that you ought to do so. In addition, you are treated, with great politeness, in ways which are calculated to heighten this feeling of not-belonging. The Ecolint graduate has been a stranger in a strange land for much of his life, and he knows how being a foreigner works. What he is not used to is being a stranger in his own land.
>
> (Dormer, 1979, 1)

It would be advisable to shorten this overly lengthy quote.

And again, by Richard, an interviewee of Fail, et al (2004, 327):

> Of course England was home so it was always going back to what was familiar . . . but it became increasingly unfamiliar as these two years went on, but I never stopped to think about it at all, because theoretically it still had that role as home. We were 'abroad' quote, unquote, therefore England was home and I never really stopped to examine that . . . Britain was horrendous . . . because what I hadn't realized, but what had clearly happened, is that X had become home, without any effort on my part, because I just lived there, it was all I knew. Other people had gone to school here and been brought up in a very British culture, British television and British everything, British beer, and here I turn up, English with a posh English accent . . . I was

(Continued)

> supposed to be English, I don't look foreign, I don't sound foreign and yet I am foreign, and I didn't get this at all . . . it must have affected me in some serious way, . . . because I felt disassociated from where I was from these people who seemed to represent values different from those I had and that's alright . . . if I'd gone to any other country, it would have been fine, because that's what you expect, but I didn't go to any other country, I went to the one which was supposed to be mine and it wasn't. . . . It was quite a shock because . . . it's like an earthquake, what you thought to be secure, you find just isn't . . .

This feeling of not belonging can be a disadvantage and an advantage. On the one hand, as TCKs may feel that they are not part of the group, as a defense mechanism, may marginalize themselves in the group so as not to have to face unknown, unfamiliar social situations (Purnell, Hoban, 2014). This feeling of not fitting in and not being able to identify with the majority may also lead to feelings of depression or anxiety, and thus to counseling if it is available. There are services for specifically TCKs in such circumstances. Another characteristic of TCKs is that they "tend to avoid solving interpersonal problems" because they know that they will be leaving soon anyway and that the conflict will, by itself, disappear. They also may begin to avoid long-term friendships for the same reason: they will be leaving soon (Gillies, 1998, 1). As Finley (2014) said in his doctoral dissertation, "With each new relocation comes the death of old relationships and the birth of new ones; however, the feelings of rootlessness versus maintaining permanent ties could prove devastating for both the children and parents." They may develop a "sense of urgency," an awareness that they have very little time, and may thus view small talk as a "waste of time," preferring to jump straight into the meat of subjects, perhaps scaring off potential friendships (Finley, 2014, 40). Maslow, in his hierarchy of needs, expressed that children

This paradox is sometimes discussed in terms of encapsulated vs. constructive marginality.

(Continued)

who move, "those who find themselves without roots (rootlessness)," and who therefore make and break relationships quickly, may have a difficult time fulfilling the third tier of his hierarchy of needs, a tier which states that humans need to know that they are loved and belong (Finley, 2014). If they have trouble fulfilling the third tier, then the highest tier, self-actualization, the fulfillment of potential, is harder to attain.

The advantages, like many of the disadvantages, also lie within the attitude. Finley's doctoral research (2014) on military children, now adults, indicates that most of them would not undo any of their experiences; they would not want to change anything. They are thankful for the experiences and value them. So this feeling of not belonging is not necessarily negative; the experiences that these people have had many times formulates an "increased intercultural communication competence and open-mindedness" (Moore & Barker, 2012, 554). A TCK may be enthusiastic and positive about their experiences and may wish to share them and live a very mobile lifestyle in the future. Because TCKs move a lot and seem to have to deal with "chronic change," this develops within them a "a strong sense of inner confidence and self-reliance;" they don't run away or hide when a new situation arises, but rather they proceed along with caution, testing the waters to see what the new rules and expectations are. They are not apt to "panic and/or feel helpless" (Finley, 2014, 36). Tarique and Weisbord (2013) observed in their studies that TCKs have "rich international experience and exposure to diversity in childhood" that can "produce in them a high level of dynamic cultural competence" (Tarique & Weisbord, 2013, 5). This can lead to the ability to bridge social and cultural gaps in everyday as well as business life (Finley, 2014). In today's highly integrated and intercultural world, these types of skills are high in demand. They are also generally very linguistic, speaking more than one language and open to more language study (Finley, 2014; Tarique & Weisbord,

> This tendency has been examined in terms of social sensitivity (Lyttle, Barker, & Cornwell, 2011).

(Continued)

2013). Many times, however, as shown previously, this ability to integrate into many cultures comes with an emotional price. It is not an easily acquired skill (Fail, et al. 2004). A qualitative study done by Barker and Moore (2012) found that many of the interviewees had the ability to switch between two or more cultural identities, depending on what culture the person was in at the time.

> I'm like a hybrid, right? I can function in both cultures. So I can go to Brazil and nobody would ever notice that I've been living in the U.S. for my whole life, and a lot of times here in US people are surprised when I tell them that I was born and raised in Brazil.

Though others expressed one identity unique to only themselves, in which they lived and operated in consistency wherever they might reside, this identity, formed by the various experiences living abroad and repatriations (re-entry and adjustment into their parent's home country), was also multicultural and efficient for living in many environments (Purnell & Hoban, 2014). However, this group, as opposed to the former, did not change identities and actions automatically like cultural chameleons. Rather, they perceived themselves as living with a static personality and cultural identity. This in no way means that the first group was confused or split in their personalities but that they naturally accommodated themselves to every situation as it came along. Some of Barker's and Moore's interviewees did, however, express confusion and a sense of being "in-between' (Moore & Barker, 2012, 558).

Having a consistent (hybrid) cultural identity does not necessarily mean that one's personality remains unchanged over time.

Conclusion

In conclusion, TCKs, despite, as well as because of, their mobile, rootless lifestyle and identity, have much to offer. As mentioned before, not only do they have a plethora of experiences and knowledge that can benefit the globalizing world, but they also understand the viewpoints of these

(Continued)

differing cultures. For example, if they had lived in Nepal or any other majority Hindu country, they might understand that the swastika, a symbol of genocide and evil to most of the world, is to those of the Hindu mindset, a symbol of peace or well-being. They may also have what Pollock calls a "three-dimensional worldview," using the example of tacks in a riot. While most people, when thinking of a riot, might mention the angry crowd or guns, a TCK who has actually experienced a riot might remember the tacks that flattened the tires of the cars on the street. They have a gritty, reality-based view of the world. TCKs also are ready to learn from and understand cultures other than their own. They have a built-in empathy that gives them an interest in people other than themselves, as well as the appreciation and comprehension of some of the deeper levels of why things are done differently in other cultures. As mentioned previously, because of their mobile history, they are also less prejudiced, adaptable, and more apt to blend in rather than to find the differences between themselves and the outgroup. They also have a sense that life is to be lived in the *now,* in the present, because this opportunity may never come again. It is a very carpe-diem mindset, useful for accomplishing goals, both in the short-term and in the long-term. Finally, because of their need to survive, TCKs usually develop quite sharp observational skills. They are able to see what is proper and what is not at a faster pace than someone else would, merely because of their experiences of being thrown into a culture and being forced to manage, sometimes learning the hard way first (Pollock, 2009).

In this brief review of literature, I have sought to express the prevailing views in research of the formation of the cultural identity of those that live, as children, outside of their passport cultures for significant periods of time, namely, Third Culture Kids. I found many of the articles and other literature to be repetitive in content, with only few deviations and variations from the general consensus of what and who TCKs are, so if

---

Margin note: Several studies have shown that third-culture individuals tend to be more open-minded than monocultural individuals, e.g. Dewaele & Van Oudenhoven (2009) and Lam & Selmer (2004).

Margin note: This student author does an excellent job of describing key characteristics of third-culture individuals and their cultural identity, as confirmed by several researchers and other authors.

(Continued)

this review is also repetitive, it is because of this reason.

There is room for further research in many aspects of TCK identity—for instance, how personal faith or family relationships help avoid the crisis of rootlessness.

References

Adler N.J. (1981). Re-entry: Managing cross-cultural transitions. *Group & Organization Studies (Pre-1986) 6*(3), 341.

Dormer, R.J. (1979). We are the Rootless Ones. *Ecolint Newsletter*, 13.

Fail H., Thompson J. & Walker G. (2004). Belonging, identity and third culture kids: Life histories of former international school students. *Journal of Research in International Education 3*(3), 319–338. doi:10.1177/1475 240904047358

February 18, 2011. Surprise Me: Transition model by David Pollock. Retrieved from: http://everydaysurprises.blogspot.fi/2011/02/transition-model-by-david-pollock.html

Finley W.G., Jr. (2014). *A narrative inquiry of adult third culture kids from military backgrounds*. (Ph.D., Walden University). *ProQuest Dissertations and Theses.* (1615343810).

Gillies W.D. (1998). Third culture kids. *Childhood Education 75*(1), 36–38.

Moore A.M. & Barker G.G. (2012). Confused or multicultural: Third culture individuals' cultural identity. *International Journal of Intercultural Relations 36*, 553–562. doi:http://dx.doi.org/10.1016/j.ijintrel.2011.11.002

Pollock, D.C. & Van Reken R.E. (2009). *Third culture kids: The experience of growing up among worlds (revised edition)*. Boston, MA, USA: Nicholas Brealey.

Purnell L. & Hoban E. (2014). The lived experiences of third culture kids transitioning into university life in Australia. *International Journal of Intercultural Relations 41*, 80–90. doi:http://dx.doi.org/10.1016/j.ijintrel.2014.05.002

Sussman N.M. (2000). The dynamic nature of cultural identity throughout cultural transitions: Why home is not so sweet. *Personality & Social Psychology Review (Lawrence Erlbaum Associates) 4*, 355–373.

Sussman N.M. (2002). Testing the cultural identity model of the cultural transition cycle: Sojourners return home. *International Journal of Intercultural Relations 26*, 391–408. doi:http://dx.doi.org/10.1016/S0147-1767(02)00013-5

Tarique I. & Weisbord E. (2013). Antecedents of dynamic cross-cultural competence in adult third culture kids (ATCKs). *Journal of Global Mobility 1*, 139–160. doi:http://dx.doi.org/10.1108/JGM-12-2012-0021

Zhou Y., Jindal-Snape D., Topping K. & Todman J. (2008). Theoretical models of culture shock and adaptation in international students in higher education. *Studies in Higher Education 33*, 63–75. doi:10.1080/03075070701794833

PART 4
INTERCULTURAL CONTEXTS

Part 4 focuses on Intercultural Communication Contexts. The following three chapters that place intercultural communication in different communicative contexts. As with Part 3, you will also find a student paper at the end of each chapter.

In Chapter 21, "Intercultural Communication Competence," Carmencita Del Villar explores how intercultural communication links to communicative competence. In Chapter 22, "Intercultural Communication and Organizations," Chin-Chung Chao and Dexin Tian discuss the growing links between organizations and interculturality. In Chapter 23, "Intercultural Communication and Health," Diyako Rahmani and Cheng Zeng look into how our health and health care are intrinsically linked to intercultural communication.

21 INTERCULTURAL COMMUNICATION COMPETENCE

Carmencita Del Villar, University of the Philippines, Diliman, The Philippines

Chapter Outline

- Definitions of Intercultural Communication Competence
- Dimensions of Intercultural Communication Competence
- Ways to Improve Intercultural Communication Competence
- Research into Intercultural Communication Competence
- Student Paper

The picture above shows a gathering of participants at the Summer Institute for Intercultural Communication (SIIC) organized by the Intercultural Communication Institute (ICI) in Portland, Oregon. Every summer, hundreds of participants from around the world go to the SIIC to learn about intercultural communication and gain more competence in interacting with people from different cultures. In this day and age when intercultural contact is ubiquitous, SIIC participants believe competence is vital to them as teachers, researchers, administrators, businesspersons, counselors, medical practitioners, students, or travelers.

Indeed, whatever your roles and statuses in life, intercultural communication competence is important to you. In your everyday life, you engage in all kinds of communication from the moment you wake up in the morning to the time you close your eyes at the end of the day. Whether you know it or not, communicating with someone from another culture is definitely among the kind of communication you do. Common examples of intercultural communication are: your classmate is an exchange student from Korea, one of your teachers belongs to the Baby Boomer generation, your math teacher is Sri Lankan, your school's canteen supervisor is Vietnamese, your bus driver is Japanese, the occasional taxi you ride is driven by a Russian immigrant, the owner of the convenience store across the street is an Indian, another classmate is from another region of your country, your grandmother is 65 years old, and your new group mate is from the opposite sex. Other examples of intercultural communication that have important implications in your life are: the worsening conflict in the Middle East, the increasing demand for oil and water in China, the rapidly increasing world population, and the fast growing migration of people. Wherever you are and whatever your situation, knowledge of intercultural communication competence is now as essential as any of the basics you need to learn to exist in this world.

This chapter explains the basics of intercultural communication competence by providing the following:

- Definitions of intercultural communication competence
- Dimensions of intercultural communication competence
- Ways to improve intercultural communication competence
- Research into Intercultural Communication Competence

A sample student paper, with suggestions from the teacher, is also included to help beginning students given the task of making their research paper.

Hopefully, after reading this chapter, you will have gained important foundations needed to become an interculturally competent person.

Definitions of Intercultural Communication Competence

There are various definitions of the term intercultural communication competence provided by experts in the field of Intercultural Communication. Different definitions indicate experts themselves disagree on certain issues as to which components make up the concept or which component is the most important. As Deardorff (2008) observed, there is no consensus among experts as to which one component best describes intercultural communication competence. Lustig and Koester (2010) concurred with Deardorff that there is still lack of agreement among experts when it comes to conceptualizing Intercultural Communication Competence, although they see some agreements when it comes to certain basic features. In the following sections, let us examine some of the definitions. Try to identify similarities among them.

Chen and Starosta (1998) defined **intercultural communication competence** as "effective and appropriate interaction between people who belong to particular environments. [It is] the ability to effectively and appropriately execute communication behaviors to elicit a desired response in a specific environment (p. 241)". Chen and Starosta's definition, according to them, resembles that of Spitzberg and Cupach (1984) in that they both stress the concept as being context-specific behavior. They further explained that "competent persons must not only know how to interact effectively and appropriately with people and environment, but also know how to fulfill their own communication goals using this ability" (p. 242). Unlike interpersonal communication, intercultural communication becomes more complex in the sense that there are additional "cultural factors" to consider. As we know, culture, or people's way of life, involves differences in people's values and perceptions of their world and those differences influence how people communicating with each other view themselves and others. So, using Chen and Starosta's views, when we try to determine one's intercultural communication competence, we should look into "the breadth and depth of the impact of culture on communication behavior" (p. 242) and relevance of that behavior on the others. We can see from Chen and Starosta's definition that it has the following elements: *Effective, appropriate, particular environments, goals* and *desired response*. This means for one to have competence in an intercultural encounter, one must be *effective* in one's communication. This involves using language and nonverbal codes that are *appropriate* to the situation. In addition, one must be familiar with the way bodily actions are used. **Particular environments** refer to the cultures of the participants. This suggests that during the encounter, the cultures of both participants, the host and the visitor, influence their behaviors. The communicator *goals* also influence how one behaves. One is motivated to say one's message in a particular way for one to reach one's goals. The **desired response** is what the communicator hopes to achieve at the end of the interaction. Let us consider the following examples. See what happens and try to determine why the misunderstandings occur. Try to identify which of the elements in Chen and Starosta's definition are present and which are not.

Example 1: Two American professors travel to South Korea to organize an international conference. The hosts are Korean professors from a local university. Prior to the trip, the American professors exchange emails with their Korean counterparts to make the initial arrangements. In their emails, the Americans use direct language, do not go through the formalities of greetings, are persistent and want things accomplished according to their time schedule. The Koreans, on the other hand, prefer to go through the formalities of greetings by referring to everybody's well-being and how nice the weather is. To them, the Americans' behavior of being direct and persistent about results is unacceptable. Because of that, the Koreans refuse to cooperate completely. Moreover, to the Koreans, not answering an email already means agreement so emailing back is redundant and a waste of time. To the Americans, immediacy in answering emails is the appropriate thing to do. This kind of interaction between the two parties goes on for a while. The Americans demand answers while the Koreans refuse to comply. Finally, when the Americans arrive in Korea, they are not greeted at the airport and are ignored for a couple of days. When the Koreans finally agree to meet them on their campus, the Americans are made to wait for more than 30 minutes. Instead of meeting the

Americans face to face, the Korean professors send a student to inform them that the professors are busy and that he was sent to meet with them.

Example 2: Upon entering a Korean home, the foreign guest does not remove his shoes and proceeds to walk into the living room. The Korean host is stunned and thinks the guest is rude.

Another definition is the one provided by Samovar, et al. (2010). They defined intercultural communication competence as "having the ability to interact effectively and appropriately with members of another linguistic-cultural background on their terms" (p. 384). Note that in this definition, it is not only the ability to communicate effectively and appropriately that is given emphasis but also the other culture as suggested by the term another linguistic-cultural background. To Samovar and colleagues, the important elements are: *effective, appropriate,* and *linguistic-cultural background*. This means that for one to be competent in the intercultural interaction, one must be *effective* in one's communication, use *appropriate language* and bodily action, and be familiar with the other person's *cultural background*. In this definition, being effective and appropriate are not enough; knowledge of the other culture is given importance. Let us consider the following examples of an intercultural interaction. Try to assess why the misunderstandings happen between the interactants. See if you can identify which elements are present and which are not.

Example 1: Two females, an American and a Filipina, share an apartment. The Filipina asks her roommate for help because her window is stuck and will not open. The American tries but fails to open it. She suggests they should call the maintenance people right away to have the window fixed. The Filipina, not wanting to cause any inconvenience, says that it is ok, she will just take care of it later, and that her roommate should not worry about it. Whereupon the American raises her voice and exclaims "No, it is not ok. Why do you keep saying it is ok when it is not? Why don't you want to assert your rights? Why are you so apprehensive? We pay for this apartment and we have every right to demand good service immediately!"

Example 2: An American, after a short conversation with his Chinese friend, says "see you later" and leaves. Where upon the Chinese spends the whole afternoon patiently waiting for the return of her American friend.

Lustig and Koester's (2010) definition of intercultural communication competence tends to favor the work of Spitzberg (1988) as he defined the concept as an "interaction that is perceived as effective in fulfilling certain rewarding objectives in a way that is also appropriate to the context in which the interaction occurs" (p. 68). They favor this definition because it allows for a better understanding of intercultural communication competence in that it uses the key word "perceived," which illustrates that competence is determined by the people involved in the communication event. It further means competence is a "social judgment" about how well the person communicates with others and not just one's perception of oneself. In addition, the definition explains that the event is specific to that time and place where it happens. Thus, competence is affected by the judgment of the people involved in the event, as well as the time and place where it happens. It also involves the appropriate behaviors that match the expectations of the event. Behaviors become effective if they are seen as appropriate by the participants in the event. Other important elements of intercultural communication competence are the objectives the participants want to achieve and the verbal and nonverbal messages they use to achieve those objectives. The important elements of Lustig and Koester's definition are: perception, effective, appropriate, objectives, verbal and nonverbal messages, context, and social judgment. Consider the following examples of an intercultural communication event. What are the reasons for the miscommunication? Try to find out which important elements are present and which are missing.

> **Example 1:** On the first day of classes in an American classroom, a Thai student enters and greets her professor by using his formal title. She says "Good morning, Professor Smith." Whereas an American student addresses the professor by his first name and says "Morning, John." The Thai student thinks the American classmate is disrespectful.
>
> **Example 2:** In an international airport in South Korea, a Japanese tourist while standing and looking for her flight schedule is bumped by a Korean man. She almost loses her balance by the force of the collision but the man just walks away as if nothing happens. The Japanese is shocked by the Korean's behavior.

Neuliep's (2006) definition of **intercultural competence** is "the degree to which one effectively adapts one's verbal and nonverbal messages to the appropriate cultural context" (p. 441). This means that when one communicates with a person from a different culture one needs to adapt one's message to the other person's culture to be effectively understood. This kind of adaptation requires that one possess some knowledge about the other person's culture, have enough motivation to communicate with him or her, and have the appropriate language and nonverbal skills. Competence is measured by how effectively one is able to communicate as perceived by the other person rather than one's own perception of one's qualities. It also varies depending on the situation. This means being competent in one situation does not necessarily make one competent in the next. What is appropriate in one culture may not be appropriate in another. The important elements of Neuliep's definition are *effective*, *appropriate*, *adaptation*, *verbal* and *nonverbal language*, and cultural context. Consider the following examples. See if you can identify the reasons why the misunderstandings happen. Which important elements are present and which are missing?

> **Example 1:** A Japanese professor, in a speech, announces that his wife is ugly. People in the audience of mixed cultures react to the professor's

remark differently. Some find the remark uncalled for while others find it funny. The Japanese in the audience find the remark very appropriate.

Example 2: An Australian man and a Filipina woman are having a conversation. The man keeps moving closer while the woman, feeling uncomfortable, keeps moving farther away.

Bennett and Bennett (2004) defined intercultural competence as "the ability to communicate effectively in cross-cultural situations and to relate appropriately in a variety of cultural contexts" (p. 149). Their definition emphasized that "no behavior exists separately from thought and emotion" (p. 149). They termed this union of thought and emotion as the "intercultural mindset and skillset" (p. 149). **Mindset** means the person is knowledgeable about the new culture, his or her own culture, differences between the two cultures, and is able to use this knowledge to relate with others. This mindset also includes a healthy dose of "curiosity and tolerance for ambiguity" (p. 149) to encourage more interaction and discovery about the other culture. This means one is open to learning about other cultures and is broadminded enough to accept the uncertainty that usually happens in intercultural interactions. The "**skillset**," on the other hand, is the ability to assess one's communication as well as miscommunications to be able to improve future interactions. The important implication of the Bennett and Bennett definition is that knowledge, attitude, and behavior must all be present to account for intercultural communication competence. As we can see from the definition, the important elements are *knowledge*, *attitude*, *appropriateness*, *behavior*, and *cultural situation*. Let us look at the following examples. What do you think are the reasons for the misunderstandings in these interactions? See if you can identify which elements are missing.

Example 1: A Japanese business person, after being introduced to a Singaporean business person, hands over his card by holding it carefully with the tips of his thumbs and forefingers, card facing the receiver, and bows his head. Whereupon the receiver grabs it with one hand, puts a notation on it, and shoves it into his pocket. The Japanese feels offended by the Singaporean's behavior.

Example 2: During a monthly lunch meeting of the faculty in one department in a Philippine university, an American friend of the department chairman drops by to pay a short visit. Seeing that there is a lunch meeting going on, he greets the chairman and says he will just return after the meeting. The chairman, being a polite Filipino, invites the American to come in and join them for lunch. The American promptly enters the room, sits on a vacant seat beside the chairman and starts to eat. The whole staff is stunned by the American's behavior but tries not to show it.

Kim (2001) mentions a number of terms to refer to **intercultural communication competence** among which are intercultural competence, intercultural skills, intercultural effectiveness, interpersonal communication competence, communication competence, and interpersonal competence. In all these terms, Kim noted interaction is essential, together with other "generic abilities" such as participants' competence, knowledge of one's biases, interests, abilities in verbal and nonverbal codes, awareness of cultural practices, knowledge of communication system, ability to manage differences, and ability to manage uncertainty. So, for competence to be achieved in the intercultural level, the following are essential elements: *interaction, knowledge of self, interests, abilities, verbal and nonverbal codes, awareness of the other culture*, and *ability to manage differences and uncertainty*. Consider the following examples of an intercultural event. Determine why misunderstandings happen. See which important elements are present and which are not.

> **Example 1:** A Filipino goes to the US for a visit. He notices people are generally friendly and easily strike up a conversation. A stranger he meets on the elevator greets him "good morning." The cashier at the grocery counter smiles and says "How are you doing today?" As he leaves the counter, the cashier bids him "Have a good day!" These simple conversations surprise him because he is not used to this kind of pleasantry towards strangers. Where he comes from people pretty much keep to themselves around strangers.
>
> **Example 2:** A professor gives a lecture to a group of Muslim students. She gestures vigorously with her left hand. The students feel offended.

Recognizing the need to develop a "consensual definition of Intercultural Communication Competence," Deardorff (2008, p. 32) launched a Delphi study involving a panel of 23 international experts in the field of intercultural communication. After a series of questions, she was able to "generate . . . refine . . . and reach an agreement on key characteristics of the concept." Results reveal intercultural communication competence is "the ability to communicate effectively and appropriately in intercultural situations based on one's intercultural knowledge, skills, and attitudes" (Deardorff, 2008, p. 33). Other definitions include "the ability to shift one's frame of reference appropriately, the ability to achieve one's goals to some degree, and the ability to behave appropriately and effectively in intercultural situations" (Deardorff, 2008, p. 34). As we can see, these definitions reflect the important elements of "communication and behavior in intercultural situations" (Deardorff, 2008, p. 35). So, for competent intercultural communication to happen, the following elements must be present: *effective and appropriate communication, knowledge of the other culture, knowledge of one's self, one's abilities and one's attitudes*. Consider the following examples of intercultural interactions. Can you find out why misunderstandings happen? Which elements in the definition are present and which are not?

> **Example 1:** An American mother introduces her young son to an elder Japanese woman and says, this is my son Paul. She then introduces the

elder to her son by saying, "Paul, this is Eriko." The Japanese elder is offended because the American did not use her title of respect (Mrs. Sato) when introducing her to the young boy. Calling her by her first name is a sign of disrespect.

Example 2: In an international conference, an American presenter wonders why there are no listeners in his session whereas the session in the next room is packed. He discovers there is a Korean presenter next door and all his Korean colleagues are there to listen and lend support.

In summary, we can see the definitions above have some overlapping elements and absence of others. It is not easy to make a tally of the common elements because one element may be termed differently by the other definitions. The last definition by Deardorff (2008), however, seems to cover all the elements of the previous definitions.

Dimensions of Intercultural Communication Competence

To help better understand the concept of intercultural communication competence, let us examine some of its key components. Chen and Starosta (1989) proposed there are four important components of intercultural communication competence. These are **personality attributes, communication skills, psychological adaptation,** and **cultural awareness.**

Personality attributes comprise self-concept, self-disclosure, self-awareness, and social relaxation. These traits develop as a result of one's experiences within his/her culture and in part from his/her heredity. Chen and Starosta (1989) described self-concept as the way one sees him/herself. An important part of self-concept is self-esteem which is how one evaluates oneself. One who values oneself highly feels more comfortable relating not only with oneself but also with others. Self-disclosure is how willing one is to share information about oneself. Intercultural communication naturally has a high level of uncertainty and appropriate disclosure can help lessen that uncertainty. The third personality attribute, self-awareness, is the ability to be aware of oneself and this improves one's adjustment to others because one becomes perceptive to one's own behavior. The fourth personality attribute, social-relaxation, allows one to learn to relax to help make the intercultural interaction more comfortable.

Communication skills include both the verbal and nonverbal behaviors that make our interactions possible. These behaviors include message skills, behavioral flexibility, interaction management, and social skills. Message skills involve having adequate knowledge of the host culture's language and nonverbal behavior. Behavioral flexibility is the ability to choose the appropriate behavior needed for the intercultural interaction. The third communication skill, interaction management, is knowing how to properly participate in a conversation. The fourth communication skill, social skills, includes empathy and identity maintenance which involve knowing how the other person feels and understanding their own and other's identity.

Psychological adjustment involves one's ability to deal with the stress that comes with being in a new environment. In the beginning, an individual may have feelings of frustration, alienation, and ambiguity as he or she adjusts to the new culture. Frustration may happen when one expects to see the familiar but sees something unfamiliar instead. Or one may feel alienated when he or she misinterprets an unfamiliar behavior. Or one may feel ambiguous and very uncertain when he or she simply does not understand the nuances of the foreign language. These are some of the feelings one may experience when adjusting to a different culture. But with enough time and patience, one would eventually adjust.

Cultural awareness refers to a deeper understanding and responsiveness to the new culture. This kind of awareness takes time because it involves not only knowing something about the new culture but being perceptive to what lies beneath the surface. When one is new to a culture one sees the observable things like fashion, music, food, architecture and people's behavior and not the deeper meanings that explain the observable such as social values, customs, norms and systems. One who is serious in developing cultural awareness must invest time and effort in doing so.

Samovar, et al. (2010) advanced five components that make a competent intercultural communicator: **motivation to communicate, an appropriate fund of knowledge, appropriate communication skills, sensitivity**, and **character**. **Motivation to communicate** means one is highly motivated to improve one's ability to communicate and goes beyond one's personal experiences to learn about others.

An appropriate fund of cultural knowledge is when one is knowledgeable not only about one's own culture but about those that one interacts with. **Appropriate communication skills** means one is able to use one's skills to reach goals in interaction. **Sensitivity** means one is receptive and aware of others. **Character** refers to one's trustworthiness, honesty, respect, and goodwill.

Lustig and Koester (2010) described three components that make up intercultural communication competence. These are: **context**, appropriate and effective behavior, sufficient knowledge, motivations, and skilled actions. Context refers to both the relationship of the people involved and the context within which the intercultural interaction happens. One may therefore be competent in one situation where one is with certain people and not competent in another situation with a different set of participants. Appropriateness and effectiveness refer to the acceptable behavior that leads to the desired result. Knowledge, motivations, and actions refer to the combination of the right information needed for the event, one's feelings and attitude toward the host culture, and the correct behavior to carry out the goal.

Neuliep (2006) mentioned the three components in Spitzberg and Cupach's model of Interpersonal Communication Competence and added his own four components. These are knowledge, affective, psychomotor and situational features. These four components influence each other. Knowledge refers to what one knows about the culture one is interacting with. Affective refers to how motivated one is in participating in the intercultural event. Psychomotor is how the knowledge and affective components are carried out. This includes one's use of language and bodily action. Situational features refer to the event in which the intercultural exchange happens. These may be the context, their previous experience with each other, and their statuses among others.

Kim (2001) forwarded three interrelated components intercultural communication competence: cognitive, affective, and operational. The cognitive component refers to the mental ability to understand messages, verbal and nonverbal, of the host culture. The affective component has to do with the emotion and the motivation to adapt to the host culture. The operational component is the behavioral dimension that expresses the cognitive and the affective components.

Recognizing the lack of agreement among experts, Deardorff (2008) presented her own list of intercultural communication competence components, which had an 80% to 100% acceptance rate by her Delphi panel. Note that the first in the list is accepted by all members of the panel. Below are the top ten components:

1. Understanding others' worldviews
2. Cultural self-awareness and capacity for self-assessment
3. Adaptability
4. Skills to listen and observe
5. General openness toward intercultural learning and to people from other cultures
6. Ability to adapt to varying intercultural communication and learning styles
7. Flexibility
8. Skills to analyze, interpret, and relate
9. Tolerating and engaging ambiguity
10. Deep knowledge and understanding of culture (one's own and others')

In summary, we can again see an overlapping of the different dimensions and the absence of others. The reason for this may be that the dimensions may be termed differently by different experts. Deardorff's (2008) list of dimensions seems to provide a more complete picture by covering all the other dimensions as suggested by the experts in her Delphi study. The implication of Deardorff's study is that although experts see or term the components differently, they all agree on the most important ones.

Ways to Improve Intercultural Communication Competence

With our knowledge of what Intercultural Communication Competence is and the important components that make up a competent intercultural interaction, we are now ready to take steps in improving our own competence. Experts on the subject suggest different ways. Let us examine the suggestions forwarded by Samovar, et al. (2010). First, be aware of your culture, which means we should understand our own culture because it gives much information about where the beliefs, attitudes, and values we now hold come from.

Second, examine your personal attitudes, or study your attitudes, stereotypes, and opinions that influence the way you view other cultures. Being aware of such things exposes us and helps us understand why we communicate the way we do with other cultures. Third, understand your communication style to find out how you communicate with others and how this communication is seen by others. Fourth, monitor yourself; essentially we should be aware of how we behave and be receptive to the way people respond to our behavior.

In addition to the four suggestions mentioned above, Samovar, et al. (2010) added three more. Fifth, we should be empathic, or try to know and feel how others feel, and work at improving this by being attentive, communicative with our feelings, and to use only acceptable behaviors, and to learn to accept differences. Sixth, we should practice effective listening; try to listen well to lessen misunderstandings especially when the interactants come from different cultures. Finally, develop communication flexibility, which is having the ability to adapt your behavior to people from cultures that are different from yours. This also calls for being tolerant and nonjudgmental when you encounter differences.

Lustig and Koester (2010) offered two tools to help one become interculturally competent: the **BASIC (Behavioral Assessment Scale for Intercultural Competence)** and the **D-I-E (Description, Interpretation, Evaluation) tool**. The first tool, the BASIC (Koester & Olebe 1988), is a tool for examining one's actual communication behavior. It has eight steps.

1. Display of respect—show respect for the other person
2. Orientation to knowledge—show that one realizes people are different and should not be judged according to their culture of origin.
3. Empathy—show one understands how others feel.
4. Interaction management—show skills in managing turn-taking in conversations.
5. Related to the group problem-solving activities—show through behaviors that one is comfortable about working with others in group problem-solving activities.
6. Relational role behavior—show one is concerned about interpersonal harmony.
7. Tolerance for ambiguity—show one can handle ambiguity, and that one is able to adapt to the feelings that come with ambiguity.
8. Interaction posture—to use non-evaluative and nonjudgmental actions in responding to others. This calls for the use of descriptive rather than interpretative or evaluative messages. This last step is better explained by the second tool, the D-I-E tool.

The second tool, the D-I-E tool (Description, Interpretation, and Evaluation) is based on the assumption that in processing information, people tend to make a "mental shorthand" by jumping to interpretations and evaluations without paying attention to the "specific sensory information" they receive (Lustig and Koester, 2010, p. 240). This shorthand may lead to misunderstandings because the other culture's meanings may be different from the interpretations and evaluations one makes. The D-I-E tool trains one to differentiate among statements one makes: whether they are statements of description, interpretation, or evaluation. Making descriptive statements can be used to describe what one sees and hears without making judgments or opinions. The advantage of doing this is that one becomes open to different possible meanings of the event rather than just the shorthand meaning one has. In the process of being aware of different meanings, one then has the chance to sift through different interpretations and find the most appropriate one, especially in an intercultural interaction.

Research into Intercultural Communication Competence

Because ICC is important to everyone, researchers have been conducting studies about it. Let us now take a quick survey of what some researchers have discovered about the relevance of intercultural communication competence in relationships, education, the workplace, medical practice, and organization.

ICC and Intercultural Effectiveness

Research has shown the relationship between ICC and intercultural effectiveness. Let us look at some studies in this regard. Bradford, et al. (1997) conducted a meta-analysis of 16 studies on ICC and provided empirical support that there was a strong correlation between ICC and intercultural communication effectiveness. They qualified that ICC and intercultural communication effectiveness were "equivalent." Their results also indicated that knowledge and skills in intercultural communication were predictors of ICC.

Another study focused on ways to lessen ethnocentrism and discovered that when people were more sensitive to other cultures and were multicultural, they also tended to have reduced ethnocentrism. This study by Dong, et al. (2008) was conducted in the United States and had for its participants 419 young adults.

Two researchers (Arasaratnam & Doerfel, 2005) from the US identified what they called key components of ICC as seen by people from 15 different cultures. Through face-to-face interviews with their respondents, they were able to identify two important components of ICC: knowledge and motivation. Other components discovered were skills in listening, experience in interacting with people from other cultures, having a "global outlook," and "other-centered" style of communication.

ICC and Education

More than in any other contexts, it is in educational institutions where the importance of communicating effectively with people from different cultures is most apparent. Let us take a look at some studies that illustrate this.

One interesting study was conducted by two researchers, Mirzaei and Forouzandeh (2013), about the possible relationship between intercultural communication competence and the motivation of Iranian students learning English as a foreign language. One hundred and eighty students taking Bachelor of Arts in English literature and Master of Arts in Teaching English as a Foreign Language participated in the study. Results showed a strong positive correlation between the two variables. Their findings suggested that if students had high intercultural communication competence, they also had high motivation to study English as a foreign language. Their study also had an important implication on the educational system and suggested that ICC training be incorporated in both the BA in English Literature and the MA in Teaching English as a Foreign Language curriculum.

Kerssen-Griep and Eifler (2008) conducted a longitudinal study into how effective an academic mentoring program was in training new teachers in communicating with students from other cultures. The White pre-service teachers were trained and observed over a period of eight months as they taught an African American cultural group. Statistically significant improvements were observed among the new teachers in their interactional ability, and mindful and skillful communication with their students.

Zimmerman's study (1995) of 101 international college students studying in an American school revealed that among the dimensions of ICC, communicating with American students was the most important factor that helped international students improve their perception of their communication competency.

In Romanowski's study (2011), high school Polish students were subjected to an experimental training that aimed to increase their intercultural exposures and to make them more aware of intercultural differences. At the end of the training, students were able to become familiar with the verbal and non-verbal language of the cultures they were exposed to which in turn allowed them better understanding and adjustment. As a result, the high school Polish students learned to appreciate and accept differences in culture, increase their intercultural sensitivity, and consequently their ICC. The study concluded that increased exposure and sensitivity to other cultures resulted in higher levels of ICC.

Briguglio (1987) described the importance of developing intercultural communication competence among undergraduate students at the Curtin University of Technology (Australia), through planned training that consisted of directed discussions and exploration of cultural issues in intercultural communication. She emphasized teaching techniques that included cultural diversity and development of ICC as opposed to simple interactions among students in multicultural classrooms.

ICC in Business and the Workplace

ICC too is seen as vital in the business world. A number of studies proved this to be true. Two professors from the US and the Philippines conducted a study to find out if ICC was associated with the multicultural team performance of American and Filipino managers in multicultural workplaces (Matveev & Del Villar 2014). Respondents included 71 MBA students from an American university and 93 Filipinos from a Philippine university. Results showed there was a significant positive correlation between ICC and multicultural team performance. This means that if respondents had high ICC levels they also performed better in multicultural teams.

Chaisrakeo and Speece (2004) argued that in the sales business, ICC played an important role in the salesperson's success in dealing with clients. They proposed a model to make success possible and that involved not only the salesperson's negotiating style but also knowledge of the organizational and national cultures.

Looking at intercultural communication competence in the workplace, Mao and Hale (2015) argued that Chinese employees who were more interculturally sensitive to other cultures tended to be more satisfied with the way they communicated with others in the organization. They also tended to use "control and solution-oriented conflict management styles." Overall, these employees tended to be more effective within their workplace compared to those who were less interculturally sensitive.

In another study in the Philippines, Del Villar (2010) found Filipinos who were more interculturally competent were more willing to communicate with others, had higher oral communication competence, and were less interculturally apprehensive. This study involved 941 respondents from 24 colleges of a state university who were administered a battery of tests to determine their scores in the different variables of the study. Extending the same study and applying it to 15 multinational corporations in the Philippines, Del Villar (2012) confirmed the same findings that intercultural communication competence was positively correlated with communication competence, willingness to communicate, and negatively correlated with intercultural apprehension.

Another study also looked into the importance of ICC in business. Bush, et al. (2001) recognized that in the recent years, the market has already become culturally diverse and this called for not only appropriate communication skills but also appropriate intercultural communication competence on the part of the sellers. They proposed marketers should have "adaptive selling behaviors" as well as "intercultural dispositions" to help improve their ICC.

ICC and Technology

In another study, Vannoy and Chen (2014) looked into the influence of using Skype as a means of communicating to understand other people's culture. For the duration of four weeks, 100 Americans and 60 Taiwanese subjects communicated with each other. At the end of the test period, the researchers found that the use of Skype influenced better intercultural communication competence among the participants.

ICC and Health/Healthcare

In the healthcare professions, researchers have recognized that communicating effectively with patients from different cultural groups is important. A study (Gibson & Zhong, 2005) explored the role of ICC in the healthcare context and examined how the healthcare providers' ICC influenced their relationships with their patients. Ninety-one patients and 45 healthcare providers were included in the survey. Results showed there was a correlation between the healthcare providers' ICC and the way their patients perceived them. Among the important elements that contributed to ICC were empathy, bilingualism, and intercultural experience.

Similarly, Rosenberg and Richard (2006) discovered knowledge and skill in ICC were important for doctors, especially those with patients from another culture. In their study of 24 patients and their doctors, they discovered that the doctors only had elementary knowledge of ICC and relied only on their interpersonal skills thereby causing distress among their patients. The researchers recommended ICC training for doctors to make their doctor–patient relationship in multicultural situations more successful.

Redmond and Bunyi (1993) studied the relationship of ICC to stress and effectiveness in handling stress as experienced by students in a Midwestern university in the US. Results showed that among the dimensions of ICC, adaptation and social decentering were the best indicators of lower levels of stress. This illustrated that if a person had adapted himself to the event and has shifted his perspectives to the other person, he would experience lower levels of stress. Further, if a person had high levels of communication effectiveness, adaptation and social integration, he would also tend to be more effective in managing his stress. All the qualities mentioned are dimensions of ICC.

Sensation-seeking, a personality trait that is associated with risk-taking and adventure, was correlated with ICC in a study conducted by Arasaratnam and Banerjee (2011). Their findings showed that there existed a positive relationship between the two variables and a negative correlation between sensation-seeking and ethnocentrism. Some implications of the study included: to sensation-seekers, a more socially acceptable alternative to risky behavior was intercultural contact; those with positive attitude towards foreigners were more motivated to communicate; because high sensation-seekers were motivated to seek foreign contacts they had more opportunities to develop ICC.

ICC and Relationships

Through the years, intercultural communication has resulted in multicultural relationships. Some studies have shown how important ICC is in these relationships. Bibb (2007) examined what "cross-national couples" did to make their relationships successful. Such topics as conflict negotiation, experiences with marginality, and cultural adaptation were assessed. Interviews were conducted with 66 respondents who were in a relationship with somebody from another culture. Results revealed a number of factors responsible for their successful relationship: intercultural skill, curiosity about each other's cultures, knowledge about their partner's country, and communication skill. Among the factors given, communication with one another was considered the most important.

Chi and Suthers (2015) studied ICC from a "relational perspective using social network analyses." In their research, they defined ICC as having the "ability to develop meaningful intercultural relations with host and other nationals." A multicultural community with 280 members was studied. Results showed that if one had more social relations or were "well-connected" in the local community one's experience with acculturation was also better. They concluded that in the case of the community they studied, ICC was a group rather than an individual attribute. When the community was cohesive its members also tended to adapt easily to each other.

From this quick survey of some studies on ICC, we can see how important it is in helping improve communication among people in different contexts. There are still hundreds of similar studies available in intercultural journals. As a student of intercultural communication, it would be beneficial for you to start reading more about those studies.

In summary, the road to intercultural communication competence is not an easy one and may take years to develop. But taking the first steps now by listening to what experts say, and benefitting from what they have studied, may be the best course of action anyone interested in intercultural communication could take.

Key Terms

BASIC	Character	Communication skills
Cultural awareness	Desired response	D-I-E
Intercultural communication competence	Intercultural competence	Particular environments
Mindset	Motivation to communicate	Personality attributes
Psychological adaptation	Sensitivity	Personality strength
		Skillset

Activities

Activity 1: "Show and Share."

Adapted from an activity in the session on Teaching Intercultural Communication by Drs. Stella Ting-Toomey and Leeva Chung, Summer Institute of Intercultural Communication, 2013, Portland, Oregon.

Objectives of the activity:

- To serve as an ice-breaker
- To allow students to get to know themselves and others better.
- To serve as a springboard for discussions about perceptions and influence of culture on perceptions.

Procedure:

- The teacher displays colorful clippings from magazines, postcards, or photos around the classroom.
- Students are given about five minutes to go around the room and choose one picture they like.
- Students are given another five-ten minutes to talk about the picture. He/she explains why the picture appeals to him or her. He/she may relate the picture to his/her life experiences.
- The class may ask questions about the sharing or may share their own perceptions of the picture. Different and similar perceptions may be used as examples to learn about influences of culture on perceptions.
- The teacher may also choose a picture and do her own sharing.

Debriefing:

- The teacher can ask what the students learned about themselves and about their classmates.
- Students can share what discoveries they made from the experience, if any.

Activity 2: "Fly on the wall"

Objectives:

- To help students become aware of other cultures by looking at different practices and behaviors.
- To help students make sense of differences observed.
- To help process what was observed by sharing with the class.

Procedure:

- The class is assigned to bunch up into groups of two (or any number depending on the class size).
- The groups are assigned to choose and visit one student organization inside the campus.
- The groups spend at least two visits with their chosen organizations to observe practices that are unique to it.

- During visits, the group may take down notes describing the unique practices observed.
- The group may also interview members of the organization to help understand the origin and reasons behind the unique practices.
- The group then reports to the class about their findings.

Debriefing:

- The teacher can ask what the students learned about themselves and about their chosen organization.
- Students can share what discoveries they made from the experience.
- The class can discuss the influence of culture on the practices and behavior of an organization.

Activity 3

Same as Activity 2 but this time the groups can visit different churches/religious buildings.

Activity 4: "e Pen Pal"

Objectives:

- To help widen students' experience with interacting with other students from other cultures.
- To allow students to apply concepts of ICC learned in the classroom.

Procedure:

- The teacher coordinates with other ICC teachers from other countries and arranges to have their students exchange emails.
- For the duration of the semester, each student is assigned an "e pen pal."
- Exchanges between e pen pals are shared with the class.
- Learning and experiences are related to concepts of ICC discussed in class.

Debriefing:

- Periodically, the teacher can ask what the students learned about themselves and about other cultures through their e pen pals.

References

Arasaratnam, L. & Banerjee, S. (2011). Sensation-seeking and intercultural communication competence: A model test. *International Journal of Intercultural Relations*, 35, 226–233. Available from: www.elsevier.com/locate/ijintrel

Arasaratnam, L. & Doerfel, M. (2005). Intercultural communication competence: Identifying key components from multicultural perspective. *International Journal of Intercultural Relations*, 29, 137–163.

Bennett, J. & Bennett, M. (2004). Developing intercultural sensitivity an integrative approach to global and domestic diversity. In Landis, D., Bennet, J., & Bennett, M. (eds.) *Handbook of intercultural training* (3rd ed.), pp. 147–165. Thousand Oaks, CA: Sage Publications.

Bibb, S. (2007). Intercultural Intimacy: An examination of cross-cultural couples and the implications for intercultural communication competence. *Capstone Collection*. Paper 2101. http://digitalcollection.sit.edu/captstone/2101.

Bradford, L., Allen, M., & Beisser, K. (1997). *An evaluation and meta-analysis of intercultural communication competence research*. Available from: https://www.researchgate.net/publication/234594736_An_Evaluation_and_Meta-Analysis_of_Intercultural_Communication_Competence_Research [accessed Jun 18, 2015].

Briguglio, C. (1987). Empowering students by developing their intercultural communication competence: a two-way process. Available from: http://www.researchgate.net/publication/228350736

Bush, V., Rose, G., & Gilbert, F. (2001). Managing culturally diverse buyer-seller relationships: The role of intercultural disposition and adaptive selling in developing intercultural communication competence. *Journal of the Academy of Marketing Science*, 29, 391–404.

Chaisrakeo, S. & Speece, M. (2004). Culture, intercultural communication competence, and sales negotiation: A qualitative research approach. *The Journal of Business & Industrial Marketing*, 19, 267.

Chen, G.M. & Starosta, W. (1998). *Foundations of intercultural communication*. Boston, MA: Allyn & Bacon.

Chi, R. & Suthers, D. (2015). Assessing intercultural communication competence as a relational construct using social network analysis. *International Journal of Intercultural Relations*. Available from: https://www.researchgate.net/publication/274096215_Assessing_intercultural_communication_competence_as_a_relational_construct_using_social_network_analysis [accessed June 18, 2015].

Deardorff, D. (2008). Intercultural competence: A definition, model, and implications for education. In V. Savicki (ed.), *Developing intercultural competence and transformation: Theory, research, and application in international education* (pp. 32–53). Sterling, VA: Stylus.

Del Villar, C. (2010). How savvy are we?: Towards predicting intercultural sensitivity. *Human Communication*, 13, 197–215.

Del Villar, C. (2012). Intercultural sensitivity of Filipinos in multinational corporations in the Philippines. *Human Communication*, 15, 59–84.

Dong, Q., Day, K., & Collaco, C. (2008). Overcoming ethnocentrism through developing intercultural communication sensitivity and multiculturalism. *Human Communication*, 11, 27–38.

Gibson, D., & Zhong, M. (2005). Intercultural communication competence in the healthcare context. *International Journal of Intercultural Relations*, 29, 621–634.

Hannaway, J. (1985). Managers, managing: The working of an administrative system. *Administrative Science Quarterly*, 35, 727–729.

Kerssen-Griep, J., & Eifler, K. (2008). When cross-racial contact transforms intercultural communication competence: White novice teachers learn alongside their African American high school mentees. *Journal of Transformative Education*, 6, 251–269.

Kim, Y.Y. (2001). *Becoming intercultural. An integrative theory of communication and cross-cultural adaptation.* Thousand Oaks, CA: Sage Publications.

Koester, J., & Olebe, M. (1988). The behavioral assessment scale for intercultural communication effectiveness. *International Journal of Intercultural Relations 12,* 233–246. In Lustig, M., & Koester, J. (2010). *Intercultural competence interpersonal communication across cultures.* (6th ed.) Boston, New York, San Francisco: Allyn & Bacon.

Lustig, M., & Koester, J. (2010). *Intercultural competence interpersonal communication across cultures* (6th ed). Boston, MA: Allyn & Bacon.

Mao, Y. & Hale, C. (2015). Relating intercultural communication sensitivity to conflict management styles, technology use, and organizational communication satisfaction in multinational organizations in China. *Journal of Intercultural Communication Research, 44,* 132–150.

Matveev, A., & Del Villar, C. (2014). Assessing intercultural communication competence of Filipino and American managers. *GSTF Journal of Business Review (GBR) 3*(3), 46–51.

Mirzaei, A., & Forouzandeh, F. (2013). Relationship between intercultural communicative competence and L2-learning motivation of Iranian EFL learners. *Journal of Intercultural Communication Research, 42,* 300–318.

Neuliep, J. (2006). *Intercultural communication a contextual approach* (3rd ed.) Thousand Oaks, CA: Sage Publications.

Redmond, M., & Bunyi, J. (1993). The relationship of intercultural communication competence with stress and the handling of stress as reported by international students. *International Journal of Intercultural Relations, 17,* 235–254.

Romanowski, P. (2011). Individual orientations towards intercultural differences on the basis of a study conducted among Polish students of English philology. Paper presented to the First International Conference on Foreign Language Teaching and Applied Linguistics (FLTAL'11), May 2011. International Burch University, Sarajevo. URL: http://eprints.ibu.edu.ba/id/eprints/575

Rosenberg, E., & Richard, C. (2006). Intercultural communication competence in family medicine: lessons from the field. *Patient Education and Counseling, 61,* 235–245.

Samovar, L., Porter, R., & McDaniel, E. (2010). *Communication between cultures.* Australia: Wadsworth Cengage Learning.

Spitzberg, B. (1988). "Communication competence: Measures of perceived effectiveness." In Tardy, C. (ed.), *A handbook for the study of human communication,* Norwood, NJ: Ablex, (pp. 67–105)

Spitzberg, B. & Cupach, W. (1984) *Interpersonal Communication Competence.* Beverly Hills, California: Sage.

Vannoy, S. & Chen, C. (2014). Intercultural communication competence via IP services applications: A modified task-technology fit perspective. *Journal of Global Information Technology Management, 15*(3), 55–80. Available from: https://www.researchgate.net/publication/274096215_Assessing_intercultural_communication_competence_as_a_relational_construct_using_social_network_analysis [accessed June 18, 2015].

Zimmerman, S. (1995). Perceptions of intercultural communication competence and international student adaptation to an American campus. *Communication Education, 44* (4), 321–335.

Student Paper

Assignment for the two to three-page paper on intercultural communication:

- Define intercultural communication. Use any of the definitions found in our reference materials.
- Explain its elements.
- Give an example of an intercultural communication event you have observed or participated in.
- Identify the elements of intercultural communication in the event.
- If needed, refer to the cultural orientations discussed in class to explain differences in cultures.

A Filipino exchange student's first day of classes in an American classroom

For this paper, I have chosen a definition given by C. Dodd where she states that intercultural communication is the sending and receiving of messages within a context of cultural differences producing differential effects.

The definition shows that there are six elements in an intercultural communication. These are the sender, receiver, message, context, culture and effects. Sender is the one initiating the interaction. He is the one sending the message. Receiver is the listener or the recipient of the sender's message. During the interaction, the receiver can also be the sender when he takes his turn to speak. The message is what the sender wants to say. The context is the place or time where the event happens. Culture is where the participants come from. Where they come from says a lot about the values, beliefs, and attitudes they hold. And effects are changes that happen as a result of the intercultural event. According to the definition of C. Dodd,

---

If the definition was taken directly from the book. Use quotation marks. Include page number when using direct quotation.

(Continued)

> the elements found in interpersonal communication are the same elements in intercultural communication. This possibly means that what happens in an interpersonal communication can also happen in an intercultural communication except that there is an additional element, culture, that is found in the latter. This can also mean that because there is an additional element, intercultural communication can be more complex than interpersonal communication. If an ordinary interpersonal communication is complex because of the differences between the two communicators, then intercultural communication can be much more complex because of the involvement of culture. To illustrate this point, take note of the following example which I personally experienced last year when I went to the United States as an exchange student.
>
>> On the first day of classes, the professor entered the classroom and greeted the students with a warm and friendly "Hi everyone." Some students greeted the teacher back by saying "Hi George." Others simply ignored him. I was stunned! The students addressed their teacher by his first name! This was unthinkable. Where I came from, no one addresses the teacher by his or her first name. Doing that would be an ultimate display of disrespect. Teachers, like our elders, are supposed to be highly respected and should be addressed accordingly. That same morning, after giving a short orientation about the requirements of the course, the professor proceeded to lecture about President Obama's foreign policy in Asia after which he invited the class to express their thoughts. Almost everyone vigorously spoke about their opinions without any encouragement from the teacher. Most of them lambasted the government and their president. Because I was new to the class, and my opinion was contrary to what they were saying, I simply listened. After everyone has conveyed their views, the professor turned to me and asked, "How about you, Ken? What is

(Continued)

> your opinion?" I froze! Not only was I shy, I also did not want to offend my American teacher and classmates with my opposing opinions. With much tentativeness, I politely answered the teacher by saying "Sir, I'm sorry. I do not have an opinion."
>
> Let us identify the elements in my story:
>
> - The professor was the sender of the message when he entered the classroom and warmly greeted his students.
> - His message was "Hi everyone!"
> - The students were the receivers when they heard their professor's greeting. They were also the senders when they greeted their teacher "Hi George!"
> - The classroom was the context. Included in the context were: the first day of classes and the time of the day.
> - Culture includes that of the teacher's (American), the students' (American), and that of the exchange student (Filipino).
> - Effects can be the Filipino exchange student's reaction to what he observed, students' reactions to their teacher's invitation to express their opinions, the Filipino exchange students feelings of unease, and his refusal to express his opinion.
>
> So, we can see from my illustration that all the six elements were present making this not only an interpersonal communication but also an intercultural communication. As C. Dodd explained, intercultural communication is the sending and receiving of messages within a context of cultural differences producing differential effects.

You may go deeper in your discussion by including an explanation of the nature of the two cultures. You might want to use direct and indirect as well as high-power and low power cultural orientations to explain the behaviors of the American teacher, American students, and the Filipino exchange student in the classroom.

Include a complete reference list at the end of the paper (author, year, title of book or article, publisher, journal).

22 INTERCULTURAL COMMUNICATION AND ORGANIZATIONS

Chin-Chung Chao, University of Nebraska-Omaha, USA and Dexin Tian, Yangzhou University, China

Chapter Outline

- Globalization and Its Impacts
  - History of Globalization
  - Definitions of Globalization
  - Impacts of Globalization
- Types of Organizations and Organizational Cultures
  - Literature Review of the Researches on Organizations in Intercultural Settings
  - Types of Organizations
  - Organizational Cultures
  - Factors That Influence Organizational Cultures
- Cultural Variations in Organizations
  - High- and Low-Context Cultures
  - Polychronic Time and Monochronic Time
  - Six Cultural Dimensions
  - Holism
- Flows of Organizational Communication
  - Downward Communication
  - Upward Communication
  - Horizontal Communication
- Cross-Cultural Adjustment and Cross-Cultural Training
  - Cross-Cultural Adjustment
  - Cross-Cultural Training
  - Cross-Cultural Competence
- Chapter Summary
- Student Paper

In today's globalized world, all of us are citizens of the global village. The above picture shows the type of **diversity** we are encountering on a daily basis, in a classroom, on a business trip, and at work. We see several national flags in the upper part of the picture, which are by no means representative of all the countries in the entire world, but are used simply to create the impression of diversity. There are altogether 11 young people, male and female from various ethnic backgrounds on both sides of a middle-aged man, probably their boss, in the picture. They all look confident, energetic, and happy. However, are they aware of and ready for the challenges in the increasingly diversified world? Let us first provide them with an old saying "when in Rome, do as the Romans do" and then begin our discussion about intercultural communication and organizations with the story about the adage.

The classic adage originated from Bishop Augustine. According to Morris, et al. (2014), history recorded that Augustine, Bishop of Milan was writing to Januarius, Bishop of Naples with the above advice about an impending trip to their organization's headquarters in Rome. At the time, Christians in Rome fasted on Saturday, but Christians in other cities did not do so. To face the intercultural dilemma and avoid potential offense, Augustine suggested adapting to the local norm of fasting when they stayed in Rome and resuming their conventional norm when coming back home to Milan and Naples. Although Bishop Augustine adopted adaptation as a solution to the intercultural dilemma, people in today's increasingly globalized businesses and **organizations** face much more complex intercultural challenges.

Globalization is changing the ways of operation and means of communication in all organizations today. It is becoming more and more common for trans-national organizations to maintain international interactions with their clients over the telephone, by e-mail, via video-conference, or face-to-face. Globalization has also brought intercultural challenges at home. The workforces of organizations have been growing culturally diverse as a result of increased immigration, multiethnic identification, and multicultural policies and ideologies. Even managers of local enterprises need to learn about cultural differences in order to communicate and connect with their employees from various cultural backgrounds.

According to the US Census Bureau (2015), between 2000 and 2025, the Hispanic population will increase by 11.2% and become the largest minority group in the United States. While the number of Caucasians will decrease by approximately 19%, all other minority groups will increase by 9%. Meanwhile, the world population will grow rapidly in developing countries while remaining stable or even decreasing in the developed countries. This is why Rodrik (1997) noted, "the most serious challenge for the world economy in the years ahead lies in making globalization compatible with domestic social and political stability" (p. 2).

As a result, organizations today find it necessary to increase their cultural awareness and enhance their **intercultural competence** to communicate correctly, effectively, and appropriately across cultural boundaries in this globally connected world. To help readers gain a better understanding of communication and intercultural communication in organizations and to enable organizations to think globally and act locally, we discuss intercultural communication in organizations from the aspects of globalization and its impacts, types of organizations and organizational cultures, cultural variations in organizations, flows of organizational communication, and cross-cultural **adjustment** and cross-cultural training in this chapter.

Globalization and Its Impacts

In this section, we first describe the history of globalization. Then, we provide definitions of globalization. Finally, we discuss the impacts of globalization on communication in cross-cultural organizations. As a double-edged sword, globalization may bring benefits and harms to domestic and international businesses. Necessary knowledge and sufficient understanding of globalization can lead organizations to maximum benefits and minimum losses.

History of Globalization

For years, globalization has been a hot topic, and it shows no signs of going away anytime soon. Although it is still contested when and where globalization started, it is for sure the world is becoming smaller and the effect is seen in all aspects of social life. This process can be termed as globalization, which has taken place quite a number of times in human history. Globalization occurred with the trading routes between ancient China and Europe, in the contacts between India and its neighboring countries, and during the interactions and conflicts among Muslims, Jews, and Christians early in human history. History witnessed bigger scales of globalization with the rise of the Portuguese, Spanish, Dutch, and British maritime empires and their colonization in different parts of the world in the 16th and 17th centuries. Waves of globalization were facilitated and accelerated with the introduction of new modes of transport like railroads and steamships and telecommunications like radio and television in the 18th and 19th centuries. These waves of globalization have revolutionized the world in major aspects and became instrumental in maximizing the utilization of time and space. This trend was followed in the 20th century, with transportation becoming much faster and safer thanks to innovations in electronics and telecommunications. As a result, the world has been experiencing a drastic change with the advent of the internet and mobile phones in the 21st century. In a word, the world has become a "global village" (McLuhan, 1964, p. 6) as predicted by Marshall McLuhan, the guru of communication studies back in the 1960s.

Definitions of Globalization

Globalization has been defined in various ways, and most definitions bear reference to the interconnectedness of political entities, economic relationships, and modes of communication. With economic relationships in focus,

Kennedy (1993) defined globalization "as primarily integrative structures," meaning the "local and national governments eventually cede control of policy to the global institutions such as the World Bank or the International Monetary Fund" (IMF) (p. 47). To the IMF, globalization is "the result of human innovation and technological progress," and "the increasing integration of economies around the world, particularly through trade and financial flows" (Clack, 2006, p. 4). *New York Times* columnist Thomas Friedman (1999) defined globalization as follows:

> It is the inevitable integration of markets, nation-states and technologies to a degree never witnessed before—in a way that is enabling individuals, corporations and nation-states to reach around the world farther, faster, deeper and cheaper than ever before and in a way that is enabling the world to reach into individuals, corporations and nation-states farther, faster, and deeper, cheaper than ever before.
>
> (pp. 7–8)

Friedman emphasizes the functions of globalization which integrates markets, nation-states, and technologies in such a way that individuals, corporations, and nation-states can be connected and reached in maximum scope, rate, and depth. Optimistic about the effects of globalization, Friedman urges active participation and integration into the globalization process.

With more and more individuals traveling to foreign countries or working in foreign companies and organizations, it is essential to know more about the cultures of foreign countries and endeavor to communicate well and work together. If individuals and organizations are unaware of cultural differences and do not know the efficient ways to get along and get business done, it can and does lead to poor performance and lost deals. Since we are working in an interconnected global economy now, it is high time we fully understood the impacts of globalization for good people relationships and lucrative business outcomes.

Impacts of Globalization

Globalization does not just refer to an economic phenomenon. Its ripple effects reach all cultural aspects of any society in the world today. Ideas, customs, and cultural movements follow closely after the exchange of goods across national boundaries. Surely, globalization exerts its immediate and obvious impacts through both pros and cons. According to Batterson and Weidenbaum (2001), globalization:

1) accelerates economic growth by increasing the standards of living;
2) benefits consumers with higher income and lower-priced products and services;
3) increases employment and improves the working conditions of workers;

4) helps cleaning up and protecting the environment;
5) helps developing nations with booming economies and millions out of poverty;
6) helps protecting human rights by linking economic freedom with political freedom;
7) fosters the growth of democratic governments throughout the world; and
8) guarantees the quality of life in terms of life expectancy, literacy, human health, leisure, and living standards.

In contrast, globalization also:

1) subjects many people to financial crises and poverty in the name of corporate greed;
2) increases record corporate profits while the conditions of the poor continue worsening;
3) offshores jobs to developing countries with poor working conditions and abuses of workers' rights;
4) exploits local environments for corporate profits and contributes to global warming;
5) subjects developing nations trapped in debt and millions of people in poverty;
6) supports a world trade in human bondage and slavery estimated in the millions;
7) threatens the sovereignty of nation-states with world trade and finance bodies; and
8) threatens public health, local economies, and the social fabric of farmers.

(p. 18)

Regarding organizations, globalization has demonstrated profound and far-reaching impacts, bringing about major organizational changes. Dani Rodrik (1997), professor of international political economy at Harvard's Kennedy School of Government, found that globalization reduces the barriers to trade and investment and accentuates the asymmetries between organizations able to cross international borders and those unable to do so. Meanwhile, globalization engenders conflicts within and between nations over domestic workplace practices and international norms. These two aspects of change are directly related to five emerging trends: globalization, diversity, **flexibility**, **flattening**, and **networks**, each of which leads to a pair of tensions.

First of all, globalization brings about greater **convergence** in consumers' tastes and preferences. As the first pair of tensions, globalization does not appeal to every organization in every country. While some organizations are more globally-oriented, others remain more locally-oriented. Due to diversity, organizational members have to work together with colleagues and customers from various countries and cultures. As the second pair of tensions, there are both advantages and disadvantages in both workplace and marketplace diversity. Proponents of organizational diversity, also called heterogenists, emphasize the advantages. Opponents or homogenists single out the disadvantages. Flexibility requires leaders and employees in organizations develop a wider repertoire of skills and strategies while working with diverse groups of people. However, some leaders and employees are comparatively more flexible. Since the world is flattening as described by Friedman (2006), organizations are getting flattened by decentralizing the decision-making mechanism so as to respond to customers, stakeholders, and markets at the quickest speed possible and with the best possible decisions. To this end, some organizations are getting decentralized, but others remain highly centralized. Networks are the results of **horizontal communication** within and between organizations. Within organizations, it is faster to communicate directly and horizontally. Between organizations, which are usually down-sized, close ties or networks are established as social mechanisms of coordination in place of legal mechanisms, which are slow and costly. Horizontal communication and networks of social mechanisms of coordination are found in more interdependent organizations as compared with more traditionally independent ones. Rodrik's (1997) findings can be summarized in Table 22.1:

Table 22.1 Trends and Tensions in Organizational Change

Trends	Tensions
Globalization	Global versus Local
Diversity	Heterogeneity versus Homogeneity
Flexibility	Flexibility versus Stability
Flat	Centralization versus Decentralization
Networks	Interdependence versus Independence

After Rodrik (1997).

In brief, globalization has made way for free trade and business, and it has created cross-cultural communication between various parts of the world. On the one hand, globalization is making this world a better place to live in. It is improving the political scenarios in more and more countries, and it is resolving the social problems of poverty and unemployment. On the other hand, globalization is westernizing the local customs and values of the developing countries while modernizing those nations. The power play may lead to linguistic, cultural, and traditional genocide if we do not keep a check of the cons of globalization and let **diffusion** go wild. To embrace globalization and stay competitive, organizations need to adapt themselves to the trends of changes while dealing with the above five pairs of tensions.

Types of Organizations and Organizational Cultures

After discussing globalization and its impacts, we present the major types of organizations, discuss organizational cultures, and elucidate the factors that influence organizational cultures in the following section. However, we begin this section with a brief literature review of the research on organizations in intercultural settings so as to clarify the academic backdrop and pave the way for our further discussion about other relevant aspects concerning intercultural communication in organizations.

Literature Review of the Research on Organizations in Intercultural Settings

With the corporate world becoming more and more interrelated and international, there has been a significant amount of literature on cross-cultural management. Cross-cultural management refers to "the study of the behavior of people in organizations located in cultures and nations around the world" (Adler, 1983, p. 226), focusing on the organizational behavior, especially interactions of peoples across countries and cultures. According to Adler, et al. (1986), "as the world enters the Pacific century, the differing impacts of Occidental and Oriental cultures on **managerial interaction** have become highly significant" (p. 306). They found that early scholarships on cross-cultural management focused on 1) cross-cultural variance; 2) cultural determination; 3) convergence versus divergence; 4) intercultural interaction; and 5) synergy from cultural diversity. Among the studies on Oriental cultures, most of them have been done on Japan and a few on other countries like South Korea and China. Some studies found Japanese managers and workers demonstrate a strong sense of identity with their work groups, an ethic of cooperativeness, a high dependence on the larger entity, a strong sensitivity to status, and active respect for the interests of individuals and for each individual as a person. Meanwhile, ethnic Chinese managers tend to honor a tight set of business rules, emphasize hard work, thrift, and competitiveness, as well as a strong belief in Confucian familism. Other studies found a long-range planning horizon, commitment to lifetime employment, and collective responsibility at the heart of the Japanese management system. The Chinese revealed a strong relationship between mind-sets and productivity, stressed equal sharing to such a degree that poor performance and good performance were rewarded equally, and became accustomed to the norm of avoiding standing out in any way. Yet, most of the scholarship was still based on Western theoretical models, which "fail to account for differences between Occidental and Oriental cultures and mind-sets" (Adler, et al., 1986, p. 306).

Based on their review of the empirical studies investigating the overseas adjustment of **expatriate** managers in the 1970s and 1980s, Mendenhall and Oddou (1985) summarized four dimensions of literature as follows. First, the self-oriented dimension dealt with 1) reinforcement substitution, replacing pleasure- and happiness-seeking activities in the home culture with similar activities in the host culture; 2) stress reduction, with the help of such methods as meditating, writing in diaries, and engaging in favorite pastimes; and 3) technical competence, as a result of the feelings of expertise in the jobs in foreign lands. Second, the other-oriented dimension encompasses the ability to develop relationships and the willingness to communicate with the host nationals. Third, the perceptual dimension concerns the abilities of the expatriates to understand and interpret the cultural reasons for the host-national's behaviors non-judgmentally and non-evaluatively. Finally, studies on the cultural toughness dimension reveal it is more difficult to adapt to the cultures of India, Pakistan, Southeast Asia, the Middle East, North Africa, and Liberia, and expatriates sent to these countries are likely to suffer from higher levels of stress (pp. 40–43).

Focusing on cross-cultural organizational behavior, Gelfand, et al. (2007) found culture was not the main focus in the studies on organizational behavior in the 1960s and 1970s. Existing research was generally atheoretical, descriptive, and methologically problematic, and organizational behavior theories were developed and tested on Western samples. It was with the advent of culture typologies (Hofstede, 1980) in the 1980s that scholars began studying national cultures to uncover the cultural boundaries of some Western organizational behavior models. Japanese models, such as quality control circles were among the research results. In the two decades around the year of 2000, "cross-cultural theory and research have taken on the central role," and "a large wave of cross-cultural research was witnessed across all areas of the field" (Gelfand, et al., 2007, p. 482). There have been such major studies as dynamic cultural theory (Hong, et al., 2000), organizational contexts (Aycan, et al., 2000), new taxonomies of cultural values (House, et al., 2004), and research methods combining **emic** (or culture specific) with **etic** (or universal) perspectives on cultural differences (Morris, et al., 1999).

Finally, Littrell and Salas (2005) emphasized the reasons, purposes, and strategies of cross-cultural training in present-day organizations. There are at least three reasons for continued cross-cultural training: the heavy financial losses associated with expatriate assignments, the lack of conclusive answers concerning the effectiveness of cross-cultural training, and the continuing diversity at the work place. In order to improve expatriates' rate of success in their foreign assignments, cross-cultural training aims to equip the expatriates with the knowledge, skill, and attitudes needed for cross-cultural adjustment, effective on-the-job performance, and interactions with the host nationals. Seven strategies of cross-cultural training are listed: 1) didactic, providing factual information about the working conditions, living environments, and cultural differences in the host countries; 2) attribution, developing attitudes and skills necessary for explaining the host national behavior from the host-culture point of view; 3) cultural awareness, educating the trainees about their own cultures so as to appreciate the differences between the home culture and host culture; 4) cognitive-behavior modification, assisting the expatriates in developing the habitual behaviors desired in the host culture; 5) interaction, making sure the incoming expatriates are learning from the expatriates whom they are replacing; 6) language, training those expatriates who will be immersed in a culture speaking a foreign language; 7) experiential, providing the expatriates with activities likely to be encountered during the foreign assignments and having them participate in the activities so as to learn by doing. Having finished the literature review, we continue talking about intercultural communication and organizations for classroom discussions and future application on various cross-cultural occasions.

Types of Organizations

According to Gardner, et al. (2001), an organization is a social unit of people structured and managed to meet a need or pursue some collective goals. Typically, organizations involve highly differentiated social systems, and individuals are divided into divisional units, functional specialties, work groups, and status levels. Due to diversity, organization employees have to "work competently with the expanding **heterogeneity,** including gender, age, race, religion, and ethnicity" (Barker & Gower, 2010, p. 296). According to Cox (1991), organizations can be classified into three types along a continuum based on the degree of employee diversity: monolithic, plural, and multicultural. In a monolithic organization, the employees are homogenous, with a limited number of minority employees. In a plural organization, minority employees are moderate in number, but they generally hold lower level jobs. In a multicultural organization, minorities should be represented at all levels of the organization, but this is only an ideal so far. As a result of the employee diversity, affirmative action plans may be in place, but they are rarely enforced. Instead, minority employees are pressed to assimilate into the mainstream culture or monolithic workgroups under frequent prejudice and discrimination. Ideally, multicultural organizational employees "have the best chance for treating workgroup members fairly, that is, respecting differences and valuing each person for special skills or knowledge" (Larkey, 1996, pp. 467–470).

As a new way of organization, multinational companies result from today's economic structures, which are turning global and adapting to the global economy. Operating in two or more countries, multinational companies or organizations are economic and technical entities which tend to produce goods and services abroad. Different from other organizations, multinational organizations usually have their employees composed of people from various geographical, religious, linguistic, and political backgrounds. To coordinate routine activities and to keep their competitive edge in the global economy, organizations including transnational ones make communication or intercultural communication the central means to devise, disseminate and pursue their organizational goals.

According to Kelleher, et al. (1996), since the 1980s many traditional organizations have flattened their structures. Traditionally, the **hierarchical** structure of Taylor's (2006) theory was followed, and organizations delegated authority in a pyramidal, hierarchical structure, with power concentrated primarily among the few individuals at the top (see Figure 22.1). Hannaway (1985) found evidence suggesting hierarchical level and environment uncertainty may affect the communication behavior of organization members (as cited in Verma, 2013). Thus, senior managers usually take more part in conversations and meetings than do lower level managers under conditions of high uncertainty (see Case Study 1).

Case Study 1: Uncertainty and Meetings

> The new director, Mr Rohtas sensed some kind of politics in the environment. The strong lobby of the old director was trying to fail the system. For one month Mr Rohtas simply observed the situation. A kind of uncertainty prevailed in the environment. He started with meetings. The old lobby deliberately avoided. Gradually, he held meetings after meetings where he showed concern for their advice as well, saying "Hello Ms Anu! What is your suggestion?" or "What kind of administrative role, you feel you can handle and do wonders, Mr Vikas?" Soon, the things improved and environment became congenial to a great extent. Wasn't communication through meeting an effective way to normalise the environment of uncertainty? Wouldn't this methodology help in different ways make working conditions better?
>
> (Verma, 2013, p. 65)

To provide innovative, high-quality products, and instantaneous services to customer demands, more and more organizations have shifted authority downward and given employees increased autonomy and decision-making power. Team structures and network structures are typical examples. Team-structured organizations emphasize interpersonal relations by linking formal and informal group relations to influence an employee's behavior or performance. Independent or semi-independent organizations nowadays tend to choose network structures so that they can share resources, information, and manpower, and responsibility for joint projects (see Figure 22.2 and Figure 22.3).

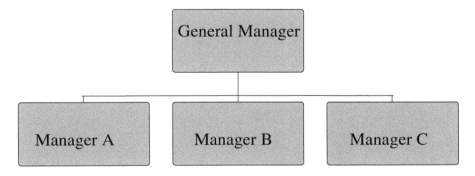

Figure 22.1 A Traditional Hierarchical Organization
(*Source:* After Kelleher, McLaren, and Bisson (1996))

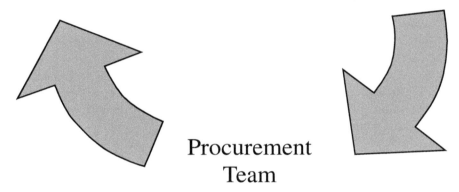

Figure 22.2 A Team-Structured Organization
(Source: After Kelleher, McLaren, and Bisson (1996))

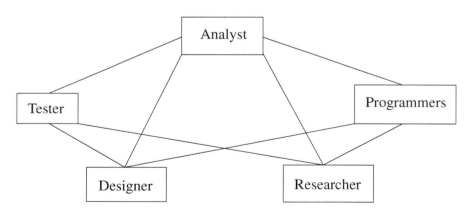

Figure 22.3 A Network-Structured Organization
(Source: After Kelleher, McLaren, and Bisson (1996))

Meanwhile, virtual organizations and organizations structured in matrix have also come into being. Briefly, virtual organizations can be described as "a network of independent firms that join together in the Internet-connected virtual space to produce a service or product" (Mowshowitz, 1997, p. 32). According to Sy and D'Annunzio (2005), a **matrix** is a grid-like structure and a matrix-structured organization is meant to share its resources to address multiple business dimensions using multiple command structures (see Figure 22.4). It is also meant to organize the employees in terms of their specialties according to the structure of projects. However, the project structure may not match the organizational structure. Besides, individual employees may find it troublesome to respond to multiple bosses. Thus, it may be difficult to control the progress of a project.

Organizational Cultures

According to Whalen (2014), it was Roger Harrison who first held the idea that organizations have cultures that can be identified, categorized, and managed. Davis (1984) coined the term **"corporate culture"** in the 1970s, and Pettigrew (1979) first used the term "organizational culture" in academic literature. The term was used to explain the economic successes of Japanese businesses which motivated their workers to nurture the commitment to a common set of core values, beliefs, and assumptions. Kerr and Slocum (2005) defined organizational culture as a system of shared assumptions, values, and beliefs that show people what is appropriate and inappropriate behavior. These values have been found to have a strong influence on employee behavior as well as organizational performance (Marcoulides & Heck, 1993; Ogbonna & Harris, 2000; Ouchi, 1981).

Actually, the concept of organizational culture exists along a continuum with the process approach at one end and classification approach at the other (Lim, 1995). The process approach follows Schein's (1990) model, in which culture consists of three levels: 1) artifacts, referring to the most visible and tangible aspects such as the physical, social, and environmental components of an organization; 2) values, meaning the deeply-held beliefs or shared

Project \ Specialties	Program	Graphics	Databases	Quality	Test
Project A		X	A	X	X
Project B	X		X	X	X
Project C	X			X	X

Figure 22.4 A Matrix-Structured Organization
Source: After Sy and D'Annunzio (2005)

principles, standards, and goals that determine behavioral patterns within an organization; and 3) assumptions, representing the unconscious level of cultural or organizational beliefs about human nature and reality.

The classification approach observes Hofstede's (1980/81; 2001) model of cultural dimensions, which will be discussed in detail in the next section. Based on their studies (Hofstede, et al., 1990), scholars have determined six dimensions of organizational cultures, which can be used "to describe the larger part of the variety in organizational practices" (Hofstede, 2011, pp. 19–21) in the following six dyadic dimensions:

Process-oriented vs. results-oriented

Process-oriented cultures are dominated by technical and bureaucratic routines while results-oriented cultures by a common concern for outcomes. Associated with the culture's degree of homogeneity, there were vast differences in perception among the process-oriented cultures, but almost everybody perceived their practices in about the same way in results-oriented cultures.

Job-oriented vs. employee-oriented

Job-oriented cultures assume responsibility for the employees' job performance only, while employee-oriented cultures assume a broad responsibility for their members' overall wellbeing. Hofstede et al. (1990) showed this orientation is part of a culture and not just a choice for an individual manager.

Professional vs. parochial

Professional members, who are usually highly educated, identify primarily with their profession whereas parochial members derive their identity from the organization they work for. This dimension is also known as the "local vs. cosmopolitan" or internal vs. external frame of reference.

The open system vs. closed system

This dimension refers to the common style of internal and external communication and to the ease with which outsiders and newcomers are admitted. Empirical evidence of systematic difference shows that organizational cultures also contain elements from national cultural differences.

Tight vs. loose control

This dimension deals with the degree of formality and punctuality within the organization, based on the function of the organization's application of technology.

Pragmatic vs. normative

The last dimension describes the degree of flexibility or rigidity of dealing with the environment, especially the customers. This dimension measures the degree of customer orientation, which has been extensively researched in the marketing literature.

Now, read Case 2 and find out the type or types of organizational cultures the people in the conversation find themselves in:

Case Study 2: A Conversation Concerning the Setting up of a Communication Lab

> Director: "Why don't you purchase Software A instead of Software B?"
> Dr Shyma: "Sir, Software A is outdated while Software B is far advanced."
> Director: "But the approval for Software B will take time, while I have to show on papers that the lab has been established." (Note: The tone here is non-cooperative and of an accusation. Obviously, it will create a defensive climate. A climate of control implies that the senior's view is the only valid one. What if the director said the following?)
> "O.K. In that case you make a proposal, explaining the advantages of Software B over Software A and let us forward the proposal."
> (Verma, 2013, p. 66)

Factors That Influence Organizational Cultures

According to Griffith and Harvey (2000), an organizational culture can be defined as "an ordering characteristic that is reflected in the employees' attributes and understanding, policies and practices implemented, and overall conditions of the work environment" (p. 90). Organizational culture is usually influenced by the following factors: 1) the diversity of the workforce, such as the proportion of local nationals, expatriates, and third-country nationals; 2) the policy **compatibility** between the home country and the host country organization; 3) the length of time the subsidiary has been in operation; 4) the ownership structure of the subsidiary such as sole ownership or shared ownership; 5) the degree of national cultural distance among network members; 6) the level of constraining government regulations such as mandatory employee quotas; and 7) the relative strategic importance of the subsidiary perceived by the home country management (Griffith & Harvey, 2000).

It is clear there are multiple factors that influence organizational cultures. This also explains why cross-cultural communication with employees overseas involves complex and vexing problems. For a better understanding of organizational cultures, Griffith and Harvey (2000) proposed a perceptual mapping of competing organizational cultural values. The mapping consists of a vertical axis and a horizontal axis which are crossed at the center. At the top of the vertical axis is "flexibility" and at the bottom "control." At the left of the horizontal axis is "internal" and at the right "external."

In the mapping, flexibility means the level of **decentralization**, control means the level of **centralization**, internal means maintaining existing cultural systems, and external means adapting to the local or home country cultural systems. The vertical axis illustrates the organizational preference towards the level or degree of flexibility/control dimension. The horizontal axis illustrates the internal/external dimension of organizational culture.

Cultural Variations in Organizations

Cultural variations are cultural differences. Many theoretical frameworks have been introduced in the study of cultural variations. Here, we focus on Hall's high- and low-context cultures and M-time and P-time orientations, Hofstede's cultural dimensions, and holism as a result of collective academic efforts. Although the cultural dimensions of Hall and Hofstede have been criticized for utilizing geographical borders between nation-states as boundaries for cultures, no scholar has provided convincing demonstration to completely discard them so far. Moreover, studies of communication practices and patterns today "still resonate with the cultural dimensions proposed decades ago" (Würtz, 2006, p. 276).

High- and Low-Context Cultures

First, context refers to "the information that surrounds an event," which is "bound up with the meaning of that event" (Hall & Hall, 2003, p. 200). On a scale from high to low context, the cultures in the world can be divided into **high-context cultures**, in which "most of the information is already in the person, while very little is in the coded, explicit, transmitted part of the message," whereas **low-context cultures** are those in which "the mass of the information is vested in the explicit code" (Hall, 1976, p. 79). Japanese, Chinese, Arabs, and Mediterranean peoples belong to high-context cultures while Americans, Germans, Swiss, and Scandinavians belong to low-context cultures.

Polychronic Time and Monochronic Time

Due to years of exposure to other cultures, Hall (1983) divided the time orientations in various cultures into **polychronic time** or P-time and **monochronic time** or M-time. P-time refers to "the model of involvement in several things at once," while M-time means the time orientation in which "events are scheduled as separate items—one thing at a time" (p. 43). P-time orientation is usually observed in Mexico, Japan, China, and some other Mediterranean countries. M-time orientation is usually witnessed in the United States, Canada, France, and other north European countries.

While it is characteristic of P-time cultures to be oriented to people, M-time cultures are oriented to tasks, schedules, and procedures. Thus, proper reporting can enable a P-time administrator to manage a surprising number of subordinates, but organizations run on the P-time model are often limited in size, and "are slow and cumbersome when dealing with anything that is new or different" (Hall, 1983, p. 46). An M-time organization can grow much larger than the P-time model, but its weaknesses "lie in its blindness to the humanity of its members and extreme dependence on the leader to handle contingencies and stay on top of things" (p. 46).

There is a caveat in the understanding of P-time and M-time orientations. While American time is mostly monochronic, which dominates the official worlds or business, government, and sports, etc., one finds P-time takes over at home, especially in those traditional homes where everything revolves around women. The Japanese are polychronic when looking and working inward to themselves, but they shift to the monochronic mode when they are dealing with the outside world. The French are "monochronic intellectually but polychronic in behavior" (Hall, 1983, p. 54).

Case Study 3: Are the Japanese Polychronic or Monochronic?

> On a recent trip to Japan, I was contacted by a well-known colleague who had translated one of my earlier books. He wanted to see me and asked if he could pick me up at my hotel at twelve fifteen so we could have lunch together. I had situated myself in the lobby a few minutes early, as the Japanese are almost always prompt. At twelve seventeen, I could see his tense figure darting through the crowd of arriving business people and politicians who had collected near the door. Following greetings, he ushered me outside to the ubiquitous black limousine with chauffeur. . . . (Between lunch and 3:00pm, my colleague arranged an interview for a magazine, a meeting with Mr. X, a book publisher, some pictures taken during the interview and the talk with Mr. X, and having lunch with him as well as an outstanding student, whose examination scores were 200 points above the average.).
>
> (Hall, 1983, pp. 55–57)

Six Cultural Dimensions

Based on their studies (Hofstede, 1991, 2001; Hofstede & Bond, 1988; Hofstede, et al., 2010), six cultural dimensions were labeled to explain cultural variations in the world. Each country could be positioned through an index score on each of the six dimensions. One may find the index score of a particular country or in contrast with another country by going to the Hofstede Center at http://geert-hofstede.com/united-states.html.

Below are the six cultural dimensions:

1. **Power Distance** (PD) is related to the extent to which the less powerful members or organizations and institutions accept and expect the unequal distribution of power. PD index scores are higher for East European, Latin, Asian, and African countries, and they are lower for Germanic and English-speaking Western countries.

2. **Uncertainty Avoidance** (UA) is related to the degree of a society's tolerance for uncertainty and ambiguity. UA scores are higher in Latin American countries, Southern and Eastern Europe countries including German speaking countries, and Japan. They are lower for Anglo, Nordic, and Chinese culture countries.
3. **Individualism** (IDV) vs. **Collectivism** is related to the degree to which individuals are integrated into groups. In individualistic societies, the stress is put on personal achievements and individual rights. In contrast, in collectivistic societies, individuals act predominantly as members of a lifelong and cohesive group or organization. Individualism prevails in developed and Western countries whereas collectivism prevails in less-developed and Eastern countries.
4. **Masculinity** (MAS) vs. **Femininity** refers to the distribution of values or division of emotional roles between women and men. Masculine cultures value competitiveness, assertiveness, materialism, ambition, and power while feminine cultures place more value on the relationships and quality of life. Masculinity is extremely low in Norway (8) and Sweden (5). In contrast, masculinity is very high in Japan (95), and in the Anglo world, masculinity scores are relatively high with 66 for Britain. In Latin America, Venezuela has a 73 point score whereas Chile has 28.
5. **Long-Term** (LTO) vs. **Short-Term Orientation** (STO) refers to the choice of focus for people's efforts in the future, present, or past. Higher LTO scores are found in East Asia, with China having 118, Hong Kong 96, and Japan 88. Scores are moderate in most European countries, with Britain and the United States being short-term oriented. A very short-term orientation is found in African and some Islamic countries.
6. **Indulgence** vs. **Restraint** is related to the gratification or control of basic human desires related to enjoying life. Indulgence scores are higher in Latin America, the Anglo world, and Nordic Europe. Restraint is more frequently found in East Asia, Eastern Europe, and the Muslim world.

Holism

Differences in social orientation cause differences in cognition between East Asians and Westerners. East Asians are more interdependent and holistic than Euro-Americans. The pattern of attention tends to be more diffused in interdependent cultures; in contrast, the pattern of attention tends to be more focused in independent cultures. East Asians are inclined to attend more to relationships between elements, background, and context. On the contrary, Westerners tend to focus on central objects and highly salient individual elements of complex scenes. Interdependence "has been shown to be linked to holistic cognition" (Varnum, et al., 2008, p. 321). According to Lim (2009), **holism** is a tendency to see everything as a whole rather than as separate components. Holistic cultures are undergirded by the following three relationship features.

First, relations in holistic cultures are prescriptive and people are not free to choose their relationships. As a result, relations take precedence over individual choices and even determine the members' roles in the society. Second, relations are whole-oriented. This means members are expected to work towards the general goals of the whole. Individuals are expected to sacrifice their needs for those of the whole. Finally, relations are complementary. In holistic cultures, individual members tend to work together. They may perform different tasks and roles, but their tasks and roles complement each other. Together, they attempt to accomplish the larger group or societal objectives. Below is a case which challenges your decision on the distinction between cultural dimensions.

Case Study 4: Which Cultural Dimension Is at Work?

> In the classroom building, Dr Priya reached the class late by two minutes. The dean on round pointed it out by saying: "Madam, what is this? You are late by two minutes. This will not be tolerated." Sir! I have two lectures back to back. Shifting from the 2nd floor to the 5th floor takes some time." "That's no excuse," responded the dean. (What if the dean finally responded as follows?) "Ok. Looks like we have a problem here, and I'll look into it later."
>
> (Verma, 2013, p. 66)

Flows of Organizational Communication

Regardless of the type of organization, communication is the essential element that maintains and sustains organizational activities. Just as Verma (2013) remarked, "communication is one of the important variables, held responsible for rise and fall, success and failure, progress and regression of any organization" (p. 63). In other words, organizational communication is central to organizational success. Organizational communication is defined as "the process by which individuals stimulate meaning in the minds of other individuals by means of verbal and nonverbal messages in the context of a formal organization" (Richmond & McCroskey, 2008, p. 20). This means organizational communication is dynamic and flows in certain modes. Before talking about the flows of organizational communication, it is necessary to have a clear understanding of the functions of communication and communication networks in an organization.

In their book entitled *Organizational Communication for Survival: Making Work, Work*, Richmond and McCroskey (2008) listed six functions of organizational communication: 1) informative: providing the organizational personnel with necessary information so they can complete their jobs in an effective and efficient manner; 2) regulative: communication directed toward regulative policies within an organization or messages about maintenance of the organization; 3) integrative: communication focused on coordination of tasks, work assignments, and group or unit coordination toward a common goal; 4) management: communication directed toward establishing relations with the personnel, getting to know them better, getting them to do what is needed; 5) persuasive: communication from supervisors meant to influence employees to complete expected jobs, and 6) socialization: communication aimed at integrating all personnel into the communication networks for surviving and progressing in the organizations.

Richmond and McCroskey (2008) described two types of communication networks: formal and informal. The former refers to communication that follows the formal, established, official lines of contact, the chain of command, or the hierarchical structure of the organization, while the latter means communication that follows the grapevine. Grapevine communication does not mean gossip; instead, it is the informal communication linking relationships among employees and management, which tells you who is really talking to whom and about what.

Having clarified the functions of communication and communication networks in an organization, we describe the three major flows of formal communication networks in an organization according to Lunenburg (2010).

Downward Communication

Downward communication transmits information from higher to lower levels or from the top to the bottom of an organization. It is generally effective when upper levels of management are highly motivated to make it work. Canary (2011) identified five purposes of downward communication: 1) implementation of goals, strategies, and objectives: information communicated about new strategies and goals for specific targets and expected behaviors; 2) job instructions and rationale: directives on how to do a specific task and how the job relates to other activities in the organization; 3) procedures and practices: messages defining the organization's policies, rules, regulations, benefits, and structural arrangements for expected uniformity in organizational practices; 4) performance feedback: progress reports or individual performance appraisals in accordance with organizational standards and goals; 5) socialization: organizational activities such as picnics, parties or other special ceremonies to motivate organizational members to adopt the institution's mission and cultural values.

Upward Communication

Upward communication is usually initiated by those at the lower levels of the organization. It can be successful only when those at the higher levels are willing to allow the communication to be effective. Thus, effective upward communication displays the following features: it is: 1) positive: positive communication is more likely to go up the system than negative communication; 2) timely: a message must be sent at the appropriate time to be allowed to go on up the system; 3) supportive: messages that support the current policy are much more likely to be given attention than those that are incompatible with current policy; 4) directed to the right person: it is essential that messages be forwarded to those people who can act on them, or else communication will be ineffective; and 5) with intuitive appeal: messages that have intuitive appeal are much more likely to go up the system than those that don't. Intuitive appeal is an idea that sounds good (Lunenberg, 2010).

Horizontal Communication

While downward and upward communication are considered vertical communication, communication that flows across the organization is regarded as **horizontal communication**. There is more horizontal than vertical communication in an organization on a daily basis because there are more employees than managers and employees at the same level feel more comfortable talking with one another than with people at different authority levels. Horizontal communication falls into one of three categories (Canary, 2011): 1) intradepartmental problem solving: interactions taking place between members of the same department for task accomplishment; 2) interdepartmental coordination: interdepartmental interactions facilitating the accomplishment of joint projects or organizational tasks; and 3) expert advice: training or consultation from specialists in various fields to an organization's employees or managers.

From the above, we can see that the three directions—downward, upward, and horizontal—establish the framework for the communication flows of an organization. These communication flows are depicted in Figure 22.5.

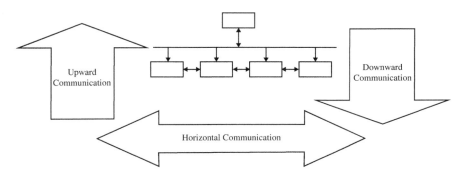

Figure 22.5 Downward, Upward, and Horizontal Communication
Source: Lunenburg (2010)

*Case 5: How Do You Comment on the Following
Grapevine Gossip via E-mail?*

> Sally Reeds, a medical secretary for the department of neurology at Western Heights Hospital in Colorado, turned on her computer and found an e-mail from her friend and co-worker, Justin Zeels, a social worker in the same hospital. Justin wrote that Dr. Sites, Medical Director of Neurology, was found under a bench outside the ER. The hospital security allegedly reported that Dr. Sites was completely intoxicated, and he was rushed home. Sally spiced up the tale and immediately e-mailed 10 of her friends. This morning, Sally looked up and saw Dr. Sites seeing his patients as if nothing had happened. She confronted him and asked him how he could possibly face everyone after what happened last night. Dr. Sites looked confused until a copy of Zeels' e-mail was thrust into his hands by another staff member. After reading it, Dr. Sites became livid and fired Justin for spreading such a malicious rumor. Meanwhile, Maria Hummingshire, another medical secretary, who saw the entire incident, ran to her computer to e-mail the latest to her friends.
>
> (Guo & Sanchez, 2005)

Cross-Cultural Adjustment and Cross-Cultural Training

As a result of globalization, many companies are now operating in more than one country. Such trans-national companies or multicultural organizations aim to create global competitiveness by reducing production costs and exploiting international market opportunities. However, according to Okpara and Kabongo (2011), these multicultural organizations are having difficulty retaining expatriates for their global operations. For instance, "20–40% of all expatriates sent on foreign assignments return home prematurely," and one chief reason lies in "the inability of the managers and the expatriates to adapt to the host-country's culture" (p. 22). Besides, these organizations are also faced with the challenge of blending employees from their parent countries with the host countries who may come from different cultural backgrounds. To adjust themselves to the new cultural environments and ensure greater productivity, both managers and their employees in trans-national organizations need to receive cross-cultural training programs and become interculturally competent.

Cross-Cultural Adjustment

According to Black (1988), cross-cultural adjustment refers to the process of adaptation to living and working in a foreign culture. It is the perceived degree of psychological comfort and familiarity an individual has while living or working in a new culture. There are three facets of expatriate adjustment: 1) work adjustment, which includes supervision, responsibilities, and performances; 2) general adjustment, which encompasses life conditions in a new culture; and 3) relational adjustment, which consists of interactions with members of the host community. This typology is composed of three factors: 1) individual: including the individual's adjustability and prior international experience; 2) contextual: including the length of time the individual spent in the host country, the partner's social support, and the organization's logistic support; and 3) organizational: including any job-related variables such as role clarity and role discretion, organizational social support, organizational cultural similarity between the home-country and the host-country, and cross-cultural preparation. Black's (1988) typology has been academically applied and empirically confirmed (Black & Gregersen, 1991; Cerdin, 1999; Parker & McEvoy, 1993).

Cross-Cultural Training

The purpose of cross-cultural training is to educate and prepare members of one culture to interact effectively and appropriately with members of another culture. Gertsen (1990) classified cross-cultural training into two categories: 1) conventional training, in which information is transmitted through a unidirectional communication; and 2) experimental training, in which the trainer gets the trainees to participate by simulating real-life and hands-on situations. Meanwhile, two other dimensions of culture should be combined in the training, namely, getting the trainees to acquire the awareness of cultural differences and become sensitive and competent in one particular culture. Brislin (1979) introduced three techniques for cross-cultural training: 1) **cognitive**: corresponding to a dissemination of information by using non-participative sessions on a foreign cultural environment; 2) **affective**: aiming to provoke individual reactions of the trainees so as to teach them to deal with critical cultural incidents; and 3) behavioral: improving the trainees' ability to adapt to the host-country's communication style and establish positive relationships with members of another culture. A number of scholars (Black, et al., 1992; Tung, 1987; Waxin & Panaccio, 2005) have adopted and verified Brilin's model.

Cross-Cultural Competence

Cross-cultural **competence** is defined as "the degree to which you effectively adapt your verbal and nonverbal messages to the appropriate cultural context" (Neuliep, 2012, p. 424). Bean (2006) summarized four dimensions of cross-cultural competence: 1) systemic: requiring effective policies and procedures, monitoring mechanisms and sufficient resources to foster culturally competent behavior and practice at all levels; 2) organizational: requiring skills and resources to meet client diversity, with an organizational culture which values, supports, and evaluates cultural competency as integral to core business; 3) professional: requiring cross-cultural competence standards to guide the work and life of individual employees; and 4) individual: requiring the maximization of knowledge, attitudes, and behaviors within an organization that supports individuals to work with diverse colleagues and customers. Cross-cultural competence is not innate; instead, it is learned through education, training, and experience. Although individuals and organizations cannot choose or change their native and host cultures, they can choose and acquire necessary intercultural competence for their personal and organizational goals.

Chapter Summary

This chapter began with an introduction to globalization and its impacts. Globalization connects people and organizations all over the world. It impacts every aspect of our daily life and influences the business world both positively and negatively. Organizations, especially those aiming at the international markets, need to be fully aware of the double-edged sword effects of globalization, understand their own strengths and weaknesses, and then try to fit in while looking at the big picture. What followed was a discussion about the major types of organizations and organizational cultures preceded by a brief literature review of the research on organizations in intercultural settings. Knowledge of the types and trends of organizational structures prepares newcomers to find their way at work and insiders to accomplish their tasks as expected. Awareness of the differences in organizational cultures facilitates both green hands and old hands in their thorough understanding of what is valued and how they should progress in both familiar cultural contexts at home and new cultural environments abroad if their organizations are trans-national or cross-cultural in nature. The discussions about cultural variations in organizations and flows of organizational communication in the following two sections theoretically and technically prepare those in cross-cultural organizations in their interactions with people or business partners, especially those from other cultures by understanding their partners' thinking patterns and norms of behavior. In the era of highly developed information and communication technologies, organizations need to keep themselves abreast of the newer, faster, and more effective ways of communication and bring both routine and newly-introduced means of communication and cross-cultural communication into full play. Finally, the chapter ends with a discussion about cross-cultural adjustment and cross-cultural training. Aware of the reasons, purposes, and strategies of cross-cultural training and making an effort to become interculturally competent, both managers and employees in multinational organizations can be ensured to interact and deal with their cross-cultural partners effectively, appropriately, and lucratively.

Key Terms

Adjustment	Affective	Centralization
Cognitive	Collectivism	Compatibility
Competence	Convergence	Corporate culture
Cultural dimension	Decentralization	Diffusion
Diversity	Downward	Emic
Etic	communication	Expatriate
Femininity	Flattening	Flexibility
Global village	Globalization	Heterogeneity
Hierarchical	Hierarchical	High-context culture
Holism	Horizontal	Individualism
Intercultural competence	communication	Low-context culture
Managerial interaction	Masculinity	Matrix
Monochronic time	Polychronic time	Organizational culture
Power Distance	Uncertainty Avoidance	Upward communication

Activities

1. Divide students into groups of three or four. Instruct groups that they have to create an organizational culture model (Schein's Onion Model can be the base for their model) based on the characteristics of a selected organization. Each group has to write at least three examples for each level. Then ask them to discuss: a) Why is it important to understand the values of the organization? b) How do you feel about the organizational culture of the organization in relation to its multicultural workforce? and c) After completing this activity, do you think that your organization embraces the idea of a multicultural perspective of organizational culture? Yes or No? Justify your claim.

2. Ask students to look at the qualities in the Intercultural Exercise (Lambert & Myers, 2005) and describe the most important quality and why they chose it. Then, ask them to identify the most difficult quality and why. Discuss how using these qualities makes the difference by relating back to the lecture material. In addition, invite students to consider using intercultural communication skills in the workplace, so that they can be more effective in their roles.

    Qualities in the Intercultural Exercise:

    ____ To be persistent
    ____ To learn from interacting
    ____ To respect other cultures
    ____ To be aware of stereotypes
    ____ To be aware of one's own limitations

___ To be aware of one's own culture
___ To tolerate ambiguity
___ To relate to people
___ To be able to communicate well
___ To be non-judgmental
___ To practice empathy
___ To be flexible
___ To listen and observe
___ To adjust based on others' reactions

References

Adler, N. J. (1983). Cross-cultural management research: The ostrich and the trend. *Academy of Management Review*, 8, 226–232.

Adler, N. J., Doktor, R., & Redding, S. G. (1986). From the Atlantic to the Pacific century: Cross-cultural management reviewed. *Journal of Management*, 12, 295–318.

Aycan, Z., Kanunggo, R. N., Mendonca, M., Yu, K., Deller, J., Stahl, G., & Kurshid, A. (2000). Impact of culture on human resource management practices: A ten country comparison. *Applied Psychology: An International Review*, 49(1), 192–221.

Barker, R. T., & Gower, K. (2010). Strategic application of storytelling in organizations: Toward effective communication in a diverse world. *Journal of Business Communication*, 49, 295–312.

Batterson, R., & Weidenbaum, M. (2001). The pros and cons of globalization. Center for the Study of American Business, Washington University in St. Louis. Retrieved from https://www.heartland.org/policy-documents/pros-and-cons-globalization

Bean, R. (2006). Cross-cultural competence and training in Australia. *Cultural Competence in the Health Care Industry*, 14(1), 14–22.

Black, J. S. (1988). Work role transitions: A study of American expatriate managers in Japan. *Journal of International Business Studies*, 19, 277–294.

Black, J. S., & Gregersen, H. B. (1991). Antecedents to cross-cultural adjustment for expatriates in Pacific Rim assignments. *Human Relations*, 44, 497–515.

Black, J. S., Gregersen, H. B., & Mendenhall, M. E. (1992). Toward a theoretical framework of repatriation adjustment. *Journal of International Business Studies*, 23, 737–760.

Brislin, R. W. (1979). Orientation programs for cross-cultural preparation. In A. Marsella, G. Tharp, & T. Ciborowski (eds.), *Perspectives on Cross-cultural Psychology*. Orlando, FL: Academic Press.

Canary, H. (2011). *Communication and organizational knowledge: Contemporary issues for theory and practice*. Florence, KY: Routledge.

Cerdin, J. L. (1999). *La Mobilité Internationale: Réussir l'Expatriation*. Paris, France: Editions d'Organisation.

Clack, G. (2006). The challenges of globalization. *eJournal of USA*, 11(1), 1–5.

Cox, T. H., Jr. (1991). The multicultural organization. *Academy of Management Executive*, 5, 34–47.

Davis, S. M. (1984). *Managing corporate culture*. New York, NY: Harper & Row.

Friedman, T. (1999). *The Lexus and the olive tree: Understanding globalization*. New York, NY: Farrar, Straus & Giroux.

Friedman, T. (2006). *The world is flat: A brief history of the twenty-first century*. New York, NY: Farrar Straus & Giroux.

Gardner, M. J., Paulsen, N., Gallois, C., Callan, V. J., & Monaghan, P. G. (2001). Communication in organizations: An intergroup perspective. In W. P. Robinson & H. Giles (eds.), *The new handbook of language and social psychology* (2nd ed., pp. 561–584). Chichester, UK: John Wiley & Son.

Gelfand, M. J., Erez, M., & Aycan, Z. (2007). Cross-cultural organizational behavior. *Annual Review of Psychology*, 56, 497–514.

Gertsen, M. (1990). Intercultural competence and expatriates. *International Journal of Human Resource Management*, 1, 341–362.

Griffith, D. A., & Harvey, M. G. (2000). Executive insights: An intercultural communication model for use in global inter-organizational networks. *Journal of International Marketing*, 9(3), 87–103.

Guo, K. L., & Sanchez, Y. (2005). *Workplace communication*. Retrieved from http://healthadmin.jbpub.com/Borkowski/chapter4.pdf

Hall, E. T. (1976). *Beyond culture*. Garden City, NY: Anchor.

Hall, E. T. (1983). *The dance of life: The other dimension of time*. New York, NY: Doubleday and Company.

Hall, E. T., & Hall, M. R. (2003). Key concepts: Understanding structures of culture. In M. G. Serapio & W. F. Cascio (eds.), *Readings and cases in international management: A cross-cultural perspective*. New York, NY: Sage.

Hofstede, G. (1980). *Culture's consequences: International differences in work-related values*. Beverly Hills, CA: Sage.

Hofstede, G. (1980/1981). Culture and organization. *International studies of management & organization*, 10(4), 15–41.

Hofstede, G. (1991). *Culture and organizations: Software of the mind*. London, UK: McGraw-Hill

Hofstede, G. (2001). *Culture's consequences: Comparing values, behaviors, institutions, and organizations across nations* (2nd ed.). Thousand Oaks, CA: Sage.

Hofstede, G. (2011). Dimensionalizing cultures: The Hofstede model in context. *Online Readings in Psychology and Culture*, 2(1), 1–25.

Hofstede, G., & Bond, M. H. (1988). The Confucius connection: From cultural roots to economic growth. *Organizational Dynamics*, 16(4), 4–21.

Hofstede, G., Hofstede, G. J., & Minkov, M. (2010). *Cultures and organizations: Software of the mind* (3rd ed.). New York, NY: McGraw-Hill

Hofstede, G., Neuijen, B., Ohayv, D. D., & Sanders, G. (1990). Measuring organizational cultures: A qualitative and quantitative study across twenty cases. *Administrative Science Quarterly*, 35, 286–316.

Hong, Y., Morris, M. W., Chiu, C., & Benet-Martinez, V. (2000). Multicultural minds: A dynamic constructivist approach to culture and cognition. *American Psychology*, 55, 709–720.

House, R. J., Hanges, P. W., Javidan, M., Dorfman, P., & Gupta, V. (eds.). (2004). *Culture, leadership, and organizations. The GLOBE Study of 62 Societies*. Thousand Oaks, CA: Sage.

Kelleher, D., McLaren, K., & Bisson, R. (1996). *Grabbing the tiger by the tail: NGO's learning for organizational change*. Ottawa: Canadian Council for International Cooperation.

Kennedy, P. (1993). *Preparing for the twenty-first century*. New York, NY: Random House.

Kerr, J., & Slocum, J. W. (2005). Managing corporate culture through reward systems. *Academy of Management Executive, 19,* 130–138.

Lambert, J., & Myers, S. (2005). *Trainer's diversity source book: 50 ready-to-use activities, from icebreakers through wrap ups.* Alexandria, VA: Society for Human Resource Management.

Larkey, L, K. (1996). Toward a theory of communicative interactions in culturally diverse workgroups. *Academy of Management Review, 21,* 467–470.

Lim, B. (1995). Examining the organizational culture and organizational performance link. *Leadership and Organizational Development Journal, 16*(5), 16–21.

Lim, T. (2009). Face in the holistic and relativistic society. In F. Bargiela-Chiappini and M. Haugh (eds.), *Face, communication and social interaction* (pp. 250–268). London: Equinox.

Littrell, L. N., & Salas, E. (2005). A review of cross-cultural training: Best practices, guidelines, and research needs. *Human Resource Development Review, 4,* 305–334.

Lunenburg, F. C. (2010). Formal communication channels: Upward, downward, horizontal, and external. *Focus on Colleges, Universities, and Schools, 4*(1), 1–7.

Marcoulides, G., & Heck, R. (1993). Organizational culture and performance: Proposing and testing a model. *Organization Science, 4,* 209–225.

McLuhan, M. (1964). *Understanding media.* Berkeley, CA: Gingko Press.

Mendenhall, M., & Oddou, G. (1985). The dimensions of expatriate acculturation: A review. *Academy of Management Review, 10,* 39–47.

Morris, M. W., Leung, K., Ames, D., & Lickel, B. (1999). Views from inside and outside: Integrating emic and etic insights about culture and justice judgments. *Academic Management Review, 24,* 781–796.

Morris, M. W., Savani, K., Mor, S., & Cho, J. (2014). When in Rome: Intercultural learning and implications for training. *Research in Organizational Behavior, 34,* 189–215.

Mowshowitz, A. (1997). Virtual organization. *Communication of the ACM, 40*(9), 30–37.

Neuliep, J. W. (2012). *Intercultural communication: A contextual approach* (5th ed.). Thousand Oaks, CA: Sage.

Ogbonna, E., & Harris, L. (2000). Leadership style, organizational culture and performance: Empirical evidence from UK companies. *International Journal of Human Resources Management, 11,* 766–788.

Okpara, J. O., & Kabongo, J. D. (2011). Cross-cultural training and expatriate adjustment: A study of western expatriates in Nigeria. *Journal of World Business, 46,* 22–30.

Ouchi, W. (1981). *Theory Z.* Upper Saddle River, NJ: Addison-Wesley.

Parker, B., & McEvoy, G. M. (1993). Initial examination of a model of intercultural adjustment. *International Journal of Intercultural Relations, 17,* 355–379

Pettigrew, A. (1979). On studying organizational culture. *Administrative Science Quarterly, 24,* 570–581.

Richmond, V., & McCroskey, J. C. (eds.). (2008). *Organizational communication for survival: Making work, work.* New York, NY: Pearson.

Rodrik, D. (1997). *Has globalization gone too far?* Washington, DC: Institute for International Economics.

Schein, E. (1990). Organizational culture. *American Psychologist, 45*(2), 109–119.

Sy, T., & D'Annunzio, L. S. (2005). Challenges and strategies of matrix organizations: Top-level and middle-level managers' perspectives. *Human Resource Planning*, *28*(1), 39–48.

Taylor, F. W. (2006). *The principle of scientific management*. New York, NY: Cosimo Classics.

Tung, R. L. (1987). Expatriates' assignments: Enhancing success, minimizing failures. *Academy of Management Executive*, *1*(2): 117–126.

U.S. Census Bureau. (2015). *Current population survey*. Washington, DC: GPO. Retrieved from http://www.census.gov

Varnum, M., Grossmann, I., Katunar, D., Nisbett, R. E., & Kitayama, S. (2008). Holism in a European cultural context: Differences in cognitive style between central and east European and westerners. *Journal of Cognition and Culture*, *8*, 321–333.

Verma, P. (2013). Relationship between organizational communication flow and communication climate. *International Journal of Pharmaceutical Sciences and Business Management*, *1*(1), 63–71.

Waxin, M. F., & Panaccio, A. (2005). Cross-cultural training to facilitate expatriate adjustment: It works! *Personnel Review*, *34*(1), 51–68.

Whalen, T. B. (2014). Utilizing the social transaction theory of social ontology to understand organizational culture change. *Journal of Business & Economics Research*, *12*(1), 37–42.

Würtz, E. (2006). Intercultural communication on websites: A cross-cultural analysis of websites from high-context cultures and low-context cultures. *Journal of Computer-Mediated Communication*, *11*(1), 274–299.

Student Paper

Cultural Diversity Training and Management in Organizations

Giovanni Consolino

A Description of the Term Paper

The paper must contain original research on a topic related to organizational communication (e.g., conflict, group relationships, organizational culture, diversity in organizations, empowerment, leadership, crisis communication, public relations). You need to gather data/information by interviewing at least two members of an organization and making observations as permitted. As a guideline, aim for at least 2 hours of interviewing and observing to carry out this study. In

(Continued)

your report, you should discuss 1) what you intended to study, 2) how you went about studying what you studied, 3) what you found out, and 4) your conclusions, especially in relation to concepts and theories covered in class. The purpose of this component is to see how real people in real organizations are dealing with organizational communication issues. This paper involves reporting and reflecting upon your observations and should reveal a technical and not just common-sense understanding of course material.

The rapid growth of a culturally diverse workforce in corporate America has emphasized an increase of multicultural collaboration in the workplace. In this sense, cultural diversity has recently become a prominent area of research. In the last three decades, numerous scholars have focused on the role of diversity to better understand organizations (Fatima Oliveira, 2013; Oetzel, McDermott, Torres, & Sanchez, 2012). Through diversity, organizations can facilitate best practices among their employees. Similarly, many scholars have examined the importance of being competent communicators in multicultural contexts (Arasaratnam, Banerejee, & Dembek, 2010; Liu 2014; Neuliep, 2012). Using effective communication with people from different cultures has become a necessity. Moreover, a recent study has emphasized the role of organizational leadership to comprehend how diversity is implemented in organizations (Ng & Sears, 2012). Certainly this has an impact on how training programs or management must be able to meet the needs of the global workforce.

With a heterogeneous work environment, it is then crucial for organizations to have a culture that encourages diversity. Given the above-mentioned considerations, it can be asserted that cultural diversity is entrenched in various aspects of the life of an organization. Hence, diversity represents a complicated yet unique component that warrants attention. The following literature review includes five main areas: defining organizational

(Continued)

culture, cultural diversity in organizations, communication and cultural diversity, intercultural communication competence in culturally diverse organizations, and transformational leadership in culturally diverse organizations.

Literature Review

Defining Organizational Culture

Organizations are complex domains where individuals become part of a common work environment. In this sense, culture represents a fundamental aspect in the life of organizations as a way to share daily practices. Schein (1990) described organizational culture as:

> A pattern of basic assumptions, invented, discovered, or developed by a given group, as it learns to cope with its problems of external adaptation and internal integration, that has worked well enough to be considered valid and, therefore is to be taught to new members as the correct way to perceive, think, and feel in relation to those problems.
>
> (p. 111)

This definition embodies the arduous scope of organizational culture whereby people depend on a mutual set of basic assumptions to understand organizational practices. Through his model, Schein (1990) identified three principal levels of culture: artifacts, values, and basic underlying assumptions. All together these levels reveal the meaning of organizational culture. Artifacts entail physical characteristics that can be observed in an organization, such as: annual reports, building architecture, dress code, philosophy statement, and technology (Schein, 1990). In essence, values are symbolic representations of a culture that shape organizations. The third and most important level is represented by basic underlying assumptions, which encompasses individuals' assumptions

---

Giovanni clearly introduced his topic and set the general context for the study. In addition, he proved that his research was invited. Furthermore, he summarized existing literature regarding his research interests – role of diversity and communication competence in multicultural contexts. Lastly, he used a preview to help readers understand what would be covered in the literature review.

(Continued)

regarding their feelings and perceptions of the workplace (Schein, 1990). Exploring basic assumptions can enable organizations to interpret implied meanings of organizational culture among employees.

Schein's model provides a valuable framework with distinct levels to understand organizational cultures. Looking at culture from a communication perspective, Miller (2012) claimed that cultural formation is based on individuals' understanding of culture as a social process. In other words, employees interpret organizational culture relying on their personal and cultural backgrounds. Likewise, Schein (1990) concurred that culture is learned through a socialization process whereby members of an organization internalize values and assumptions. Hence, it is crucial that organizational members have a common understanding of the cultural values and assumptions entrenched in the culture where they operate. This last aspect becomes even more complicated when considering people from different backgrounds who work in the same organization. As Mafela (2013) emphasized, "culture is a particular way of life that encompasses the values, premises, and practices in terms of which members of a community order their interaction" (p. 125). In this view, communication plays a pivotal role in understanding how people from different cultures can perceive and interpret organizational culture in the workplace. By taking a critical stance to examine intercultural communication, Buzzanell (2011) addressed the necessity to create a dialogue that aims at unraveling taken-for-granted realities to create depth and breadth in cultural understandings.

To further explain how intercultural communication has an impact on organizational culture, there are two types of cultural dimensions that need to be examined, individualism and collectivism (Lim, Kim, & Kim, 2011). These two areas are essential to comprehend how people are integrated into groups. Individualistic cultures place an emphasis on the individual; therefore, personal development is the

(Continued)

main focus (Neuliep, 2012). Thus, members that belong to this cultural dimension tend to focus on personal achievement and independence from family ties. Typical individualistic cultures are countries like the United States, Australia, and Germany. In their study, Lim et al. (2011) found that individualism is a common feature of American identity. On the other hand, collectivistic cultures give more importance to have a strong bond within social groups (Hall et al., 2004). Countries that best represent this cultural dimension are China, Japan, Mexico, and Saudi Arabia. Through these two cultural dimensions, it is possible to delineate clear distinctions between members of different cultures.

Recent studies have used organizational culture to understand cultural diversity in organizations (Randel & Early, 2009). Essentially, organizational culture constitutes a valuable characteristic to assess whether diversity is important in organizations. In their study, Randel and Early (2009) found that employees of respect-oriented organizational cultures keep their subjective opinions in the way they perceive members' diversity. In this sense, diversity becomes more tacit by not recognizing differences among members. Further, this finding exemplifies the difficulty in comprehending how diversity is enacted through organizational culture. In this regard, Dixon and Dougherty (2010) suggested that organizational culture cannot underestimate the role of divergent meanings. This statement becomes even more relevant when talking about diversity. In fact, an organizational culture must be tailored to the needs of its employees, so that they can fully identify with it. Thus, exploring the concept of diversity is pivotal to comprehend the multicultural landscape of organizations.

Cultural Diversity in Organizations

In recent years, there has been a considerable demographic transition in the United States (Irizzary & Galant, 2006). This change implies that organizational scholarship needs to further explore

(Continued)

the role of diversity in the workplace. Allen (1995) postulated that the increase of diversity in the organizations has theoretical and practical implications for organizational communication scholars. Consistent with the surge of diversity, communication research can exemplify the implementation of effective practices in the workplace. The concept of diversity has always been associated with multiculturalism to indicate a set of various personal and cultural characteristics within a social context (Cumber & Braithwaite, 1996). In a broad way, diversity in the workplace originally incorporated the following characteristics: race, gender, age, religion, country of origin, and economic status (Allen, 1995; Mor Barak, 2011). This conceptualization of diversity seems quite oversimplified to address its complexity in an organizational context. For this reason, more applicable definition of diversity will be provided later.

In their qualitative study of diversity management in healthcare, Irizzary and Gallant (2006) found that patients of diverse cultures and racial groups felt isolated and discriminated against by employees. This finding reinforces the need to address diversity among organizational members. Another study examined college students' perceptions of cultural diversity in two universities. By interviewing a culturally diverse sample of 27 participants, Cumber and Braithwaite (1996) found that students had different meanings of cultural diversity. While a Native American student declared that diversity entails respecting people's cultural background, a white American student stated that diversity is constituted by a social context wherein multiple cultures are accepted (Cumber & Braithwaite, 1996). Through these definitions, it is possible to understand how members of different cultures ascribe different meanings to cultural diversity. Furthermore, in the same study, several participants indicated that for them diversity meant that people would not give up to their sense

(Continued)

of cultural identity (Cumber & Braithwaite, 1996). In this sense, diversity can be seen as an opportunity to assimilate to a new social context without abandoning one's own identity.

In accordance with Cumber and Braithwaite's research, a recent study looked at diversity by exploring the challenges of a multicultural classroom (Guo, Cock-Wootten, & Mushi, 2014). Diversity has certainly become a crucial component to promote collaborative education. In utilizing a case study to analyze students' meaningful discussion about diversity, Guo et al. (2014) suggested that diversity does not indicate the preference of a value system or culture over another, but rather the ability to recognize a variety of points of view. Therefore, diversity is about giving voice to members of all cultures, so that they are able to express themselves in a social context.

Looking at the issue of diversity, Hon and Bruner (2000) interviewed twenty-eight practitioners and five executives of various public relations firms to understand diversity integration. In this view, diversity represents part of a strategic management plan to enhance public relations. Specifically, one-third of participants "describe their organization as aware of diversity issues, but lacking in true commitment" (Hon & Brunner, 2000, p. 318). Moreover, only four out of thirty-three participants stated that diversity was fully embedded in the management plan of their organization (Hon & Brunner, 2000). An organization can have norms and policies that encourage diversity, but they may not be implemented in a practical manner. Regarding the importance of diversity, two participants concluded "cultural differences bring things to the table that a homogeneous group never would" (Hon & Brunner, 2000, p. 331). In other words, diversity can benefit organizations because it provides people with different perspectives that enhance organizational practices. Essentially, diversity enables people to move out from their comfort zone to explore different alternatives and perspectives.

(Continued)

In a similar way, Cox and Blake (1991) proposed six important advantages that can be gained through the insightful management of cultural diversity: cost (high costs for recruiting and training new employees), best personnel from a large pool, better marketing due to cultural sensitivity, better creativity and problem-solving through a wider range of perspectives, and greater flexibility to react to environmental changes (as cited in Miller, 2012). This means that cultural diversity can provide organizations and their members a multiple benefits. In addition, communication research can represent a prolific terrain to inquire how interaction among organizational members can promote effective diversity practices in the workplace.

Communication and Cultural Diversity

As stated previously, diversity has drastically increased in the last few years. This has brought multiple perspectives in the workplace as well as concerns about the role of communication. Two distinct forms of communication that have been found in the literature are ethnocentric communication and cosmopolitan communication (Grimes & Richard, 2003). These two communication forms reveal different characteristics that interactants can display in an intercultural setting. According to Grimes and Richard (2003), ethnocentric communicators perceive that there are cultural groups with different ways of understanding. Thus, these communicators are aware of multiple interaction forms. However, they are not open to change their way because they think their way is the best (Grimes & Richard, 2003). Then, ethnocentric communicators may feel that their cultural practices are better than those of other cultures. Conversely, cosmopolitan communication entails a sense of appreciation toward others (Grimes & Richard, 2003). It seems that communication is used to foster harmony between cultural differences. In fact, Grimes and Richard (2003) argued that

(Continued)

cosmopolitan communicators do not give up their ways of understanding, but they simply treat others as natives. Here, communication becomes an equal opportunity of expression among people of different cultures. In a similar way, individuals who use a cosmopolitan style "will be more creative, culturally sensitive, grounded, group-oriented, and aware of hidden assumptions" (Grimes & Richard, 2003, p. 23). People that employ cosmopolitan communication tend to be more flexible; therefore, they can easily adapt to cultural differences. In particular, this suggests that individuals must be able to effectively communicate with members from different cultural backgrounds. Being competent communicators is an essential skill that individuals must gain to use and adapt to proper intercultural communication in a social context.

Intercultural Communication Competence in Culturally Diverse Organizations

Intercultural communication competence represents a prominent area of research among scholars (Arasaratnam et al., 2010; Liu, 2014; Neuliep, 2012). This is principally due to the advent of globalization with people from different cultures collaborating in the same social context. In this view, it is essential that individuals exhibit effective and appropriate communication toward members of other cultures. According to Neuliep (2012), intercultural communication competence represents an individual's ability to adapt his or her verbal and nonverbal messages to a specific cultural context. It is then crucial that an individual makes a personal effort to succeed in an intercultural interaction.

Most recent studies have identified five fundamental characteristics of competent intercultural communicators: empathy, intercultural experience, positive attitude towards other cultures, motivation, and listening (Arasaratnam et al., 2010).

(Continued)

These areas constitute key qualities necessary to achieve intercultural competence. Empathy refers to the ability to understand people's feelings and emotions. Intercultural experience can include experience living abroad, having intercultural friends, and acquiring intercultural communication training (Arasaratnam et al., 2010). A positive attitude toward other cultures entails an individual's tendency to respect people from different cultures. Motivation is defined as the need to understand and learn about other cultures. Lastly, listening can be considered as being actively involved in an intercultural interaction or conversation.

Arasaratnam et al. (2010) claimed that people who are eager to understand different cultures tend to be very engaged listeners. Being an active listener demonstrates a sense of interest and curiosity when communicating with people from different cultures. Similarly, this conveys a positive impression to foster proper intercultural contact between interactants. In a survey study among a culturally diverse sample of 400 college students, Arasaratnam (2006) found a significant correlation between positive attitude toward other cultures and cultural empathy. Hence, this study emphasizes the importance of personal behavioral characteristics to achieve intercultural competence. Another study including a sample of 165 freshmen undergraduate college students concluded that students generally respect cultural differences; however, they may feel uncomfortable communicating with individuals from different cultures (Liu, 2014). In essence, intercultural competence is an essential yet intricate skill to acquire. In this sense, it is important to note that intercultural experience plays a pivotal role in acquiring intercultural competence.

Using interviews among 19 American students who studied abroad for a short period of time, Penington and Wildermuth (2005) found that students' intercultural experience positively changed their

(Continued)

lives. Thus, it can be inferred that studying abroad represents a valuable experience to gain intercultural competence. Further, most students mentioned that living in other countries enabled them to develop effective cognitive and behavioral skills (e.g., listening carefully, experiencing not being a member of the host culture, and gaining self-knowledge) (Penington & Wildermuth, 2005). As students experienced a different culture, they were able to adjust themselves by expressing appreciation and willingness to learn about the new environment and its members. Ultimately, this served students to engage themselves in proper intercultural communication. Further, research on leadership could help to explain how leaders have an impact on promoting the attainment of intercultural communication competence among organizational members. Since leaders carry out the mission and philosophy of an organization, they must have a thorough understanding of the pivotal role of exhibiting proper intercultural communication. In this view, one type of leadership that has been linked to intercultural communication and cultural diversity is transformational leadership.

Transformational Leadership in Culturally Diverse Organizations

According to Burns (1978), transformational leadership is a process whereby leaders are capable of motivating their followers in an intrinsic way, so that they can achieve their full potential. These types of leaders aim at adapting themselves to what their subordinates need. In particular, transformational leadership is comprised of four main factors: idealized influence, inspirational motivation, intellectual stimulation, and individualized consideration (Northouse, 2016). Idealized influence refers to leadership's values and morals that convey a common mission among individuals. Inspirational motivation reflects a leader's ability to exemplify values and objectives

(Continued)

to stimulate followers to achieve more than their own self-interests (Northouse, 2016). Through intellectual stimulation, leaders properly engage followers to think outside of the box to solve a problem, so that they can work more effectively. Individualized consideration entails the ability of a leader to help and recognize subordinates' personal achievements to grow in the organization (Northouse, 2016). These factors are key for transformational leaders to enable their followers to prosper in an organization.

Moreover, Gandolfi (2012) proposed that transformational leaders can display effective communication in a global workplace. This means that transformational leadership embodies an approach whereby a leader can inspire positive change among subordinates from different cultural backgrounds. To achieve this, these types of leaders exhibit excellent cognitive and behavioral skills (i.e., empathy, providing ongoing guidance to their subordinates, and using metaphors to convey a strong vision among followers) (Gandolfi, 2012). Looking at the characteristics of this leadership approach, it could be possible to understand if leadership plays a pivotal role in encouraging diversity in organizations.

Likewise, Ng and Sears (2012) used transformational leadership as a lens to study CEOs' social values in relation to diversity practices. Examining organizational leadership is fundamental to predict diversity management practices in an organization. Ng and Sears (2012) asserted that transformational leaders have high moral standards that lead them to care about individuals' rights and dignity. Basically, transformational leaders truly focus on employees' well-being in the workplace. In a survey conducted among 572 participants of various Canadian corporations, including CEOs and Human Resources Executives, it was found that transformational leadership is directly related to the implementation of diversity practices (Ng & Sears, 2012). Thus, this study emphasizes how leaders play an active role in promoting

(Continued)

diversity. In addition, Ng and Sears (2012) suggested that transformational leaders possess necessary skills in persuading organizational members to have the moral responsibility to manage diversity in the workplace. Overall, these results extend the scope of leadership to take a more inclusive view of diversity, so that it can be encouraged throughout the whole organization.

Previous literature has emphasized the impact of organizational culture to guide organizational members to identify themselves with the workplace (Miller, 2012; Schein 1990). With the phenomenon of globalization, people from different cultures have been able to become part of a very diverse environment. For this reason, organizational cultures have become more multifaceted and ambiguous (Dixon & Dougherty, 2010; Miller, 2012). For instance, members of individualistic cultures can have a different interpretation of organizational values and practices in comparison to members of collectivistic cultures. This is due to the fact that each culture reflects a specific way of life with different communication forms (Hall et al., 2004; Mafela, 2013).

In this view, it is important to recognize that intercultural communication competence is a necessary skill for individuals nowadays, comprising specific cognitive and behavioral areas (e.g., empathy, positive attitude, and motivation) (Arasaratnam, 2006; Arasaratnam et al., 2010; Gandolfi, 2012; Liu; 2014; Neuliep; Penington & Wildermuth, 2005). In essence, prior research has been able to delineate which areas individuals must focus on to develop and achieve intercultural communication competence. Additionally, several studies addressed that diversity training or management still remains an underdeveloped area in the organizational communication scholarship (Cumber & Braithwaite, 1996; Guo et al, 2014; Hon & Brunner, 2000). Hence, there is the necessity to fill this void in order to shed more light on cultural diversity.

The literature review provided sufficient background to understand the nature of research conducted in his area of interest that included cultural dimensions, organizational culture, interpretation of diversity, benefits of diverse organizations, ethnocentric and cosmopolitan communication, intercultural communication competence, and transformational leadership in culturally diverse organizations. However, the literature can be strengthened by describing a more detailed justification of what the author is going to do specifically and outlining his specific research questions in the end of the review.

(Continued)

Methodology

Organizational Context

Mutual Corporation is a large financial institution with seven location nationwide and more than 5,000 employees. With a considerable amount of international individuals from all around the world, this organization represents one of the best examples of multicultural workforce in Corporate America. The purpose of my research was to understand cultural diversity in the workplace through the personal account of employees.

Research Participants

Participants for this study were three international employees. All participants worked in different departments of Mutual Corporation. Himal, a 24-years old business analyst originally from Nepal, worked in the organization for one year. Nicole, a 27-years old business analyst from Bulgaria, has worked in the organization for three years. Lastly, Max, a 30-years old business analyst from West-Africa, has been in the institution nearly four years.

Qualitative Approach

To collect data, individual semi-structured interviews were used. This type of interview encompasses a flexible set of questions whereby employees were able to easily express their opinions about diversity in the workplace. In order to gain an insightful use of the data, I used an appropriate interview protocol, which comprised two main parts. The first part required participants to report demographic information. The second section delved into the interview questions about these areas: organizational culture, meaning of diversity, corporate training and diversity, and the role of leadership in relation to diversity. Some of the following questions were discussed:

(Continued)

> - Could you describe the culture of your department or area in your organization?
> - How, if at all, does the culture of your organization promote diversity?
> - What does diversity mean to you?
> - What are your perceptions of diversity in regards to the management of your company?
> - How does leadership play an active role in fostering diversity?
>
> Each interview was audio-recorded and transcribed *verbatim* for data analysis, which revealed similarities and differences among participants' narratives. Analyzing employees' stories allowed me to gain a descriptive framework to understand their perspectives of cultural diversity in their organization.
>
> ### Implications of Findings for Diversity Training/Management
>
> After analyzing the data, I immediately noticed how the culture of the organization is tailored to its employees. Employees concurred that the institution is comprised of a diverse workforce that reflects a welcoming environment. Participants' stories described Mutual Corporate as an organization that is close to the needs of its organizational members. In this regard, interviews highlighted the values related to the culture of the organization: caring environment, people-orientation, and community. Moreover, employees stated that leadership values diversity by giving equal opportunity to everyone who wants to work at Mutual Corporate.
>
> However, employees' accounts indicated that there was no presence of diversity training at the beginning of the job. Additionally, Max and Nicole clearly pointed out that diversity can have a positive impact on the image of the organization. While Nicole declared that diversity training can benefit collaboration between American and international employees, Max concluded that the

The method section is clearly stated. Giovanni introduced his organizational context, participants, the method of semi-structured interviews for his data collection, and the interview questions. It is well-organized and easy to follow. However, it would be useful for others to replicate his study if he could provide more detailed information about the specific processes for data collection and data analysis. For instance, what sampling method and criteria were used to select participants for this study? What method and process were used for the data analysis? Did he use any verification strategies for his data analysis? And did he encounter any ethical considerations?

(Continued)

> The findings are interesting that have revealed the culture of the organization and the need for diversity to be implemented in organizations. However, Giovanni can strengthen the findings and discussion section by providing an overview of his themes/sub-themes, using quotations to provide adequate evidence for each theme/concept that he analyzed, providing enough of his own analysis to make key points about themes, and including content-based literature at appropriate points to assist in interpretation.

institution could certainly improve diversity by giving employees an opportunity to tell their story (e.g., advertisement or employee profile on the company website).

In accordance with the finding of past literature, this research highlights that diversity is not implemented in most organizations. Thus, this paper aimed to serve as a genuine invitation for more culturally conscious discussions about guiding management and corporate to a more inclusive and practical understanding of diversity, so that it can be improved in organizations.

Conclusion

To summarize, recent research has pointed out that organizational leadership plays a pivotal role to comprehend the nature of cultural diversity (Ng & Sears, 2012). Since management carries out the mission and philosophy of an organization, it is crucial that managers can use a more effective and inclusive implementation of diversity in the workplace. In this regard, Mor Barak (2011) declared that effective diversity practices improve the environment of an organization contributing to the following aspects: valuing individuals differences, creating a more inclusive workplace that reflects the needs of the surrounding community, and enhancing individuals' collaboration despite of cultural boundaries. Therefore, this paper would like to call for managers to understand the needs of a culturally diverse workforce, to design training programs that include diversity, to improve multicultural teamwork, and to build a more culturally diverse environment in their organization.

> Giovanni revealed the implications of what was done in his study and concluded it well.

References

Allen, B. J. (1995). Diversity and organizational communication. *Journal of Applied Communication Research*, 23, 143–155. doi:10.1080/00909889509365420

Arasaratnam, L. A. (2006). Further testing of a new model of intercultural communication competence. *Communication Research Reports*, 23, 93–99. doi:10.1080/08824090600668923

(Continued)

Arasaratnam, L. A., Banerjee, S. C., & Dembek, K. (2010). Sensation seeking and the integrated model of intercultural communication competence. *Journal of Intercultural Communication Research*, 39, 69–79. doi:10.1080/17475759.2010.526312

Buzzanell, P. M. (2011). Interrogating culture. *Intercultural Communication Studies*, 20(1), 1–16.

Cumber, C. J., & Braithwaite, D. O. (1996). A Comparative study of perceptions and understanding of multiculturalism. *Howard Journal of Communications*, 7, 271–282.

Dixon, M. A., & Dougherty, D. S. (2010). Managing the multiple meanings of organizational culture in interdisciplinary collaboration and consulting. *Journal of Business Communication*, 47, 3–19.

Fatima Oliveira, M. (2013). Multicultural environments and their challenges to crisis communication. *Journal of Business Communication*, 50, 253–277. doi:10.1177/0021943613487070

Gandolfi, F. (2012). A conceptual discussion of transformational leadership and intercultural competence. *Review of International Comparative Management*, 13, 522–534.

Grimes, D., & Richard, O. C. (2003). Could communication form impact organizations' experience with diversity? *Journal of Business Communication*, 40, 7–27.

Guo, S., Cockburn-Wootten, C., & Munshi, D. (2014). Negotiating diversity: Fostering collaborative interpretations of case studies. *Business Communication Quarterly*, 77, 169–182. doi:10.1177/2329490614530464

Hall, M., De Jong, M., & Steehouder, M. (2004). Cultural differences and usability evaluation: Individualistic and collectivistic participants compared. *Technical Communication*, 51, 489–503.

Hon, L., & Brunner, B. (2000). Diversity issues and public relations. *Journal of Public Relations Research*, 12, 309–340.

Irizarry, C., & Gallant, L. (2006). Managing diversity: Interpretation and enactment in a health care setting. *Qualitative Research Reports in Communication*, 7, 43–50.

Lim, T., Kim, S., & Kim, J. (2011). Holism: A missing link in individualism-collectivism research. *Journal of Intercultural Communication Research*, 40, 21–38. doi:10.1080/17475759.2011.558317

Liu, S. (2014). Becoming intercultural: Exposure to foreign cultures and intercultural Competence. *China Media Research*, 10(3), 7–14.

Mafela, M. (2013). Cultural diversity and the element of negation. *Intercultural Communication Studies*, 22, 124–133.

Miller, K. (2012). *Organizational communication: Approaches and processes* (6th ed.). Boston, MA: Wadsworth Cengage Learning.

Mor Barak, M. E. (2011). *Managing diversity: Toward a globally inclusive workplace* (2nd ed.). Los Angeles, CA: Sage.

Neuliep, J. W. (2012). *Intercultural communication: A contextual approach.* (5th ed.). London, UK: Sage Publications, Inc.

Ng, E., & Sears, G. (2012). CEO leadership styles and the implementation of organizational diversity practices: Moderating effects of social values

(Continued)

and age. *Journal of Business Ethics*, 105, 41–52. doi:10.1007/s10551-011-0933-7

Northouse, P. G. (2010). *Leadership: Theory and practice*. (5th ed.). Thousand Oaks, CA: Sage.

Oetzel, J. G., McDermott, V. M., Torres, A., & Sanchez, C. (2012). The impact of individual differences and group diversity on group interaction climate and satisfaction: A test of the effective intercultural workgroup communication theory. *Journal of International & Intercultural Communication*, 5, 144–167. doi:10.1080/17513057.2011.640754

Penington, B., & Wildermuth, S. (2005). Three weeks there and back again: A qualitative investigation of the impact of short-term travel/study on the development of intercultural communication competency. *Journal of Intercultural Communication Research*, 34, 166–183.

Randel, A. E., & Earley, P. (2009). Organizational culture and similarity among team members' salience of multiple diversity characteristics. *Journal of Applied Social Psychology*, 39, 804–833. doi:10.1111/j.1559-1816.2009.00461.x

Schein, E. H. (1990). Organizational culture. *American Psychologist*, 45, 109–119. doi:10.1037/0003-066X.45.2.109

23 INTERCULTURAL COMMUNICATION AND HEALTH

Diyako Rahmani and Cheng Zeng, University of Jyväskylä, Finland

Chapter Outline

- A Review of History and Methodology
- Health Communication Defined
- Health Communication in Different Contexts
  - Interpersonal Health Communication
    - Provider–Patient Relationships
    - Family Relationships
    - Romantic Relationships
  - Intergroup Communication
  - Intercultural Communication
- Major Issues in Health Communication
- Risk Behaviors
- Mass Media
  - Media Theories in Health Communication
    - Cultivation Theory
    - Agenda Setting
    - Framing
- Future Directions
- Chapter Summary
- Student Paper

A Review of History and Methodology

The world has witnessed a great deal of attention to and investment in health care. Our knowledge of treating illnesses and managing our environment has increased significantly, genetics and biomedicine have opened up new horizons in treatment of diseases such as cancer, and for the first time many dangerous contagious diseases have been controlled and restricted. Moreover, new media and the internet have taken information exchange to a new level. While health care professionals were previously sources of public knowledge on health issues, nowadays a quick search for any disease can provide a huge amount of information, videos, pictures, and even treatments. Historically, to perform any kind of medical tests, one had to go to medical centers where professional devices measured different aspects of one's health, while nowadays a drop of saliva or blood can be enough for some of the most advanced medical tests at home. A search in the health care and fitness categories of Google Play, Google app store for Android operation system, lists more than 600 free and paid applications. As health issues become an increasingly prominent concern, the ways these issues are communicated are getting more important.

Health Communication Defined

Health communication is a fast-developing field of communication that investigates and provides information about how we communicate health issues in health care situations. Based on the various approaches to health communication, different definitions have been proposed. While health care authorities look at health communication as a set of strategies to influence and promote health care knowledge and conditions of individuals and communities (Schiavo, 2007), a social constructionist perspective sees health communication as a way of explaining the symbolic usage of the sociocultural relationships in health care for the audience who are often unaware of such social and political relationships (Sharf & Vanderford, 2003). To sum up numerous existing definitions of health communication, Schiavo (2007) presented the following definition:

> Health communication is a multifaceted and multidisciplinary approach to reach different audiences and share health-related information with the goal of influencing, engaging, and supporting individuals, communities, health professionals, special groups, policymakers and the public to champion, introduce, adopt, or sustain a behavior, practice, or policy that will ultimately improve health outcomes.
>
> (p. 7)

These different approaches/definitions of health communication are rooted in the multidisciplinary and interdisciplinary nature of this field. Distinct aspects of education, promotion, marketing, and information have formed this multidisciplinary field (Waisbord & Obregon, 2012). E-health is a good example of this multidisciplinary genealogy, where expertise from media studies, medical science, computer science, and social science are needed to secure the success of a project (Suggs & Ratzan, 2012).

As previously mentioned, many people believe the final outcome of health communication is changing individual beliefs and behaviors about health issues. Risky behaviors such as tobacco, alcohol, and drug use, unhealthy diet, lack of physical activity, risky traffic behaviors, and unsafe sexual behaviors are all considered to be major reasons for death, and changing such behaviors can reduce the emotional, and economic expenses of such behaviors (Noar, et al., 2007). This behavioral approach to health communication is another important feature of this field of study. Behaviors are the manifestations of cultural norms such as the way people communicate and take care of their health issues. Any changes toward promotion of community health care conditions should eventually result in changes in how individuals behave in relation to health issues. Also, social changes will take place when there are changes on the individual, group, and community levels.

Moving toward change in health behaviors is a characteristic of the latest stage of health communication evolution. Research has distinguished four different stages in the formation and evolution of health communication (Piotrow, et al., 2003). The first period is the "clinical era" where people are directed toward health care centers, where they receive health care services and information. In the second period, the "field era," health information reaches people through a variety of information, education and communication products via the community level, clinics and health centers. Subsidized products that encourage people to adopt special health behaviors is a characteristic of the third period, namely the "social marketing era"; and this is when the last period, "strategic behavior change," comes into focus.

Media studies is one of the main disciplines that has influenced health communication (Mello, 2015). Media can influence the public and its decisions and behaviors through education and propagandizing healthy behaviors. A good example of the role of media in prompting healthy behaviors is health campaigns. Mass media are one of the most important parts of a successful health campaign. For example, Valente (1996) showed a mass media campaign was associated with behavioral change in Bolivia. Different (mass) media theories investigate and explain the role of media in health communication, among them cultivation theory (Gerbner & Gross, 1976), media agenda setting (McCombs & Shaw, 1972), and media framing theory (Goffman, 1974).

It is also worth mentioning that health communication is studied at the community, national, international, and global levels. For example, while HIV/AIDS threatens public health all over the world, and is a question of global concern, research has shown it is important to take contextual differences into consideration in treating HIV/AIDS in different places (Airhihenbuwa & Obregon, 2000). This contextualization of health care can take place on the level of local or national cultures. At the same time, although the international activities to control epidemic diseases, such as Zika, include multiple countries, a global health issue affects the health conditions of most people in the world (Waisbord & Obregon, 2012).

Health Communication in Different Contexts

Health communication has been studied in different contexts such as interpersonal, intergroup, and intercultural/cross-cultural communication. Health communication among people regardless of their social and group identities is interpersonal communication. When we take into consideration the social identity of the participants we study communication at the intergroup level. Studying communication behaviors of participants from different cultural backgrounds is an intercultural/cross-cultural communication approach.

Interpersonal Health Communication

The relationship between patients and providers includes different aspects of an interpersonal relationship and health is an important factor in many such occasions (Duggan, 2006). Along with the provider–patient, romantic relationships and family relationships are among the most studied relationships. In the following section, each one is reviewed.

Provider–Patient Relationships

Patient–provider interaction is a key area of study in health communication (Thompson, 2003) and essential to health care delivery (Korsch, 1989). In recent years the **provider–patient** relationship shifted from a medicine-centered relationship to a comprehensive approach including psychological

Figure 23.1

considerations and social elements such as aging (Lambert, et al., 1997). Moreover, more cases of chronic diseases, demanding quality and the advent of managed care resulted in an increase in the importance of the provider–patient relationship (Lambert, et al., 1997). As a trend of research, provider–patient studies aim at both assessment and improvement of communication skills (Thompson, 2003) that result in better treatment and satisfaction for both the providers and patients. Other outcomes related to provider–patient interactions are patients' compliance with the prescribed treatments and instruction, medical malpractice suits, and time spent in medical visits (Belle Brown, et al., 2003).

Due to the significance of the patient–provider relationship, medical schools are increasingly requiring students to strengthen their communication skills, but also there are different programs to teach patients how to communicate during health care communication (Duggan, 2006) and to use various communication skills, such as disclosure. Although some research reports self-disclosure by physicians has no effect on successful patient-physician partnerships (McDaniel, et al., 2007), other studies show physicians' self-disclosure is associated with patient satisfaction ratings for surgical visits (Beach, et al., 2004), patients' self-disclosure can give them more access to social and material support (Neville Miller & Rubin, 2007) and it is crucial in keeping the balance in information sharing during provider–patient interaction. Thus, self-disclosure is a key to patients' well-being, as it helps with prevention of hypertension, diseases, and increases resistance to illness (Gillotti, 2003).

Demographic variations such as sex and age are also important in provider–patient relationships. Previous research has shown female providers on average spend two more minutes communicating with patients and pay more attention to patient-centered communication through partnership, positive talking, and psychological and emotional sensitivity (Roter & Hall, 2004). There are also specific considerations in provider–patient communication when the patient is a child or an older adult. While communicating with older adults, ageism is a potential problem. Ageism is stereotyping expectations about older adults, rather than perceiving individually, which can create distance between the provider and patient and lead to failures in communication (Ryan & Butler, 1996). Along with the communicational role of professional providers, recent research has focused on other caregivers such as family members and friends also involved in the process of communication with older adults (Alpert & Womble, 2015).

Communicating with children as patients can be even more difficult due to the possible lack of cognitive capabilities and the fact that medical procedures can be challenging for children, for example in the case of vaccinations that temporarily worsen health conditions (DiMatteo, 2004). On the other hand, ethical and legal issues necessitate involving parents or legal guardians of children, something that changes the dyadic conversation of the provider–patient into group communication (Guttman & Salmon, 2004).

Family Relationships

Another important area is to study how family members communicate health issues within families. A caregiving relationship, i.e. taking care of a sick family member, is one of the most studied and obvious family relationships. However, the intersection of family studies and health communication is much wider, as family members are the first agents of the formation of health beliefs, attitudes and approaches in other family members (Baiocchi-Wagner, 2015) and usually they are among the first groups to be informed and sought for advice about health issues (Sharf & Vanderford, 2003). Thus, family health communication research focuses on different variations of the intra-family relationship such as the parent-child relationship or marital relationships.

Family communication research has shown the family can mediate in and affect sickness processes and side-effects such as allostatic load, depressive disorders, and health promoting/compromising behaviors (Jones, et al., 2004). For example, in the short term, family can help with mobilizing resources, in the case of an acute stressor to maintain homeostasis. However, family can also expose its members to permanent stressors and conflicts especially during childhood. Generally, family communication about health issues can help members to decide about the utilization of health care services, compliance with treatment prescriptions, and health promoting techniques (Baiocchi-Wagner, 2015).

Another important family issue is how the family communicates end-of-life decisions, organ donation choice, and related issues. Interpersonal communication within families has a direct effect on people's willingness to communicate about organ donation and its related processes (Scott & Quick, 2012). Age, religion, attitude toward organ donation, and recall of media content about organ donation are also among the factors that affect communicating organ donation choice among family members (Newton, et al., 2010).

End-of-life decision communication within families can help with managing the difficult situations families face when about to lose a member, especially, considering the fact that end-of-life decisions mostly include orders related to life support withdrawal (Lamba, et al., 2012). However, communicating about such decisions is a complex procedure, which results in varying outcomes. The people who achieve the outcomes they seek are those with capabilities in not only communicating about end-of-life decisions, but also higher quality communication about those decisions (Scott & Caughlin, 2014). Closely related to end-of-life decisions is communication among family members coping with death. Communicating grieving and sharing difficult situations people experience due to losing a loved one are necessary for the health and well-being of individuals. The death of a family member can disturb the balance in a family system, while it can also strengthen the feelings of commitment and appreciation for life among family members (Bosticco & Thompson, 2005). Based on the kinship for the dead and the age of the bereaved family members, people take different strategies to deal with the loss of a family member.

Romantic Relationships

Health is an important component for couples in **romantic relationships** (Duggan, 2006). One of the main areas of research in this field is how couples communicate about sex, namely **sexual communication**, defined as "a means by which individuals come to select potential partners for sexual relations, and through which the meaning functions, and effects of sexual relations are negotiated" (Metts & Spitzberg, 1996, p. 49). Sexual communication is important to sexual decision making, preventing sexually transmitted diseases, and discussing contraception (Widman, et al., 2006). Common topics of sexual communication among couple are sexual histories, sexual likes and dislikes, and sexual fantasies (Widman, et al., 2006).

Widman et al. reported factors such as relationship length, satisfaction and commitment, and individual factors such as gender, age, and self-silencing can predict communication openness in sexual communication (2006). However, sometimes people find it difficult to discuss sexual communication issues such as contraception due to a partner's negative reaction toward the discussion, the desire for a longer relationship, and self and partner's reputation (Coleman & Ingham, 1999).

Sexual education is also an important element of sexual communication. Families in general and parents in particular are among the adolescent's main sources of information about sexual relationships (Williams, et al., 2015). In a parent-adolescent relationship, various factors such as the parent's belief system, the content of sex-related communication, style and process of communication, and modeling and indirect socialization influence communication, socialization, and teaching about sex (Lefkowitz & Stoppa, 2006). Parents with religious tendencies need to provide the adolescent with both religious and practical guidance regarding sexual health (Williams, et al., 2015). A variation in the content and topic of the sexual communication between parents and offspring can influence interpersonal communication. While some parents are more comfortable talking about dating and less explicit sexual behaviors, they may choose to use less direct styles to talk about intercourse and other forms of explicit sexual relationships; however there should still be positive intergenerational communication to have effective sexual communication. The style of intergenerational sexual communication can also be indirect in cases where parents are remarried or dating someone else and the adolescent is exposed to the sexual behavior of the parent as model of sexual behavior.

Another area of interpersonal health communication research deals with how lesbian, gay, bisexual, and transgendered people (LGBTs) communicate within-the-context-of/about health care. LGBTs have their own unique and different medical and psychological health needs (Harrison & Silenzio, 1996). Previous research has shown many LGBTs have higher drug and alcohol consumption to reduce social distress, are often targets of hate and bias crime, and have a higher rate of suicide than heterosexuals (Bonvicini & Perlin, 2003). One major problem in LGBT healthcare is that the patient is often assumed to be heterosexual, many LGBT healthcare risks are not addressed (Bonvicini & Perlin, 2003), and due to homophobic views, many LGBTs conceal their sexual identity and tendencies (Harrison & Silenzio, 1996). To reduce and better understand disparities between heterosexuals and LGBTs, the latter group should be able to disclose their sexual identity (Cahill & Makadon, 2013).

Intergroup Communication

Communication also investigates health communication between/across different (cultural) groups. Although there is an interpersonal aspect of interaction in health care, in relationships such as provider–patient, the behaviors are strongly governed by intergroup relationships and the norms attached to each group of the providers or patients (Watson & Gallois, 1998). Examples of health intergroup communication are communication between LGBTs and other groups, Caucasians and Blacks on healthcare issues, and between patients and nurses in a healthcare setting (Dougherty, et al., 2011). An intercultural example of such communication is the way immigrants and refugees communicate health care issues. Understanding cultural differences in the beliefs and perceptions of people about health care is an important step in the development of an effective treatment procedure, and neglecting such variations could lead to dangerous outcomes. For example, previous research has shown there is a difference between the communication behaviors of Black and White Americans during medical visits; thus it is important to consider the role of intercultural differences such as race and ethnicity during medical visits. Research in this field proposes to increase the intercultural awareness and sensitivity of providers and to have health care interventions and campaigns targeted at patients (Johnson, et al., 2004). Also, racially concordant medical visits are reported to be longer and result in higher patient satisfaction compared to racially discordant ones (Cooper et al., 2003).

The perception of group members about in-group (social identities) and out-group members (stereotypes) affects the way people understand diseases and communicate about them (Harwood & Sparks, 2003). For example, once the group identity as a smoker is established, there is a lower chance of quitting, in comparison with the people who smoke the same amount, but they do not label (identify) themselves as smokers. Social identity and organizational context determine the functions of individuals' communication style, thus they can cause ineffective communication in the case of intergroup conflict, such as when groups have opposing interests and values (Hewett, et al., 2009).

Different theories investigate intergroup healthcare communication, but two of the most common theories are social identity theory (SIT) (Tajfel & Turner, 1986) and communication accommodation theory (CAT) (Gallois, Ogay, & Giles, 2005). SIT posits that individuals' behaviors are influenced by their group membership. The three main assumption of SIT are: 1) people define their identity based on their interaction with groups, 2) based on the valence of their social identity related to the group, people evaluate their role in the group, and 3) the relationship with out-group influences people's evolution of their in-group. CAT, on the other hand, emphasizes communication strategies, tactics, and behaviors used to achieve group identities, which according to SIT are the motivations for intergroup dynamics. In other words, CAT applies an interpersonal approach to intergroup interactions of group members.

Intercultural Communication

Culture in a nutshell includes ideas, beliefs, values, and perceptions formed over time and passed down from generation to generation about life, the world and human beings who are similar to or different than us. Based on cultural information, individuals develop certain verbal and non-verbal behaviors to deal with the questions they face in their surrounding world. Through contact in an intercultural context, behaviors from different cultural mindsets come together and affect and are affected by each other. Differences in cultural values and the way people understand medical issues challenge health communication. Misperceptions caused by different cultural backgrounds can lead to increased rates of illness and death among members of indigenous and minority groups (Ring & Brown, 2002). A review of cross-cultural and intercultural research in occupational rehabilitation and work disability prevention revealed that pain, communication and therapist-patient relationship, and intercultural competence are major topics (Côt, 2013). The same study concluded that due to immigration and other forms of intercultural contact, we are more in need of currently-missing culturally appropriate health care interventions and training programs.

In the patient–provider relationship, intercultural issues play an important role, and intercultural awareness of the individuals, especially providers, improves the quality of health care services and the effectiveness of treatments, which, in turn, are related to levels of intercultural anxiety and cultural sensitivity (Ulrey & Amason, 2001). However, cultural differences make it difficult for people to express themselves and comprehend one another. One example is the communication between Hawaiians and Native Americans and their white American health care providers. While in the modern medical community, members communicate in a time-efficient manner to diagnose and prescribe to deal with as many patients as possible, Native Americans typically take their time to tell stories and use metaphors and/or humor to communicate with providers (Kalbfleisch, 2009). Another example of such discrepancies in understanding and perception of health care notions is the Hmong. The Hmong's medical and treatment system is more based on spiritualism and shamanistic rituals rather than modern medical methodologies (Conquergood, 2005).

Immigrants, minority group members and asylum seekers face severe challenges in their health communication with providers from the dominant cultural groups. A critical reading of communication interactions among the family and child nurses with immigrants in Australia represented a reproduction and domination of a neo-colonial discourse of white Western communication styles (Grant & Luxford, 2011). Even though immigrants in general are at risk of impaired communication in health contexts, female immigrants are more likely to be in danger, as is the case with female South Asian immigrants in the US (Tsai & Lee, 2016). These women have less health literacy and language skills, which leaves them with less access to proper health care.

Intercultural differences in health care will result in conflict and it is important to manage such conflicts. An increase in cultural sensitivity is one way to resolve these issues (Ulrey & Amason, 2001). Cultural sensitivity is recognition and appreciation of different cultural ideas, beliefs, values, and perceptions of individuals from different cultural backgrounds (Dennis & Giangreco, 1996). Cultural sensitivity works on surface and deep structures. Surface structures target the fitness of a health care intervention, increasing the acceptance of the intervention messages among the people of target groups, whereas deep structures incorporate contextual social, cultural, historical, and environmental factors to convey the salience of the intervention (Resnicow, et al., 1999). Dealing with ideas and beliefs about health care issues such as believing certain illnesses are punishment from God or the result of the "evil eye" will belong to the deep structural approach (Resnicow, et al., 2000).

Major Issues in Health Communication

Risk Behaviors

Various studies on a wide range of health issues have reported that health communication results in weak behavioral changes. In everyday life we still witness individuals continue to engage in risky health behaviors such as smoking, conducting unsafe sexual behaviors, consuming unhealthy diets, and so forth. It is almost common knowledge these behaviors involve substantial health hazards and thus should be avoided. But why do people mindfully ignore scientific results and choose not to follow medical advice? To understand these "irrational" behaviors, it is important to study people's perception of risks and how perception affects people's health behaviors.

Early health studies proposed that high-risk perceptions are associated with health-protective behaviors. In testing this assumption, studies reported mixed results. One reason for the inconsistent finding is a lack of differentiation between cognitive and emotional risk/vulnerability perceptions. Previous studies on risk perceptions predominantly focused on only the cognitive dimension of risk perceptions, while the affective feelings of vulnerability remain less researched. People are not always rational in perceiving risks. For example, many may still consider driving a car to be safer than flying in a plane. In this sense, psychological approaches are central to understanding how worry, fear, and anxiety shape one's health behaviors (Harrington, 2015). Recent empirical studies confirm the important role of emotional responses to risks and found the emotional aspect often complements the cognitive aspect in risk assessments. In a study of breast cancer, Rimal and Juon (2010) reported higher levels of anxiety lead to more information seeking and cancer screening behaviors. Individuals do not simply change because they have more information. It is important to consider the interactions of cognitive and affective dimensions of risk perceptions to be more persuasive in health interventions.

Seen as a vulnerable group, adolescents and young adults have been the focus of many risk behaviors studies. Studies have found various biological, socio-cultural, and psychological factors that exert influence on risk-taking behaviors of adolescents. The primary forces in risk-taking behaviors are often biological. Zuckerman (1983) found adolescents with a higher level of sensation seeking are more prone to substance abuse. While biological factors help clarify individual risk-taking behaviors, socio-cultural elements are important in explaining group dynamics among adolescents. Peer cultural, the first and foremost socio-cultural element, is often the determining factor in whether adolescents engage in risk-taking behaviors. For example, peers are typically the ones who provide and solicit the use of cigarettes, alcohol, and substances. In addition, risk-taking behaviors are more appealing to adolescents because such behaviors promote autonomy and independence (Levitt, et al., 1991). In addition to peer influences, parental factors such as ties with children, authoritarian parenting vs. indulgent parenting; attitudes towards risky behaviors are also significant in either encouraging or discouraging adolescents' risk-taking behaviors. Despite the importance of biological and socio-cultural factors, researchers argue additional factors need to be explored to explain why some adolescents engage in risk-taking behaviors in low-risk environments while some are resistant to risky behaviors in high-risk environments. Pursuing this line of research, a few studies have found adolescents' risk-taking behaviors are greatly influenced by psychological factors such as internal stress, boredom, and sensation seeking. The risk-taking behaviors of adolescents could be to fight against stress or boredom and the risk-associated acts make things fun (Levitt, et al., 1991).

Fostering risk resistance behaviors is not an easy task, particularly among adolescents. Old habits die hard and the potential consequences of risk-taking behaviors are fatal. Three steps suggested by Harrington (2015) to promote public health are: understanding the motivations, developing meaningful intervention programs, and influencing public policies. Future research should continue to expand our understanding of health related behaviors to build a better and healthier society.

Culture is a determining factor in interpreting and managing health related risks. The way people understand diseases is closely linked to their cultural health beliefs, which has a direct impact on their health-seeking behaviors. For example, a number of studies have shown Asians living in the UK are less likely to visit health professionals for psychological issues due to the social stigma surrounding mental illnesses (Currer, 1986). Risky behaviors are often associated with national culture. While smoking among women in Mexico is low, Bethel and Schenker (2005) found Hispanic women who are more acculturated into US culture are more likely to be current smokers. Moreover, a study exploring risky behaviors among secondary students in the US and El Salvador found US adolescents reported higher levels of substance use and sexual intercourse (Springer, et al., 2007). The authors suggested this difference was due to the fact that engaging in risky behaviors in the US is vital for adolescents to promote closeness and trust with each other, whereas in Central America religious activities and sports are more prominent in social bonding among teens. Another comparative study of health behaviors between Spaniards and Germans reported Germans are more proactive in seeking health information and have higher expectations in getting involved in health decisions (Bodemer, et al., 2012).

Understanding the role of culture in health communication can not only help enhance the effectiveness of health campaigns but also eliminate the disparities between subgroups. Within a nation, ethnic differences in health behaviors are evident. For example, previous research on sexual intercourse among adolescents from grades 9–12 reported African-American males were the most sexually active while Asian-American girls were the least sexually active and tend to engage in sex activity at an older age (Cavazos-Rehg, et al., 2009). Obesity, a prominent health crisis in the US, is manifested disproportionally among different ethnic groups. Among adolescents from 6–18 years old, African-American and Hispanic-American children are more likely to be overweight compared to Caucasian children (Wang & Tussing, 2004). Researchers generally agree that socioeconomic status factors such as family income and patients' educational levels are significant in child feeding and food preference. In addition, studies have demonstrated cultural factors may contribute to differences in child obesity too. African and Latino mothers tend to perceive being overweight as normal and they usually are more concerned if their children are underweight as opposed to overweight (Sherry, et al., 2004). Thus, it is essential to promote the facts about obesity to minority mothers to close the gap in health outcomes between different ethnic groups.

Mass Media

Historically, health information dissemination has relied on traditional channels such as newspapers, radio, and TV to reach the mass public. Due to the popularity of the internet, an increase in its use in health communication has been witnessed over the last two decades. Gradually, new media is replacing traditional channels and becoming the primary source for health information. A survey conducted in the US in 2005 revealed 42% of internet users consider the internet as the most reliable source for health information (Harrington, 2015). Health topics that have received significant media attention are smoking, heart diseases, cancer, sex-related behaviors, and drug use. Health messages evoke cognitive or emotional responses by either promoting healthy behaviors (e.g. eat more vegetables; use condoms) or discouraging unhealthy behaviors (e.g. don't smoke; don't sit for too long). Usually less effective than commercial campaigns, health campaigns often encourage individuals to make short-term sacrifices for long-term benefits. Repetition has been the most used strategy in health campaigns to increase public awareness of certain diseases. However, audiences exposed to such messages are generally passive and reluctant to change behaviors. Research suggests health campaign messages can be effective when they are creative and well designed.

Simply repeating monotonous health messages is usually not effective in changing attitudes and behaviors. Thus, more and more practitioners prefer to rely on an Entertainment-Education model to draw audiences' interest and attention when disseminating health information. Entertainment-Education (EE) refers to the process of using popular media narratives such as drama, comedy, music, or dance to promote health education (Beacom & Newman, 2010). Research shows the EE approach has been largely employed and successful in addressing topics such as: HIV/AIDS, alcohol and drug abuse, eating disorders, assault, etc. (Valente & Bharath, 1999). The paramount concern for an EE approach is the accuracy of the information. This is particularly crucial when we know little about some diseases or when scientific opinions on certain health issues are divided. In these cases, an accurate presentation of the health issue helps provide information from different perspectives and encourages patients to engage in healthy behaviors. On the other hand, the entertaining values of health messages are not to be underestimated. Characters in entertaining messages are effective in inviting emotional involvement and identification from the viewers. For example, "Grey's Anatomy," which was one of the top-rated TV shows with routinely 20 million viewers, was a successful case of embedding health information in the plots. Studies revealed viewers' knowledge of certain health issues covered in the show was significantly increased and that knowledge is likely to be retained by the viewers for a long time (Rideout, 2008). To better understand how TV shows like "Grey's Anatomy" and other media have shaped our health knowledge, attitudes, and behaviors, it is essential to examine media theories that illustrate media effects and the ways we learn from the media.

Media Theories in Health Communication

Cultivation Theory

Cultivation theory argues our perception of reality is influenced by our media consumption (Gerbner & Gross, 1976; Gerbner, et al., 1986). Studies employing cultivation theory have predominantly focused on how television exposure "cultivates" attitudes and values. Watching TV is one of the most time-consuming leisure activities and it is also a vital source for health information. Much of the health-related information on television is misleading or inaccurate. In an early study, Cassata, Skill, and Boadu (1979) found in soap operas half of the characters have health concerns; miscarriages and death in pregnancy were common for women, and women were more likely to develop mental illnesses. People exposed to TV routinely tend to gain more knowledge of health issues and at the same time perceive a higher vulnerability to those diseases

(Snyder & Rouse, 1995). For instance, Lemal and Van den Bulck (2009) reported women who had frequently been exposed to breast cancer content in TV were more likely to be afraid of being diagnosed with breast cancer.

TV food commercials often aim to persuade people to purchase foods that are energy-dense and nutrient-poor. Many of these commercials are placed during children's programming time periods, which have a negative impact on children's food preferences (Byrd-Bredbenner, et al., 2003). As a less formal and serious form of TV programming, late night comedies tend to discuss health issues in a humorous way, which could be a "superficial yet nonetheless important" (p. 149) way to raise public awareness (Compton, 2006).

Agenda Setting

One crucial line of mass communication research is to explore the role and effects of media. **Agenda setting** theory mainly focuses on media's ability to raise the importance of certain issues among the public (McCombs & Shaw, 1972). The theory assumes topics highlighted in media will be perceived as significant by the audience. However, it is important to note that not all issues presented in media have the same effects on the public. Issues are more likely to exert influence on the audience when they: 1) affect a minority group, 2) have received dense coverage in a short time, 3) are concrete, and 4) are dramatic (Soroka, 2002). Originally used only in political contexts, media as a powerful tool of persuading the public has been widely addressed in health communication. For example, in the 1980s the Japanese government persuaded (through media campaigns) 75–90% of the Japanese that smoking in public places should be regulated (Ministry of Health & Welfare, 1993). In addition, the media coverage of HIV/AIDS in Africa led to an increase in perceived importance of prevention and intervention programs. On the other hand, diseases such as tuberculosis and measles, which received little media coverage, have been neglected by the public and policymakers for years (Pratt, Ha, & Pratt, 2002).

Framing

Agenda setting deals with the frequency of media topics while framing focuses on the tones used when reporting those topics. **Framing** "is to select some aspects of a perceived reality and make them more salient in a communicating text, in such a way as to promote a particular problem definition, causal interpretation, moral evaluation, and/or treatment recommendation for the item described" (Entman, 1993, p. 52). Agenda setting and framing as a package are employed by media professionals to tell the public not only "what" to think about but also "how" to think about it. For example, a labor strike can be framed either as a "disruption" or a productive activity for employee rights (Simon & Xenos, 2000).

Framing is often considered as an extension of agenda setting, which defines the issues and articulates points of view regarding the issues (Scheufele & Tewksbury, 2007). In a study exploring how obesity is framed in media,

Lawrence (2004) collected *New York Times* articles from 1985–2003 about obesity and identified three major themes: 1) obesity is an individual matter that is caused by personal exercise times and food choices; 2) obesity is a biological health problem that can be treated with medicines; and 3) obesity is an environmental epidemic that is created by corporate and public policy. When obesity is framed more as an individual issue, the public would think obese people are blamed for their own problems because they fail to control what they eat and how much they exercise. On the other hand, food corporations and the government are seen as the root cause for obesity if an environmental frame is used. In this sense, obesity is a social phenomenon that is created by unhealthy food providers, poor regulations on food manufacturing, insufficient P.E. classes in school, and so on.

Mass media is a powerful tool to inform the public about health and medical issues. One major limitation of current studies is previous research on the role of mass media in health communication has predominantly been conducted in the US. As nations have vastly different media systems, the media coverage in each country is likely to differ. A few scholars have attempted to shed light on the cross-cultural differences in health media and individual health seeking behaviors from different perspectives. In a study exploring the relationship between media consumption and self-assessed health in 25 European countries, Blom, et al. (2016) found exposure to radio and newspapers is positively associated with better health while TV exposure was negatively related to healthy outcomes. In addition, people who frequently use the internet reported higher levels of self-assessed health in Europe across different media systems. Moreover, in exploring the differences in online health information in different languages, Tozzi, et al. (2010) reported, as opposed to English websites, health information about the human papillomavirus immunization on Italian websites has lower accessibility, credibility, and content ratings.

More individuals are turning to the internet, especially social media, for health-related information nowadays (Oh & Kim 2014). A few studies have documented the cross-cultural differences in how individuals use the internet for health information. Oh and Kim (2014) found Korean students demonstrated higher trust in social media and tend to use more social media for health information than their American counterparts. In the same line of research, a comparative study reported Koreans and Hong Kongers reported significantly higher levels of social networking site use for health information than Americans (Song, et al., 2016). Moreover, in terms of information seeking behaviors, Song et al. (2016) indicated Americans tend to use more expertise-based websites, whereas Asians value more experienced-based information. Thus, online health information needs to be tailored according to the cultural contexts.

Future Directions

One area of future research is to understand how people develop their perceptions about health care (Thompson, 2003). The way we perceive something about our health will affect how we react to it. For example, a difference in perceptions of how critical an illness is can lead to delays in dealing with the problem. Individuals, who perceive the risk of salt in heart disease to be high, possibly are more likely to decrease salt consumption than those who have a moderate perception of this risk. People may even have totally different cognitive perceptions of illness; for example, they may attribute their illness to spiritual or supernatural causes. These cultural differences call for more research in the field of intercultural health communication to have a better understanding of the nature of interaction between people from different cultural backgrounds in health care contexts.

Health communication research helps promote the health care system and encourages disease prevention, patient self-care, etc. (Kreps, et al., 1998). Future health communication scholarship should continue to pay attention to promoting public health with a focus on disadvantaged populations. Marginalized groups such as ethnic minorities, women, elderly, people with HIV/AIDS, etc. often have special needs and adopt different health behaviors than mainstream populations (Kreps, 1996). Thus, it is imperative to take the role of culture into consideration to provide effective health care and information to at-risk populations.

Chapter Summary

Health communication is a developing field dealing with communication styles and processes in the context of health care. This interdisciplinary field has received much attention in recent years due to the huge effect it can have on the health conditions of society. Health communication has been studied in different fields and contexts. As more people are using the internet and smart phones, and other kinds of media, their relationship with health issues and how they affect their health habits have all become important topics of study. It is also essential to pay attention to cultural differences and various cultural approaches to health care, especially in intercultural contexts, since neglecting such differences could result in higher amounts of risky behaviors and physical and financial costs.

Key Terms

Agenda-setting	Cultivation	Framing
Health communication	Provider–patient	Romantic relationships
Sexual communication		

Activities

1. In a group of 3–5 people discuss what your main sources of health information are and how much health information you get from the media.

Provide a list of different sources and compare it to those of other groups in your class.
2. Identify the steps you take when you realize you are sick. What elements will affect your decision to see or not to see a health care professional?
3. Suppose you have a serious disease. In a group of 3–5 people discuss what kind of health care professional you are more likely to talk with about your condition. How would you discuss the disease with your family? What cultural issues affect these decisions?

References

Airhihenbuwa, C.O., & Obregon, R. (2000). A critical assessment of theories/models used in health communication for HIV/AIDS. *Journal of Health Communication*, 5, 5–15. doi:10.1080/10810730050019528

Alpert, J.M., & Womble, F.E. (2015). Coping as a caregiver for an elderly family member. *Health Communication*, 30, 714–721. doi:10.1080/10410236.2013.879560

Baiocchi-Wagner, E. (2015). Future directions in communication research: Individual health behaviors and the influence of family communication. *Health Communication*, 30, 810–819. doi:10.1080/10410236.2013.845492

Beacom, A.M., & Newman, S.J. (2010). Communicating health information to disadvantaged populations. *Family Community Health*, 33, 152–162.

Beach, M.C., Roter, D., Rubin, H., Frankel, R., Levinson, W., & Ford, D.E. (2004). Is physician self-disclosure related to patient evaluation of office visits? *Journal of General Internal Medicine*, 19, 905–910. doi:10.1111/j.1525-1497.2004.40040.x

Belle Brown, J., Stewart, M., & Ryan, B.L. (2003). Outcomes of patient–provider interaction. In T.L. Thompson, A.M. Dorsey, K.I. Miller & R. Parrott (eds.), *Handbook of health communication* (pp. 141–161). Mahwah, NJ: Lawrence Erlbaum Associates.

Bethel, J.W., & Schenker, M.B. (2005) Acculturation and smoking patterns among Hispanics: a review. *American Journal of Preventive Medicine*, 29, 143–148.

Blom, N., Zanden, R., Buijzen, M., & Scheepers, P. (2016). Media exposure and health in Europe: Mediators and moderators of media systems. *Social Indicators Research*, 126, 1317–1342. doi:10.1007/s11205-015-0933-6

Bodemer, N., Müller, S.M., Okan, Y., Garcia-Retamero, R., & Neumeyer-Gromen, A. (2012). Do the media provide transparent health information? A cross-cultural comparison of public information about the HPV vaccine. *Vaccine*, 30, 3747–3756. doi:10.1016/j.vaccine.2012.03.005

Bonvicini, K.A., & Perlin, M.J. (2003). The same but different: Clinician–patient communication with gay and lesbian patients. *Patient Education and Counseling*, 51, 115–122.

Bosticco, C., & Thompson, T. (2005). The role of communication and story telling in the family grieving system. *Journal of Family Communication*, 5, 255–278.

Byrd-Bredbenner, C., Grasso, D., & Finckenor, M. (2001). Nutrition messages on prime-time television programs. *Topics in Clinical Nutrition*, 16, 61–72.

Cahill, S., & Makadon, H. (2013). Sexual orientation and gender identity data collection in clinical settings and in electronic health records: A key to ending LGBT health disparities. *LGBT Health*, *1*, 34–41.

Cassata, M. B., Skill, T. D. & Boadu, S. L. (1979). In sickness and in health. *Journal of Communication*, *29*, 73–80.

Cavazos-Rehg, P. A., Krauss, M. J., Spitznagel, E. L., Schootman, M., Bucholz, K. K., Peipert, J. F., Sanders-Thompson, V., Cottler, L. B., & Bierut, L. J. (2009). Age of sexual debut among US adolescents. *Contraception*, *80*, 158–162. doi:10.1016/j.contraception.2009.02.014

Coleman, L. M., & Ingham, R. (1999). Exploring young people's difficulties in talking about contraception: How can we encourage more discussion between partners? *Health Education Research*, *14*, 741–750. doi:10.1093/her/14.6.741

Compton, J. (2006). Serious as a heart attack: Health-related content of late-night comedy television. *Health Communication*, *19*, 143–151. doi:10.1207/s15327027hc1902_6.

Conquergood, D. (2005). Health theatre in a Hmong refugee camp: Performance, communication, and culture. In M. A. Abbas, J. N. Erni & W. Dissanayake (eds.), *Internationalizing cultural studies: An anthology* (pp. 79–94). Oxford, UK: Blackwell.

Cooper, L. A., Roter, D. L., Johnson, R. L., Ford, D. E., Steinwachs, D. M., & Powe, N. R. (2003). Patient-centered communication, ratings of care, and concordance of patient and physician race. *Annals of Internal Medicine*, *139*, 907–915.

Côt, D. (2013). Intercultural communication in health care: Challenges and solutions in work rehabilitation practices and training: A comprehensive review. *Disability & Rehabilitation*, *35*(2), 153–163. doi:10.3109/09638288.2012.687034

Currer, C. (1986). Concepts of mental well- and ill-being: the case of mothers in Britain. In C. Currer & M. Stacey (eds). *Concept of health, illness and disease* (pp. 319–327). Leamington Spa: Berg.

Dennis, R. E., & Giangreco, M. F. (1996). Creating conversation: Reflections on cultural sensitivity in family interviewing. *Exceptional Children*, *63*, 103–116.

DiMatteo, M. R. (2004). The role of effective communication with children and their families in fostering adherence to pediatric regimens. *Patient Education and Counseling*, *55*, 339–344.

Dougherty, D. S., Baiocchi-Wagner, E., & McGuire, T. (2011). Managing sexual harassment through enacted stereotypes: An intergroup perspective. *Western Journal of Communication*, *75*, 259–281. doi:10.1080/10570314.2011.571654

Duggan, A. (2006). Understanding interpersonal communication processes across health contexts: Advances in the last decade and challenges for the next decade. *Journal of Health Communication*, *11*, 93–108. doi:10.1080/10810730500461125

Entman, R. M. (1993). Framing: Toward clarification of a fractured paradigm. *Journal of Communication*, *43*, 51–58.

Gallois, C., Ogay, T., & Giles, H. (2005). Communication accommodation theory: A look back and a look ahead. In W. B. Gudykunst (ed.), *Theorizing about intercultural communication* (pp. 121–148). Thousand Oaks, CA: Sage.

Gerbner, G., & Gross, L. (1976). Living with television: The violence profile. *Journal of Communication*, *26*, 172–194. doi:10.1111/j.1460-2466.1976.tb01397.x

Gerbner, G., Gross, L., Morgan, M., & Signorielli, N. (1986). Living with television: The dynamics of the cultivation process. In J. Bryant & D. Zillmann (eds.), *Perspectives on media effects* (pp. 17–48). Hillsdale, NJ: Erlbaum.

Gillotti, C. M. (2003). Medical disclosure and decision-making: Excavating the complexities of physician-patient information exchange. In T. L. Thompson,

A. M. Dorsey, K. I. Miller & R. Parrott (eds.), *Handbook of health communication* (pp. 163–181). Mahwah, NJ: Lawrence Erlbaum Associates.

Goffman, E. (1974). *Frame analysis: An essay on the organization of experience*. Boston, MA: Northeastern University Press.

Grant, J., & Luxford, Y. (2011). 'Culture it's a big term isn't it?' An analysis of child and family health nurses' understandings of culture and intercultural communication. *Health Sociology Review*, 20(1), 16–27. doi:10.5172/hesr.2011.20.1.16

Guttman, N., & Salmon, C. T. (2004). Guilt, fear, stigma and knowledge gaps: Ethical issues in public health communication interventions. *Bioethics*, 18, 531–552. doi:10.1111/j.1467-8519.2004.00415.x

Harrington, G. N. (2015). *Health communication: Theory, method, and application*. New York, NY: Routledge.

Harrison, A. E., & Silenzio, V. M. B. (1996). Comprehensive care of lesbian and gay patients and families. *Clinic Review Articles*, 23, 31–46.

Harwood, J., & Sparks, L. (2003). Social identity and health: An intergroup communication approach to cancer. *Health Communication*, 15, 145–159.

Hewett, D. G., Watson, B. M., Gallois, C., Ward, M., & Leggett, B. A. (2009). Intergroup communication between hospital doctors: Implications for quality of patient care. *Social Science & Medicine*, 69, 1732–1740.

Johnson, R. L., Roter, D., Powe, N. R., & Cooper, L. A. (2004). Patient race/ethnicity and quality of patient-physician communication during medical visits. *American Journal of Public Health*, 94, 2084–2090.

Jones, D., Beach, S., & Jackson, H. (2004). Family influences on health: A framework to organize research and guide intervention. In A. Vangelisti (ed.), *Handbook of family communication* (pp. 647–672). Mahwah, NJ: Lawrence Erlbaum Associates.

Kalbfleisch, P. J. (2009). Effective health communication in native populations in North America. *Journal of Language and Social Psychology*, 28, 158–173. doi:10.1177/0261927X08330607

Korsch, B. M. (1989). Current issues in communication research. *Health Communication*, 1, 5–9. doi:10.1207/s15327027hc0101_1

Kreps, G. L. (1996). Communicating to promote justice in the modern health care system. *Journal of Health Communication*, 1, 99–109.

Kreps, G. L., Bonaguro, E. W., & Query, J. L. (1998). The history and development of the field of health communication. In L. D. Jackson, & B. K. Duffy (eds.), *Health communication research: A guide to developments and direction* (pp. 1–15). Westport, CT: Greenwood Press.

Lamba, S., Murphy, P., McVicker, S., Harris Smith, J., & Mosenthal, A. C. (2012). Changing end-of-life care practice for liver transplant service patients: Structured palliative care intervention in the surgical intensive care unit. *Journal of Pain and Symptom Management*, 44, 508–519. http://dx.doi.org/10.1016/j.jpainsymman.2011.10.018

Lambert, B. L., Street, R. L., Cegala, D. J., Smith, D. H., Kurtz, S., & Schofield, T. (1997). Provider–patient communication, patient-centered care, and the mangle of practice. *Health Communication*, 9, 27–43. doi:10.1207/s15327027hc0901_3

Lawrence, R. G. (2004). Framing obesity: The evolution of news discourse on a public health issue. *The Harvard International Journal of Press/Politics*, 9, 59–75. doi:10.1177/1081180X04266581

Lefkowitz, E. S., & Stoppa, T. M. (2006). Positive sexual communication and socialization in the parent-adolescent context. *New Directions for Child and Adolescent Development*, 2006, 39–55. doi:10.1002/cd.161

Lemal, M., & Van den Bulck, J. (2009). Television news exposure is related to fear of breast cancer. *Preventive Medicine*, 48, 189–192. doi:10.1016/j.ypmed.2008.11.011

Levitt, M. Z., Selman, R. L., & Richmond, J. B. (1991). The psychosocial foundations of early adolescents' high-risk behavior: Implications for research and practice. *Journal of Research on Adolescence*, 1, 349–378. doi:10.1111/1532-7795.ep11298101

McCombs, M., & Shaw, D. L. (1972). The agenda-setting function of mass media. *Public Opinion Quarterly*, 36, 176–187. doi:10.1086/267990

McDaniel, S. H., Beckman, H. B., Morse, D. S., Silberman, J., Seabaurn, D., & Epstein, R. M. (2007). Physician self-disclosure in primary care visits: Enough about you, what about me? *Archive of Internal Medicine*, 167, 1321–1326. doi:10.1001/archinte.167.12.1321

Mello, S. (2015). Media coverage of toxic risks: A content analysis of pediatric environmental health information available to new and expecting mothers. *Health Communication*, 30, 1245–1255. doi:10.1080/10410236.2014.930398

Metts, S., & Spitzberg, B. H. (1996). Sexual communication in interpersonal contexts: A script-based approach. In B. R. Burleson (ed.), *Communication yearbook* (19th ed., pp. 49–51). Thousand Oaks, CA: Sage.

Ministry of Health and Welfare (1993). *Kitsuen to kenko (Smoking and health)*. Tokyo, Japan: Health Promotion and Fitness Foundation.

Neville Miller, A., & Rubin, D. L. (2007). Factors leading to self-disclosure of a positive HIV diagnosis in Nairobi, Kenya: People living with HIV/AIDS in the sub-Sahara. *Qualitative Health Research*, 17, 586–598. doi:10.1177/1049732307301498

Newton, J. D., Burney, S., Hay, M., & Ewing, M. T. (2010). A profile of Australian adults who have discussed their posthumous organ donation wishes with family members. *Journal of Health Communication*, 15, 470–486. doi:10.1080/10810730.2010.492559

Noar, S. M., Benac, C. N., & Harris, M. S. (2007). Does tailoring matter? Meta-analytic review of tailored print health behavior change interventions. *Psychological Bulletin*, 133, 673–693.

Oh, S., & Kim, S. (2014). College students' use of social media for health in the USA and Korea. *Information Research*, 19, 283–300.

Piotrow, P. T., Rimon, J. G. I., Payne Merritt, A., & Saffitz, G. (2003). *Advancing health communication: The PCS experience in the field*. Baltimore, MD: Johns Hopkins Bloomberg School of Public Health, Center for Communication Programs.

Pratt, C. B., Ha, L., & Pratt, C. A. (2002). Setting the public health agenda on major diseases in Sub-Saharan Africa: African popular magazines and medical journals, 1981–1997. *Journal of Communication*, 52, 889–904. doi:10.1111/j.1460-2466.2002.tb02579.x

Resnicow, K., Baranowski, T., Ahluwalia, J. S., & Braithwaite, R. L. (1999). Cultural sensitivity in public health: Defined and demystified. *Ethnicity & Disease*, 9, 10–21.

Resnicow, K., Soler, R., Braithwaite, R. L., Ahluwalia, J. S., & Butler, J. (2000). Cultural sensitivity in substance use prevention. *Journal of Community Psychology*, 28, 271–290.

Rideout, V. (2008). Television as a health educator: A case study of Grey's Anatomy. Menlo Park, CA: Henry J. Kaiser Family Foundation. Retrieved from: https://kaiserfamilyfoundation.files.wordpress.com/2013/01/7803.pdf

Rimal, R. N., & Juon, H.-S. (2010). Use of the risk perception attitude framework for promoting breast cancer prevention. *Journal of Applied Social Psychology*, 40, 287–310.

Ring, I. T., & Brown, N. (2002). Indigenous health: Chronically inadequate responses to damning statistic. *Medical Journal of Australia*, 177, 629–631.

Roter, D. L., & Hall, J. A. (2004). Physician gender and patient-centered communication: A critical review of empirical research. *Annual Review of Public Health*, 25, 497–519. doi:10.1146/annurev.publhealth.25.101802.123134

Ryan, E. B., & Butler, R. N. (1996). Communication, aging, and health: Toward understanding health provider relationships with older clients. *Health Communication*, 8, 191. doi:10.1207/s15327027hc0803_1

Scheufele, D. A., & Tewksbury, D. (2007). Framing, agenda setting, and priming: The evolution of three media effects models. *Journal of Communication*, 57, 9–20.

Schiavo, R. (2007). *Health communication: From theory to practice*. San Francisco, CA: Jossey-Bass.

Scott, A. M., & Caughlin, J. P. (2014). Enacted goal attention in family conversations about end-of-life health decisions. *Communication Monographs*, 81, 261–284. doi:10.1080/03637751.2014.925568

Scott, A. M., & Quick, B. L. (2012). Family communication patterns moderate the relationship between psychological reactance and willingness to talk about organ donation. *Health Communication*, 27, 702–711. doi:10.1080/10410236.2011.635135

Sharf, B. F., & Vanderford, M. L. (2003). Illness narratives and the social construction of health. In T. L. Thompson, A. M. Dorsey, K. I. Miller & R. Parrott (eds.), *Handbook of health communication* (pp. 9–33). Mahwah, NJ: Lawrence Erlbaum Associates.

Sherry, B., McDivitt, J., Birch, L., Cook, F., Sanders, S., Prish, J., Francis, L. A., & Scanlon, K. (2004). Attitudes, practices, and concerns about child feeding and child weight status among socioeconomically diverse white, Hispanic, and African-American mothers. *Journal of the American Dietetic Association*, 104, 215–221.

Simon, A., & Xenos, M. (2000) Media framing and effective public deliberation. *Political Communication*, 17, 363–376.

Snyder, L. B., & Rouse, R. A. (1995). The media can have more than an impersonal impact: The case of AIDS risk perceptions and behavior. *Health Communication*, 7, 125–145.

Song, H., Omori, K., Kim, J., Tenzek, K. E., Morey Hawkins, J., Lin, W. Y., Kim, Y. C., & Jung, J. Y. (2016). Trusting social media as a source of health information: Online surveys comparing the United States, Korea, and Hong Kong. *Journal of Medical Internet Research*, 18, 3. doi:10.2196/jmir.4193

Soroka, S. (2002). *Agenda-setting dynamics in Canada*. Vancouver: UBC Press.

Springer, A., Kelder, S., Orpinas, P., & Baumler, E. (2007). A cross-national comparison of youth risk behaviors in Latino secondary school students living in El Salvador and the USA. *Ethnicity and Health*, 12, 69–88. doi:10.1080/13557850601002155

Suggs, L. S., & Ratzan, S. C. (2012). Global E-health communication. In R. Obregon, & S. Waisbord (eds.), *The handbook of global health communication* (pp. 251–273). Malden, MA: Wiley-Blackwell.

Tajfel, H., & Turner, J. C. (1986). The social identity theory of intergroup behavior. In S. Worchel, & W. G. Austin (eds.), *Psychology of intergroup relations* (2nd ed., pp. 7–24). Chicago, IL: Nelson-Hall.

Thompson, T. (2003). Provider–patient interaction issues. In T. L. Thompson, A. M. Dorsey, K. I. Miller & R. Parrott (eds.), *Handbook of health communication* (pp. 91–93). Mahwah, NJ: Lawrence Erlbaum Associates.

Tozzi, A., Buonuomo, P., degli Atti, M., Carloni, E., Meloni, M., & Gamba, F. (2010). Comparison of quality of internet pages on human papillomavirus immunization in Italian and in English. *Journal of Adolescent Health*, 46, 83–89. doi:10.1016/j.jadohealth.2009.05.006

Tsai, T., & Lee, S. D. (2016). Health literacy as the missing link in the provision of immigrant health care: A qualitative study of southeast Asian immigrant women in Taiwan. *International Journal of Nursing Studies*, 54, 65–74. doi:10.1016/j.ijnurstu.2015.03.021

Ulrey, K. L., & Amason, P. (2001). Intercultural communication between patients and health care providers: An exploration of intercultural communication effectiveness, cultural sensitivity, stress, and anxiety. *Health Communication*, 13(4), 449–463. doi:10.1207/S15327027HC1304_06

Valente, T. W. (1996). Mass-media-generated interpersonal communication as sources of information about family planning. *Journal of Health Communication*, 1, 247–266. doi:10.1080/108107396128040

Valente, T. W., & Bharath, U. (1999). An evaluation of the use of drama to communicate HIV/AIDS information. *AIDS Education and Prevention*, 11, 203–212.

Waisbord, S., & Obregon, R. (2012). Theoretical divides and convergence in global health communication. In R. Obregon & S. Waisbord (eds.), *The handbook of global health communication* (pp. 9–33). Malden, MA: Wiley-Blackwell.

Wang, Y., & Tussing, L. (2004). Culturally appropriate approaches are needed to reduce ethnic disparity in childhood obesity. *Journal of the American Dietetic Association*, 104, 1664–1666.

Watson, B., & Gallois, C. (1998). Nurturing communication by health professionals toward patients: A communication accommodation theory approach. *Health Communication*, 10, 343–355. doi:10.1207/s15327027hc1004_3

Widman, L., Welsh, D. P., McNulty, J. K., & Little, K. C. (2006). Sexual communication and contraceptive use in adolescent dating couples. *Journal of Adolescent Health*, 39, 893–899.

Williams, T. T., Pichon, L. C., & Campbell, B. (2015). Sexual health communication within religious African-American families. *Health Communication*, 30, 328–338. doi:10.1080/10410236.2013.856743

Zuckerman, M. (1983). A biological theory of sensation seeking. In M. Zuckerman (ed.), *Biological bases of sensation seeking, impulsivity and anxiety* (pp. 37–76). Hillsdale, NJ: Lawrence Erlbaum Associates, Inc.

Student paper

How Health Care Is Communicated to Immigrants in Finland

Anni Harjula & Tiina Hakkarainen
Health Communication KVVS208
Department of Communication: University of Jyväskylä 2016

In this analysis we will discuss the current situation in Finland regarding how health and health care are communicated to immigrants. More in detail,

(Continued)

we will focus on how health care is delivered to immigrants and refugees and what kinds of obstacles and difficulties they have faced, or they will possibly face. The theory of planned behavior (Ajzen, 1985) is used in the analysis. In the first section of the analysis, we will review the case and provide an overview of the current health communication situation in Finland between immigrants and Finnish health care providers. This is followed by a review of the theory of planned behavior (Ajzen, 1985), after which we apply the theory to explore how health and health care are communicated to immigrants in Finland. In the last section of the paper, implications of our analysis are discussed.

> This is a nice and organized preview of the paper. It provides enough information about how different sections of the paper are connected and discussed.

Review of the Case

According to a recent study conducted by the Finnish Immigration Service (2015), the most asylum applicants came from Iraq, Afghanistan, Somalia, Syria, and Albania. Relatively, few studies have been made on the subject – however many of those have particularly studied Somalis in Finland, which may seem surprising as the number of Somalis is the third largest of all groups. The subjects vary from e.g. contraception use among Somali refugee women (Degni, Koivusilta, & Ojanlatva, 2006) to more general healthcare issues. For instance, Mölsä, Hjelde and Tiilikainen researched the changing conceptions of mental distress among Somalis (2010), followed by Kuittinen et al. (2014) and their study of the mental health of older Somali refugees and native Finns in Finland. Mölsä et al., discovered that "Islamic understandings of healing, including notions of jinn spirits and treatment, continue to be important in exile" (2010, p. 276), which drastically differs from the Finnish concept.

In this analysis we will discuss more in depth about these kinds of different cultural and/or religious beliefs, their possible consequences and

(Continued)

furthermore, other possible adversities, such as language barriers and other cultural behaviors that may affect health care outcomes once in Finland.

In today's world, there are more immigrants than ever previously recorded, and during the past few decades the number has increased rapidly. It has been estimated, that should the immigrant growth rate continue to increase at the same pace, by 2050 there would be 405 million international migrants (IOM, 2010). In 2010, the global overview of international migrants was estimated to be 214 million, the United States being the country with the largest foreign-born population, and they still host the largest migrant stock of any country worldwide (IOM, 2010). In Finland, however, the situation is very different. Even though the number of refugees or asylum-seekers has grown dramatically, Finland is not facing a crisis, despite the common belief, having made 7466 decisions in total in 2015 (IOM, 2010). For example, in comparison with the US and their immigrant number of 42.8 million, we are talking about completely different numbers and levels of issues – which is of course also related to the size of the country, population, and so forth (Finnish Immigration Service, 2016).

However, this is not to say that Finland would not be influenced by the migrant crisis in Europe at all. Since 2015, we have been witnessing more and more migrants and refugees, who have made the journey to Finland to seek asylum or better living standards. According to the Finnish Immigration Service (2016), there were only 326 asylum-seekers in January 2015, whereas half a year later, in September 2015, the number of asylum seekers in Finland was already 10,836. This means the health care landscape in Finland has changed at least up to a certain extent, and health communication situations occur increasingly in an intercultural context. The changed health care landscape brings along new issues that the Finnish society – as well as immigrants – need to address. Health

(Continued)

disparities between immigrants and Finnish people exist. The National Institute for Health and Welfare (2016) states "Compared with the population as a whole, the health and wellbeing of immigrants are generally in a poorer state. These may have been weakened by unemployment and small income, perceived discrimination and difficulties in the use of health care services and social services". Bearing the current situation in mind, it becomes important to ask how do we communicate health and health care to immigrants in Finland, and how could we do it better.

The well-being and general health of a refugee is often shaped by interactions with clinicians in care settings that lack of ethno-cultural match (Koehn, 2005). The relationship between the health care perspectives of asylum-seekers and their attending Finnish physicians showed little correspondence in a survey conducted by Koehn (2005). The study showed that "the perspectives of interviewed physicians and asylum seekers consistently diverged across critical healthcare-related issues: physical and mental health status and illness explanations, contributors to mental health problems and symptoms, and the value attributed to ethno-culturally familiar health beliefs and healthcare practices" (p. 67). Kuittinen et al. (2014) also pointed out after their study, that Somalis in Finland reported high illiteracy rates and poor language proficiency, which could furthermore indicate relatively low acculturation status and that older Somalis are highly dependent on the immigrant community within Finland.

Review of the Theory of Planned Behavior

In our analysis, we will apply the theory of planned behavior, which was developed by Ajzen in 1985 in his article "From intentions to actions: A theory of planned behavior". Originally, the theory is a revised version of the theory of reasoned action, which was proposed by Ajzen and

> The introduction section includes a proper review of the case, and the purpose of study. However, it would be more reader-friendly if based on the present discussion, there was a clear expression of the purpose at the end of this section.

(Continued)

> Choosing a proper theory to be applied to study is an important step of doing a research. A proper theory should be able to elucidate the expected answers out of doing a research. What we expect to see is a justification for choosing this specific theory for this paper. This justification comes in the next section along with the application of the theory to study. But it is always nice to know the significance of the choices from the beginning.

Fishbein in their book "Belief, attitude, intention, and behavior: An introduction to theory and research" (1975). The theory of reasoned action proposes any persuasive messages should take an individual's beliefs into account. According to the theory of reasoned action, this is because an individual's beliefs directly affect intentions toward a behavior (Fishbein & Ajzen, 1975). An individual's intentions toward a behavior, in turn, will determine whether he or she will perform such behaviors.

The theory of reasoned action proposes an individual's intent to perform a behavior is based on 2 variables, an individual's attitude toward the behavior and subjective norms (Fishbein & Ajzen, 1975). First, an individual's attitude toward the behavior depends on his or her beliefs about the consequences of the behavior. A person evaluates whether performing the behavior makes sense. In other words, he or she considers whether performing the behavior will produce the intended outcome – thus, will the behavior do what it promises to do, which, in turn, tells the person whether the behavior is worth performing or not. Second, subjective norms are based on the person's normative beliefs. Subjective norms refer to social pressure the person feels regarding the behavior. Individuals' intention to perform the behavior is affected by their perceptions of how other people around them – such as family members, friends, or the whole society – feel about such behavior. They evaluate whether the behavior is socially acceptable; whether other people wish them to perform the behavior or not. The theory of reasoned action suggests the more positive the attitude individuals have toward the behavior, and the more positively they believe the behavior is perceived by other people, the more likely it is they will perform the behavior.

The theory of reasoned action was later revised to the theory of planned behavior by Ajzen (1985). The theory of planned behavior proposes the same

(Continued)

variables – attitude toward the behavior and subjective norms – as introduced in the theory of reasoned action. However, perceived behavioral control is proposed as an additional element to the theory of planned behavior (Ajzen, 1985). Perceived behavioral control is based on control beliefs individuals hold regarding the behavior. It refers to the perception individuals have about their ability to perform the behavior, as well as how much control they perceive to have over the behavior. They evaluate how easy or difficult it is for them to perform the behavior, and whether they are able to do it. The more confident individuals are about their ability to perform the behavior, the more likely it is that they will perform the behavior. Ultimately, the theory of planned behavior explores the relationship between cognition and behavior (Croucher, 2016). Attitude toward the behavior, subjective norms and perceived behavioral control affect the person's behavioral intentions, and finally predict whether they will perform the behavior or not. According to the theory, any persuasive messages aiming to change behaviors should take the person's behavioral beliefs, normative beliefs, and control beliefs into account (Ajzen, 1985).

> Up to here the authors have reviewed the history of the theory and its related important notions and concepts.

The theory of planned behavior has been applied to a plethora of studies in health communication. First, plenty of research can be found that has explored health communication and young people. For example, the theory of planned behavior has been applied to studies that have explored the barriers to parent-adolescent communication about sex (Malacane & Beckmeyer, 2016), the influence of parental communication and perception of peers on adolescent sexual behavior (Sneed, Tan, & Meyer, 2015), the role of peer communication in college student's sexual health (Rittenour & Booth-Butterfield, 2006), parent-adolescent communication about marijuana use (Huansuriya, Siegel, & Crano, 2014), the effects of a peer education protocol to reduce binge drinking among adolescents

> This kind of categorization into first, second, etc. makes the text reader-friendly and easier to understand. A good idea!

(Continued)

(Planken & Boer, 2010), the effects of social support on social networking sites on increasing physical activity of college students (Zhang et al., 2015), and the power of persuasive messages promoting oral health and dental check-ups among young adults (Anderson, Noar, & Rogers, 2013).

Second, plenty of research has been conducted to investigate health communication and women. For instance, the theory of planned behavior has been applied to studies that have explored the process of designing a contraceptive choice campaign targeted to women (Sundstrom, DeMaria, Meier, Jones, & Moxley, 2015), preconceptions influencing women's perceptions of information on breast cancer screening (Henriksen, Guassora, & Brodersen, 2015), health promoting behaviors and faith-based support among African American women (Drayton-Brooks & White, 2004), the role of social networks as increasing family planning knowledge among African American women (Blackstock, Mba-Jonas, & Sacajiu, 2010), health-care providers' perceptions of communicating recommendations to obese pregnant women (Grohmann et al., 2012), and the effects of a HIV/AIDS intervention for illiterate rural females in Ethiopia (Bogale, Boer, & Seydel, 2011).

Third, plenty of research can be found that have explored health communication and organ donation. Specifically, the theory of planned behavior has been applied to studies that have investigated college students' intention to register as organ donors in Japan, Korea, and the US (Bresnahan et al., 2007), the effects of viewing an entertaining education program on cornea donation intention (Bae, 2008), intentions of becoming a living organ donor among Hispanics (Siegel, Alvaro, Lac, Crano, & Dominick, 2008), and Hispanic Americans' willingness to discuss living organ donation with their family members (Siegel, Alvaro, Hohman, & Maurer, 2011).

Finally, the theory of planned behavior has been applied to a variety of studies that have investigated several other health-related issues. For example, there were studies that have explored

(Continued)

the effects of health media on intentions to avoid unprotected sun exposure (Lovejoy, Riffe, & Lovejoy, 2014), health information seeking on the Internet (Marton & Wei Choo, 2012), the use of health-related ICT among older adults (Heart & Kalderon, 2013), parents preventing childhood obesity (Andrews, Silk, & Eneli, 2010), the factors determining the use of a diabetes risk-screening test (Nijhof, Hoeven, & de Jong, 2008), and the development of a mass media campaign to increase physical activity and nutrition in the US (Maddock, Silbanuz, & Reger-Nash, 2008).

Applying the Theory to the Case

As the theory review suggests, the theory of the planned behavior (Ajzen, 1985) can be used to explore a multitude of different health communication situations – and the topic of our analysis is not an exception. The theory of planned behavior offers us great ways in which we can investigate how health and health care are communicated to immigrants in Finland. In addition, the theory develops our understanding of how we could reduce health disparities between native-born Finnish people and immigrants; in other words, how we could promote health and health care to immigrants in a more efficient and appropriate way.

According to the theory of planned behavior, we should first have a closer look at immigrants' attitudes toward health-related behavior. We often take Western medicine for granted, and consider it is the only way to deliver health care. However, immigrants may have beliefs regarding health and health care that are culturally different from Western beliefs. For instance, there is no concept of epilepsy in the Hmong culture; instead epileptic seizures are explained by a spirit that takes over one's body (Fadiman, 2012). In her book, Fadiman (2012) described how Hmong refugee parents living in the West preferred to adhere to the beliefs and rituals of their ancestors instead of accepting

---

Side comments:

Anni and Tiina have done a nice job in reviewing the theory evaluation and its application to health communication. Categorization and review of studies related to each area is appreciable.

This is a nice transition paragraph from the general scope of the theory to a particular case of this study.

This section contains three reasons why the theory of planned behavior is a proper one for this study. The justifications and application of the theory have been done thoroughly and they yielded eye-catching implications as they are listed in the last section.

(Continued)

Western medical care for their daughter who suffered from epilepsy. In addition, there are many other cultural differences and aspects to for example organ donation. Wong (2010) studied the factors limiting deceased organ donation in Malaysia, India, and China, and identified six main themes of concern. Wong (2010) discovered that perceived religious prohibitions, cultural methodologies, fear of disfigurement, fear of surgery, distrust of the medical system, and family disapprovals were the main concerns across all the three groups. According to Wong (2010), an in-depth understanding of cultural and religious factors in South-East Asia is lacking, something important in order to provide appropriate strategies to promote acceptance of organ donation. The underlying idea is that if the behavior proposed by a Finnish health care provider does not make sense to the immigrant and if they do not believe the behavior works for them, it is less likely that they will act as suggested.

Second, the theory of planned behavior guides us to explore immigrants' subjective and societal norms. For example, in many cultures there are different kinds of religious beliefs that determine what acceptable behavior is, and what is not. For instance, a terminally ill patient in Finland can decide together with a doctor when he or she wishes to quit treatment. However, for many Muslims, one's body is not necessarily all their "own" – in Hayward and Madill's study (2003), Muslim participants raised concerns about material intactness and debated whether the body, after death, would be returned to Allah physically or metaphysically. Hindu participants in Wong's study (2010) believed that the body should not be modified, as they will need it to remain intact for their next life (the thought of reincarnation), thus may be more reluctant to donate organs than Westerners. In China, the participants were more likely to think that once an organ is removed from the body, one would not have that particular organ when they entered the spiritual world (Wong, 2010). This could be

(Continued)

the reason why people are not considered as eligible to make life and death decisions, or as Hayward and Madill stated, "For many Muslims, feeling confident that they are behaving in accordance with Islam may be their *highest context* in organ donation" (2003, p. 397). It is also good to bear in mind that ways to communicate health are different in individualistic and collectivistic cultures. In Finland, a health care provider tells the news directly to the patient, but in many other cultures, the health care provider discusses with family members of the patient, and lets them to inform their loved one. Other examples of culturally different norms would be birth control and abortion. In many cultures fertility is favored over birth control, and abortion is considered as socially unacceptable. In addition, in many cultures (obviously, up to a certain extent in Finnish culture too) mental illnesses are considered taboo, which can prevent the immigrant from seeking mental health care. According to the theory of planned behavior, some immigrants' may occasionally be reluctant to perform the behavior proposed by Finnish health care providers because it contradicts the norms of their own ethnic community. Another potential scenario could be that the proposed health-related behavior appeals to the immigrants, but they decide not to perform it due to the fear of being judged by members of their own community. Obviously, the same goes the other way around as well: one might be judged by Finnish people in case they decide to follow norms that are not part of the Finnish culture.

Third, the theory of planned behavior suggests we should analyze immigrants' perceived behavioral control. There are many elements involved in a health communication situation in an intercultural context that affect the perception the immigrant has about his ability to perform the behavior. Obviously, the lack of common language can make the communication situation difficult and uncomfortable. The immigrant's lack of adequate language

(Continued)

> skills in Finnish or Swedish may cause misunderstandings, confusion and uncertainty in health communication situations, which could be avoided by utilizing their rights as a Finnish resident to interpreting services (National Institute for Health and Welfare, 2016). However, there might be a lack of competent interpreters out there, especially if the immigrant speaks a more exotic language. Even if an interpreter would be involved, there is always the danger of something being lost in translation. The immigrants may have to learn a plethora of new ways of communicating in a health communication situation, ranging from how to make an appointment with a doctor, where exactly to go to when feeling sick, how to get his medicine, or how to follow the doctor's instructions, and those tasks already can differ a lot from their original health care system. Often, immigrants may also have lower income than Finnish people, which can lower their self-efficacy. It is much more challenging to take care of one's health – for instance, to go to regular health check-ups, or to buy expensive medicine if the person cannot financially afford to do that. The theory of planned behavior suggests if the proposed health-related behavior feels difficult or uncomfortable to perform, it is likely it will not be done.
>
> ### Implications
>
> The analysis has several implications. The theory of planned behavior suggests we need to focus on the immigrants' behavioral beliefs, normative beliefs, and control beliefs in case we wish to reduce health disparities in the Finnish society, and promote health and health care in a more efficient and appropriate way. This is because the immigrants' beliefs affect their behavioral intentions, which in turn predict whether they will perform the proposed health behavior or not.
>
> First, we should bear in mind that the proposed health-related behavior has to make sense to the

Application of the theory to the study is OK. However, still Anni and Tiina could bring more examples of the Somali immigrants, or any other major group of immigrants in Finland to see how they may have cultural clashes with the Finnish mainstream culture in the context of health communication.

(Continued)

patient. However, as our analysis suggests, some immigrants' may have different cultural beliefs related to health than Finnish people do. Thus, cultural awareness and knowledge of Finnish health care providers should be increased by organizing training and education programs for them. Cultural training and education should be provided to immigrants' too, so they can learn about Finnish culture, and the health care system in the country.

Second, we should consider that the proposed health-related behavior has to be socially accepted by immigrants' social networks. As explained in our analysis, sometimes immigrant communities may have different norms that contradict Finnish norms, and prevent them from doing the proposed health-related behavior. Bearing this in mind, it could be useful that immigrant communities – not only individual immigrants – would be involved in the attempt of promoting health and health care.

Third, immigrants should perceive they are able to perform the proposed health-related behavior. However, as our analysis suggests, health communication situations can sometimes be difficult for multiple reasons. For example, the lack of language skills and the unfamiliar health care system may lower immigrants' perceived behavioral control. Thus, health and health care should be made easier, more accessible, and affordable for immigrants. Finnish language courses should be organized, and appropriate interpreting services should be offered for immigrants. In general, immigrants should be provided with assistance regarding how to navigate in the Finnish health care system.

In this analysis, we analyzed the current situation in Finland regarding how health and healthcare are communicated to immigrants. The theory of planned behavior by Ajzen (1985) offers a good theoretical basis to investigate the topic. Our analysis revealed there are many issues involved in health communications situations between immigrants and Finnish health care providers. For

> Anni and Tiina have proposed cultural awareness (sensitivity) and providing the immigrants with education. You can relate these solutions to what is previously mentioned in the chapter.

(Continued)

example, different cultural beliefs and norms, as well as inadequate language skills, lower income, and difficulties in use of Finnish health care services can hinder the health communication process and lead to poorer health outcomes among immigrants. Towards the end of the paper, we also discussed the implications of the analysis. We suggested ways to promote better health and health care to immigrants, which would reduce health disparities between immigrants and Finnish people. We found out in our analysis that communication is a key to accomplish this goal. In order communicate health in a more efficient and appropriate way, Finnish health care providers – as well as immigrants – should focus on becoming more aware of and understanding those beliefs of each other that guide the behavior.

> This paragraph is a nice conclusion for the paper and it covers what they brought in the study. Well-done Anni and Tiina, it is a nice job ☺

References

Ajzen, I. (1985). From intentions to actions: A theory of planned behavior. In J. Kuhl & J. Beckmann (eds.), *Action control: From cognition to behavior* (pp. 11–39). New York, NY: Springer-Verlag.

Anderson, C. N., Noar, S. M., & Rogers, B. D. (2013). The persuasive power of oral health promotion messages: a theory of planned behavior approach to dental checkups among young adults. *Health Communication*, 28, 304–313. doi:10.1080/10410236.2012.684275

Andrews, K. R., Silk, K. S., & Eneli, I. U. (2010). Parents as health promoters: A theory of planned behavior perspective on the prevention of childhood obesity. *Journal of Health Communication*, 15, 95–107. doi:10.1080/10810730903460567

Bae, H.-S. (2008). Entertainment-education and recruitment of cornea donors: The role of emotion and issue involvement. *Journal of Health Communication*, 13, 20–36. doi:10.1080/10810730701806953

Blackstock, O. J., Mba-Jonas, A., & Sacajiu, G. M. (2010). Family planning knowledge: The role of social networks and primary care providers as information sources for African American women. *American Journal of Sexuality Education*, 5, 128–143. doi:10.1080/10627197.2010.491060

Bogale, G. W., Boer, H., & Seydel, E. R. (2011). Effects of a theory-based audio HIV/AIDS intervention for illiterate rural females in Amhara, Ethiopia. *AIDS Education and Prevention*, 23, 25–37. doi:10.1521/aeap.2011.23.1.25

Bresnahan, M., Lee, S. Y., Smith, S. W., Shearman, S., Nebashi, R., Park, C. Y., & Yoo, J. (2007). A theory of planned behavior study of college students' intention to register as organ donors in Japan, Korea, and the United States. *Health Communication*, 21, 201–211. doi:10.1080/10410230701307436

(Continued)

Croucher, S. M. (2016). *Understanding communication theory: A beginner's guide*. New York, NY: Routledge.

Degni, F., Koivusilta, L., & Ojanlatva, A. (2006). Attitudes towards and perceptions about contraceptive use among married refugee women of Somali descent living in Finland. *European Journal of Contraception & Reproductive Health Care*, 11, 190–196. doi:10.1080/13625180600557605

Drayton-Brooks, S., & White, N. (2004). Health promoting behaviors among African American women with faith-based support. *ABNF Journal*, 15, 84–90.

Fadiman, A. (2012). *The spirit catches you and you fall down: A Hmong child, her American doctors, and the collision of two cultures*. New York, NY: Farrar, Straus & Giroux.

Finnish Immigration Service (2015). Maahanmuuttoviraston myöntämät ensimmäiset oleskeluluvat ja Suomen kansalaisuuden saaneet 2015. Retrieved from: http://www.migri.fi/download/64996_Tilastograafit_2015_valmis.pdf?3f9905c2de6cd388

Finnish Immigration Service (2016). Asylum applicants 1.1.-31.12.2015. Retrieved from http://www.migri.fi/download/64990_Tp-hakijat_2015.pdf?99f9f8aa8930d388

Finnish Immigration Service (2016). Asylum applicants 1.1.-31.3.2016. Retrieved from: http://www.migri.fi/download/65778_EN_tp-hakijat_tammi_2016.pdf?4cca869f1474d388

Finnish Immigration Service (2016). Statistics on asylum and refugees. Retrieved from: http://www.migri.fi/about_us/statistics/statistics_on_asylum_and_refugees

Fishbein, M. & Ajzen, I. (1975). *Belief, attitude, intention, and behavior: An introduction to theory and research*. Reading, MA: Addison-Wesley.

Grohmann, B., Brazeau-Gravelle, P., Momoli, F., Moreau, K., Zhang, T., & Keely, E. J. (2012). Obstetric health-care providers' perceptions of communicating gestational weight gain recommendations to overweight/obese pregnant women. *Obstetric Medicine*, 5, 161–165. doi:10.1258/om.2012.120003

Hayward, C., Madill, A. (2003). The meanings of organ donation: Muslims of Pakistani origin and white English nationals living in North England. *Social Science & Medicine*, 57, 389–401. doi:10.1016/S0277-9536(02)00364-7

Heart, T., & Kalderon, E. (2013). Older adults: Are they ready to adopt health-related ICT? *International Journal of Medical Informatics*, 82, 209–231. doi:10.1016/j.ijmedinf.2011.03.002

Henriksen, M. J. V., Guassora, A. D., & Brodersen, J. (2015). Preconceptions influence women's perceptions of information on breast cancer screening: a qualitative study. *BMC Research Notes*, 8, 1–9. doi:10.1186/s13104-015-1327-1

Huansuriya, T., Siegel, J. T., & Crano, W. D. (2014). Parent–child drug communication: Pathway from parents' ad exposure to youth's marijuana use intention. *Journal of Health Communication*, 19, 244–259. doi:10.1080/10810730.2013.811326

IOM. (2010). *World Migration Report, 2010–The future of migration: Building capacities for change*. New York, NY: World Organization for Migration.

(Continued)

Koehn, P. H. (2005). Medical encounters in Finnish reception centres: Asylum-seeker and clinician perspectives. *Journal of Refugee Studies, 18*, 47–75. doi: 10.1093/refuge/fei003

Kuittinen, S., Punamäki, R-L., Mölsä, M., Saarni, S. I., Tiilikainen, M., & Honkasalo, M-L. (2014). Depressive symptoms and their psychosocial correlates among older Somali refugees and native Finns. *Journal of Cross-Cultural Psychology, 45*, 1434–1452. doi:10.1177/0022022114543519

Lovejoy, J., Riffe, D., & Lovejoy, T. I. (2014). An examination of direct and indirect effects of exposure and attention to health media on intentions to avoid unprotected sun exposure. *Health Communication, 30*, 261–270. doi: 10.1080/10410236.2013.842526

Maddock, J. E., Silbanuz, A., & Reger-Nash, B. (2008). Formative research to develop a mass media campaign to increase physical activity and nutrition in a multiethnic state. *Journal of Health Communication, 13*, 208–215. doi:10.1080/10810730701807225

Malacane, M., & Beckmeyer, J. J. (2016). A review of parent-based barriers to parent–adolescent communication about sex and sexuality: Implications for sex and family educators. *American Journal of Sexuality Education, 11*, 27–40. doi:10.1080/15546128.2016.1146187

Marton, C., & Wei Choo, C. (2012). A review of theoretical models of health information seeking on the web. *Journal of Documentation, 68*, 330–352. doi:10.1108/00220411211225575

Mölsä, M. E., Hjelde, K. H., & Tiilikainen, M. (2010). Changing conceptions of mental distress among Somalis in Finland. *Transcultural Psychiatry, 47*, 276–300. doi:10.1177/1363461510368914

National Institute for Health and Welfare (2016). Health and wellbeing. Retrieved from https://www.thl.fi/en/web/immigrants-and-multiculturalism/health-and-wellbeing

National Institute for Health and Welfare (2016). Services. Retrieved from https://www.thl.fi/en/web/immigrants-and-multiculturalism/services

Nijhof, N., Hoeven, ter, C. L., & de Jong, M. D. T. (2008). Determinants of the use of a diabetes risk-screening test. *Journal of Community Health, 33*, 313–317. doi:10.1007/s10900-008-9099-3

Planken, M., & Boer, H. (2010). Effects of a 10-minutes peer education protocol to reduce binge drinking among adolescents during holidays. *Journal of Alcohol and Drug Education, 54*, 35–52.

Rittenour, C. E., & Booth-Butterfield, M. (2006). College students' sexual health: Investigating the role of peer communication. *Qualitative Research Reports in Communication, 7*, 57–65.

Siegel, J. T., Alvaro, E. M., Hohman, Z. P., & Maurer, D. (2011). "Can you spare an organ?": Exploring Hispanic Americans' willingness to discuss living organ donation with loved ones. *Health Communication, 26*, 754–764. doi:10.1080/10410236.2011.566831

Siegel, J. T., Alvaro, E. M., Lac, A., Crano, W. D., & Dominick, A. (2008). Intentions of becoming a living organ donor among Hispanics: A theory-based approach exploring differences between living and nonliving organ donation. *Journal of Health Communication, 13*, 80–99. doi:10.1080/10810730701807142

(Continued)

> Sneed, C. D., Tan, H. P., & Meyer, J. C. (2015). The influence of parental communication and perception of peers on adolescent sexual behavior. *Journal of Health Communication*, *20*, 888–892. doi:10.1080/10810730.2015.1018584
>
> Sundstrom, B., DeMaria, A. L., Meier, S., Jones, A., & Moxley, G. E. (2015). "It makes you rethink your choice of the pill": Theory-based formative research to design a contraceptive choice campaign. *Journal of Health Communication*, *20*, 1346–1354. doi:10.1080/10810730.2015.1018650
>
> Wong, L.-P. (2010). Factors Limiting Deceased Organ Donation: Focus Groups' Perspective From Culturally Diverse Community. Elsevier Inc. doi:10.1016/j.transproceed.2009.11.053
>
> Zhang, N., Campo, S., Yang, J., Janz, K. F., Snetselaar, L. G., & Eckler, P. (2015). Effects of social support about physical activity on social networking sites: Applying the theory of planned behavior. *Health Communication*, *30*, 1277–1285. doi:10.1080/10410236.2014.940669

PART 5
CONCLUSION

Part 5 concludes this textbook. The concluding chapter of this textbook, Chapter 24, "The Bases for Intercultural Communication in a Digital Era" by Shiv Ganesh, Mingsheng Li, and Franco Vaccarino, offers a critique of current theories and approaches to intercultural communication and interculturality. The authors also propose ways in which the discipline can move forward into the future.

24 THE BASES FOR INTERCULTURAL COMMUNICATION IN A DIGITAL ERA

Shiv Ganesh, Mingsheng Li, and Franco Vaccarino, Massey University, New Zealand

Chapter Outline

- Changing Environments for Intercultural Communication
  - Going Beyond Dichotomies
- Expanding Bases of What Counts as Intercultural Communication
  - New Bases, New Constructs
  - Social Media, Globalization and Culture Formation
- Where to From Here?

As several contributors to this book have observed, we continue to be 'stuck' in Eurocentric, largely 20th century notions of interculturality. In this concluding chapter, we want to take up this theme in much more detail, following from some implicit claims by several authors that our theories and methods in intercultural communication research are dominated by a list of 'usual culprits' and that we continue to deal with a largely Eurocentric and dichotomized set of theories of intercultural communication.

Therefore, we argue in this chapter for the need to upend our assumptions about the bases of intercultural communication, literally turn our map of the world upside down, and radically reconfigure how we conceptualize, theorize, teach and practise intercultural communication in order to deal with the complexities and challenges of the current age. The chapter proceeds first by examining the case for change and reviewing our prevailing biases and bases for conceptualizing intercultural communication, before looking at how we can expand these bases, how the digital era makes intercultural communication simultaneously more easy on one hand and more fraught and complex on the other, and the renewed need for intercultural training.

Changing Environments for Intercultural Communication

We begin with the observation that much current research and teaching in intercultural communication is based on an identity-difference dichotomy that stretches across functionalist, interpretive, and critical paradigms of inquiry (Martin & Nakayama, 2013). Starting from early studies of cross-cultural similarities and difference, moving into critical studies of intercultural identity (Bardhan & Orbe, 2012), and continuing into organizationally-inspired accounts of global convergence and divergence (Stohl, 2001), the tension between identity and difference in intercultural communication has informed and shaped the field in very fundamental ways. Grappling with, accepting and attempting to move beyond this dichotomy continues to be a core concern of much intercultural communication inquiry.

Likewise, scholars continue to grapple with Eurocentrism, in the form of deep assumptions about the nature of individuals, the role of culture and the shape of difference. Scholars have been concerned about such dichotomized and Eurocentric understandings of intercultural communication for decades. Yum (1988) optimistically maintained that as more and more non-Western scholars and researchers undertake studies and research in intercultural communication, they would likely become increasingly dissatisfied with the dominant model in intercultural communication based on Eurocentric research philosophies and traditions. The traditional model assumes individuals are autonomous, independent, stable, consistent, and bounded, and this is incompatible with an alternative model in the rest of the world that suggests that individuals are not independent entities; they are interdependent, well connected with others, with a sense of belonging and affiliation. Gergen (1973) attributed this incompatibility to the arbitrary labelling of terminology based on Western taken-for-granted normative assumptions, rather than on cultural and ethnographic perspectives.

More recently, Littlejohn and Foss (2005) espoused a similar view that current human communication theory in general is but a Eurocentric enterprise with a strong Western bias, without integrating and embedding non-Western ideas into its philosophical foundations. Kim (2002) pointed out that 'culture is the most basic and far-reaching context in which communicative processes are engaged and thus formed' (p. 28) and she complained that intercultural communication research in the past half century has deviated from this cultural perspective in its conceptual frameworks. She suggested that the understanding of human communication involves multiple cultural perspectives and forces that shape and internalize thoughts and influence behaviour, rather than the normative system or any single theoretical framework that leads to 'inherent myopia' (p. 183). To understand a specific culture and the behaviour of its members, it is important to formulate a valid cultural framework with explanatory principles with reference to that culture (Fiske, et al., 1998). Gordon (1999) also emphasized that cultural studies should take multicultural perspectives instead of a unicultural Western model of communication that was dominated by American and European research traditions and theorizing. Kim (2002) made 'a strong and urgent call for increasing diversity', to reformulate the traditional field of communication, and shift from an Anglo-centred field to a multipolar field, multiculturalism, and alternative cultural perspectives (p. 3). Barker (2002) has also supported the view that cultural studies should even invalidate the Eurocentric model based on cultural hegemony and cultural imperialism for three reasons: the global flow of cultural discourses is no longer a one-way traffic, formerly Western hegemonic cultural discourses flowing from the West to the East, from the North to the South, are no longer a form of domination, and crucially, that Globalization does not lead to homogenization of identity only, but also to hybridization, creolization, cultural juxtaposing, disjuncture, and fragmentation.

Going Beyond Dichotomies

Teaching and research in intercultural communication has been dominated by Western models of value orientations that focus on conceptual dichotomies, such as Hall's (1989) model that comprises high versus low contexts, or monochronic versus polychronic cultures, and the model by Hofstede (1980) that includes individualism versus collectivism, high versus low power distance, high versus low uncertainty avoidance, and masculinity versus femininity. These models have had a huge impact on intercultural communication teaching and research around the world. However, several scholars continue to question not only the dichotomization inherent in these approaches but also their generalizability. In Kim's (2002) view, 'individualism and collectivism exist in all cultures and... individuals hold both individualistic and collectivistic values' at both individual and cultural levels (p. 187). She observed that even in highly individualistic Western cultures, the behaviour of most people does not fit the prevailing theoretical descriptions: they may not be self-reliant, self-confident, independent, and self-sufficient.

For instance, Chinese culture is labelled as a collectivistic, high power distance, and high context culture. However, when Western researchers visit China and stay in China for a period of time, they realize that although the Chinese behave differently from Westerners in many ways, such as business etiquettes, relationships, manners, they are not as collectivistic or polychronic as Westernized researchers, who come in attuned to difference, might think. Certainly, people in China often challenge those in power and speak what they mean, just as people in low context cultures do. In a formal setting, the Chinese are strictly punctual and well-focused on the agenda, rather than doing many things at a time. In the 'individualistic' New Zealand, by contrast, people are both individualistic and collectivistic, all depending on the situation. In the New Zealand workplace, there is a strong sense of *esprit de corps*, and teamwork and collective endeavours are highly visible. Some New Zealand individuals are also found to be polychronic in their behaviour. For example, university students, while listening to lectures, respond to emails, send text messages, search for information online, and watch videos. Power distance is also apparent in New Zealand companies, organizations, government agencies, and higher education institutions. If there are differences in communication, these differences are situationally and idiosyncratically determined. They do not fall squarely into the value orientation patterns promulgated by either Hall or Hofstede.

The dichotomous Western-centric models therefore need to be challenged. These models assume that cultural values, interpretations, and meanings are strictly attached to a physical place, or nation, or country; moreover, that they are static. However, according to Barker (2002), 'globalization is implicated in the global production of the local within and the localization of the global' (p. 73). The boundary of local and global is continuously changing and being blurred in the process of accelerated globalization. One can simultaneously identify with the local and global 'cultural processes of integration and disintegration, which are independent of inter-state relations' (Barker, 2002, p. 133), and thus take on hybrid identities such as diasporas in New Zealand and Australia. Barker was certain that these processes of cultural flows are filled with uncertainties, chaos, contingencies, and disorder, rather than order, stability, systematicity, and linear determinations and patterns.

It is therefore obvious that it is unrealistic to use Western-centric models to explain what is happening around the world, and we should jump out of the trap of Hall's and Hofstede's models that sees culture as place-bound, stable, consistent, and over-generalized. And so the authors in this edited collection should be applauded for taking intercultural communication out of its usual circuits and understanding it anew in multiple contexts. Kim (2002) pointed out that cultural studies should take into consideration cultural synergy that enables researchers to change their mind-sets by transcending their cultural blind spots, constraints, and the concepts of hegemony, and by being exposed to different cultural values, traditions, ideologies, perceptual frameworks, and philosophies. Barker (2002) argued that in cultural studies, there is no universal transcendental truth; 'truth is culture-bound, contingent and specific to the historical and cultural conditions of its production' (p. 64). He insisted that 'cultural studies should not understand theory as a grand narrative but as a local tool' to examine the democratic pluralist tradition that accommodates value differences, diversity, and liberty (p. 65). Barker (2008) has also suggested that cultural studies should undo 'the binaries of Western philosophy' (p. 36), involving the dismantling of hegemonic theoretical models and conceptual hierarchical oppositions such as individualism versus collectivism, high context and low context cultures, and monochronic and polychronic cultures so as to explore their blind spots, constrains, and irrationalities.

Expanding Bases of what Counts as Intercultural Communication

One way of responding to Barker's (2008) call and moving beyond Eurocentric and dichotomized understandings of intercultural communication, is for all of us to commit to expanding the bases of how we conceive of culture itself. By 'base' we refer to the social category that forms the foundation upon which a particular culture is built. Traditionally, scholars in intercultural communication have tended to work with four bases of culture: race, ethnicity, nationality and language, each of which has begun to become increasingly problematic in the current era.

In the past, people were classified and divided into racial groups on the basis of various biological and physical characteristics, which generally resulted from genetic ancestry. This classification has been, and continues to be controversial as racial categories vary significantly across the world, and there does not seem to be absolute agreement around the exact definition of each category. The concept of race is now recognized as being 'constructed in fluid social and historical contexts' (Martin & Nakayama, 2013, p. 191), and therefore not biologically essential or rigid. It is perfectly reasonable for people to identify with multiple races: indeed, this is often the case in New Zealand, where people sometimes identify as *both* Māori and Pakeha (European).

Another relatively controversial foundational base for intercultural communication inquiry is ethnicity. Ethnicity refers to a group or groups that people identify with or feel they have a sense of belonging and affiliation. Members identify with each other based on their common or shared cultural experiences and contexts. From a static, assigned category, however, like race, ethnicity is becoming a more fluid and dynamic construct. Individuals can self-identify with a particular ethnic group where they feel a sense of shared common origins, such as customs, culture, religion, or language. Sometimes this is highly controversial, especially when such identification becomes deception, but we want to suggest that ethnic identification, in terms of explicit identification with a particular culture, has always been a tacit choice.

Intricately connected to an ethnic group's identity is the language people use, and this is a third major base of much intercultural communication research and theory. Language is a central part of our identity and our culture as it reflects and constructs our values and helps us mark our social and cultural boundaries. Language is an important tool that humans use to construct and exchange meaning with others, and our culture aids in the construction of meaning. Liu, et al. (2011, p. 135) add that language is a cultural tool that needs to be placed within its social context in order for it to be understood. The preferred communication style of a particular culture is also reflected in their language use. Nationality is the fourth popular base for studies of intercultural communication. It could refer to an ethnic group of people with a shared culture, language or identity, but not defined by political borders. However, nationality can also refer to the legal relationship between an individual and a particular country, nation, or state. It can be an individual's country of birth or another country where that individual has citizenship. While studies of intercultural communication have long used nationality as a base or a proxy for understanding identity, for several years now, scholars have been arguing that international and intercultural differences should be understood as related but distinct constructs (Nakayama, 2008).

New Bases, New Constructs

Recently, intercultural communication scholars have been discussing several other bases upon which cultures form. Croucher (2013), for example, examined some historically central constructs in communication studies such as communication apprehension and willingness to communicate with reference to *religion* as a basis for intercultural difference, looking at major differences in how Catholics and Muslims in France enacted both constructs. Several scholars have understood *gender* as a basis for the formation of culture, looking at different cultures enacted by women and men. Julia Wood (2010) for example, has argued that women and men are socialized into very different cultures from the time they are born, even though they grow up in the same neighbourhood or even the same house. Class too is historically central to the way that cultures form, yet completely unstudied in intercultural communication. Paul Willis (1977), for instance, did a now famous ethnographic study of working class cultures, looking at how cultural factors and norms reinforced how working class men aspired to and stayed in working class jobs, thereby restricting their social mobility.

We suggest that the focus upon race, ethnicity, language and nationality as bases for intercultural communication is as much a product of the dichotomized and Eurocentric traditions as anything else, and therefore if we want to move beyond Eurocentricism, we need to shift and expand our understanding of the bases upon which cultures form. As Wood (2010) has argued, the basis upon which cultures can form is endless, and includes categories such as age, sexuality and (dis)ability. However, it is only in recent years that scholars have started to look at these categories as sites of *inter*cultural communication. The *Journal of International and Intercultural Communication*, for instance, ran a groundbreaking special issue on LGBTQ cultures only a few years ago (Chávez 2013). In recent years, scholars, particularly feminist researchers, have begun to look at how different categories such as age, race and gender intersect in various ways to produce unique cultures, subcultures and countercultures. In the current age, such intersections are both mobilized and accentuated by digital cultures (which itself is a basis for identity formation), so it is worth discussing digital and social media in some detail, as the implications for intercultural communication are immense (see Shuter, 2012).

Social Media, Globalization and Culture Formation

With globalization rapidly augmenting the compression of time and space in an ever-changing world where distances between different points have contracted and shrunk 'into a much smaller interactive field' (Chen & Zhang, 2010, p. 805), there has been a stronger sense of interdependence and interconnectedness among individuals and countries, as well as a stronger sense of difference. This has affected and impacted on all cultural, social, political, economic, and spiritual aspects of human life. Within an increasingly interwoven world, this interconnectedness draws global citizens from all parts of the world into a sense of belonging within a 'global village' (McLuhan & Fiore, 1968) or a 'global community' (Holt, 2000). In addition, with the advancement of technology and communications and the rapid development of new social media, there is a more intimate connection with 'wired cities' (Dutton, et al., 1987), 'virtual communities' (McChesney, 1996), and 'cyber-communities' (Cooks, 2000). Anderson (2006, p. 184) notes that 'People are re-forming into thousands of *cultural tribes of interest*, connected less by geographic proximity and workplace chatter than by shared interests.'

With the compression of time and space, individuals from various parts of the world can connect and interact with each other within seconds using a range of interconnected digital devices, as they are now free of 'the constraints of physical proximity and spatial immobility' (Buckingham, 2008, p. 147). This freedom allows a range of diverse forms of communication to be instantly and easily available as well as allowing the users to control whatever is shared and viewed. With its digital, interactive, and virtual nature, social media has become part of the everyday lives of many 21st century citizens. Chen (2012, p. 1) points out that this new media 'has brought human interaction and society to a highly interconnected and complex level'.

Intercultural communication constitutes a very significant component of this interconnected complexity as new media challenges 'the very existence of intercultural communication in its traditional sense' (Chen, 2012, p. 1) and also affects how cultures are formed, the bases upon which those cultures form, and how individuals from different cultures subsequently encounter each other. Socially, culturally and digitally, globalization has had a substantial impact on individuals' sense of community (Chen & Starosta, 2000). According to Chen and Zhang (2010, p. 796), globalization 'has redefined the meaning of community with a new look at inclusiveness and collective sense of identity.' Globalization processes, including social media and digital communication, have introduced new possibilities to include individuals and communities in intercultural as well as international communication. These new possibilities also challenge traditional ways of understanding culture. With increased possibilities of exchanging information and knowledge globally, 'new forms of intercultural communication are being developed; new cultural identities are being (re)created and (re)defined through the impact of cultural diversity in the digital domain' (Primorac & Jurlin, 2008, p. 71).

As discussed earlier, digital media are themselves a basis for culture formation as well as a means for it. Cvjetièanin (2008, p. 105) states that 'digital culture transforms the cultural field, encourages new forms of creative expression and offers a new perspective to intercultural communication.' Digital culture transforms the way we understand our world, and quoting the title of Marc Le Glatin's (2007) book, digital culture is *'un séisme dans la culture'* (a cultural earthquake).

Where to From Here?

If the bases upon which cultures are forming are multiplying, intersecting and accelerating, how do we apprehend and deal with these new challenges? It is crucial in our globalized world to work with an updated notion of intercultural communication training that takes into account the increasingly rapid changes in and multiplying bases of cultural formation. While individuals are now more aware of differences than ever before, they continue to neither realize nor recognize how these differences impact on their interactions and behaviours with people from different cultures, or just how quickly those differences can change in the first place! In order to navigate cultural differences, similarities and flux, individuals continue to need to become culturally competent. Wilson, et al. (2013, p. 900) defined cultural competence as 'the acquisition and maintenance of culture-specific skills required to (a) function effectively within a new cultural context and/or (b) interact effectively with people from different cultural backgrounds'. Bennett (2008, p. 97) defines becoming competent as acquiring 'a set of cognitive, affective, and behavioral skills and characteristics that support effective and appropriate interaction in a variety of cultural contexts'. *Mindset* refers to, *inter alia*, knowledge and one's awareness of operating within a particular cultural context, culture-general and culture-specific knowledge, frameworks, worldviews, values, and norms; and *heartset* refers to attitudes, motivation, openness, tolerance of ambiguity, and flexibility. *Skillset* refers to abilities or repertoire of behaviour, including gathering appropriate information, listening, adapting, building relationships, managing social interactions, and empathizing.

As globalization amplifies, intercultural communication training becomes more important, for individuals in the workplace, staff and students at educational institutions, individuals going on various international assignments, expatriates, migrants and refugees. In other words, there is a growing need for citizens in all parts of the world to receive intercultural communication training. Intercultural communication training should raise awareness about the bases of cultural formation and their relationship with the construction of different cultural norms, break down cultural barriers, and increase self-awareness and communication skills when engaging with individuals from other cultures. Pusch, et al. (1981, p. 73) pointed out that one of the historical purposes of intercultural training has been to 'provide a functional awareness of the cultural dynamic present in intercultural relations and assist trainees in becoming more effective in cross-cultural situations'. Through intercultural communication training, individuals should be able to 'integrate alternate frames of reference' (Paige, 1993, p. 172) into their lives in order to function more effectively in the global village and thus also move away from a Eurocentric orientation. Bennett (2004) pointed out that as individuals become more interculturally competent, there seems to be a move from ethnocentrism to *ethnorelativism*, a term he coined to highlight that the experiences of an individual's beliefs and behaviours are merely one organization of reality among a range of feasible possibilities.

What constitutes effective training for the 21st century global citizen to become interculturally competent? Bhawuk (1998) stated that intercultural communication training programmes should be based on cultural theories, and some theories that have been proposed to integrate the knowledge, attitude and behaviour components include the culture learning theory and the social identification theory (Ward, 2004). Bennett and Castiglioni (2004, p. 250) highlighted that intercultural communication training should include 'physical self-awareness' in order to have a deeper understanding of 'the embodied feeling' for culture. Furthermore, Ward (2004) maintained that cultural knowledge and cultural attitude are not adequate to prepare individuals to deal with a range of intercultural situations, and she recommends that intercultural communication programmes should include social skills in order to bring about behavioural changes. Bennett's (2008) mindset, heartset, and skillset approach to intercultural competence contains the vital ingredients that need to be integrated into any intercultural communication training programme as 'knowledge, attitude and behavior must work together for development to occur' (Bennett & Bennett, 2004, p. 149). As cultural formation, reformation and deformation continue apace in the current age, the need for training has never been more apparent.

References

Anderson, C. (2006). *The long tail. How endless choice is creating unlimited demand.* London, UK: Random House.

Bardhan, N., & Orbe, M. (2012). *Identity research and communication: Intercultural reflections and future directions.* New York, NY: Lexington.

Barker, C. (2002). *Making sense of cultural studies: central problems and critical debates.* London, UK: Sage.

Barker, C. (2008). *Cultural studies: theory and practice.* Los Angeles, CA: Sage.

Bennett, J. M. (2008). Transformative training: Designing programs for culture learning. In M. A. Moodian (ed.). Contemporary leadership and intercultural competence: Understanding and utilizing cultural diversity to build successful organizations (pp. 95–110). Thousand Oaks, CA: Sage.

Bennett, J. M., & Bennett, M. J. (2004). Developing intercultural sensitivity: An integrative approach to global and domestic diversity. In D. Landis, J. M. Bennett & M. J. Bennett (Eds.), *Handbook of intercultural training* (3rd ed., pp. 147–165). Thousand Oaks, CA: Sage.

Bennett, M. & Castiglioni, I. (2004). Embodied ethnocentrism and the feeling of culture: A key to training for intercultural competence. In D. Landis, J. Bennett, & M. Bennett (eds.), *Handbook of intercultural training* (3rd ed., pp. 249–265). Thousand Oaks, CA: Sage.

Bennett, M. J. (2004). Becoming interculturally competent. In J.S. Wurzel (ed.), *Toward multiculturalism: A reader in multicultural education.* Newton, MA: Intercultural Resource Corporation.

Bhawuk, D. P. S. (1998). The role of culture in cross-cultural training: A multimethod study of culture-specific, culture-general, and culture theory-based assimilators. *Journal of Cross-Cultural Psychology*, 29, 630–655.

Buckingham, D. (2008). *Youth, identity, and digital media.* Cambridge, MA: The MIT Press.

Chávez, K. R. (2013). Pushing boundaries: Queer intercultural communication. *Journal of International and Intercultural Communication*, 6, 83–95.

Chen, G. M. (2012). The impact of new media on intercultural communication in global context. *China Media Research*, 8(2), 1–10.

Chen, G. M., & Starosta, W. J. (2000). *Communication and global society: An introduction.* In G. M. Chen & W. J. Starosta (eds.), Communication and global society (pp. 1–16). New York, NY: Peter Lang.

Chen, G. M., & Zhang, K. (2010). New media and cultural identity in the global society. In R. Taiwo (ed.), *Handbook of research on discourse behavior and digital communication: Language structures and social interaction* (pp. 795–815). Hershey, PA: Idea Group Inc.

Cooks, L. (2000). Conflict, globalization, and communication. In G. M. Chen & W. J. Starosta (eds.), *Communication and global society* (pp. 257–277). New York, NY: Peter Lang.

Croucher, S. M. (2013). Communication apprehension, self-perceived communication competence, and willingness to communicate: A French analysis. *Journal of International and Intercultural Communication*, 6, 298–316.

Cvjetièanin, B. (2008). Challenges for cultural policies: the example of digital culture. In A. Uzelac & B. Cvjetièanin (eds.). *Digital culture: The changing dynamics* (pp. 103–112). Zagreb, Croatia: Institute for International Relations.

Dutton, W. H., Blumer, J. G., & Kraemer, K. L. (eds.). (1987). *Wired cities: Shaping the future of communications.* Boston, MA: G. K. Hall.

Fiske, A. P., Kitayama, S., Markus, H. R., & Nisbett, R. E. (1998). The cultural matrix of social psychology. In D. T. Gilbert, S. T. Fiske, & G. Lindzey (eds.), *The handbook of social psychology* (Vol. 2, pp. 915–981). Boston, MA: McGraw-Hill.

Gergen, K. J. (1973). Social psychology as history. *Journal of Personality and Social Psychology*, 26, 309–320.

Gordon, R. D. (1999). A spectrum of scholars: multicultural diversity and human communication theory. *Human Communication*, 2, 1–18.

Hall, E. T. (1989). *Beyond culture.* New York, NY: Anchor Books.

Hofstede, G. (1980). *Culture's consequences: international differences in work-related values.* Beverly Hills, CA: Sage.

Holt, R. (2000). 'Village work': An activity-theoretical perspective toward global community on the Internet. In G. M. Chen & W. J. Starosta (eds.), *Communication and global society* (pp. 107–141). New York, NY: Peter Lang.

Kim, M.-S. (2002). *Non-Western perspectives on human communication: implications for theory and practice.* Thousand Oaks, CA: Sage.

Le Glatin, M. (2007). *Internet: un séisme dans la culture?* Toulouse, France: Éditions de l'Attribut.

Littlejohn, S. W., & Foss, K. A. (2005). *Theories of human communication* (8th ed.). Belmont, CA: Thomson/Wadsworth.

Liu, S., Volčič, Z., & Gallois, C. (2011). *Introducing intercultural communication: Global cultures and contexts.* London, UK: Thousand Oaks, CA: Sage.

Martin, J. N., & Nakayama, T. K. (2013). *Intercultural communication in contexts* (6th ed.). New York, NY: McGraw-Hill.

McChesney, R. W. (1996). The internet and U.S. communication policy-making in historical and critical perspective. *The Journal of Communication*, 46, 98–124.

McLuhan, M., & Fiore, Q. (1968). *War and peace in the global village*. New York, NY: Bantam.

Nakayama, T. (2008). On (not) feeling rebellious. *Journal of International and Intercultural Communication*, 1, 1–2.

Paige, R. M. (1993). Trainer competencies for international and intercultural programmes. In R. M. Paige (ed.), *Education for the intercultural experience* (2nd ed., pp. 169–199). Yarmouth, Maine: Intercultural Press Inc.

Primorac, J., & Jurlin, K. (2008). Access, piracy and culture: the implications of digitalization in Southeastern Europe. In A. Uzelac & B. Cvjetièanin (Eds.). *Digital culture: The changing dynamics* (pp. 71–90). Zagreb, Croatia: Institute for International Relations.

Pusch, M. D., Patico, A., Renwick, G. W., & Saltzman, C. (1981). Cross-cultural training. In G. Althen (ed.), *Learning across cultures* (pp. 72–103). Washington, DC: National Association for Foreign Student Affairs.

Shuter, R. (2012). Intercultural new media studies: The next frontier in intercultural communication. *Journal of International and Intercultural Communication*, 41, 219–237.

Stohl, C. (2001). Globalizing organizational communication: Convergences and divergences. In F. Jablin & L. Putnam (eds.), *The new handbook of organizational communication* (pp. 323–375). Thousand Oaks, CA: Sage Publications.

Ward, C. (2004). Psychological theories of culture contact and their implications for intercultural training and interventions. In D. Landis, J. M. Bennett & M. J. Bennett (eds.), *Handbook of intercultural training* (3rd ed., pp. 185–217). Thousand Oaks, CA: Sage.

Willis, P. (1977). *Learning to labor*. New York, NY: Columbia University.

Wilson, J., Ward, C., & Fischer, R. (2013). Beyond culture learning theory: What can personality tell us about cultural competence? *Journal of Cross-Cultural Psychology*, 44, 900–927.

Wood, J. (2010). *Gendered lives: Communication, gender and culture*. Boston, MA: Cengage Learning.

Yum, J. O. (1988). The impact of Confucianism on interpersonal relationships and communication patterns in East Asia. *Communication Monographs*, 55, 374–388.

INDEX

Aboriginal Australians 59
accented speech 157
acculturating individuals 207, 209, 213, 217, 219, 221–2, 227
acculturation: complex perspectives on 219–20; one-dimensional perspectives on 212–15; relationships between components of 213; selective processes of 220–1; two-dimensional perspectives on 215–19; use of term 207, 212
acculturation attitudes 220, 222
acculturation theories 122, 207; Acculturation Strategies theory 215–20, 233
adaptation: mutual 165; see also intercultural adaptation
adaptation and acculturation studies 39
addressivity 131
adolescents: and identity 99–100; and risky behavior 325–6, 341
affectionate communication 162
affirmative action 26, 278
affordances 141, 181
Africa: Chinese culture in 45; cultural diversity of 30
African-Americans: cultural identity of 118, 122; and health care 342; social identity of 102, 184; as subculture 84
African American Vernacular English (AAVE) 139
African-descended South Americans 15, 18
African languages 27
ageism 319
agenda setting 328
aggressiveness 185, 190, 193
Algerians, in France 105–6
Alice's Adventures in Wonderland 97–8
amae 55, 198–200, 203

ambiguity, tolerance for 186, 252, 256–7
Amerindians see Native Americans
animosity 172–3, 175–7
anthropology: social 207; in South America 15–16
antibodies, cultural 43
anxiety uncertainty management theory 158
apartheid 26, 28
apology behavior 198–204
appreciation, expressing 162
Arab Americans 118
Arabic culture: and conflict styles 191; and Islam 68
Arabic language 138
Arab-Israeli conflict 33–4
Argentina 15–18
art, cultural differences in 82
ascription 98–9, 117, 120–5
Asia: Australia's trading relations with 60; see also East Asia
Asian Americans 117, 121, 162, 236, 326
assimilation: and immigration policies 215; minority groups fighting 117; in South America 16
assimilation orientation to acculturation 212, 215–16, 233
asylum-seekers 29, 323, 337–9
Augustine, Saint 271
Australia: cultural history of 58–60; international students in 160
Australians, conflict styles of 191
autonomy-embeddedness continuum 90
avowal 98, 120–1, 123–5

Bakhtin, Mikhail 131–2
BASIC (Behavioral Assessment Scale for Intercultural Competence) 257

behavioral control, perceived 341, 345, 347
behavioral flexibility 254
beliefs, and culture 80
benevolence 49, 185–6
biases, self-serving 192
bicultural individuals 218–19, 222, 225
bilingual intercultural education 17–18, 20.n2
Bolivia 14, 16–19, 317
Buddhism 69, 71–3
Burkina Faso 30
business, intercultural communication competence in 259–60

CAJ (Communication Association of Japan) 54–5
Cameroon 30–1
Cantonese dialect 141
Carbaugh, Donal 132–3
Cartesian dualism 72
Casmir, Fred 222
CAT (communication accommodation theory) 322–3
categorical perception 135, 143
Catholic Church 51, 62–3, 106
centralization 284
CEOs, social values of 308
child-caregiver interaction 134
children, as patients 319
China: family structure in 83; in Hofstede's dimensions 187; intercultural communication research in 42–5; Pearl River Delta Region languages 141; post-colonial context of 41–2
Chinese character emoticons 151
Chinese culture: and conflict 182–3, 191; in Hofstede's model 357; intimate relationships in 161–2
Chinese language: in Hong Kong 105; Mandarin 130, 135–6, 141; mixed-code conversation in 141–2; see also Cantonese dialect; Taiwanese dialect
Chinese people: communication styles of 147; in Indonesia 140; in Malaysia 68–9; as managers 276; as migrants to US 122; online conversation between 149–51
Christianity: in France 104, 106; intercultural communication in 62–4; in Korea 48; in Malaysia 69; in South America 15

class: and culture 360; and racial stratification 15
closed systems 282
CMC (Computer-Mediated Communication) 141, 146–7
code-switching 140
collectivism: Hofstede's use of term 87; in Korean culture 49–50; in Swedish culture 221; see also individualism-collectivism spectrum
Collier, Mary Jane 27, 98
Colombia 14, 16–18
colonialism 16, 25, 41
communalism 10
communication: between Muslims 67–8; Chinese words for 42; and culture 82, 249; definitions of 4–5; ethnocentric and cosmopolitan 304–5, 309; and identity 98, 100; and intercultural adaptation 213; key elements of 5; and Third Culture Building 222–3; transactional approach to 5–6
communication anxiety 157–8
communication-between-cultures 41–2
communication flexibility 257
communication networks 287–8
communication process 6, 23
communication skills: in health communication 319; and intercultural competence 254
communication studies: in China 42; in Japan 53–6
communication styles: Chinese and American 147; indigenous to Japan 55; other-centered 258
Communication Theory of Identity 115–17
communication traits 39
competence, elements of 249
compromise 108–9, 179, 187, 190–2
conduct manuals 200
conflict: cultural rules around 182, 184; dual concern model of 190; and intercultural communication 10; personal and situational elements of 180–1; and values 185; see also intercultural conflict; interpersonal conflict
conflict styles 108–9, 189–95, 260
Confucianism 48, 69, 276
Confucius Institutes 45

context: as cultural dimension 88; in intercultural communication competence 255
contextualization cues 130
cosmopolitanism 217, 282
Côte d'Ivoire 30
country-animosity 175–6
cross-cultural adjustment 213, 272, 290–1
cross-cultural communication: and globalization 275; Japanese studies of 56; use of term 7; within organizations 283
cross-cultural competence 291–2
cross-cultural research 183, 277
cross-cultural training 272, 277, 290–2
Croucher, Stephen 5, 64, 83, 88, 102, 104, 106, 217, 360
cultivation theory 317, 327
cultural awareness 4, 254–5, 271, 277, 347
cultural chameleons 225, 241
cultural competence, defined 121, 362
cultural differences: and conflict 184, 194; discussing 177; emic and etic perspectives 277; and intercultural relationships 160–1, 165; political management of 22–3
cultural dimensions: critique of dichotomous models 357–8; Hall's model 88; Hofstede's model 86–8, 100, 282–7, 300–1, 309
cultural discourse analysis 132–4
cultural diversity: in Europe 23; exposure to 210; and globalization 271; in Iran 37–8; in Israel 34; in organizations 298–9, 301–5, 309–11; at work 163–5 (see also employee diversity)
cultural frame-switching 218
cultural hegemony 41, 357
cultural hybrids 225, 236; see also third culture individuals
cultural identity 101–2; and diversity 303; in Israel 35; multiple types of 120; reinvention of 18; in South Africa 27; third-culture 224, 232
Cultural Identity Negotiation Theory 115, 122–3
Cultural Identity Theory 114–16, 119–26
cultural imperialism 217, 357

cultural interactions, global history of 40, 41
cultural norms 69, 107, 200, 317, 362
cultural practices, uniqueness of 132
cultural sensitivity 304, 323–4
cultural similarity 159, 291
cultural/social identity see social identities
cultural toughness 277
cultural universals 64
culture: bases of 359; and communication behavior 82, 249; definitions of 27, 78–9, 114, 119; dominant 84–5, 100–1, 104, 106, 109, 222; in health communication 326; impact on individuals 183; in intercultural communication research 39; and nation 14–15; reproduction of 181–2; as social process 300; three-layered model of 79, 80–4
culture confusion 210
culture learning theory 363
culture shock 43, 157, 208–10, 227; reverse 209, 235

Dalai Lama 71–2
decentralization 33, 284
decoding 6, 71
deculturation 212–13, 215, 221
denotative and connotative meanings 129–30
dialogue, and language 131–2
dichotomies, going beyond 355–7
D-I-E (Description, Interpretation, Evaluation) 257–8
digital culture 360–1
disagreements 164, 179–82, 184, 192, 195
distinctiveness, positive 106–7
diversity: critical 27; see also cultural diversity
diversity management and training 302, 308–9, 311
downward communication 288
Durkheim, Émile 82, 102
dynamic cultural theory 277

East Asia: conflict styles in 191; embeddedness in 90; and emotional expression 147; and holism 286–7; long-term orientation 88; management culture in 276; marriage beliefs in 162; power distance in 87

education, and intercultural communication competence 258–9
Ehime Maru incident 198–204
Einstein, Albert 131
emancipative values 187–8
emoticons / Emoji 141–2, 144, 146–53
emotional expression 147, 190–1
empathy: and intercultural communication competence 261, 305–6; Korean equivalents of 51; and TCKs 242
employee diversity 278, 283, 298, 302, 311–12
employee-oriented cultures 282
emptiness (Shunyata) 72
encoding 6, 71
enculturation 212, 221
end-of-life decisions 320
English language: Iranian learners of 39, 259; in Japan 53–4, 56; in Korea 48; plasticity of 22; in West Africa 30
Entertainment-Education model 327
epilepsy 83, 343–4
ethnic attitudes 174
ethnic diversity: and health behavior 326; in Malaysia 69; in South Africa 25–7; in West Africa 30–1
ethnic friendships 121
ethnic groups, use of term 85
ethnic identity 102, 359
ethnicity, use of term 102
ethnocentric communication 304
ethnocentrism: and cultural adaptation 208; defining 175–6; and intercultural relationships 158–9, 165; use of term 10; ways to reduce 258; and willingness to communicate 172–7
ethnolinguistic identity theory (ELIT) 104–7, 109
ethnorelativism 362–3
Eurocentrism 71, 355–8, 360, 362
Europe: intercultural communication in 22–3; multiculturality of 21–2
European Union: free movement within 21; migration to 3–4, 29, 85; and multiculturalism 8
expatriates: children of 224; cultural adaptation of 206–7, 290; as managers 276
expectations: in intercultural relationships 160; for self-disclosure 64
Extended U-Curve Model 209, 210
eyes 77

face and facework 107–8, 188–9, 198, 202
Facebook Messenger 148
Face Negotiation Theory (FNT) 107–10, 189
family communication 219, 320–1
fandoms 85, 86
Fanon, Frantz 41
Finland: cultural peculiarities of 80, 82; healthcare for immigrants to 336–48; in Hofstede's dimensions 187; identities in 101–2; multiculturalism in 9; refugees to 85
foreign languages: in communication studies 54; and conflict 184; emoticons in 151; fear of embarrassment in 157; learning 164
framing 328–9
France, Muslims and Christians in 104–6, 184, 360
French language, in West Africa 30
Friedman, Friedman 273
friendship, cultural meanings of 160

Ganesha 81
Geertz, Clifford 78, 102
gender: and culture 360; and emoticons 147–8, 152
gender identity 103
gender role expectations 163
German language 138
Ghana 30, 185
global competence 56
globalization: and culture formation 360–1; definitions of 272–3; and global competence 56; history of 272; impacts of 273–5, 292; and intercultural communication 43, 155, 271, 362; and localization 358
global village 271–2, 361–2
Gordon, Milton 212
grammar 130, 134, 203
grapevine communication 288, 290
Great Commission 62–3
"Grey's Anatomy" 327
group biases 104
group boundaries, closed 106–7
group identities: in Northern Ireland 124; seeking new 103
Guangdong Province 141
Gudykunst, William B 7, 56, 73, 78, 80, 81, 85, 156, 158

Hall, Edward T. 7, 88–9, 136, 357–8
Haredi Jews 33, 35
harmonious relationships: in Buddhism 73; in Confucian culture 48; as cultural value 89–90; in Islam 68–9; in Japanese culture 82, 182, 198–9, 201; in Korean culture 48, 50
Harry Potter 131
health behaviors: changing 317, 326–7; of immigrants 343, 346–7; of marginalized groups 330; risky 324–6
health beliefs, cultural differences in 83, 323–4, 343–4, 346
healthcare: developing perceptions of 329–30; diversity management in 302; intercultural communication competence in 261; recent developments in 315–16
health communication: contexts of 318–24; cultural differences in 338, 343, 345–7; defined 316–17; evolution of 317; and face negotiation theory 109; major issues in 324–7; media theories in 327–9; research in 330; and theory of planned behavior 341
health information 317, 326–9, 331, 343
heartset 362–3
hierarchical organizations 278, 279
hierarchy: of needs 239–40; racial 2, 26, 89
hierarchy-egalitarianism continuum 51, 87–90, 107, 186
high-context culture 88; CMC in 147; Korea as 50–1; in organizations 284
Hinduism 25, 69, 81, 242, 344
history, shared 80
HIV/AIDS 317, 327–8, 330, 342
Hmong 83, 84, 323, 343
Hofstede, Geert: attitudes to nations and cultures 183; cultural variability research 86–7, 100, 186–7; definition of culture 78; and face negotiation theory 189–90; see also cultural dimensions, Hofstede's model of
holism 73, 83, 284, 286–7
home culture: and assimilation 213–14; escaping 181; re-adaptation to 209; use of term 207
home-culture identity 216, 221
Hong Kong: language in 105, 141; McDonald's in 132
Hopi language 136

horizontal communication 275, 289
host culture: competence acquisition in 213; receptivity to acculturation 216–17, 220; use of term 207
human identity 81, 99
humor 147, 163–4, 212, 323
Hu Zhengrong 44

idealized influence 307
identities: formation of 99; types of 80–1, 99–103; use of term 98–9
identity-difference dichotomy 356
identity expectancy 189
identity gaps 116–17, 127
identity theories 103–9, 115–16
illness: cognitive perceptions of 330; cultural interpretations of 323–4; and self-disclosure 319
iman 67
immigrants: global flows of 338; and healthcare 322–4, 336–48; hidden 225; see also asylum-seekers; refugees
indexical signs 137
India: caste system in 84; communalism in 10
indigenismo 16
individualism, in Western cultures 48–9
individualism-collectivism continuum 87, 186, 286; and apology behavior 200, 202; and CMC 147; and conflict style 190–1; critique of 357; and Face Negotiation Theory 107–9, 189–90; and health communication 345; and Japanese research 56; and organizational culture 300–1
Indonesia 60, 68, 140
indulgence-restraint 87–8, 187, 286
INGOs (international nongovernmental organizations) 176
ingroup/outgroup designations 103–4, 176
ingroups: and collectivism 87; in identity theories 104; personal identity in 81; use of term 99
integration orientation to acculturation 215, 217–19, 233
intellectual stimulation 307–8
interactional resources 139
interaction management 254, 257
interaction posture 257
interactive acculturation model 222
intercultural adaptation: Extended U-Curve Model 209, 210; Integrative

Theory of 212–15, 214; managing stress of 211; predicting successful 210; of third culture individuals 225; use of term 206
intercultural communication: anxiety and uncertainty in 158; approaches to identity in 100; classroom example of 268–9; common examples of 247–8; cultural bias in research on 355–8; definitions of 7, 172–3, 267; expanding bases of 358–60; in Face Negotiation Theory 108; in majority Muslim countries 68; miscommunication with 133–4; need for 8–10; new media challenging 361; and organizational culture 300; politicization of 18; training in 362–3; use of term 120–1; willingness for 173–4; within African nations 30–1; within Iran 38–9
intercultural communication competence: activities 262–4; in culturally diverse organizations 305–7, 309; definitions of 248–54; dimensions of 254–6; Iranian research on 39; research into 258–62; ways to improve 256–8
intercultural competence: definitions of 251–3; education to develop 38, 271; level of 121
intercultural competence, of third-culture individuals 240
intercultural conflict: advice for 193–4; secular and emancipative values in 188
intercultural effectiveness 258
intercultural events 253, 256, 267
Intercultural Exercise, qualities in 293–4
intercultural experience 30–1, 166, 209, 261, 305–7
intercultural friendships 156, 159–61, 166, 224, 306
intercultural health communication 323–4
intercultural identity 214, 216, 356
interculturality 1, 17, 355
intercultural learning 93, 256, 296
intercultural personhood 218
intercultural relationships: benefits of 156, 165; communication challenges in 157–9; dating and marriage 161–3 (see also romantic relationships); at work 163–5; see also intercultural friendships

intercultural research 183, 193, 214, 323
intercultural skills 156, 225, 252, 262
intercultural transformation 214
intercultural understanding 22–3, 73
interdependent origination 2, 71–3
interethnic communication, use of term 7
intergroup behavior, and identity 107
intergroup communication: openness to 105; use of term 183
intergroup health communication 322–3
international communication, use of term 7–8
International Communications (China) 44
international students: adaptation issues for 161; stereotypes of 158
international teaching assistants (ITAs) 158–9
internet: and globalization 272; and health information 316, 326, 329; see also CMC
interpersonal communication: and identity 98; and intercultural communication 249, 268; use of term 213
interpersonal conflict: and cultural differences 10, 164; and Hofstede's dimensions 187; as unavoidable 179–80
interpersonal health communication 318–22
interracial couples 123, 161
intimacy 50, 150, 160–3, 234–5
Iran 37–9, 111, 259
Islam: cultural differences within 68; in Iran 37–8; key elements of 66–7; patience in 83; and understandings of health 337, 344–5; see also Muslims
Israel 32–5, 185
IWTC (intercultural willingness to communicate scale) 174

Japan: communication as academic discipline in 53–5; group membership in 202; intercultural communication research in 53–6; relations with United States 200
Japanese culture: apology behavior in 198–201; conflict styles in 182, 191; marriage beliefs in 162; peculiarities

of 82; tea ceremony in 82; time orientation in 285
Japanese management system 276
Japanology 55
Jeong 51
job-oriented cultures 282
JSMR (Japan Society for Multicultural Relations) 55

Kim, Y. Y. 156, 189, 211, 212, 213, 215, 216, 218, 222, 252, 253, 256
Korea see North Korea; South Korea
Korean culture: and conflict styles 191; and emoticons 150; global reach of 51.n3; values of 47–51
Korean language 47–8, 50
kua wen hua (跨文化) 42

language: and categorical perception 135–6; and culture 132; definition of 130–1; and identity 138–9, 359; in intercultural communication 39, 129–30; new and mixed forms of 139–40; online 141; and social identity 105; in time and space 131–2; see also foreign languages
language barriers: and intercultural relationships 160–1; and migrant health 345–6
language ideology 137–8, 143
language proficiency 53, 159, 206, 339
language socialization 134–5
Latin America: ethnicity in 15; inequality in 19
Latino cultures 121, 162, 217, 326
LGBT community 34–5, 321–2, 360
linguistic-cultural background 250
linguistic diversity 15, 139
listening: effective 257; engaged 306
Llull, Ramon 64
long-short-term orientation 49, 87–8, 186–7, 286
love, expression of 162–3, 166
low-context culture 88; CMC in 147; in organizations 284

Macau 141
McDonald's corporation 132
macro-cultural systems 82
Malaysia, religious diversity in 69
management, cross-cultural 226, 276–8, 312
managerial interaction 276

Mandela, Nelson 26–7
marginality: encapsulated and constructive 239; experiences with 262
marginalization orientation to acculturation 215, 217, 233
marriage: cultural differences in 84; intercultural 161–2, 223
Martin, Judith 7, 26, 98
masculinity-femininity dimension 86–7, 186, 286
mass communication 213
mass media: and acculturation 213; and cultural interactions 41; and health communication 317, 326–9; privatization of 33
mastery-harmony continuum 89–90
matrix-structured organizations 281
Mbeki, Thabo 27
meaningfulness 162
media studies 107, 316–17
Meir, Golda 34
mental health 325, 327, 339, 345
message skills 254
mestizo peoples 15–16, 19, 20.n1
microcultures see subcultures
migration, cross-national 29–30; see also asylum-seekers; immigrants; refugees
military children 225, 237, 240
mindfulness 2, 71–3, 108
mindset 242, 252, 362–3
minority groups: cultural identity of 117–18; in ELIT 104–6; in France 102; and healthcare 323; in Israel 35; persecution of 8, 85; in South America 16, 19
minority status 85, 124
missionaries, Christian 63–4
mixed codes 141, 143
Monnet, Jean 21
monochronic time 88–9, 284–5
monocultural communication 174
motivation: to adapt 256; and anxiety 158; to communicate 251, 255, 305–6; inspirational 307–8; to learn English 259; for moving abroad 215
multicultural classrooms 259, 303
multicultural identities 226
multiculturalism: in Australia 59–60; cultural change in 222; and diversity 302; and intercultural communication 8–9; in Israel 32, 34
multicultural organizations 278, 290

multinational companies 163–4, 278
Muslims: and communication 67–9; negative stereotypes of 9; religious identity of 102, 104; in South Africa 25; in United States 85; see also Islam

Nakayama, Thomas 7, 98, 356
national identity 9, 17, 27, 30, 100–2, 110
nationality: as base of culture 7, 359–60; as cultural identity 120; in Israel 34; as social identity 103; in West Africa 29
Native Americans 14–19, 136, 139, 302, 323
negative face 188
networks: global 173; organizational 274–5, 279; social 78, 87, 186, 342, 347
network-structured organizations 280
new media 43–4, 316, 326, 361
New Zealand 59, 206, 357–9
Nigeria 30, 185, 296
noise 6
nonverbal behaviors 166, 254, 323
nonverbal communication 146
nonviolence 2, 71–3
Nordic countries, cultural peculiarities of 83–4, 87–8, 90, 286
Northern Ireland 124
North Korea 47; see also Korean culture

Oberg, Kalervo 208
obesity 326, 328–9, 343
open systems 282
organ donation 320, 342, 344–5
organizational behavior, cross-cultural 277
organizational change, trends and tensions in 275
organizational communication: flows of 287–8, 289; Japanese research on 55
organizational cultures: and communication 165, 279; cross-cultural competence in 291, 309; defined 281, 299; dimensions of 281–3, 299–301; factors influencing 283–4
organizational identity 164
organizations: authority within 278–81, 279–80; cultural variations in 284–5; diversity in 272, 274–6, 299, 309; types of 276, 278
outgroups: animosity towards 176; discrimination against 184; use of term 99

Palestinian Arabs 33–5
Papua New Guinea 134, 140
parochial members 282
passport culture 233–4, 237, 242
patience 83, 255
personal communication 213
personal identities 81, 99, 103, 184, 195
personality attributes 254
personal space 89
phonemes 135
planned behavior, theory of 337, 339–47
polychronic time 88–9, 284–5, 357
positive face 188–9
post-colonial context 16, 40–2
power, in acculturation 222
power distance 86–7, 186, 285; and Face Negotiation Theory 107; Korea and US compared 49; limitations of concept 357–8
prejudice: and ethnocentrism 10; as psychological noise 6
problem-solving 190, 192, 304
process-oriented culture 282
professional identity 118
professional members 282
pronouns, as shifting indexicals 137, 138
provider-patient relationships 318–19, 322–3
proxemics 89
psychological adjustment 214, 218, 254–5

Quakers 137
Quechua people 16, 19
queueing 132
Qur'an 66–8, 83

race: conversations about 177; use of term 102
racial groups 26–7, 302, 359
RAEM (Relative Acculturation Extended Model) 219, 220, 222
rational community 23
reality, internal models of 79–80
reasoned action, theory of 339–41
referential signs 137
referents 5, 48
refugees: to Australia 59; European reactions to 22, 29; and healthcare issues 322, 339; integration of 216; use of term 207
relational truthfulness 202
religion, and culture 82–3, 102, 360

religious identity 102
religious traditions 64, 182, 184, 188, 193
repatriation 233, 235, 241
resocialization 209–10
results-oriented culture 282
risk perceptions 324–5
ritual performance 133
rituals: and culture 79–80, 82; of Iran 37–8; Islamic 67–8, 102
romantic relationships: and health communication 321; intercultural 156, 162
rootlessness 237, 239–40, 243
Russian language, in Israel 33–4

Sami 84, 101
Sapir, Edward 135–6
Saussure, Ferdinand de 130, 132, 143
Schein's Onion model 281–2, 293, 300
Schwartz, Shalom, and cultural values 49, 89, 90
secular values 187–8
self-awareness: cultural 256; physical 363
self-clarity 236
self-concept 98, 109–10, 118, 254
self-construal 108–9, 183, 189
self-disclosure: differing expectations of 64; and intercultural communication competence 254; in intercultural friendships 160–1, 165; of physicians 319; in the workplace 164
self-esteem 103, 235–6, 254
Senegal 30
sensation-seeking 261, 325
sense-making 180
sensitivity, and intercultural communication competence 38, 255
separation orientation to acculturation 215–17, 233
settler colonialism 58–9
sex, and gender 103
sexual communication 321–2, 341
shibboleth 138
SIETAR (Japan) 55
signified 5, 130
signifier 5, 130
signs: referential and indexical 137; use of term 5, 130
SIIC (Summer Institute for Intercultural Communication) 247
sincerity 201–3

Singapore 88, 191, 206, 252
six-word memoirs 124
skillset 252, 362–3
Skype 148, 260
small talk 133
smoking 324–6, 328
smoothing conflict style 190
social communication 213
social constructionism 316
social decentering 261
social groups: and language 139–41; use of term 85
social identities: and health communication 322; open and threatened 105; use of term 80–1, 99
social identity theory (SIT) 103–4, 109, 184, 322, 363
Social Information Processing Theory 141
social interactions: and Face Negotiation Theory 107; ritualized 133, 143
social judgments 250–1
social media: and culture formation 361; and health information 329; and language 141–3; mixed codes on 142; SIT in 104
social relaxation 254
social sensitivity 225–6, 240
social skills 254, 363
social strata 134
sojourners 206–7, 216, 234
Somalis, in Finland 85, 337, 339, 350
South Africa: historical background of 25–6; as Rainbow Nation 26–8
South America: bilingual education in 17–18; indigenous people of see Native Americans; intercultural communication studies in 14–15, 19; population sectors of 15–16
South Korea: cultural index of 49; economy of 47–8; see also Korean culture
space, as cultural dimension 88–9
Special Broadcasting Service (SBS) 60
speech genres 131–2, 143
sports fandom 85
stereotypes: and health communication 319, 322; and intercultural relationships 156, 158–9, 165; use of term 9–10
stress: communication coping with 212; effectiveness in handling 261; reducing 212, 277

Stress-Adaptation-Growth Dynamic 211, 212
subcultures 84–6, 91, 221–2, 360
subjective norms 340–1
sunao 198, 201–3
swearing 142
Swedish people: living in US 220–1; in US 224
symbolic anchors 133
symbolic markers 16, 141
synergy, cultural 358
syntax 130–1, 134

Taiwanese dialect 135–6, 160
TCKs (Third Culture Kids) 224–5, 232–43
team-structured organizations 279, 280
technology, intercultural communication competence in 260
television, health information on 326–9
terminology, cultural bias in 356
territoriality 89
text messages 144
Thai culture: and conflict styles 191; and emoticons 150
third culture: and intercultural friends 159; use of term 222, 224
Third Culture Building 222–4, 223
third culture individuals 218, 224–7, 234, 242; see also TCKs
Three Bonds and Five Relationships (三綱五倫) 48
time culture: monochronic and polychronic 88–9, 284–5; Native American 136–7
Ting-Toomey, Stella 7, 44, 73, 100, 107, 108, 109, 156, 189, 190, 262
toasting 133
tourists, intercultural adaptation of 206
tradition, as cultural value 49, 88–9, 185–6
traditional societies 50, 188
transformational leadership 299, 307–9
transnational communities 217
Trekkies 85–6
Trump, Donald 101
trust, building 164
Turkish culture, and conflict styles 191–2

U-Curve Theory 208, 210, 232–3, 235
uncertainty: in intercultural relationships 158, 165; in meetings 279
uncertainty avoidance 88, 186, 286; in Korean culture 49–51
understanding, shared 71, 131
United States: compared to Japan 56; conflict styles of 191; cultural index of 49; cultural peculiarities of 80, 82–3; ethnic differences in 84, 163, 271; forms of English in 82, 139–40; in Hofstede's dimensions 187; intercultural communication in 8, 14–15; international students in 155–7; nationalism in 101; social groups in 85
upward communication 288–9
USS Greenville 198, 203
utterances 131

value clusters 49
value hierarchies 90, 185
values, and culture 80, 86, 89, 90, 184–6
virtual organizations 281
vision, surplus of 131–2
vitality 105–6
vowel shifts 140

Waddle, Scott 199, 202–3
W-curve model 209, 235
WeChat 141–2
West Africa 2, 29–31
Western medicine 83, 343–4
white privilege 100
Whorf, Benjamin 136
withdrawing conflict style 190
women: and gender roles 103, 163, 188, 285; and health communication 324–7, 330, 342; in Korean culture 50–1; in minority groups 117; use of emoticons 151
workforces, diverse see employee diversity
World Values Survey 187–8
worldview: and culture 79–81; three-dimensional 242

young adults 162, 258, 325, 342

Zionism 33